# SOUL F(

## Gandhi's Writings on Peace

Edited by
V. Geetha

**TARA**
PUBLISHING

Soul Force: Gandhi's Writings on Peace
Copyright © 2004

For this edition
Tara Publishing Ltd., UK < www.tarabooks.com/uk >
and
Tara Publishing, India < www.tarabooks.com >

For the extracts from the *Collected Works of Mahatma Gandhi*
Navajivan Trust, Ahmedabad

Design: Rathna Ramanathan, Minus 9 Design

Production: C. Arumugam

Printed and bound by Multi Vista Global Ltd, Chennai, India

ISBN: 81-86211-85-3

To the memory of my uncle, A.V. Santhanam

# Contents

# Introduction

Mohandas Gandhi's life continues to attract hagiographers, historians, political scientists and peace scholars. Yet another book on the great man's life and work therefore needs to state its case, explain if it purports to offer one more reading of a rare life, or is looking to do something else.

This is a book of extracts from Gandhi's writings on non-violence and peace. The extracts are framed by editorial notes and annotations. The intent is not to merely deconstruct a great life, or offer a new scholarly reading of Gandhi. Rather, the book seeks to restore him to history and by the same token to the living present. From a life that was so richly led, it seeks a sign for the times.

## A Point of View

I came to Gandhi with mixed feelings. I had grown up with images of him as the great 'Mahatma'. Eventually I learnt to view him through the critical lens of those who were of his time, but who held widely divergent views on politics, social change and justice. It has not been easy for my generation, who grew up in the 1970s, to think beyond the well-founded critiques of Gandhi, advanced by men such as Dr. Ambedkar and E. V. Ramasamy (see below). Their contentious and critical reading of Gandhi and his life effortlessly unpacked his moral and political philosophy, and political practice—to reveal a man whose religious faith and ethical worldview appeared hostile to modern liberal notions of rights and justice. But yet I felt compelled to return to Gandhi, attracted chiefly by his luminous prose, so reminiscent of some of the loveliest passages in the New Testament, and just as haunting.

Reading Gandhi against the grain was both pleasurable and frustrating. I found much that humbled and disarmed my critical mind, yet there was also enough to frustrate an easy acceptance and admiration. His penetrative critique of violence and its effects on both the perpetrator and the victim, his refusal to concede that just ends could be reached through violent means, his belief that violence is intrinsic to an unrestrained pursuit of materialistic progress and his insistence that ultimately hatred and destruction ought to be countered with not merely a pacifist politics, but an ethics of compassion, were immensely compelling. But there were exasperating moments as well, especially when Gandhi resorted, as he sometimes did, to tedious moral rhetoric to insist on the force of his 'truth'; or when he insisted—often in the face of contrary actual historical evidence—that given a chance, authority and power would reform and redeem themselves.

Unwilling to reconcile admiration and affection with critical anger, but convinced that I had to sift through my ambiguous responses with greater care, I returned to what has always moved me most about Gandhi's life: his plaintive last years, when he wandered the refugee camps of a partitioned country, wondering why his creed of non-violence had failed. This Gandhi, Lear-like in his tragic ardour, and obdurate in his commitment to peace, seemed a fit figure to speak from across the years that divide him from us. For this was not the apostle of peace, but its humblest pilgrim: a man whose ideas could help illuminate—even if they do not help resolve—some of the most agonising moral and political questions of our time, when both oppression and justice appear to demand unprecedented destruction, death and loss of dignity.

This book, then, explores Gandhi's responses to violence, as they emerged in the context of specific historical situations. It constructs its narrative in and through Gandhi's own words— from letters, speeches and writings in English, Gujarati and Hindustani. The story that unfolds in these pages marks not only those moments of triumph and prophecy that Gandhi won for peace, but also those impasses and failures which were as much a part of the evolving saga of non-violence, as Gandhi thought and lived it.

## Reading a Life

I have framed Gandhi's life through a favoured literary and spiritual trope: as a burdened moral journey in historical time. Gandhi himself provides the sanction for such a reading. Amongst his favourite texts were John Bunyan's *Pilgrim's Progress* and Thomas a' Kempis' *Imitation of Christ*, both of which narrate the paradoxical story of a mortal being's questing for transcendence. Unwilling to abandon the present and yet refusing to surrender his choices to the anxieties of history, Gandhi lived as a missionary of faith does—subjecting himself to moral and spiritual tests, relying only on his ineffable 'inner voice', as he called it, to resolve his quandaries of the hour. He was not entirely opposed to modern instruments of law and rule, nor did he reject secular solutions to questions of injustice and oppression. But he did not consider them adequate. As he often remarked, justice without compassion was not justice at all. Likewise, for him, a legal affirmation of equality was not significant, until it was suffused with the spirit of generous love. His Jewish critic and admirer, Hayim Greenberg, a Zionist labour leader from New York once observed:

... if there really are reincarnations, Gandhi was ... probably a reincarnation of Asoka, of that Indian Emperor who, three centuries before the Christian era, sought to embody his vision of the Kingdom of Heaven through historical realisation, in a new social creation, in legislation, in the framework of a state. ... Asoka aimed ... to establish a state in which there would be no contradiction between "the measure of law" and "the measure of mercy", to use Hebrew terms, where law itself would be suffused with mercy. Upon *ahimsa*, upon the three-thousand-year-old ideal which sprang up in a unique form in India, upon the principle of not-killing, not-injuring, not-causing-pain, upon the idea of an all-embracing loving-kindness, he sought to build up the constitution and the mechanism of the state. And it is in this "paradoxical" way that Gandhi also set out to make his life's journey in our generation.

## The Inheritance

Gandhi chose to be non-violent. As he recounts in his autobiography, it was a learnt virtue, and one that he tested several times in his long life. His mother's piety and his wife Kastuba's devotion and firmness of resolve, as she both supported and opposed her obdurate husband and his difficult ways, impressed him deeply and convinced him of the virtues of patient sufferance and iron tolerance. There were direct spiritual influences too: the Jainism of his native Gujarat which held non-killing or *ahimsa* to be an insuperable ideal; the devotional Vaishnavism of his mother's family, centred on the worship of the god Krishna, which taught him to envisage the divine as essentially compassionate, and counselled love and charity to all living creatures; the traditions of Jewish and Islamic martyrdom which he knew intimately from his days in South Africa; and finally and most importantly, the life of Christ and the message of the Sermon on the Mount which touched his heart and soul in his early youth.

Like many others of his generation, Gandhi also looked to the *Bhagavad Gita*, which had come to be privileged—from the nineteenth century onwards—as an important and decisive Hindu text by modern Hindus. But his reading of the Gita was soundly heretical: unlike his contemporaries who found in it a sanction for a virile and masculine nationalism, he read it as a text that taught liberation from the violence of mortality, of the body and its needs.

Gandhi's political and public expressions of non-violence were complex and varied. Non-violent opposition to wrong and evil—whether of British imperial authority in South Africa and India or the cruelty of caste Hindu society—encompassed passive resistance, Non-cooperation and civil disobedience, three different stages and modes of non-violent resistance to wrongly held authority and unjust laws. Gandhi cited various inspirations: Henry David Thoreau, the British suffragettes, the medieval English peasant revolutionary Wat Tyler, the Puritan writer John Bunyan and Christ himself, who called on men and women to resist evil in faith, and not in anger. All these heroic figures were important, because they were also eminently practical in their espousal of their creed and faith—they lived what they believed.

Non-violence was affirmed as truth and the struggle one waged—in opposition to unjust authority, laws, ill-conceived prejudices, blind hatred, aggression—was satyagraha, the war of truth. To prove the truth of one's innocence, of the injustice visited upon oneself, a person suffered privation and hurt, appealing thereby to the oppressor's conscience. The oppressor was not to be scorned, judged or reviled, but loved. Here too Christ was an inspiration. Gandhi's favourite verse from the New Testament was *Corinthians* I, 13:

Charity suffereth long, and is kind; charity envieth not, charity vaunteth not itself, is not puffed up, doth not behave itself unseemly, seeketh not her own, is not easily provoked, thinketh no evil; rejoiceth not in iniquity, but rejoiceth in the truth; beareth all things, believeth all things, hopeth all things, endureth all things.

He also recalled in this context the martyrdom of the Islamic Imams Hossein and Hussein, who consented to die that their faith may live and whose love for the world translated as a willingness to die. It is important to note here that Gandhi's sense of the civic derived from these traditions, rather than the decidedly secular ones of the Modern Age.

Non-violence that suffered injustice was however not to be taken to mean passivity or cowardice. Rather, it demanded great moral effort to remain steadfast in one's wearing of pain. Such discipline as a person cultivated required, in turn, the active eschewing of bitterness and anger, and the renunciation of the desire to prove oneself right. In Gandhi's world, truth was to be established not through argument but by moral living. As he often remarked, it would not do to kill for affirming one's truth; rather a person had to learn to die for it. Tolstoy was clearly Gandhi's mentor here.

Gandhi defined the qualities of an ideal satyagrahi in fairly clear-cut terms: he or she had to be schooled into knowing the ways of non-violence and the war of truth. Referring once to himself, he admitted that his public presence—as an apostle of peace—had come about as a result of his carefully tending his erring self:

I may not write merely to excite passion. The reader can have no idea of the restraint I have to exercise from week to week in the choice of topics and my vocabulary. It is a training for me. It enables me to peep into myself and make discoveries of my weaknesses. Often my vanity dictates a smart expression or my anger a harsh adjective. It is a terrible ordeal but a fine exercise to remove these weeds. The reader sees the pages of *Young India* fairly well dressed up and sometimes with Romain Rolland, he is inclined to say 'what a fine old man this must be'. Well, let the world understand that the fineness is carefully and prayerfully cultivated. …When that fineness has become perfectly natural, i.e., when I have become incapable of evil and when nothing harsh or haughty occupies, be it momentarily, my thought-world, then and not till then, my non-violence will move all the hearts of all the world.

Fundamentally, a satyagrahi had to learn to engage sensitively with the violence of living, with bodily needs which human beings have been able be fulfil only through acts that destroyed one life form or another. These needs therefore had to be regulated, restrained and ultimately overcome. Needs included the appetites and thus all desire had to be purged of the urge to self-satisfaction. Cleansing also possessed a more material significance in Gandhi's lexicon. Convinced that the Hindu caste order's obsession with purity and pollution was linked to its inability to deal with the phenomenon of waste and refuse, Gandhi thought and wrote a great deal about personal hygiene and sanitation. A good satyagrahi was one who not only lived minimally but also took responsibility for community sanitation. Cleaning toilets was, for Gandhi, not merely a civic task, but a deeply symbolic one

The school for the satyagrahi was to be the ashram: a community of renouncers who were not slaves to want, and who were concerned about the world. These were men and women who consciously did not observe caste and community ties and lived by a common ethic to which they were all equally bound. In the ashram one learnt to eat and live simply, practise sexual abstinence, unless, of course, a person wished to marry. But even then sexual love was to be kept within confines and enjoyed only for the purpose of producing a child. At other times, it was to be sublimated into a general human affection. Importantly, Gandhi insisted that celibacy was as much for women, as for men. He disagreed that women were merely sexual beings and observed that if only men learnt to disregard lust, they could be better companions to their women. The ashram was also a place to raise children, practise vocations that required the use of the hand and the body as much as of the mind and soul, and a refuge for those who were ailing, or in need of emotional or spiritual succour.

## Performance

Gandhi's original philosophy and practice of non-violence were honed and sharpened by his keen understanding of violence and its many social and historical guises. At one level, violence inhered in the very act of living. But this was a condition that had to be suffered and transformed. At another level, violence was symptomatic of life in the present, of modern life that knew—

and knows—neither sensual restraint nor spiritual humility. Gandhi wrote eloquently against what he understood as the logic of his time: a society driven by profit and mind-numbing pleasure, and rendered intemperate by the limitless expansion of human needs. At a third level, violence signified the breakdown of communication, it imposed itself where dialogue had broken down, where different points of view confronted each other with mutual suspicion, hostility and aggression. He argued that killing all those who held a different view of the world only further reaffirmed the memory of those who die, and legitimised their cause. Whether states did this, or individuals, violence demanded action on its own terms and therefore merely served to perpetrate division and antagonism.

Gandhi always addressed violence in its contingent forms: his opposition to it was specific, defined and disciplined. He was not worried about the success or failure of his campaigns. He suspended them if his supporters crossed the line of civil suffering he had drawn and sought to inflict hurt on those who opposed them. He heeded his 'inner voice' in such matters and did not consider public or even peer opinion. He never failed to point out that, for him, non-violence was not a policy, but a creed. His followers did not always actively interrogate him—his moral reasoning was beyond reproach and efficacious. In his striving for the ideal he never lost sight of the practical need of the hour.

Gandhi was not unaware of his charisma. He possessed a fine sense of the dramatic and developed a repertoire of public rituals to communicate his truth. Fasting, spinning, walking on foot for miles: his public rites of passage breathed a rich yet everyday symbolism. But his performances were not always salutary and sometimes threatened to erode the very principles on which they were based. This was particularly evident in his encounter with Dr. Ambedkar, anti-caste and 'untouchable' leader, who challenged his politics and questioned his ethics. Gandhi's moral world was somewhat bruised by these charges, as his strong sense of the 'truth' of his position came into conflict with his sense of himself as the privileged bearer of that truth.

## Critics

Gandhi's contemporaries, especially those who disagreed with the premises of his world view, were sharply critical of his politics and ethics. There were two kinds of critics: the thinkers and leaders of the anti-caste movements in southern and western India who looked to modern secular ideals to define their sense of the good and the just. Then there were the socialists, both within and outside the Indian national movement, who considered his ideas as legitimising the essentially upper class and caste character of Indian nationalism. Of these two criticisms, the first bears consideration at length, since those who advanced it did not merely discard Gandhi's moral reasoning as 'claptrap', as some socialists did, but offered their own visions of how these two realms ought to be linked.

Dr. Ambedkar from neighbouring Maharashtra, and E. V. Ramasamy, anti-caste radical and founder of the iconoclastic Tamil Self-respect Movement both held Gandhi to be a dangerous ideologue. They objected to his deploying the language of faith in the realm of politics and argued that moral arguments in the modern period needed to anchor themselves in a secular location. For Dr. Ambedkar, the realm of the law and later the rational compassion of the Buddha appeared fit guarantees of ethical action that sought to engage with the world and its sorrows. For Ramasamy, a self-critical rational disposition towards the world and an existential desire to serve suffering humanity dictated the nature of the ethics that one might yet counsel to a troubled world.

Two aspects of their critique may be recalled here. Dr. Ambedkar found Gandhi's faith in gentle suffering and moral persuasion, in the face of tyranny, misplaced and sentimental; especially when Gandhi worked this faith to challenge the 'satanic' crime of untouchability. Dr. Ambedkar argued that it was the purest moral sophistry on Gandhi's part to counsel the untouchable to suffer his fate and status with quiet calm and confident fortitude: for it made wrongs done unto the victim appear "as though they were his privileges". Dr. Ambedkar also resented Gandhi's obstinate faith in the power of conscience. He did not share Gandhi's belief that Hindus who observed caste differences and practised untouchability would, if shown the error of their ways, recognise the evil they harboured in their midst and cast it out:

Untouchability is an attitude of the Hindu. For untouchability to vanish, it is the Hindu who must change. Will he change? Has the Hindu any conscience? Is he ever known to have been fired with a righteous indignation against a moral wrong? Assuming he does change so much as to regard Untouchability a moral wrong, assuming he is awakened to the sense of putting himself right with god and Man, will he agree to give up the economic and social advantages which Untouchability gives?

Ramasamy's criticisms of Gandhi were layered and complex. What he objected to most of all was Gandhi's definition of satyagraha. He held that to insist on the truth of one's position, as Gandhi did, and yet claim that he was not being partisan was problematic. For one, it denied there existed other truths, counter-positions on the same reality. For another, it confused truth claims with moral ones. Often, it was Gandhi's moral obduracy, rather than the virtues of the truth he counselled, which compelled his followers and sometimes his critics to accept his point of view. For Gandhi's truth claims, prompted as they were by his inner voice, could not be measured except through their own forms of expression. In other words, no dialogic measure could be brought to bear on his truth.

Ramasamy's arguments may be illumined by looking at the characteristic manner in which Gandhi chose to demonstrate the validity of his truth—he often fasted for it. How could this be countered? A counter-fast would not have mattered, because it could always be discounted as a false one—since it was offered not on its own merits, but as a rebuttal. Thus, either Gandhi must be allowed to suffer and die for his truth, or the latter must be accepted as valid. In another age, a Socratic fate might have been foisted on Gandhi. But in the age of dialogue, argument and discussions, this was not to be so: out of fear that he could die, frustrated and angry at being held to ransom, and sometimes because of a genuine desire to meet his point of view, his interlocutors accepted his moral arguments.

## The Moral

Gandhi's critics point the way to a reading of Gandhi that does not baulk at the difficulties posed by a life such as his. They alert us to the perilous implications of undertaking a moral journey in a world where secular values compete with spiritual ones to construct a meaning of the moral.

The journey itself, though, was more than what it claimed for itself, in terms of truth and morality. This is what makes it so memorable. For, it was mediated through actual practices of love, suffering, intimacy, dissension and experimentation. Gandhi's lively interest in those around him, from erring children to recalcitrant political foes, translated into everyday deeds of nurture. Caring and sustained letters to personal and political friends and acquaintances contained health and dietary advice, frank discussions on sexuality, advice on knotty domestic problems, long and tedious exchanges with those who misread his creed of non-violence in one way or another ... Gandhi's writings also reveal his longing and ability to communicate even with those he disagreed with, and his searching out something in them for him to love. As Greenberg put it, his was a life "in whose soul loving-kindness was the foremost drive".

It is this journey, undertaken in an existential as well as a civic spirit, which is the subject, the moral and measure of this book.

## A Note on the Text

*Soul Force* is divided into eight chapters, which follow each other in a chronological fashion (Chapters 6 and 7 deal with events from the same period). Every chapter begins with a background note and is divided into sections, centred on a key incident, event or argument from that particular period of Gandhi's life. Each section has its own introduction. Wherever necessary, annotations and explanatory notes have been provided. With reference to words such as 'untouchable' and 'harijan', which have become historically contentious, I have retained the usage of the period in my editorial comments to avoid sounding anachronistic.

For every extract that came to be eventually included in the book, several others, equally fascinating, had to be left out. For instance, Gandhi's voluminous writings on the—for him—interlinked subjects of sexuality, violence, health and female freedom and autonomy do not find adequate representation here. Likewise, his extensive writings on sanitation and handicrafts, his views on education—all of which comment on how they relate to a life of non-violence—have been included only to the extent that they amplify the argument.

All extracts have been taken from the CD-ROM version of the Collected Works of Mahatma Gandhi (Publications Division, Government of India, n.d.) and all references in the book are to this and not the printed version of the Works ('errors' in the original extracts have not been modified, and are given as they are in the CD-ROM version).

## Acknowledgements

I would like to thank: Gita Wolf for suggesting the idea for the book and seeing it through; Arun Wolf for his critical yet receptive interest in Gandhi when he was fifteen years old, which convinced me that the young would not be averse to reading his work anew; Sirish Rao who never tired of listening to my Gandhi story for the day; K. Manoharan, who read the manuscript in record time and offered extremely useful suggestions; Karen Press for a careful and critical perusal of the final draft and Rathna Ramanathan and C. Arumugam for help with design and production.

Nalini Rajan who directed me to Hannah Arendt to clarify my understanding of Gandhi, the Librarian, The School, KFI, where I spent many hours leafing through the last volumes of the *Collected Works*, Usha and John Samuel who gifted me a copy of the New Testament just when I had begun work on this project, Peter Ruhe of the Gandhiserve Foundation for his assistance with copyright information, the Navajivan Trust for generously according permission to use extracts from the *Collected Works* and Hivos, whose support enabled the research for this book: I am deeply grateful to all of you.

And finally, my parents—Gandhians essentially—who followed the project's progress with anxious and affectionate concern, Subatra, Selvam and Sharifa, whose companionship continues to inspire all my efforts and Helmut Wolf for being helpful in many different ways—much love and many thanks.

V.Geetha

Chennai, June 30, 2004

# Chapter 1

## The South African Years: The Advent of Satyagraha
## 1893-1914

*Mohandas Karamchand Gandhi arrived in South Africa in 1893. He was twenty-five years old and trained as a lawyer.*

*South Africa was a British colony, comprising the regions of Natal, the Transvaal, Orange River Colony and the Cape Colony. It was home to several thousands of Indians, chiefly from Gujarat and the Tamil country. Many of them had been brought in to labour on the plantations and farms owned by white settlers on land forcibly taken from the native peoples of South Africa. They were 'indentured' to their employers and owed them a certain time of service, after which they were deemed free. A modest section of the Indian population—Hindus, Muslims and Christians—comprised hawkers, merchants and lawyers. There were other 'coloured' migrants too, Malay and Chinese workers who came as labourers and traders and those who were of 'mixed' origin.*

*South Africa was already an apartheid state in the making. Native peoples were ghettoised and kept subordinate; migrant Indians, coloured races and those of mixed origin suffered varying degrees of legal discrimination and social abuse. Indentured labourers worked in extremely harsh conditions and were bound to their work, until they could pay off the value of the contract that had brought them to the colony in the first place. But once they did that, they faced an uncertain future, for as 'free' subjects, they stood in danger of being deported if they and their grown-up children did not pay a stipulated tax (the poll-tax). Indian hawkers and merchants could not trade freely, were refused licenses and sometimes restricted to particular 'locations'. More generally, Indians were accused of being deceitful, thieving, insanitary in their habits and a general menace to rule and order in South Africa.*

*The migrants however were not an entirely passive community. There existed an incipient protest culture amongst Asians, especially amongst traders and those in the professions. Gandhi found himself in this restive environment which he gradually transformed and made distinctive through his unique mode of struggle. He was appalled by the manner in which racist prejudices were written into the law of the land. Confronting the law as a subject of an Empire whose moral character he trusted, he gradually evolved a resistance movement that sought to disobey unjust laws through peaceful means. Civil disobedience, which confounded the law with its own presumptions of justice, became the basis for Gandhi's 'war of truth' or satyagraha.*

*Gandhi arrived in the Transvaal, which, along with Natal, held the largest number of Indian migrants. He got involved in the Transvaal's civic life, and emerged as an able interpreter and spokesman for Indian trading interests. The plight of indentured labourers and the mean conditions in which they lived and worked moved him, but he found himself able to articulate the problems of hawkers and traders more ably. This was because he was concerned with the legal rather than the economic expressions of racial prejudice. Legal discrimination implicated all Indians, whereas economic injustice was varied and could not be countered without calling into question the Indians' right to live in South Africa.*

*Meanwhile, he worried ceaselessly about the effect of harsh environments and an uprooted existence on the moral worth of Indian labourers. His imprecations to labourers did not therefore consider merely their lack of rights, or the manner in which they were subject to racial abuse. His advice, often, took the form of counselling, and he dwelt, at length, on their lifestyle—on matters of dirt, disease, promiscuity, dissoluteness, ignorance and caste and community prejudices. Later on, as the resistance to the colonial government's policies grew, his political energies were placed at the service of indentured labour as well.*

*Though Gandhi was aware of the manner in which colonial economic exploitation and rule dispossessed native Africans and affected other* 'coloured' people, he did not see himself as competent or capable of representing their cause, nor did he wish to do so. His defiance of unjust laws was advanced from his location as a loyal subject of an Empire that had made a compact with his countrymen in India, promising to treat them fairly and without discrimination. Since this compact could not be invoked in the instance of other colonial subject populations, he did not seek to extend the Indian resistance to encompass other forms of protests against British colonial rule in South Africa.

At times Gandhi even endorsed the colonial view of the 'kaffir', as the native was referred to by white settlers, as a simple, lovable, though unpredictable savage—often upholding, through an invidious comparison, the 'civilized' Indians' claims to rights that were being denied them.

Three phases may be discerned in Gandhi's life in South Africa. From 1894-1906, he petitioned, argued, debated and interpreted the justness of Indian claims to the South African government and white settler society. In the second phase, which began in 1906 and lasted until 1911, he organized Indians in a series of struggles against unjust racially inspired laws—and which saw the advent of a political philosophy which he initially described as 'passive resistance' and then re-named 'satyagraha'. His last years in South Africa, 1913-1914, found him at his most militant, as he drew into the struggle not only traders and hawkers but also hundreds of indentured labourers and workers.

## Courageous Speech

*Gandhi's manner of public address was unique: he first spoke out against injustice in 1894, not from the point of view of a subdued petitioning subject, but as a self-assured and equal member of an Empire whose Christian temper he trusted. His early speeches and writings reveal him to be confident without being belligerent and respectful without being obsequious. What is noteworthy is that he refused the role of history's victim; instead he claimed what was due to him and other Indians by dint of their presence in South Africa, and as contributors to its productive wealth and quality of life.*

*At the same time, he refrained from claiming all rights that the colonisers enjoyed. Gandhi was acutely conscious of the peculiar circumstances of Indian migration to South Africa and did not therefore ask for rights that would compromise their very existence in the colony: the labouring class had been brought in to work on the mines and farms, the service classes had come of their own volition, and as such neither class could claim sovereign rights in a colony where a numerically small white community jealously guarded its privileges.*

*Gandhi demanded, therefore, only what might be granted to the Indians by virtue of the legal and ethical arrangements that bound them contractually to Empire in India. By the terms of the Queen Empress' proclamation of 1858, discrimination on the basis of colour and race was to be strictly eschewed. This also meant that he spoke only for the Indians, and not for the other 'coloured' people or 'kaffirs', for they were not bound by such contractual obligations. He pleaded the Indian cause in India as well, to the chagrin of South African colonists who resented his speaking of 'their' affairs before another subject population.*

*The extracts in this section reveal the early Gandhi, as he spoke, wrote, argued and entreated with the white settlers of South Africa.*

## Open Letter
## Durban, [Before December 19, 1894]

TO
THE HON. MEMBERS OF
THE HON. THE LEGISLATIVE COUNCIL AND
THE HON. THE LEGISLATIVE ASSEMBLY, DURBAN

SIRS,

Were it possible to write to you anonymously, nothing would have been more pleasing to me. But the statements I shall have to make in this letter will be so grave and important that it would be considered a sheer act of cowardice not to disclose my name. I beg, however, to assure you that I write not from selfish motives, nor yet from those of self-aggrandisement or of seeking notoriety. The one and only object is to serve India, which is by accident of birth called my native country, and to bring about better understanding between the European section of the community and the Indian in this Colony.

... To whom else could such an appeal be more aptly made, or by whom else should it be considered more seriously than you? To carry on an agitation in England is but a poor relief when it can only create a greater friction between the two peoples in the Colony. The relief, at best, could only be temporary. Unless the Europeans in the Colony can be induced to accord the Indians a better treatment, the Indians have a very bad time before them under the aegis of the Responsible Government, in spite of the vigilance of the Home Government. Without entering into details, I would deal with the Indian question as a whole.

I suppose there can be no doubt that the Indian is a despised being in the Colony, and that every opposition to him proceeds directly from that hatred. If that hatred is simply based upon his colour, then, of course, he has no hope. The sooner he leaves the Colony the better. No matter what he does, he will never have the white skin. If, however, it is based upon something else, if it is based upon an ignorance of his general character and attainments, he may hope to receive his due at the hands of the Europeans in the Colony.

The question what use the Colony will make of the 40,000 Indians is, I submit, worthy of the most serious consideration by the Colonists, and especially those who have the reins of government in their hands, who have been entrusted by the people with legislative powers. ...You can educate public opinion in such a way that the hatred will be increased day by day; and you can, if you choose so to do, educate it in such a way that the hatred would begin to subside.

I now propose to discuss the question under the following heads:

1. Are the Indians desirable as citizens in the Colony?

2. What are they?

3. Is their present treatment in accordance with the best British traditions, or with the principles of justice and morality, or with the principles of Christianity?

4. From a purely material and selfish point of view, will an abrupt or gradual withdrawal of them from the Colony result in substantial, lasting benefit to the Colony?

I

In discussing the first question, I will deal, first of all, with the Indians employed as labourers, most of whom have come to the Colony under indenture. It seems to have been acknowledged by those who are supposed to know, that the indentured Indians are indispensable for the welfare of the Colony; whether as menials or waiters, whether as railway servants or gardeners, they are a useful addition to the Colony. The work that a Native cannot or would not do is cheerfully and well done by the indentured Indian. It would seem that the Indian has helped make this the Garden Colony of South Africa. Withdraw the Indian from the sugar estate, and where would the main industry of the Colony be? Nor can it be said that the work can be done by the Native in the near future. The South African Republic is an instance in point. In spite of its so-called vigorous Native policy, it remains practically a desert of dust, although the soil is very fruitful.

... As to the Indian traders, who are miscalled Arabs, it would appear best to consider the objections raised to their coming to the Colony. From the papers, especially *The Natal Mercury* of 6-7-'94, and *The Natal Advertiser* of 15-9-'93, the objections appear to be that they are successful traders, and that, their mode of living being very simple, they compete with the European trader in petty trades. I dismiss as unworthy of consideration the generalizations from rare particular instances that the Indians resort to sharp practices. As to the particular instances of insolvency, I would only say, without meaning in the least to defend them, "Let those that are without sin first cast a stone."

... Coming to the serious objection as to successful competition, I believe it is true. But is that a reason for driving them out of the Colony? Will such a method commend itself to a body of civilized men? What is it that makes them so successful competitors? ... The chiefest element of their success, in my humble opinion, is their total abstinence from drink and its attendant evils. That habit at once causes an enormous saving of money. Moreover, their tastes are simple, and they are satisfied with comparatively small profits, because they do not keep uselessly large establishments ...

·... It will be best, also, to consider the common objection to the Indian traders and labourers. It is their insanitary habits. I am afraid I must, to my great mortification, admit this charge partially. While much that is said against their insanitary habits proceeds merely out of spite and hatred, there is no denying that in this respect they are not everything that could be desired. That, however, never can be a reason for their expulsion from the Colony. They are not hopelessly beyond reform in this branch. A strict, yet just and merciful, operation of the sanitary law can, I submit, effectually cope with the evil, and even eradicate it ...

It will, I hope, be readily admitted that they are exceptionally free from those vices which render a community a danger to society. They yield to no one in their obedience to constitutional authority. They are never a political danger. And except the ruffians who are sometimes picked out, of course unknowingly, by the immigration agents at Calcutta and Madras, they seem to be free from the highly grievous offences. ...

## II

The second head of the enquiry is the most important, viz., what are they, and I request you to peruse it carefully. My purpose in writing on this subject will have been served if only it stimulates a study of India and its people; for, I thoroughly believe that one half, or even three-fourths, of the hardships entailed upon the Indians in South Africa result from want of information about India.

... A general belief seems to prevail in the Colony that the Indians are little better, if at all, than savages or the Natives of Africa. Even the children are taught to believe in that manner, with the result that the Indian is being dragged down to the position of a raw Kaffir. Such a state of things, which the Christian legislators of the Colony would not, I firmly believe, wittingly allow to exist and remain, must be my excuse for the following copious extracts, which will show at once that the Indians were, and are, in no way inferior to their Anglo-Saxon brethren, if I may venture to use the word, in the various departments of life—industrial, intellectual, political, etc.

*(Here, Gandhi provides a variety of quotes from Orientalist scholars of Indian history and society, including Lord Macaulay, Herbert Risley and the redoubtable Max Mueller. These are not reproduced here - ed.)*

... Such is India. If the picture appears to you to be somewhat overdrawn or fanciful, it is none the less faithful. There is the other side. Let him who takes delight in separating, rather than in uniting, the two nations give the other side. Then, please, examine both with the impartiality of a Daniel, and I promise that there will yet remain a considerable portion of what has been said above untouched, to induce you to believe that India is not Africa, and that it is a civilized country in the truest sense of the term *civilization*.

Before, however, I can quit this subject, I have to crave leave to be allowed to anticipate a possible objection. It will be said: "If what you say is true, the people whom you call Indians in the Colony are not Indians, because your remarks are not borne out by the practices prevailing among the people whom you call Indians. See how grossly untruthful they are." Everyone I have met with in the Colony has dwelt upon the untruthfulness of the Indians. To a limited extent I admit the charge. It will be very small satisfaction for me to show, in reply to the objection, that other classes do not fare much better in this respect, especially if and when they are placed in the position of the unfortunate Indians. And yet, I am afraid, I shall have to fall back upon argument of that sort. Much as I would wish them to be otherwise, I confess my utter inability to prove that they are more than human. They come to Natal on starvation wages (I mean here the indentured Indians).

They find themselves placed in a strange position and amid uncongenial surroundings. *The moment they leave India* they remain throughout life, if they settle in the Colony, without any moral education. Whether they are Hindus or Mahommedans, they are absolutely without any moral or religious instruction worthy of the name. They have not learned enough to educate themselves without any outside help. Placed thus, they are apt to yield to the slightest temptation to tell a lie. After some time, lying with them becomes a habit and a disease. They would lie without any reason, without any prospect of bettering themselves materially, indeed, without knowing what they are doing. They reach a stage in life when their moral faculties have completely collapsed owing to neglect.

There is also a very sad form of lying. They cannot dare tell the truth, even for their wantonly ill-treated brother, for fear of receiving ill-treatment from their master. They are not philosophic enough to look with equanimity on the threatened reduction in their miserable rations and serve corporal punishment, did they dare to give evidence against their master. Are these men, then, more to be despised than pitied? Are they to be treated as scoundrels, deserving no mercy, or are they to be treated as helpless creatures, badly in need of sympathy? Is there any class of people who would not do as they are doing under similar circumstances?

But I will be asked what I can have to say in defence of the traders, who, too, are equally good liars. As to this, I beg to submit that the charge against them is without foundation, and that they do not lie more than the other classes do for the purposes of trade or law. ...

III

In order to answer the third question, "Is their present treatment in accordance with the best British traditions, or with the principles of justice and morality, or with the principles of Christianity?" it will be necessary to enquire what their treatment is. I think it will be readily granted that the Indian is bitterly hated in the Colony. The man in the street hates him, curses him, spits upon him, and often pushes him off the footpath. The Press cannot find a sufficiently strong word in the best English dictionary to damn him with. Here are a few samples :

"The real canker that is eating into the very vitals of the community"; "these parasites"; "Wily, wretched, semi-barbarous Asiatics"; "a thing black and lean and a long way from clean, which they call the accursed Hindoo"; "he is chock-full of vice, and he lives upon rice. ... I heartily cuss the Hindoo"; "squalid coolies with truthless tongues and artful ways". The Press almost unanimously refuses to call the Indian by his proper name. He is "Ramsamy"; he is "Mr. Sammy"; he is "Mr. Coolie"; he is "the black man". And these offensive epithets have become so common that they (at any rate one of them, "coolie") are used even in the sacred precincts of the courts, as if "the coolie" were the legal and proper name to give to any and every Indian. The public men, too, seem to use the word freely. I have often heard the painful expression "coolie clerk" from the mouths of men who ought to know better. The expression is a contradiction in terms and is extremely offensive to those to whom it is applied. But then, in this Colony the Indian is a creature without feelings!

The tramcars are not for the Indians. The railway officials may treat the Indians as beasts. ... The hotels shut their doors against them. ... Even the public baths are not for the Indians, no matter who they are. If I am to depend upon one-tenth of the reports that I have received with regard to the treatment of the indentured Indians on the various estates, it would form a terrible indictment against the humanity of the masters on the estates ... This, however, is a subject which my extremely limited experience of it precludes me from making further remarks upon.

... Now, is this treatment in consonance with the British traditions of justice, or morality, or Christianity? ... To bring a man here on starvation wages, to hold him under bondage, and when he shows the least signs of liberty, or, is in a position to live less miserably, to wish to send him back to his home where he would become comparatively a stranger and perhaps unable to earn a living, is hardly a mark of fair play or justice characteristic of the British nation.

That the treatment of the Indians is contrary to the teaching of Christianity needs hardly any argument. The Man, who taught us to love our enemies and to give our cloak to the one who wanted the coat, and to hold out the right cheek when the left was smitten, and who swept away the distinction between the Jew and the Gentile, would never brook a disposition that causes a man to be so proud of himself as to consider himself polluted even by the touch of a fellow-being.

## IV

The last head of the enquiry has, I believe, been sufficiently discussed in discussing the first. And I for one would not be much grieved in [sic] an experiment were tried to drive out each and every Indian from the Colony. In that case, I have not the slightest doubt that the Colonists would soon rue the day when they took the step and would wish they had not done it. The petty trades and the petty avocations of life would be left alone. The work for which they are specially suited would not be taken up by the Europeans, and the Colony would lose an immense amount of revenue now derived from the Indians. The climate of South Africa is not such as would enable the Europeans to do the work that they can easily do in Europe. What, however, I do submit with the greatest deference is this, that if the Indians must be kept in the Colony, then let them receive such treatment as by their ability and integrity they may be fit to receive, that is to say, give them what is their due, and what is the least that a sense of justice, unalloyed by partiality or prejudice, should prompt you to give them. ...

I have the honour to remain,
Your obedient servant,
M. K. GANDHI

From *A Pamphlet* (1: 186-204)

**Letter to *The Times of Natal***
**Durban, October 25, 1894**

TO
THE EDITOR
THE TIMES OF NATAL

SIR,

... You are pleased to acknowledge that "India possesses men of high culture, etc." and yet you would not, if you could, give them equal political power with the white man. Do you not thus make the insult doubly insulting? If you had thought that the Indians were not cultured, but were barbarous brutes, and on that ground denied them political equality, there would be some excuse for your opinions. You, however, in order to enjoy the fullest pleasures derived from offering an insult to an inoffensive people, must needs show that you acknowledge them to be intelligent people and yet would keep them under foot.

Then you have said that the Indians in the Colony are not the same as those in India; but, Sir, you conveniently forget that they are the brothers or descendants of the same race whom you credit with intelligence, and have, therefore, given the opportunity, the potentiality of becoming as capable as their more fortunate brethren in India, just as a man sunk in the depth of ignorance and vice of the East End of London has the potentiality of becoming Prime Minister in free England.

... The Indians do not regret that capable Natives can exercise the franchise. They would regret if it were otherwise. They, however, assert that they too, if capable, should have the right. You, in your wisdom, would not allow the Indian or the Native the precious privilege under any circumstances, because they have a dark skin. You would look to the exterior only. So long as the skin is white it would not matter to you whether it conceals beneath it poison or nectar. To you the lip-prayer of the Pharisee, because he is one, is more acceptable than the sincere repentance of the publican, and this, I presume, you would call Christianity ...

... "Suffer little children to come unto me," said the Master. His disciples (?) in the Colony would improve upon the saying by inserting "white" after "little". During the children's *fete*, organized by the Mayor of Durban, I am told there was not a single coloured child to be seen in the procession. Was this a punishment for the sin of being born of coloured parents? Is this an incident of the qualified citizenship you would accord to the hated "Rammysammy"? If He came among us, will he not say to many of us, "I know you not"?

Sir, may I venture to offer a suggestion? Will you reread your New Testament? Will you ponder over your attitude towards the coloured population of the Colony? Will you then say you can reconcile it with the Bible teaching or the best British traditions? If you have washed your hands clean of both Christ and British traditions, I can have nothing to say; I gladly withdraw what I have written. Only it will then be a sad day for Britain and for India if you have many followers.

Yours, etc.,

M. K. GANDHI

*The Times of Natal,* 26.10.1894 (1: 182-83)

---

*Gandhi came on a visit home to India in 1896 and returned to South Africa in early 1897. Even before he disembarked from the S.S. Courland, he was told that a hostile crowd of European settlers was waiting to 'receive him'. They were apparently enraged with him for the views he had expressed, while in India, on the incipient racism of South African society. These views had been made known through the widely distributed 'Green Pamphlet'. Gandhi and the other Indians decided to remain on board the ship until such time as they could depart without fear of assault. This is an interview which he granted while on the ship.*

### Interview to *The Natal Advertiser*
[S.S. Courland], January [13,] 1897

(Reporter:) ... Where did you prepare the pamphlet *(on Indian grievances which incited anger amongst the European settlers in South Africa - ed.)*?

(Gandhiji:) I did not prepare it in Natal. I prepared the whole of it while on the voyage home (*to India - ed.*) .

How did you secure the information it contains?

I was determined to make myself acquainted with all the facts about the Indians in South Africa, and with that object in view I had translations of the Transvaal laws supplied to me, and I asked friends in the Cape Colony and in other parts of South Africa to furnish me with any information they had on this question. So, I was fully acquainted with the facts before I decided to go to India. In the memorials which have been sent from the Indians of Natal to the Home Government, the Imperial view of the question has always been kept in the forefront.

... What was your object in publishing the pamphlet?

My object in publishing it was to place the entire facts regarding the position of the Indians in South Africa before the Indian public. The people here believe that India does not know exactly how many Indians were outside the country, and what their status was, and the object was to draw their attention to the subject, and it was with that view that the pamphlet was published.

But had you not an ulterior object?

The ulterior object was to have the status of the Indians decided to our satisfaction; that is to say, in terms with the Proclamation of 1858 (*applicable to India, which assured Indians that they would not be discriminated against - ed.*).

... What means do you propose adopting?

We desire them to go in for a constitutional agitation in India. At every meeting that has been held, resolutions have been passed authorizing the chairman to draw up memorials addressed to the Indian Government and the Home Government, drawing their attention to the position of the Indians in South Africa. These meetings have been held throughout the presidencies of Bombay, Madras and Calcutta.

Have you received any encouragement from the Indian Government on the subject?

No; I had to return before I received any reply.

Mr. Gandhi continued:

It has been said that I went to India to blacken the character of the Natal Colonists. This I must emphatically deny. It will be remembered that I addressed an "Open Letter" to the members of the Natal Parliament about two years ago, and there I gave my view of the treatment the Indians were receiving, and it was exactly that view that I placed before the Indian public. In fact, I copied an extract from that "Open Letter", word for word, into my pamphlet. It gave my view of the treatment the Indians were receiving before, and no exception was taken to that portion of the "Open Letter" when it was published here. No one then said that I was blackening the character of the Colonists, but only when that statement was repeated in India. ...

... In your Indian campaign what attitude did you adopt towards the indentured Indian question?

I have said most emphatically, in the pamphlets and elsewhere, that the treatment of the indentured Indians is no worse or better in Natal than they receive in other parts of the world. I have never endeavoured to show that the indentured Indians have been receiving cruel treatment. The question, generally speaking, is not a question of the ill-treatment of Indians, but of the legal disabilities that are placed on them. I have even said in the pamphlet that instances I have quoted show that the treatment that the Indians receive was owing to the prejudice against them, and what I have endeavoured to show is the connection between the prejudice and the laws passed by the Colony to restrict the freedom of the Indian.

... I have said that the Indians did not approach the Indian Government, the Indian public, or the Home Government, with the view to having any redress against the prejudices of these Colonists. I have said that Indians are the most hated beings in South Africa, and that they are being ill-treated; but, for all that we do not ask the Government for redress with regard to these things, but with regard to the legal disabilities that are placed upon the Indians. We protest against the legislation passed by prejudice, and redress has been asked for against them. ... It has been said in the papers that there is an organized attempt, under my leadership, to swamp the Colony with Indians. This statement is absolutely false. I have as much to do with having induced these passengers to come here as I have with inducing passengers to come from Europe. No such attempt has ever been made.

... My object throughout is not to sow dissension between the two communities, but to assist at creating harmony between the two, without the Indians having to accept any degradation of their status as conferred upon them by the Proclamation of 1858, when it was stated that all subjects of Her Majesty in India would be treated on a footing of equality without distinction of race, colour, or creed; and I submit, I am justified in requesting every Colonist to tolerate the attitude, however much they have differed from it.

*The Natal Advertiser*, 14.1.1887 (2: 4-7)

---

*Gandhi began to write and publish his own newspaper,* Indian Opinion, *in 1903. The paper appeared in English and Gujarati (and briefly in Tamil) and was consciously used to educate Indians on political matters and to address the colonists.*

### The Cinderella of the Empire

... So far as the burden of the Empire is concerned, at every step, India is called upon very naturally to give at least her own share, and that in no ungrudging spirit. Is India to take her full share of the burden only, and never receive or participate in the glory of the privileges of the Empire?

We read that, from the earliest struggles (*through which the British gained supremacy, using Indian fighters - ed.*) , she has been, shall we say, heroically performing her duty. We are told by Lord Macaulay that at the siege of Arcot, the Indian soldiers voluntarily denied themselves a portion of their own rations and gave up their rice to their English comrades, contenting themselves with merely the water in which the rice was boiled. This was not done for sentiment only, but the privations that the besieged had to suffer were so great, that the Indian soldiers considered it their duty to forgo their own portion. During the wars in Afghanistan, do we not read, in the graphic description left of them by the late Sir John Kaye, that thousands of Indians were embedded in the snow passes uncomplainingly? ...

... We are unwilling to prolong the list of these services, nor do we intend to lay any undue stress upon them. Moreover, we are not blind to the fact that the English share of the burden is far greater, far severer, far ampler in quantity than any that India has borne, but we do say that, if comparison were to be set up between the privileges also enjoyed by both, we do think that India would not come out unfavourably in the competition. We may state, ... we do not import into consideration the fact often flung in the faces of the Indian races, namely, that, after all is said and done, they are conquered, and therefore, not entitled to the same rights as real Britishers. We dismiss this from our consideration for two very sound reasons, the one given by Professor Seely in his *Expansion of Great Britain,* namely, that in the real sense of the term India is not a conquered country, but that it is British because the vast majority of its people have, perhaps for selfish reasons, accepted British rule. The second reason is, that British statesmen have times without number disavowed any connection whatsoever with the idea of inequality necessarily existing between the conquerors and the conquered, other things being equal, and they have done this more especially with regard to the British Indians.

We have, therefore, now cleared the ground for asking the Colonists a simple question: where does India come in so far as their Imperialism is concerned, if British Indians may not have simple rights of citizenship in British territory, as the Colonists here and perhaps elsewhere would have it? Is it an equable bargain that, while India is expected to bear the burden of the Empire, she may not get the benefits of that Empire? ...

...We are addressing these thoughts to the Colonists in the hope that they will receive them in the spirit in which they are given.

*Indian Opinion,* 30-7-1903 (3: 169-71)

## The Virtue of Service: Doing Good

---

*Gandhi's responses to the South African dilemma were marked by a strong moral fervour. He entreated, argued and invoked the morality of Christian faith and English practice to hold up a mirror to the rulers, in which they could recognize their virtues and act on them. And, importantly, to prove the rightness of his cause, he undertook to serve English rule—during the Boer wars (1899), when the English colonies fought the Boers, who were fiercely independent Dutch settlers, and the Zulu wars when the colonists put down a Zulu uprising (1906) —in the faith that the rulers would honour those that stood by them in times of need.*

*Significantly, he held that it was not for him as a subject of Empire to debate and judge the merits of these wars. A classic instance of turning the other cheek, this mode of dutifully suffering one's condition expanded into a strategy of passive resistance after 1906, when the Indians' war-time efforts were ill-served by government ordinances that affirmed racial preferences and divisions.*

---

**The Indian Offer**
**Durban, October 19, 1899**

TO
THE HONOURABLE THE COLONIAL SECRETARY
MARITZBURG

SIR,

About 100 English-speaking Indians of Durban met together at a few hours' notice on the 17th inst. to consider the desirability of unreservedly and unconditionally offering their services to the Government or the Imperial authorities in connection with the hostilities now pending between the Imperial Government and the two Republics in South Africa.

... We do not know how to handle arms. It is not our fault; it is perhaps our misfortune that we cannot, but it may be there are other duties no less important to be performed on the battlefield and, no matter of what description they may be, we would consider it a privilege to be called upon to perform them and would be ready to respond to the call at any time appointed by the Government. If an unflinching devotion to duty and extreme eagerness to serve our Sovereign can make us of any use on the field of battle, we trust we would not fail. It may be that, if in no other direction, we might render some service in connection with the field hospitals or the commissariat. The motive underlying this humble offer is to endeavour to prove that, in common with other subjects of the Queen-Empress in South Africa, the Indians, too, are ready to do duty for their Sovereign on the battlefield ...

... The mercantile portion of the Indian community, too, have loyally come forward, and if they cannot offer their services on the battlefield, they have contributed towards the maintenance of the dependants of those volunteers whose circumstances would render support necessary.

I venture to trust that our prayer would be granted, a favour for which the petitioners will be ever grateful and which would, in my humble opinion, be a link to bind closer still the different parts of the mighty empire of which we are so proud.

I have the honour to be,
Sir,
your obedient servant,
M. K. GANDHI

From the photostats of a typed office copy, a rough pencil draft in Gandhi's own hand, S. N. 3301-2, and *The Natal Mercury*, 25-10-1899 (2: 316-17)

---

*Gandhi visited India in 1901 and spoke widely on the various aspects of the South African problem. In this particular address, he recalls the reasons for Indians having supported the British during the Boer War.*

## Speech at Calcutta Meeting
## January 27, 1902

MR CHAIRMAN AND GENTLEMEN,

... We claimed the privileges of British subjects. Now was the time to discharge the responsibilities of that status; the local differences were to be sunk if the policy referred to at the outset was to be carried out; we had nothing to do with the question whether the war was right or wrong. That was the function of the Sovereign. Thus argued your countrymen at a great meeting convened for the purpose. Here was the opportunity to answer the oft-repeated charge in the Colony, that, if there was a war, the Indians would scuttle away like rabbits. It was resolved at that meeting to offer the services of those assembled there, free of charge, to do any work at the front for which they might be found fit. The Government, while thanking the volunteers, replied that their services were not required. In the meanwhile, there returned from England a ... medical missionary belonging to the Church of England. His name is Canon Booth, now Dean of St. John. ... He offered to train them as ambulance leaders. ...We ... telegraphed to the Government informing them as to how we were qualifying ourselves. And intimation was received from the Government that we were to help the Protector of Indian Immigrants in forming a volunteer Indian Ambulance Corps. Within four or five days, about 1,000 Indians were collected, a majority from the various estates. These were, of course, in no way bound to offer their services, nor was the slightest pressure imposed on them. It was entirely a free-will offering on their part ...

... I would not be true to myself if I did not give you an idea of the impression that was created in the minds of many of us about the life of the British soldier when at work, and especially under temporary reverses. ... Although the energy put forth was the greatest—not a minute was passed idly by anybody in those stirring times—there was perfect order, perfect stillness. Tommy was then altogether lovable. He mixed with us and the men freely. He often shared with us his luxuries whenever there were any to be had. ... There was, shall I say, a spirit of brotherhood irrespective of colour or creed. The Red Cross badge or the khaki uniform was a sufficient passport whether the bearer had a white skin or brown.

As a Hindu, I do not believe in war, but if anything can even partially reconcile me to it, it was the rich experience we gained at the front. It was certainly not the thirst for blood that took thousands of men to the battlefield. ... they went to the battlefield, because it was their duty. And how many proud, rude, savage spirits has it not broken into gentle creatures of God? ...

*The Englishman,* 28-1-1902 (2: 437-440)

---

*Gandhi wrote up his South African experiences into a book years later (*Satyagraha in South Africa, 1928*), recalling and reconstructing from memory the events of those momentous days. This extract from the book offers a slightly different interpretation on the role of Indians in the Boer wars.*

## The Boer War

... Our existence in South Africa is only in our capacity as British subjects. In every memorial we have presented, we have asserted our rights as such. We have been proud of our British citizenship, or have given our rulers and the world to believe that we are so proud. Our rulers profess to safeguard our rights because we are British subjects, and what little rights we still retain, we retain because we are British subjects. It would be unbecoming to our dignity as a nation to look on with folded hands at a time when ruin stares the British as well as ourselves in the face simply because they ill-treat us here. Any such criminal inaction could only aggravate our difficulties ... If we desire to win our freedom and achieve our welfare as members of the British Empire, here is a golden opportunity for us to do so by helping the British in the war by all the means at our disposal. It must largely be conceded that justice is on the side of the Boers. But every single subject of a state must not hope to enforce his private opinion in all cases. The authorities may not always be right, but so long as the subjects owe allegiance to a state, it is their clear duty generally to accommodate themselves and to accord their support to acts of the state.

Again, if any class among the subjects consider that the action of a government is immoral from a religious standpoint before they help or hinder it, they must endeavour fully and even at the risk of their lives to dissuade the Government from pursuing such a course. We have done nothing of the kind. Such a moral crisis is not present before us, and no one says that we wish to hold aloof from this war for any such universal and comprehensive reason. Our ordinary duty as subjects, therefore, is not to enter into the merits of the war, but, when war has actually broken out, to render such assistance as we possibly can ...

*Satyagraha in South Africa* (34: 62-3)

---

*In 1906, the Zulus under Chief Bambata ranged themselves against the colonists in what turned out to be a protracted bloody war. Once again, Gandhi arranged for an Indian volunteer team to be formed to offer medical support during the British war against the Zulus.*

### Indian Volunteers

... Wars are not fought all the time. A war breaks out, roughly speaking, once in twenty years. It is now more than twenty years since the last Kaffir rebellion broke out. There is, therefore, absolutely no risk in joining the Volunteer Corps. It can be looked upon as a kind of annual picnic. The person joining it gets enough exercise and thus keeps his body in good trim and improves his health. One who enlists as a volunteer is much respected. People love him and praise him, calling him a civilian soldier.

If the Indians are given such a status, we believe it would be a very good thing. It is likely to bring in some political advantage. Whether or not any advantage is to be derived, there is no doubt that it is our duty to enlist. Hundreds of leading whites enlist themselves and take pride in doing so. Under the prevailing law, it is open to the Government to enlist compulsorily. We ought to obey the laws designed for the defence of the country we live in. Therefore, considering the matter from any point, it is clear that, if we are able to join the Volunteer Corps, the reproach against us would be lived down, once and for all. For fifteen years now the whites have accused the Indians that, if it came to giving one's life in defence of Natal, they would desert their posts of duty and flee home. We cannot meet this charge with a written rejoinder. There is but one way of disproving it—the way of action. The time to act appears to have come now. But how is it to be done? Not by making volunteers out of the poor labourers freed from their indentures. It is the duty of the trading community to take part in the movement themselves. Many men can be trained up even if each shop offers only one man. Trade will not suffer. The condition of those who join will improve. They will gain in strength and energy and will be deemed to have done their duty as citizens ...

*Indian Opinion* 23.6.1906 (from the Gujarati) (5: 268-69)

---

*This account of Indian participation in voluntary service during the Zulu wars is from* Satyagraha in South Africa.

## The Reward of Gentleness—The Black Act

... The corps (*during the Zulu Wars - ed.*) was on active service for a month. I have always been thankful to God for the work which then fell to our lot. We found that the wounded Zulus would have been left uncared for, if we had not attended to them. No European would help to dress their wounds. Dr. Savage, who was in charge of the ambulance, was himself a very humane person. It was no part of our duty to nurse the wounded after we had taken them to the hospital. But we had joined the war with a desire to do all we could, no matter whether it did or did not fall within the scope of our work. The good Doctor told us that he could not induce Europeans to nurse the Zulus, that it was beyond his power to compel them and that he would feel obliged if we undertook this mission of mercy. We were only too glad to do this. We had to cleanse the wounds of several Zulus which had not been attended to for as many as five or six days and were therefore stinking horribly. We liked the work. The Zulus could not talk to us, but from their gestures and the expression of their eyes they seemed to feel as if God had sent us to their succour. The work for which we had enlisted was fairly heavy, for sometimes during the month we had to perform a march of as many as forty miles a day ...

*Satyagraha in South Africa* (34: 83)

## Resisting Evil: Passive Resistance

*Gandhi's distinctive mode of public action evolved in response to the racial policies of the colonial government of the Transvaal. Transvaal, along with Natal, had large numbers of Indian settlers who experienced diverse sorts of civil and legal discrimination. In 1906, the South African government of the Transvaal passed an Ordinance (also known as the Asiatic or the Transvaal Ordinance), which required Indians of all classes to re-register their presence, and submit to finger-printing, as a form of identification. Earlier, only thumb impressions were required, and chiefly from labourers who did not know to read and write. The call for fingerprinting was interpreted by Indian notables, including Gandhi, as a sign of a desire to stigmatise Indians and remind them of their inferior status in the colony. Gandhi and another Indian notables were chosen to present the Indian case against the Ordinance to the imperial government in London.*

*Gandhi's mission seemed successful but in reality it was not so. Upset with what appeared an instance of imperial doublespeak, he and his fellow Indians pledged to defy the Asiatic Ordinance and launched the first passive resistance struggle in South Africa. As it gathered momentum, passive resistance came to be re-christened 'satyagraha', or a 'war of truth'. Even as he held fast to his pledge, Gandhi remained open to negotiation and dialogue. As a passive resister, he seldom gave up on those who held power. He wished to engage their conscience and if this meant he and his men should stage a retreat and be prepared to negotiate, he did not mind doing so. Nor did he consider such measures as compromising his struggle in the cause of truth. For, as he adroitly argued, truth demanded that one act in faith and bear no ill-will towards one's adversary. In the event, though, his trust in government proved to be rather misplaced and he had to start satyagraha all over again.*

*Gandhi's last struggle in South Africa, launched against a tax that burdened indentured labourers and a court judgment that held non-Christian marriages contracted outside South Africa to be invalid, proved to be an epic one. The end of the struggle found him ready to sail home. These extracts capture dramatic moments in the history of satyagraha in South Africa.*

*Gandhi was a keen watcher of world events. In 1905 a democratic revolution in Russia weakened the powers of the Tsar considerably. To Gandhi, troubled by the legal and moral implications of the Asiatic Ordinance, Russian developments appeared to hold an augury for the future of Indians in South Africa.*

### Russia and India

... Under British rule, we draft petitions, carry on a struggle through the Press, and seek justice from the King. All this is perfectly proper. It is necessary, and it also brings us some relief. But is there anything else that we should do? And, can we do it? We shall think of these questions later. For the present, let us see what Russia is doing. The people there, both rich and poor, do not send petitions and stop there. The oppression there is such that it has given rise to a number of anarchists. They believe that all rulers are oppressive, and the State should therefore be done away with. To achieve this end, people in Russia kill the officials openly as well as secretly. In this, however, they are making a mistake. Such thoughtless adventures only serve to keep the minds of both the rulers and the ruled in a state of constant tension. All the same, it is admitted on all hands that men taking such risks must be brave and patriotic.

Even young girls set out on such adventures and court risks. A book was recently published about the lives of young women who have thus made themselves immortal. Knowing that death is certain, these fearless girls, actuated by patriotism and a spirit of self-sacrifice, take the lives of those whom they believe to be the enemies of the country, and themselves meet an agonising death at the hands of officials. Facing such risks, they serve their country selflessly. It will be no wonder if such a country succeeds in achieving freedom from tyranny. The only reason why it has not become free immediately is that such patriotism is misdirected, as we have pointed out before, and results in bloodshed. In consequence, these people cannot, according to divine law, obtain any immediate benefit.

Do our people display patriotism of this order? We have regretfully to say "No". No one can be blamed, for we have not yet been trained for this. We are children in political matters. We do not understand the principle that the public good is also one's own good. But the time has now come for us to outgrow this state of mind. We need not, however, resort to violence. Neither need we set out on adventures, risking our lives. We must, however, submit our bodies to pain, and the new Transvaal Ordinance offers an excellent opportunity. The Ordinance represents the limit of oppression. It is not for us to punish those who made that Ordinance. If we did that, we would be as much at fault as the Russians. Indians are a meek people, and we wish they will always remain so. What, then, should we do? ... If, disregarding our attempts at gentle persuasion, the Government enforces the Ordinance, Indians will not abide by it; they will not [re-]register themselves, nor will they pay fines; they will rather go to gaol. We believe that, if the Indians in the Transvaal firmly stick to this resolution, they will at once be free of their shackles. The gaol will then be like a palace to them. Instead of being a disgrace, going to gaol will enhance their prestige. And the Government, for its part, will realize that it cannot with impunity go on humiliating Indians.

What we do not do, besides addressing petitions—though we ought to do it—is that we will not sacrifice our bodily comforts. We give ourselves over to physical pleasures and cannot give them up. It is our duty to make some sacrifice for the sake of others. We do not realize that there is real beauty in this: that it is thus that we please God and do our true duty. ...

*Indian Opinion*, 8-9-1906 (from Gujarati) (5: 327-38)

---

*Following the promulgation of the Asiatic Ordinance (1906), Gandhi and a few others were deputed by the Indian community to visit London and lay their case before the imperial government. He received the sympathetic ear of several liberal Englishmen, in government and civil society. This letter, written on the eve of his return to South Africa summarises the Indian case.*

**Letter to the Press**
**Hotel Cecil, Strand, W. C.**
**November 30, 1906**

TO
THE EDITOR
THE TIMES
LONDON

SIR,

On the eve of the departure of the Indian Deputation from the Transvaal, may we trespass upon your courtesy to allow us to offer our thanks to the many supporters of the British Indian cause who have rendered us their valuable assistance in putting our case before the Imperial Government and the British public. The unfailing courtesy we have experienced from gentlemen representing different shades of opinion, from all parties, and from the Press has been a source of keenest satisfaction to us and has inspired us with a new hope. Our brief stay in London has prevented us from personally waiting on all whom we should have liked to meet. We have, however, received support and sympathy even from them.

The lesson we have drawn from the above is that we may rely upon the British sense of fair play and justice and that the cause we have the honour to espouse is absolutely just. May we restate it in a few words? We ask for no political power in the Transvaal. We do not strive for unrestricted immigration of British Indians, but we do respectfully and emphatically claim the ordinary rights of citizenship for those who are already in the country namely, freedom of ownership of land, freedom of locomotion, freedom of trade, subject to such requirements as may be necessary in the interests of the community as a whole. In short, the British Indians in the Transvaal claim the right to live in the Transvaal with self-respect and dignity. The Indian community protests against any class distinction being made, and it has exerted itself against the Asiatic Law Amendment Ordinance, because it violates in the most brutal manner the principles above laid down.

In our humble opinion we feel that if we cannot secure for our countrymen, whom we have the honour to represent, the above measure of recognition, the term "British Indian" becomes an empty platitude and "Empire" ceases to have any meaning for the British Indian. In coming to England and laying our case before the Home Government, we have no desire to offer violent opposition to the

European Colonists in the Transvaal. Ours is wholly a defensive attitude. When the local Government, in the name of the people of the Transvaal, sends to the Imperial Government for assent a piece of offensive legislation to protect and accentuate colour prejudice, we are obliged, in self-defence, to lay before the same Government the Indian side of the question. We are anxious and willing to work out our own salvation by our conduct, and by showing to the Colonists that their interests are also our interests and that our goal is the common advancement of them and us. We cannot do this if we do not get breathing time, by reason of the anti-Indian prejudice of the few being crystallized into and receiving the hallmark of legislation under the King's Sign Manual.

We are,

M. K. GANDHI

H. O. ALLY

*The Times*, 3-12-1906 (6: 188-89)

---

*Gandhi's English visit did not win him his pleas on behalf of his countrymen. The imperial government assured him that it would not assent to the Asiatic Ordinance, but in the same breath informed colonial authorities in South Africa that they would not withhold such an assent, should a self-governing South African republic demand it. Since self-government was in the offing for England's South African possessions, this effectively neutralized the imperial promise made to Gandhi. Realising this, Gandhi and his peers decided to embark on an agitation—they vowed, in the name of God, that they would not honour the Asiatic Ordinance. This summary of his position at that time is excerpted from* Satyagraha in South Africa.

### The Advent of Satyagraha

I wish to explain to this meeting that there is a vast difference between this resolution (*to defy the Asiatic Ordinance - ed.*) and every other resolution we have passed upto date and that there is a wide divergence also in the manner of making it. It is a very grave resolution we are making, as our existence in South Africa depends upon our fully observing it. ...

We all believe in one and the same God, the differences of nomenclature in Hinduism and Islam notwithstanding. To pledge ourselves or to take an oath in the name of that God or with Him as witness is not something to be trifled with. If having taken such an oath we violate our pledge we are guilty before God and man. Personally I hold that a man, who deliberately and intelligently takes a pledge and then breaks it, forfeits his manhood. ... You are all well advanced in age and have seen the world; many of you are delegates and have discharged responsibilities in a greater or lesser measure. No one present, therefore, can ever hope to excuse himself by saying that he did not know what he was about when he took the oath.

I know that pledges and vows are, and should be, taken on rare occasions. A man who takes a vow every now and then is sure to stumble. But if I can imagine a crisis in the history of the Indian community of South Africa when it would be in the fitness of things to take pledges, that crisis is surely now. There is wisdom in taking serious steps with great caution and hesitation. But caution and hesitation have their limits, which we have now passed. The Government has taken leave of all sense of decency. ... This pledge must not be taken with a view to produce an effect on outsiders. No one should trouble to consider what impression it might have upon the local Government, the Imperial Government, or the Government of India. Every one must only search his own heart, and if the voice assures him that he has the requisite strength to carry him through, then only should he pledge himself and then only would his pledge bear fruit. A few words now as to the consequences.

... It is not at all impossible that we might have to endure every hardship that we can imagine, and wisdom lies in pledging ourselves on the understanding that we shall have to suffer all that and worse. If someone asks me when and how the struggle may end, I may say that, if the entire community manfully stands the test, the end will be near. If many of us fall back under storm and stress, the struggle will be prolonged. But I can boldly declare, and with certainty, that so long as there is even a handful of men true to their pledge, there can only be one end to the struggle, and that is victory.

A word about my personal responsibility. If I am warning you of the risks attendant upon the pledge, I am at the same time inviting you to pledge yourselves, and I am fully conscious of my responsibility in the matter. ... I wish respectfully to suggest it to you that, if you have not the will or the ability to stand firm even when you are perfectly isolated, you must not only not take the pledge yourselves, but you must declare your opposition before the resolution is put to the meeting and before its members begin to take pledges and you must not make yourselves parties to the resolution. Although we are going to take the pledge in a body, no one should imagine that default on the part of one or many can absolve the rest from their obligation. Every one should fully realize his responsibility, then only pledge himself independently of others and understand that he himself must be true to his pledge even unto death, no matter what others do ...

*Satyagraha in South Africa* (34: 89-91)

---

*Gandhi spent a lot of time arguing his case for resisting the Asiatic Ordinance. Conscious that he was calling for a novel mode of struggle, he had recourse to a textured rhetoric, which counselled Indians to shed fear, act as their conscience dictated, and suffer for a common cause.*

## Tyranny of Law

... As for looking after oneself, even birds and beasts do this. The chief difference between man and beast is that man is a benevolent creature. All live happily where one feels happy in the happiness of others. But where everyone looks after himself alone, all are lost. For, as the poet says, "He who will let others go to the bottom, shall himself flounder." This is an important idea and a little reflection will show that it is true. A mother suffers discomfort to bring up her child.

In the end such a mother finds herself happy. Where the members of a family share one another's burdens and give up individual interests, the whole family is well sustained. Members of a community individually suffer to save the group as a whole and are themselves saved too. Similarly, where men undergo suffering or die for their country's sake, they truly live and bring credit to the country. Is there any Indian who seeks happiness for himself by breaking this fundamental law? These examples clearly prove that the Transvaal Indians will be victorious if, for the sake of the Indian community and for the sake of their personal honour, they endure all sufferings and face all hardships to accomplish the task they have undertaken. They will then break their bonds and win immortal fame in history.

*Indian Opinion*, 15-6-1907 (from Gujarati) (7: 2)

---

## Letter to *Rand Daily Mail*
Johannesburg, July 6, 1907

TO
THE EDITOR
RAND DAILY MAIL

SIR,

... I, personally, feel ... that the faculty of suffering for the common good has only lain dormant (*in the Indians - ed.*), and that, under stress of circumstances, it is being again quickened into life. Picketing is by no means a new thing to the Indian mind. The network of castes in India simply illustrates the use and value of that weapon, provided that it is rightly used. Ostracism and excommunication are the most powerful instruments resorted to today in India, in unfortunately trivial matters, and, if the Registration Act now enables my countrymen to realize the use of that terrible weapon for a higher purpose ...

... There is, of course, therefore, nothing strange in Indian pickets, (for them) rare self-sacrifice and courage, endeavouring to show their ignorant or weakly brethren the path of duty. At the same time, there is just as much difference today between Western pickets and Eastern, or, rather, Indian, as there is, apparently, between West and East. We have no desire to terrorise. We do not wish to compel obedience to the wish of the majority, but, like the indomitable Salvation Army lasses, we do, in our humble manner, wish with all the persuasive power of which we may be capable to inform those who do not know of what is held to be the right view of the Asiatic

Registration Act. It is, then, left open to such men either to accept the advice that may be given by us, or to accept the degrading Act and to sell themselves for a miserable existence in this country ...

*Rand Daily Mail*, 9-7-1907 (7: 50-51)

## Johannesburg Letter

... Many whites have been offering advice to Indians. When the former ask "What will you do?", many Indians say in reply, "We shall do what our leaders do." Some answer, "We shall do what others do." These are words of cowards, and they will do harm. Everyone should give the reply: "I dislike the law and so I will never submit to it. Moreover, I will not submit to it also because I have taken an oath in the name of God. I would rather go to gaol than submit to the law which would make a slave of me." He who cannot give this answer will never reach the other shore. None can swim with another's buoy. We are to swim with our own strength. Will the reader swallow dust because I choose to do so? Will he fall into a pit because I do so? Will he forsake his religion because I do so? I may stand my mother's humiliation, turn my sons into thieves, and have the fingers of myself and of my sons cut off; will the reader do likewise? Everyone will answer "Never!" In a similar spirit, everyone should answer, "I don't care what others do, but I for my part will not submit to the law."

*Indian Opinion*, 13-7-1907 (7: 55-6)

*Gandhi's experiments in resistance took courage from both religious and secular traditions of righteous suffering—the diverse examples of Buddha, Jesus, and English suffragettes fighting for the women's vote all equally ennobled his intentions to defy unjust laws.*

## Divine Law

... To submit to the unjust law will be a sin. Likewise, it will be a sin to violate the divine law. He who abides by the divine law will win bliss in this world, as also in the next. What is this divine law? It is that one has to suffer pain before enjoying pleasure and that one's true self-interest consists in the good of all, which means that we should die—suffer—for others. Let us take a few examples.

When a lump of earth is broken into dust, it mixes with water and nourishes plant life. It is by sacrificing themselves that plants sustain every kind of animal life. Animals sacrifice themselves for the good of their progeny. The mother suffers unbearable pain at the time of child-birth, but feels only happy in that suffering. Both the mother and the father undergo hardships in bringing up their children. Wherever communities and nations exist, individual members of those communities or nations have endured hardships for the common good. In the sixth century B. C., Lord Buddha, after wandering from forest to forest, braving the extremes of heat and cold and suffering many privations, attained self-realization and spread ideas of spiritual welfare among the people. Nineteen hundred years ago, Jesus Christ, according to the Christian belief, dedicated his life to the people and suffered many insults and hardships. The prophet Mahomed suffered much. People had prepared themselves for an attack on his life. He paid no heed to it. These great and holy men obeyed the law stated above and brought happiness to mankind. They did not think of their personal interest but found their own happiness in the happiness of others.

The same thing happens in political matters too. Hampden, Tyler, Cromwell and other Englishmen were prepared to sacrifice their all for the people and did not feel concerned at being robbed of all their possessions. Nor did they feel anxious when their lives were in danger. That is why the British people today rule over a large empire. The rulers of the Transvaal enjoy power because they suffered great hardships before our very eyes. Mazzini suffered banishment for the sake of his country. Today he is being revered. He is regarded as the father of Italian unity. By suffering endless hardships, George Washington made America what it is today. This again shows that one must pass through suffering before tasting happiness. For public good, men have to suffer hardships even to the point of death.

Let us go further. It is a sin to violate one's pledge—to betray manhood with which we are endowed. To save himself from the sin of incest, Yusoof Abesalam suffered gaol. Imam Hasan and

Hussein refused to acknowledge the authority of Yazid, for it would have been wrong to do so. For this reason, that is, in order to preserve their honour, they became martyrs. For the sake of honour, God's devotee, Prahlad, boldly embraced the red-hot pillar, and the child Sudhanva threw himself into the frying pan without any hesitation. For the sake of truth, Harishchandra allowed himself to be sold to a low-caste man; he gave up his throne and suffered separation from his wife and son. For the sake of his father's word, Ramachandra went into the forest. And for the sake of their right, the Pandavas left their kingdom and wandered in the forest for 14 years.

Today it has fallen to the lot of the Indian community in the Transvaal to submit to this great divine law. So persuaded, we congratulate our countrymen. They have the opportunity now to see the Indian community throughout South Africa gaining its freedom through them. How could such great happiness come to us without our going through equally great suffering? Our petition is no longer addressed to man, but to God Himself. Day and night He listens to our plaints. We do not have to seek an appointment with Him for the hearing of our petition. He hears the petitions of all at the same time. With the purest heart therefore we pray to God that our brothers in the Transvaal may be prepared to suffer fearlessly anything that may befall them in August, placing their trust in Him alone, and with only His name on their lips.

*Indian Opinion*, 27-7-1907 (from Gujarati) (7: 88-9)

---

### Brave Women

... The struggle of the Transvaal Indians is nothing when compared with the courage and the tenacity of these women (*the suffragettes - ed.*). Moreover, they have to face opposition from many women. There is a much larger number of women against than in favour of franchise for themselves. Though a mere handful, these women do not admit defeat. The more they are repressed, the more the resistance they offer. Many of them have been to gaol. They have borne being kicked and stoned by base and cowardly men.

There was a cable last week that they had resolved to intensify their struggle still further. There are taxes to be paid to the

Government by these women or their husbands. If they do not pay the taxes, whatever things they possess can be auctioned. They may even be imprisoned. The women have now resolved that they will not pay any taxes or levies till they get their rights, but will rather allow their possessions to be auctioned, and they themselves will suffer imprisonment. This courage and tenacity deserves to be emulated by the Transvaal Indians, in fact, by the whole Indian community.

The Natal Indians think it much of a hardship if their goods are to be auctioned for trading without a licence. These people do not realize that the Government cannot auction the goods of a large number of people. But what would it matter if it did ? If women can sacrifice their possessions for a matter like franchise, cannot we put up with a similar hardship while fighting for our livelihood? The movement of the suffragettes will go on for a long time, and they will keep up the agitation, resolute and tireless. They fight on with faith in truth, persuaded that, though they will not be there to enjoy the rights, if only the succeeding generations enjoy them, it will be as good as if they had themselves done so. Indians have to fight with the same spirit.

*Indian Opinion*, 28-12-1907 (from Gujarati) (8: 29)

---

*For Gandhi, the Asiatic Ordinance represented a subtle political evil, which drew upon legal strictures to validate prejudice and hatred. He did not mind that Indians had to register their presence in the colony, only that the registration was imposed on them in ways that challenged their self-respect.*

### Why Do We Oppose Law

... Why are we opposing the law? Let us now consider the answer. To many it appears that there is a fight because of the objection to giving ten finger-prints, to some, the only objectionable thing is submitting the names of mother and wife; while others say that it is painful to think of the police making a house-to-house search. ... The things referred to above are objectionable because they have been introduced with a view to insulting us. Not all yellow people suffer from jaundice. But, generally speaking, if we see an emaciated body which is yellow, we shall take it for granted that the person has got that disease. A physician will not treat the person for being yellow. He will treat him for jaundice.

We have to spot out, then, the jaundice in the law. It is this: that the white people, by introducing this law, wish to show that the Asiatics are not men but beasts; not free men, but slaves; not their equals, but their inferiors; that they are born to endure whatever is inflicted on them, that they have no right to protest; that they are not men, but cowards. [Taking of] finger-prints, etc., is only a symptom of this condition, this jaundice. Whatever the law wants us to do, it wants us to do under compulsion. The Indian, who is a man of credit, is assumed to be a thief. Assuming that we are thieves, they also consider our children to be thieves, and strike fear in them by unworthy attacks on them. In our country the words, "A European is coming", arouse terror in children from infancy. So here also this law is intended to terrorize them. If we were asked to point out in which section of the law all this occurs, it would be difficult to reply. No one can point to the flower of Deadly Nightshade and say which part of it contains the poison. The proof of the poison is in eating [its berries]; and the same is true of this law. If this law is read and fully understood by a proud and self-respecting man, it cannot but send a shudder through his body. It deprives the Indian of the very spirit of manliness in him ...

*Indian Opinion*, 30-11-1907 (from Gujarati) (7: 379-81)

---

*Resistance to the Asiatic Ordinance took the form of disobeying the law—Indians refused to register themselves, upon which many were arrested. Gandhi refused to concede that this strategy of resisting a wrongful law was detrimental to civic health.*

**Letter to *The Star***
**Johannesburg, December 30, 1907**

TO
THE EDITOR
THE STAR

SIR,

The Government are to be congratulated on boldly and honestly taking proceedings mainly against those only who have led the passive resistance movement against the Asiatic Act. That, indeed, is the only method of testing the reality and universality of Asiatic feeling. ... The arrests have synchronised with the announcement of the Royal Assent to the Immigration Act. This shows that the Government intend to use their newly-acquired power. They have now three strings to their bow, viz., imprisonment, the stopping of trade licences, and deportation. ... If I do not submit to the Asiatic Act I am deported, that is, put across the border or sent to India without a penny on me, if I do not possess private property, to shift for myself as best I can, the cost of deportation to be paid by me. And if I have a family in the Transvaal, so far as the Government are concerned, they will be allowed to die of starvation. And this, mind, is to happen to men to whom the Transvaal is their adopted home and India a foreign country for purposes of earning a livelihood. ... I do not say that those who do not comply with the law, even when non-compliance is due to the dictates of the conscience, should not be punished at all, but I do say that when the punishment is disproportionate to the offence, it savours strongly of barbarism.

... I consider myself a lover of the British Empire, a citizen (though voteless) of the Transvaal, prepared to take my full share in promoting the general well-being of the country. And I claim it to be perfectly honourable, and consistent with the above profession, to advise my countrymen not to submit to the Asiatic Act as being derogatory to their manhood and offensive to their religion. And I claim, too, that the method of passive resistance adopted to combat the mischief is the cleanest and the safest, because, if the cause is not true, it is the resisters, and they alone, who suffer.

I am perfectly aware of the danger to good government, in a country inhabited by many races unequally developed, in an honest citizen advising resistance to a law of the land. But I refuse to believe in the infallibility of legislators. I do believe that they are not always guided by generous or even just sentiments in their dealings with unrepresented classes. I venture to say that, if passive resistance is generally accepted, it will once and for ever avoid the contingency of a terrible death struggle and bloodshed in the event (not impossible) of the natives becoming exasperated by a stupid mistake of our legislators.

It has been said that those who do not like the law may leave the country. ... No, Sir, if I could help it, nothing would remove Indians from the country save brute force. It is no part of a citizen's duty to pay blind obedience to the laws imposed on him. And if my countrymen believe in God and the existence of the soul, then, while they may admit that their bodies belong to the State to be imprisoned and deported, their minds, their wills and their souls must ever remain free like the birds of the air, and are beyond the reach of the swiftest arrow. ... If, when the leaders are withdrawn, my countrymen succumb, we shall have deserved the law. Then, too, the cleanness of passive resistance, that is Jesus' teaching "resist not evil", will have been justified.

I am, etc.,

M. K. GANDHI

*The Star*, 30-12-1907 (8: 47-48)

---

*The resistance to an unjust law came to be described as passive resistance. Gandhi was, however, unhappy with the term, since it appeared limiting and negative in its connotations. This is how he came up with another term for what appeared to him a war in the cause of truth.*

## Johannesburg Letter
## Before January 10, 1908

PASSIVE RESISTANCE

The editor had invited [suggestions from readers for] a Gujarati equivalent for "passive resistance". I have received one which is not bad, though it does not render the original in its full connotation. I shall, however, use it for the present. The word is *sadagraha*. I think *satyagraha* is better than *sadagraha*. "Resistance" means determined opposition to anything. The correspondent has rendered it as *agraha*. *Agraha* in a right cause is *sat* or *satya agraha*. The correspondent therefore has rendered "passive resistance" as firmness in a good cause. Though the phrase does not exhaust the connotation of the word "passive", we shall use *satyagraha* till a word is available which deserves the prize.

*Indian Opinion*, 11-1-1908 (from Gujarati) (8: 80)

---

*Prolonged satyagraha against the Asiatic Ordinance led to Gandhi's arrest. While still in jail, he agreed to meet with an envoy from General Smuts, the Premier of the Transvaal. He offered Smuts what he and his followers had all along agreed to do: voluntarily register themselves, provided the hated Ordinance was repealed afterwards. Smuts agreed and the prisoners were released. Gandhi considered this a triumph of Satyagraha.*

## Triumph of Truth

... The Government has now promised not to apply the law to Indians on the condition that the objective of the law should be secured by the Indians themselves acting of their free will, that is, without the compulsion of that law. This condition means voluntary registration. The Indian community has time and again offered to register on its own. The Government has now at last accepted the proposal and agreed not to apply the new law to those who register voluntarily ...

... When the movement started, there were quite a few weak-minded Indians who argued, "The laws of the State are inviolable"; "It is like running one's head against a wall"; "It will do if the Government makes a few changes in the law"; "It is madness to resist the Government" and so on. Those who argued in this manner showed little faith in Khuda-Ishwar (*Muslim and Hindu names for God respectively - ed.*), swayed as they were by greed for money or other unworthy temptations. The selfsame law is now about to fall apart. It has not gone yet, but the Indians who were imprisoned have been released with the assurance that it will go. All the newspapers, without an exception, are astonished. The whites are dumbfounded and wonder how all this came about.

We consider this a victory for truth. We do not claim that every Indian adhered to truth in the course of the struggle. Nor do we claim that no one thought of his own interests during the campaign. We do, however, assert that this was a fight on behalf of truth, and that most of the leaders fought with scrupulous regard for truth. That is why there has been such a wonderful result. Truth is God, or God is nothing but Truth. We come across this idea in every religion.

... If, with some measure of truth on our side, we strive for a certain result and fail, the blame does not lie with truth but with us. If a particular result does not serve our good, God will not grant it, however much we may desire it. ... He who fights in this manner will fight only in the name of God. He will give no thought to success or failure. He is pledged only to the great task of serving Truth, doing his duty in the name of God. The outcome itself is in the hands of the Lord Almighty.

If this is a victory for truth, it is also a victory for satyagraha. Every Indian should by now be convinced that satyagraha, or passive resistance, is an infallible remedy. It can cure the most dangerous of ailments. Our success should lead at least to one result, namely, that we make full use of satyagraha. Only it should be used on proper occasions, and the people should remain united. It must also be realized that there are evils to which satyagraha cannot be applied. It can be effective only in situations where we are required to act positively. For instance, if the Government does not allow us to acquire land, satyagraha will be of no avail. If, however, it forbids us from walking along a certain foot-path, or asks us to shift to Locations, or seeks to prevent us from carrying on trade, we can resort to satyagraha. That is, if we are required to do anything which violates our religion or insults our manhood, we can administer the invaluable physic of satyagraha. There is one condition, however, to be observed, if the remedy is to be effective: we should be prepared collectively to accept hardships.

Some persons may well feel that all this is empty talk. What victory has there been to talk about? Here we are yielding on the question of giving digit-impressions. I am afraid that those who argue like this do not know the true position. This was not a struggle against digit impressions. Once the law is gone, there is no harm in our having to give the ten finger-prints. The giving of finger-prints is not in itself a disgraceful thing. But under the new law giving anything whatever is objectionable. There is no humiliation in polishing a friend's shoes as a gesture or of our free will. But polishing shoes out of fear, when ordered to do so, would amount to demeaning ourselves as menials. In other words, whether a particular thing is good or bad depends on the context. We know that there are many Indians who have mistakenly assumed that our campaign is against the giving of ten finger-prints. But such Indians should realize that there is no humiliation in giving ten finger-prints when not compelled by the law. Doing so certainly does not amount to a violation of our pledge. At the moment of writing it is not finally settled that the digit-impressions will be asked for. Every effort is being made to ensure that they will not be. But it is our duty to place the matter before the people in the proper perspective.

Digit impressions whether or not they are required should not lead to any difficulty. It is essential to present a correct idea of the object of this campaign.

*Indian Opinion*, 8-2-1908 (from Gujarati) (8: 120-22)

---

*Gandhi's compromise offer to Smuts angered several Indians, amongst whom was a Pathan (Pathans are from the north-west of the Indian subcontinent in what is today Pakistan) who attacked Gandhi in public, just when he was getting ready to take out a registration certificate.*

## My Reward

BEGINNING

For my part, I am not in the least surprised that I was assaulted. I had declared even on the 9th that, in view of the promise about the repeal of the law, I did not see any dishonour in giving finger impressions outside the law. On the contrary, I thought it was honourable to give them. When, in the meeting in front of the Mosque, there' was strong opposition to the idea of Indians voluntarily giving their finger-impressions, I asked myself what I would do if I had the real spirit of satyagraha in me, and then I declared my resolution that, if I was alive on Monday, I would positively give my finger-impressions. I still do not regret having done so; rather,

I think that I did my duty to my God and my community. ...

NO ONE TO BLAME

I do not blame anyone for the assault. Those who attacked me would have at one time greeted me and welcomed me enthusiastically. When they assaulted me, it was in the belief that I had done them and the community harm. ... If that is what they thought, is it surprising that they attacked me? If they had had some education, they would, instead of assaulting me, have adopted other means of venting their dislike of me. In either case, they would have had the same reason.

Experience tells me that some people know of only one way of expressing disapproval. For them physical strength is the one supreme thing. How then could I be angry? What point would there be in having them prosecuted? My real duty consists in disproving their charge against me. That will take time. Meanwhile, as is the way of the world, people will persist in the methods of violence. In this situation, the duty of the wise man is only to bear the suffering in patience. Why then should I be afraid of suffering? I therefore ask of God that I may remain fearless till the last. I ask my well-wishers to say the same prayer ...

*Indian Opinion*, 22-2-1908 (from Gujarati) (8: 153-55)

---

*In spite of Gandhi heeding his offer, General Smuts reneged on his promise. Though Indians registered themselves voluntarily, he refused to comply with their demand and did not repeal the Asiatic Ordinance. Gandhi was forced to accept he had been duped.*

## Speech at Mass Meeting, Johannesburg
## June 24, 1908

... Some of my countrymen tell me and, perhaps, with some justification that I did not take them into confidence, when I approached General Smuts on the strength of the letter that was placed before me in the gaol-yard, and it is better that I myself should voice their complaint I believe that, in seeing General Smuts as I saw him, I acted correctly and in accordance with my conscience, but time has shown that they were right, time has shown also that I need not have gone to General Smuts as I did. What I did was simply and solely to accept voluntary registration that was placed before him for over a year by the whole Indian community. I felt that I was yielding nothing, not a single new principle, not a single concession, in accepting this voluntary compromise. I believed that I had full instructions from my countrymen to do so, but I believed too much. I did not know what was to come after. I did not know that there was to be repudiation of the emphatic promise that was made in connection with the repeal of the Act. I know now that the compromise is not to be respected by the Government.

... I do plead guilty. I am responsible for it responsible because I had too great faith in the statesmanship of General Smuts, in his honesty, and in his integrity. If any countrymen today believe that I have sold them, they have good reason to believe so, although [there is] no justification for it, in my own estimation. They can only judge me by the results obtained. They cannot judge, the world is not today so constituted that it will judge men by the motives they ascribe to themselves, but by the result of their actions; and they judge me by the result of my action ...

*Indian Opinion*, 4-07-1908 (8: 400-03)

---

*General Smuts' betrayal led to a sustained campaign against the Ordinance. As an initial act of defiance, Indians who had taken out registration certificates, including Gandhi, decided to make a bonfire of the latter. Gandhi utilized this occasion to call for a prolonged satyagraha against the government of the Transvaal.*

### Speech at Mass Meeting, Johannesburg
### August 16, 1908

... The responsibility that devolves upon me this afternoon is a very serious responsibility. I have been taken to task, in connection with the advice that I have been giving to my fellow-countrymen for some length of time, by friends. I have been ridiculed by those who do not profess to be friends, and, yet, after due consideration, and, shall I say, prayer also, the advice that I ventured to give to my fellow-countrymen I am going to repeat this afternoon, and that advice is that, as events have taken the turn that you know in connection with our struggle, we must burn our certificates. [Applause.] I am told that I may be instrumental in imposing on my countrymen untold suffering because of the advice that I have given, if they follow that advice. I know that well, but I do know this also, that, if the burning of the certificates will impose untold suffering on you, the keeping of these certificates and submission to the Asiatic Act ... I will impose on my countrymen untold indignity, and I say with the greatest emphasis at my command that I would far rather that my countrymen suffered all they have to suffer than that they imposed on themselves indignity ...

... What is this fight that we are engaged upon? What is its significance? To my mind, its significance did not commence with a demand for the repeal of the Asiatic Act, nor does it end with the repeal of the Asiatic Act. I know full well that it is open to the Government of the Colony to give a repeal of this legislation today, to throw dust into our eyes and then embark upon other legislation, far harsher, far more humiliating, but the lesson that I wanted to learn myself, the lesson I would have my countrymen to learn from this struggle is this: that unenfranchised though we are, unrepresented though we are in the Transvaal, it is open to us to clothe ourselves with an undying franchise, and this consists in recognizing our humanity, in recognizing that we are part and parcel of the great universal whole, that there is the Maker of us all ruling over the destinies of mankind and that our trust should be in Him rather than in earthly kings, and if my countrymen recognize that position I say that no matter what legislation is passed over our heads, if that legislation is in conflict with our ideas of right and wrong, if it is in conflict with our conscience, if it is in conflict with our religion, then we can say we shall not submit to that legislation.

We use no physical force, but we accept the sanction that the legislature provides, we accept the penalties that the legislature provides. I refuse to call this defiance, but I consider that it is a perfectly respectful attitude, for a man, for a human being who calls himself man. And it is because it was necessary that British Indians should learn that lesson that the heads of the community gathered together and assembled together and said to themselves that this is the struggle, this is the method of struggle that they would place before their countrymen. It can do no harm whatsoever to the Government of the Colony, it can do no harm to those who are engaged in this struggle; it simply tests them and, if they are true, then they can only win; if they are not true, then they simply get what they deserve ...

*Indian Opinion*, 22.8.08 (9: 67-70)

---

*Following the burning of certificates, the government of the Transvaal relented a little. It accepted voluntary registrations, but refused to repeal the Asiatic Ordinance. Further, it created a new law which made it difficult for Indians to enter the Transvaal from other parts of South Africa and reside there. Gandhi undertook a visit to London (1909) to see if the imperial government could be persuaded to view the Indian case with sympathy. But he was told in clear terms that South Africa was adamant about keeping racial divides—and strictures—in place. On his return, he and his men embarked on a long and arduous period of struggle, which resulted in arrests, deportations, the separation and breakdown of families. These years (1909-1912) enabled him to refine his practice of satyagraha.*

## Who Can Offer Satyagraha?

... In a struggle of this kind, there is no room for defeat. If, on any occasion, we fail, we shall discover that the failure was due to some deficiency in the satyagrahi and did not argue the inefficacy of satyagraha as such. The point needs to be carefully grasped. No such rule can be applied to physical fighting. When two armies engage in such fighting, defeat [of either] will not necessarily be the result of the inferior fighting quality of the troops. ... For instance, one side may have better arms than the other, or may be favourably placed in the battle-field, or may command superior technical skill. There are many such extraneous factors which account for the victory or defeat of the parties to a physical fight. But such factors offer no difficulties to those fighting the battle of satyagraha. Their deficiency alone can come in their way. ... In satyagraha, the victory of a single member may be taken to mean the victory of all, but the defeat of the side as a whole does not spell defeat for the person who has not himself yielded. For instance, in the Transvaal fight, even if a majority of Indians were to submit to the obnoxious Act, he who remains unyielding will be victorious indeed, for the fact remains that he has not yielded. That being so, it is necessary to inquire as to who can offer so admirable a battle— one which admits of no defeat—which can have only one result.

... If we inquire into the meaning of satyagraha, we find that the first condition is that anyone who wants to engage in this kind of fighting should show a special regard for truth—should have the strength that flows from truthfulness. That is to say, such a man should depend on truth alone. One cannot have the best of both worlds. A man who attempts to have it so will be crushed under pressure of both kinds. Satyagraha is not a carrot, to be played on as a pipe. Anyone who thinks that it is, so that he may play on it if he can or bite it off if he cannot, will find himself lost in the end. It is absurd to suggest that satyagraha is being resorted to only by those who are deficient in physical strength or who, finding physical strength unavailing, can think of no alternative but satyagraha. Those who hold such a view, it may be said, do not know what this fight means. Satyagraha is more potent than physical strength, which is as worthless as straw when compared with the former. Essentially, physical strength means that a man of such strength fights on the battle-field with little regard for his body, that is to say, he knows no fear. A satyagrahi, on his part, gives no thought whatever to his body.

Fear cannot touch him at all. That is why he does not arm himself with any material weapons, but continues resistance till the end without fear of death. This means that the satyagrahi should have more courage than the man who relies on physical strength. Thus, the first thing necessary for a satyagrahi is pursuit of truth, faith in truth. He must be indifferent to wealth. Wealth and truth have always been in conflict with each other, and will remain so till the end of time. ... Money is welcome if one can have it consistently with one's pursuit of truth; otherwise one must not hesitate even for a moment to sacrifice it as if it were no more than dirt on one's hand. No one who has not cultivated such an attitude can practise satyagraha. Moreover, in a land where one is obliged to offer satyagraha against the rulers, it is not likely that the satyagrahi will be able to own wealth ...

A satyagrahi is obliged to break away from family attachments. This is very difficult to do. But the practice of satyagraha, if satyagraha is to be worthy of its name, is like walking on the edge of a sword. In the long run, even the breaking away from family attachments will prove beneficial to the family. For, the members of the family will come to feel the call for satyagraha, and those who have felt such a call will have no other desire left. When faced with suffering of any kind—loss of wealth or imprisonment—one need not be concerned about the future of one's family. He who has given us teeth will provide us with food to eat. If He provides for such dangerous creatures as the snake, the scorpion, the tiger and the wolf, He is not likely to be unmindful of mankind. It is not a pound of millets or a handful of corn that we hanker after, but the delights of the palate; not just the clothes that we need to enable us to bear cold, but garments of brocaded silk. If we abandon all this restless craving, there will hardly be any need for anxiety as to the means for maintaining one's family.

... This inquiry, then, leads at last to the conclusion that he alone can offer satyagraha who has true faith in religion. ... In other words, he who leaves everything to God can never know defeat in this world. Such men are not defeated in fact simply because people say that they are defeated. So also one cannot claim success simply because people believe that one has succeeded. [There can be no arguing about this;] if you know the difference, you know it, else you don't. This is the real nature of satyagraha ...

*Indian Opinion*, 29-5-1909 (from Gujarati) (9: 339-342)

---

*Satyagraha acquired an even sharper edge in the decade that followed. In 1913, the colonial government re-imposed the poll-tax on ex-indentured labourers from India—they either had to pay the tax or face deportation. This enraged Indians, since the colonial government had promised the Indian nationalist leader, Gopalakrishna Gokhale*

*who visited South Africa in 1912, that the poll-tax and the Asiatic
Ordinance would be repealed. Around this time, a Supreme Court
judgment declared all non-Christian marriages contracted outside South
Africa invalid and in a stroke declared Hindu and Muslim unions
illegal. These developments led to a breaking of laws. Women, including
Kasturba Gandhi, courted arrest. Satyagraha acquired a new impetus.*

## No Settlement

... The real object of our fight must be to kill the monster of racial
prejudice in the heart of the Government and the local whites. We
feel the presence of this monster in the Government's administration
of the new immigrant law, in its insistence on the collection of the
£3 tax from poor, miserable, helpless Indians, and in its attitude
towards our women.

The best cure for all this lies, not in securing the repeal or
amendment of the respective laws, but in rooting out the evil from
the heart. There is only one way to kill the monster and that is to
offer ourselves as a sacrifice. There is no life except through death.
Death alone can raise us. It is the only effective means of persuasion.
It is a seal which leaves a permanent imprint. We will not conquer
the whites by hating them. We can gain no victory by killing them.
We may kill a white in the body, but the monster inside will survive
and multiply. ... We are not concerned with the body of any white,
but only with the evil in his heart. The only effective way of bringing
about a change in his attitude is satyagraha. It is a divine law that
even the most hard-hearted man will melt if he sees his enemy
suffering in innocence. The satyagrahi volunteers to suffer in this
way.

There is another remedy, but it is not likely to be adopted. For
the prejudice in the heart of the whites against us, we are partly
responsible. We have several defects. We tell lies and follow wrong
courses. We give false evidence. We are dirty in our ways. We can
overcome the whites' prejudice only if we give up these bad habits.
But this is not likely to happen. The Indian who is full of faults
will not read writings of this kind. Nor can those who do make
him see reason. Satyagrahis should die for his sake as well. Their
death will be an education for these our brethren, whom ignorance

has made blind. It has always been the way of this world that the fruit of one's death is reaped by others ...

*Indian Opinion*, 13-9-1913 (from Gujarati) (10: 289-90)

---

*During this period satyagraha was offered not only by individuals, but by large groups as well. Coal-mine workers in Natal, many of whom were ex-indentured labourers or children of such labourers, struck work in protest against the poll-tax. While Gandhi conceded their cause as legitimate and led them in a long march to break the laws and get arrested, he did not wish other—non-Indian—sections of South African society to take up against the government, using the general atmosphere of discontent to their advantage. Thus, when railway workers resorted to a strike and expressed their willingness to align their cause to that of the Indians, he refused the offer.*

## Who May Be Deported?

... Seen superficially, the difference between satyagraha and brute force is so subtle that it escapes notice and both satyagrahis and non-satyagrahis, i.e., those who believe in brute force, are misled. Some of our well-wishers and friends did not like our strike (*the coal miners strike - ed.*) in Natal, as they thought we had overstepped the limits of satyagraha. Others mistakenly imagined that the recent strike of the white railway-men was satyagraha, though the difference between their aim and ours in going on strike is as great as that between North and South. If we went on strike, it was not in order to harass the Government. We only wanted to suffer—do *tapascharya*—by going to gaol. In the event, we find that our victory is at hand. That victory is also unique. We seek no political powers for ourselves. We only wish to preserve our self-respect and defend our religion. Whatever we may suffer in our own persons, we shall never seek to injure our opponent or dislodge him from office.

The railwaymen's attitude is the precise opposite of this. Their fight is not for self-respect. They have nothing to do with religion. They wanted a rise in their pay—wanted improvement in their economic condition. They went on strike not in order to get themselves gaoled but with the object of bringing pressure on the

Government. If the latter were to use force against them, they, too, would, if they could, use force in return. If it were possible, they would even overthrow the Government and install themselves in power.

In fact, that is their ultimate object. And so they have had to surrender in sheer helplessness before superior force. The Government, too, on its part, acted boldly and deported them overnight, secretly, without producing them in any court. All the world has commended its action and praised its courage. If it were to deport us, it would lay itself open to the charge of being oppressive, though we, of course, would have to submit with a smiling face. There is thus a vast difference, which every Indian should note and understand, between satyagraha and *asatya-graha.*

Satyagraha is not a game in which one might either win or lose. There is no room for failure in it. Brute force has to take its chance of success or failure. And the odds are always with the stronger party, irrespective of the rights of the case.

*Indian Opinion,* 4-2-1914, (from Gujarati) (14: 55-56)

---

*The satyagraha against unjust laws ended with the colonial government conceding certain demands: the supreme court judgment on non-Christian marriages was declared non-binding and the poll tax was repealed. Gandhi was convinced that these gains were a direct result of the Indian will to suffer. The suffering had been immense: striking workers had been shot at, several young martyrs had died in gaol and many had been deported. Considering his work in South Africa to be over, and answering to a call from Gopalakrishna Gokhale to join the nationalist struggle in India, Gandhi decided to return home (in July 1914). On the eve of his departure, he offered a definitive description of his doctrine of passive resistance, which he re-christened 'soul force'.*

### The Theory and Practice of Passive Resistance

... The term does not fit the activity of the Indian community during the past eight years. Its equivalent in the vernacular, rendered into English, means Truth-Force. I think Tolstoy called it also Soul-Force or Love-Force, and so it is. Carried out to its utmost limit, this force is independent of pecuniary or other material assistance;

certainly, even in its elementary form, of physical force or violence. Indeed, violence is the negation of this great spiritual force, which can only be cultivated or wielded by those who will entirely eschew violence. It is a force that may be used by individuals as well as by communities. It may be used as well in political as in domestic affairs. Its universal applicability is a demonstration of its permanence and invincibility. It can be used alike by men, women, and children. It is totally untrue to say that it is a force to be used only by the weak so long as they are not capable of meeting violence by violence. This superstition arises from the incompleteness of the English expression. It is impossible for those who consider themselves to be weak to apply this force. Only those who realize that there is something in man which is superior to the brute nature in him, and that the latter always yields to it, can effectively be Passive Resisters.

... A perfect Passive Resister has to be almost, if not entirely, a perfect man. We cannot all suddenly become such men, but, if my proposition is correct—as I know it to be correct—the greater the spirit of Passive Resistance in us, the better men we will become. Its use, therefore, is, I think, indisputable, and it is a force which, if it became universal, would revolutionise social ideals and do away with despotisms and the ever-growing militarism under which the nations of the West are groaning and are being almost crushed to death, and which fairly promises to overwhelm even the nations of the East. If the past struggle has produced even a few Indians who would dedicate themselves to the task of becoming Passive Resisters as nearly perfect as possible, they would not only have served themselves in the truest sense of the term, they would also have served humanity at large. Thus viewed, Passive Resistance is the noblest and the best education. It should come, not after the ordinary education in letters of children, but it should precede it. It will not be denied that a child, before it begins to write its alphabet and to gain worldly knowledge, should know what the soul is, what truth is, what love is, what powers are latent in the soul. It should be an essential of real education that a child should learn that, in the struggle of life, it can easily conquer hate by love, untruth by truth, violence by self-suffering ...

*Golden Number, Indian Opinion,* 1914 (14: 216-18)

---

*This was one of Gandhi's farewell speeches—even as he bade goodbye to South Africa, he rehearsed future themes of work and action.*

## Speech at Gujarat Sabha Function, Durban
## July 9, 1914

... I am about to leave a *bhoga-bhumi* (*land of pleasure - ed.*) for a *karma-bhumi* (*land of* [*dutiful*] *action - ed.*). For me there can be no deliverance from this earthly life except in India. Anyone who seeks such deliverance must go to the sacred soil of India. For me, as for everyone else, the land of India is "the refuge of the afflicted". I am therefore longing to return to the motherland. It is my parting prayer that you should all bear love for one another, regardless of caste or creed. I have always shown the same respect for Muslims as for Hindus. Hinduism, too, teaches this [regard for other religions], and if anyone says that in this I am not acting like a Hindu, I shall offer satyagraha against him. I make bold to say that certainly no one present here is more of a Hindu than I am, perhaps not even as much.

Whenever we have a guest, we show due respect to him. We ought to respect members of other communities in the same manner. If every Indian lived thus in amity with others, there is not the slightest doubt that we shall make great advance in South Africa.

As to the honour that has been done to me on this occasion, I have only this to say, that every time I have been honoured I have felt particularly weak and that when I have received blows I have felt accession of strength and progressed towards greater firmness of mind. Those friends, therefore, who speak ill of me these days are, to judge from results, my well-wishers. I shall have been rightly honoured only when every friend becomes a satyagrahi.

*Indian Opinion, 15-7-1914* (from Gujarati) (14: 210-11)

---

## Experiments in Ethical Living

*Around the time that Gandhi began to engage in public life, he also began an exercise in communal living. He set up Phoenix farm, a sprawling space that housed* Indian Opinion *and those who worked on it, itinerant Englishmen and Indians who wished to adopt another style of living and working, and visitors who were curious about life on the farm. At Phoenix, Gandhi learned to farm, work, live simply, practise special diets, organize alternative schooling … Later on, his German architect friend, Hermann Kallenbach, granted him the use of his Tolstoy farm, which Gandhi organized as a school for satyagrahis, especially those who fought against the Asiatic Ordinance and whose families needed a place to live and work.*

*Life on these farms was adventurous and experimental in the literal sense of the term. At different times, Gandhi adopted different practices that he wished to work with. For instance, after his experiences as part of a volunteer corps in the Zulu wars, he turned celibate and began to lead a life of continence, around which he attempted to build an entire philosophy of minimal living. Besides training the body to heed ethical practices, farm life also fostered and nurtured habits of co-existence, as diverse sorts of people came together to work out practical living arrangements. For Gandhi, living thus was of a part with his work in the outside world. He held that a life of restraint, work and responsible comradeship was indispensable for a public morality that relied on satyagraha.*

*Gandhi's experiments in ethical living drew on models of alternative living furnished by groups as disparate as the Trappist monks and vegetarian communities of the sort that were found in early twentieth century England. Tolstoy and Ruskin were important influences during this period and their thought provided Gandhi with a rich and forceful vocabulary of spare living. His novel ideas of work owed a great deal to philosophies of self-help, such as those advanced, in a different context and for different reasons, by the American 'Negro' leader, Booker T. Washington.*

*These selections from his writings on experimental living unfold as an argument for living differently.*

*An early essay, this describes Gandhi's impressions of a Trappist community.*

## A Band of Vegetarian Missionaries

... The settlement is a quiet little model village, owned on the truest republican principles. The principle of liberty, equality and fraternity is carried out in its entirety. Every man is a brother, every woman a sister. ... Both the brothers and the sisters observe a strict vow of silence and of chastity ...

... A model Trappist gets up at 2 a.m. and devotes four hours to prayer and contemplation. At six, he has his breakfast, which consists of bread and coffee, or some such simple foods. He dines at twelve, and makes a meal of bread and soup, and fruits. He sups at six in the evening and goes to bed at 7 or 8 p.m. The brothers eat no fish, flesh or fowl. They discard even eggs. ... They take no intoxicating liquors except under medical advice. ... None may keep money for private use. All are equally rich or poor.

... They believe in no colour distinctions. The Natives are accorded the same treatment as the whites. They are mostly children. They get the same food as the brothers, and are dressed as well as they themselves are. ... While the mission schools of other denominations very often enable the Natives to contract all the terrible vices of the Western civilization, and very rarely produce any moral effect on them, the Natives of the Trappist mission are patterns of simplicity, virtue and gentleness. It was a treat to see them saluting passers-by in a humble yet dignified manner.

... On the settlement there are various workshops—blacksmiths', tinsmiths', carpenters', shoemakers', tanners', etc., where the Natives are taught all these useful industries, in addition to the English and the Zulu languages. Here it may be remarked that it speaks volumes for the high-mindedness of the noble settlers that, although almost all of them are Germans, they never attempt to teach the Natives German; all these Natives work side by side with the whites.

At the sisters' cloisters, they have the ironing, sewing, straw-hat manufacturing and knitting departments, where one can see the

Native girls, dressed in clean costumes, working assiduously.

... The most prominent feature of the settlement is that you see religion everywhere. Every room has a Cross and, on the entrance, a small receptacle for holy water which every inmate reverently applies to his eyelids, the forehead and the chest. Even the quick walk to the flour mill is not without some reminder of the Cross. It is a lovely footpath. On one side, you have a magnificent valley through which runs a small rivulet which murmurs the sweetest music, and on the other, little rocks whereon are carved the various inscriptions reminding you of the scenes of the Calvary. ... The walk thus forms a continuous exercise for calm contemplation, unmarred by any other thoughts, or outside noise and bustle.

*The Vegetarian*, 18.5.1895 (1: 241-44)

---

*Phoenix farm was started to house* Indian Opinion, *the paper Gandhi and others began in 1903. However, the farm was to be more than home to a printing press. It was to embody an ideal of living, as Gandhi explained in this retrospective note.*

## Ourselves

... The object of *Indian Opinion* was to bring the European and the Indian subjects of King Edward closer together. It was to educate public opinion, to remove causes for misunderstanding; to put before the Indians their own blemishes; and to show them the path of duty while they insisted on securing their rights. This was an Imperial and pure ideal, towards the fruition of which anyone could work unselfishly. So it appealed to some of the workers.

The plan was shortly this. If a piece of ground sufficiently large and far away from the hustle of the town could be secured for housing the plant and machinery, each one of the workers could have his plot of land on which he could live. This would simplify the question of living under sanitary and healthy conditions, without heavy expenses. The workers could receive per month an advance sufficient to cover necessary expenses, and the whole profits could be divided amongst them at the end of each year. The management would thus be saved the necessity of having to find a large sum of money from week to week. The workers also could have the option of buying out their plot of land at the actual cost price.

Living under such conditions and amid the beautiful surroundings which have given Natal the name of the Garden Colony, the workers could live a more simple and natural life, and the ideas of Ruskin and Tolstoy [be] combined with strict business principles. Or, on the other hand, the workers could reproduce the artificiality of town life, if it pleased them to do so. One could hope that the spirit of the scheme and the surroundings would have an educative influence on them. There would be a closer brotherly combination between the European and the Indian workers. There was a possibility that the daily working hours could be reduced. Each could become his own agriculturist. The English workers could belie the taunt that the Englishman in South Africa would not cultivate the soil and work with his own hands. He had here all the facilities for such work, without any of the drawbacks. The Indian worker could copy his European brother, and learn the dignity and utility of healthy recreation as distinguished from constant, slaving toil for miserable gains. The incentive would be threefold to all: and ideal to work for in the shape of *Indian Opinion*; perfectly healthy surroundings to live in, and an immediate prospect of owning a piece of land on the most advantageous terms; and a direct tangible interest and participation in the scheme. Such in outline was the argument. It has been translated into action. The printing works have been removed to a large piece of ground near Phoenix Station, on the North Coast line. There are already Englishmen and Indians working here under the scheme.

It is yet too early to forecast the result. It is a bold experiment and fraught with momentous consequences. We know of no non-religious organization that is or has been managed on the principles above laid down. If it succeeds, we cannot but think that it would be worthy of imitation. We write impersonally, and no one on the staff of this journal claims any glory over the matter. We, therefore, think it but right to take the public into our confidence. Their support would encourage us very greatly, and no doubt contribute largely to the success of the scheme. We can appeal to both the great communities residing in South Africa and trust that they will assist the management to bring the scheme to the successful issue that we believe it deserves.

*Indian Opinion*, 24-12-1904 (4:145-46)

---

*Gandhi's experiments in Phoenix farm attracted people from several walks of life. Gandhi welcomed them but insisted that they examine the rules of living at the farm before they arrived there. Raojibhai Patel was one of Gandhi's earliest pupils who later on turned out to be an able acolyte.*

**Letter to Raojibhai Patel**
**Magshar Sud 8 [November 29, 1911]**

DEAR SHRI RAOJIBHAI,

I have your letter. I gather from it that you want to work in Phoenix. It is a good idea. I shall encourage you, but I doubt if you can stand the strain. In Phoenix

1. you will have to observe *brahmacharya (sexual continence - ed.)*;

2. you will be under a vow of scrupulous regard for truth;

3. you will have to do chiefly manual labour, that is, work with the hoe and the shovel;

4. if you intend to add to [your] book-learning, please forget all about it. Whatever addition comes naturally of because circumstances demand it will be welcome;

5. you should make up your mind that our duty is to strengthen character rather than acquire book-learning;

6. you should fearlessly oppose injustice from the caste or the family;

7. you should embrace absolute poverty.

You should think of joining Phoenix only if you would and can do this. You should tell yourself that life there will grow harder as the days pass and know that this is for your good. Learn to think along these lines if you decide to come over in March. Continue to write to me.

With due regards from

MOHANDAS

R. Patel, *Gandhijini Sadana* (Gujarati), Navajivan Publishing House, 1939 (12: 107)

*Gandhi was immensely interested in and inspired by Leo Tolstoy's life and work—and his experiments in Phoenix owed a great deal to the great Russian's deliberate choice of a life of simplicity, effort and labour.* Indian Opinion *carried a short history of the great writer for its Gujarati readers.*

## Count Tolstoy

It is believed that, in the western world at any rate, there is no man so talented, learned and as ascetic as Count Tolstoy. Though he is now nearly eighty years old, he is quite healthy, industrious and mentally alert.

Tolstoy was born of a noble family in Russia. His parents had enormous wealth, which he inherited. He is himself a Russian nobleman, and has, in his youth, rendered very good service to his country by fighting gallantly in the Crimean War. In those days, like the other noblemen of his time, he used to enjoy all the pleasures of the world, kept mistresses, drank and was strongly addicted to smoking. However, when he saw the carnage and bloodshed during the war, his mind brimmed over with compassion. His ideas changed; he began a study of his own religion and read the Bible. He read the life of Jesus Christ which made a deep impression on his mind ... It was also about this time that he discovered in himself a great talent for writing. He wrote a very effective book on the evil consequences of war. His fame spread throughout Europe. To improve the morals of the people he wrote several novels which can be equalled by few books in Europe. ... His writings had a great effect on his own mind. He gave up his wealth and took to a life of poverty. He has lived like a peasant for many years now and earns his needs by his own labour. He has given up all his vices, eats very simple food and has it in him no longer to hurt any living being by thought, word or deed. He spends all his time in good works and prayer. He believes that:

1. in this world men should not accumulate wealth;

2. no matter how much evil a person does to us, we should always do good to him. Such is the Commandment of God, and also His law;

3. no one should take part in fighting;

4. it is sinful to wield political power, as it leads to many of the evils in the world;

5. man is born to do his duty to his Creator; he should therefore pay more attention to his duties than to his rights;

6. agriculture is the true occupation of man. It is therefore contrary to divine law to establish large cities, to employ hundreds of thousands for minding machines in factories so that a few can wallow in riches by exploiting the helplessness and poverty of the many.

These views he has very beautifully supported by examples from various religions and other old texts. There are today thousands of men in Europe who have adopted Tolstoy's way of life. They have given up all their worldly goods and taken to a very simple life ...

*Indian Opinion*, 2.9.1905 ( from Gujarati) (4: 399-400)

---

*The following remarks on Tolstoy, extracted from an address made nearly twenty-five years later, indicate how central his imagination and thought continued to be to Gandhi's own commitment to simplicity and plain living.*

## Speech on Birth Centenary of Tolstoy

... Tolstoy drew people's attention to ... the idea of "bread labour". ... Its simple meaning is that he has no right to eat who does not bend his body and work. If every one of us did bodily labour to earn his food, we would not see the poverty which we find in the world. One idler is the cause of two persons starving, for his work has to be done by someone else. Tolstoy said that people came forward for philanthropic service, spent money for the purpose and earned titles as reward for their service, but he said it would be enough if, instead of all this, they did a little physical work and got off the backs of others. That is true indeed. In that lies humility. To do philanthropic service but refuse to give up one's luxuries is to act in the way described by Akha Bhagat (*a Gujarati poet - ed.*), "Stealing an anvil and gifting a needle".

It is not that others have not said what Tolstoy said, but there was magic in Tolstoy's language, for he acted upon what he preached. He who was accustomed to the comforts of wealth started doing physical labour. He used to work on the farm or do other labour for eight hours a day. That does not mean that he gave up literary work. In fact, after he started doing physical labour his literary work came to have greater life in it. ... Physical labour did not tell upon his health, and he believed that it sharpened his intellect. Students of his works will bear testimony that he was right ...

*Navajivan*, 16.9.28 (from Gujarati) (43: 9)

---

*Hermann Kallenbach, a wealthy German-Jewish architect, was one of Gandhi's closest friends and supporters in South Africa. He lent his sprawling Tolstoy farm for Gandhi to use—during the heyday of the satyagraha struggle, when volunteer families needed a place to live.*

**Letter to Hermann Kallenbach (Unrevised)**
**Tolstoy Farm, Lawley Station, Transvaal, November 6, 1911**

MY DEAR LOWER HOUSE,

It is on Sunday night I am writing this thought it is dated for Monday. ... A remarkable incident happened at the Farm during the week. We were making very fair headway with the fence. One day when I was not at that work, Desai came and informed me that someone had torn up the fence. This is the analysis of my mind. The thought could not have occupied more than a second. "Some evil-minded person has done it. I must inform police." "You coward. Your philosophy is skin-deep. No, the police must not be informed either for your or my sake. The fence should be re-put and someone must sleep near it, if necessary." Thus resolved I went down to the fence myself. I found that the probability was that the fence was torn up by cattle. Anyhow we fixed the poles much more strongly than before. I took with [me] plates and nails to fix on to the poles. No one slept there and there has been no further interruption. The incident, however, touched me deeply and set me thinking as to the right course of conduct. The most prominent idea that forced itself on me was that we, if we were to carry out the ideals we hold were unfit to hold more land than we *actually* used. The corollary is not that we should give up the land (though even that may not be quite so farcical as one may imagine) but that we should fence only so much as we wanted and used and no more ...

From the Original: *Gandhi-Kallenbach Correspondence*, National Archives (12: 87)

---

*Gandhi's devoted friend, Henry Polak, lent him Ruskin's* Unto this Last *to keep him company during a train journey. It affected him deeply and led him to experiment with ethical living.*

## The Magic Spell of a Book

... I believe that I discovered some of my deepest convictions reflected in this great book of Ruskin (*Unto This Last - ed.*) , and that is why it so captured me and made me transform my life. A poet is one who can call forth the good latent in the human breast. Poets do not influence all alike, for everyone is not evolved in an equal measure. The teachings of *Unto This Last* I understood to be:

1. that the good of the individual is contained the good of all.

2. that a lawyer's work has the same value as the barber's inasmuch as all have the same right of earning their livelihood from their work.

3. that a life of labour, i.e., the life of the tiller of the soil and the handicraftsman is the life worth living.

The first of these I knew. The second I had dimly realized. The third had never occurred to me. *Unto This Last* made it as clear as daylight for me that the second and the third were contained in the first. I arose with the dawn, ready to reduce these principles to practice.

*My Experiments with Truth* (44: 313)

---

# Hind Swaraj

---

*Gandhi's personal and political probing into the nature of power, ill-will and resistance resulted in a growing moral sense of the evil that attends mortal dealings. The colonial South African State furnished him with a model of untruth—it practised discrimination even though its convictions held such a practice to be wrong; it did not heed service and loyalty as virtues, it went back on its promises to suffering satyagrahis, and, importantly, it upheld racism in principle, through the law. Gradually Gandhi came to identify this rule and the larger colonial authority it represented as a form of violence, characteristic of modern civilization.*

*His criticisms of the latter acquired a distinctive edge during the course of his second visit to England (1908) to plead the cause of South African Indians, yet again. His sojourn in London was prolonged and it did not appear that he would gain the ear of the imperial government to his purpose. This made him restless and frustrated. During this time, he came across a group of Indian nationalists, who solemnly believed that a violent overthrow of British power was necessary to free India from colonial rule. Gandhi not only disagreed with this mode of struggle, he even felt that it was tainted by the very authority it wished to challenge. To disprove the effectiveness of violence and to call attention to the limited and dissembling nature of modern life which legitimized violence, he decided to write a tract.*

*Drawing on Tolstoy and Ruskin, and on the criticisms advanced by men such as Edward Carpenter, the gentle vegetarian socialist who rejected the promises of modern industrial civilization, Gandhi produced a moral indictment of modernity. In his arguments, he pursued his anathema to brute force and compulsion in any form to its logical conclusion. Hind Swaraj, as his tract was called, was no negative critique—it proposed another civilizational model to the one that was clearly dominant. As these extracts demonstrate, Gandhi's rejection of modern civilization was complex and was premised on an ethics of restraint and compassion.*

---

*Lord Ampthill was a Member of the House of Lords, former Governor of the Madras Presidency and a man sympathetic to Indian causes.*

## Letter to Lord Ampthill
## London, October 30, 1909

MY LORD,

I have for some time past been wishing to place before Your Lordship the result of my observations made here during my brief stay on the nationalist movement among my countrymen.

If you will permit me to say so, I would like to say that I have been much struck by Your Lordship's candour, sincerity and honesty of which one notices nowadays such an absence among our great public men. I have noticed too that your imperialism does not blind you to matters of obvious justice and that your love of India is genuine and great.

I have made it a point to see Indians here of every shade of opinion. Opposed as I am to violence in any shape or form, I have endeavoured specially to come into contact with the so-called extremists who may be better described as the party of violence. This I have done in order if possible to convince them of the error of their ways. I have noticed that some of the members of this party are earnest spirits, possessing a high degree of morality, great intellectual ability and lofty self-sacrifice. They wield an undoubted influence on the young Indians here. They are certainly unsparing in their efforts to impress upon the latter their convictions ...

An awakening of the national consciousness is unmistakable. But among the majority it is in a crude shape and there is not a corresponding spirit of self-sacrifice. Everywhere I have noticed impatience of British rule. In some cases the hatred of the whole race is virulent. In almost all cases distrust of British statesmen is writ large on their minds. ... Those who are against violence are so only for the time being. They do not disapprove of it. But they are too cowardly or too selfish to avow their opinions publicly. Some consider that the time for violence is not yet. I have practically met no one who believes that India can ever become free without resort to violence. I believe that repression will be unavailing.

At the same time, I feel that the British rulers will not give liberally and in time. The British people appear to me to be obsessed by commercial selfishness. The fault is not of men but of the system and the system is represented by the present civilization which has produced its blasting effect as well on the people here as on India. India suffers additionally only in so far as it is exploited in the interest of foreign capitalists. The true remedy lies, in my humble opinion, in England discarding modern civilization which is en-souled by this spirit of selfishness and materialism, is vain and purposeless and is a negation of the spirit of Christianity. But this is a large order. It may then be just possible that the British rulers in India may at least do as the Indians do and not impose upon them the modern civilization.

Railways, machinery and corresponding increase of indulgent habits are the true badges of slavery of the Indian people as they are of Europeans. I, therefore, have no quarrel with the rulers. I have every quarrel with their methods. I no longer believe as I used to in Lord Macaulay as a benefactor through his minute on education. And I do think that a great deal too much is being made of *pax Britannica*. To me the rise of the cities like Calcutta and Bombay is a matter for sorrow rather than congratulation. India has lost in having broken up a part of her village system. Holding these views, I share the national spirit but I totally dissent from the methods whether of the extremists or of the moderates. For either party relies ultimately on violence.

Violent methods must mean acceptance of modern civilization and therefore of the same ruinous competition we notice here and consequent destruction of true morality. I should be uninterested in the fact as to who rules. I should expect rulers to rule according to my wish otherwise I cease to help them to rule me. I become a passive resister against them. Passive resistance is soul force exerted against physical force. In other words love conquering hatred. I do not know how far I have made myself understood and I do not know how far I carry you with me in my reasoning. But I have put the case in the above manner before my countrymen.

The information I have given Your Lordship is quite confidential and not to be made use of prejudicially to my countrymen. I feel that no useful purpose will be served unless the truth is known and proclaimed ...

I remain, etc.,

From a photostat of the original draft in Gandhi's hand (10: 200-02)

---

*As his stay in London was prolonged, Gandhi had occasion to observe life around him. His incipient disillusionment with western civilization emerged into a full-fledged argument against it.*

## This Crazy Civilization

London has gone mad over Mr. Bleriot who flew in the air in an aeroplane and Dr. Cook who claims to have reached the North Pole. Newspapers report their achievements in great detail. People, it appears, throw away thousands of pounds after such things. Personally, I am unable to see what miracles they have achieved. No one points out what good it will do to mankind if planes fly in the air. People go crazy over every impostor making a novel claim. To me at least it appears that life would grow intolerable if there were to be too many planes in the air. We have trains running underground; there are telegraph wires already hanging over us, and outside, on the roads, there is the deafening noise of trains. If you now have planes flying in the air, take it that people will be done to death. Looking at this land, I at any rate have grown disillusioned with Western civilization. The people whom you meet on the way seem half-crazy. They spend their days in luxury or in making a bare living and retire at night thoroughly exhausted. In this state of affairs, I cannot understand when they can devote themselves to prayers ...

*Indian Opinion*, 2.10.1909 (from Gujarati) (10: 67)

---

## Terrible Civilization of the West

An English journal called *The New Age* has published a cartoon on this subject, which we reproduce in this issue. It shows an army on the march. Behind, there is a grotesque figure, that of a general. On the body of this terrible form are hanging a gun emitting smoke in every direction and swords dripping with blood, and on its head a cannon. There is the drawing of a skull on a badge hanging on one side. On the arm, moreover, there is a cross. (This cross is the emblem of a batch which looks after the wounded.) In the mouth, held in the teeth, there is a dagger dripping with blood. On the shoulder is seen a belt studded with live cartridges. The drawing is entitled "March of Civilization".

No one who reads this description of the cartoon can help becoming grave. On reflection, we cannot help feeling that Western civilization is as cruel as, perhaps more cruel than, the terrible expression on the face of the man in the cartoon. The sight which fills one with the utmost indignation is that of the cross in the midst of weapons dripping with blood. Here the hypocrisy of the new civilization reaches its climax. In former times, too, there used to be bloody wars, but they were free from the hypocrisy of modern civilization.

While drawing our readers' attention to this cartoon, we want to give them at the same time a glimpse of the divine light of satyagraha. On one side, look at the picture of civilization drawn above, a civilization grown as terrible as a wolf through its hunger for wealth and its greedy pursuit of worldly pleasures. On the other, look at the figure of a satyagrahi who, out of his loyalty to truth, to his nature as a spiritual being and out of a desire to obey God's command, submits to the suffering inflicted by wicked men, with fortitude in his breast, with a smile on his face and without a single tear in his eyes. Of the two pictures, towards which will the reader feel attracted?

We are sure it is the vision of the satyagrahi which will touch the heart of mankind, and that the effect will grow deeper as his sufferings increase. Is there anyone who, looking at this cartoon alone, does not feel in his heart that satyagraha is the only way in which mankind can attain freedom and strength? We admit, of course, that to be shot dead or hanged when trying to shoot another does test one's fortitude; but dying in the attempt to kill another does not require even a hundredth part of the fortitude and courage implicit in the suffering that a satyagrahi goes through, in the slow, prolonged torture that he calmly endures in facing a bullet without firing one in return ...

*Indian Opinion*, 2-4-1910 (from Gujarati) (10: 472-73)

## Concluding the South African Years

*Gandhi's years in South Africa were immensely important for the history of India and the cause of non-violence. In fact it was his South African work that brought him to public attention in India. In this sense, South Africa proved to be a nursery for satyagraha. When he left that country, he did so with a realisation that his work had ended: he had pioneered a novel mode of resistance, struggled as far as he could, within the limits he had set himself and what had been handed to him by history. There was of course much more to be done, but he knew that he could not continue as before. New beginnings had to be made but perhaps not by him. India awaited him and he looked forward to what he could do in his homeland.*

*Gandhi learnt to identify the injustice that he was to battle all his life in his dealings with the South African state. The peculiar circumstances of Indian migration and exile provided him with a context in which he could re-work notions of community, culture and the common good. His non-combative tone, patient argument and familiarity with the details of what he addressed, his determination to appeal to the oppressor's better nature—qualities that we tend to associate with his mature public voice—are already evident here. We also get a sense from these writings of the still raw piety that, in later years, would mellow into a generous and warm love towards even his political and ideological adversaries.*

*Gandhi's experiments in life and thought would undergo a further metamorphosis in the Indian context, adding to the complex and layered meanings that came to nest in notions of passive resistance and satyagraha. But even here it is evident that satyagraha comprised more than a set of principles that guided public action—it was also an ethos that inhered in details of everyday living, in the manner in which a person cultivated personal and public relationships, in the style of one's speech and writing, in the relentless pursuit of transparency in all aspects of life and above all a commitment to not turning to violence at any cost, and whatever the provocation. The keywords in Gandhi's lexicon of non-violence were satya (truth), tapasacharya (patient and dutiful sufferance of one's ills in good faith), and yagna (concentrated yet selfless practice of a vocation, a duty): words that would resonate for the next three decades in the Indian subcontinent.*

*The actual political gains that his struggles achieved for Indians in South Africa may be debated, as indeed they are today by South Africans of Indian origin. His strangely reticent responses to the cruel and inhuman exploitation of native South Africans, especially his offer of support to the British during the infamous Zulu wars, are likewise being interrogated. Though he did not endorse racism, and was sharply critical of legal discrimination and coercive laws, his inability to imaginatively engage with 'kaffir' life and politics, of which he was not entirely unaware, raises questions about the viability and significance of passive resistance struggles that limit themselves to particular concerns and do not seek to indict oppressive systems. In later days, when he recalled his South African days in Satyagraha in* South Africa, *Gandhi displayed a greater sensitivity to the 'native' question and was more trenchant in his criticisms of colonialism and empire.*

*In spite of these criticisms, very few dispute the fact that Gandhi's work in South Africa produced a political method that was rich in its associative meanings and marked by an earnest commitment to gentle reconciliation between races, as well as between rulers and the ruled.*

## Chapter 2

## Truth's Pilgrim: The Early Indian Years
## 1915-1919

*Gandhi returned to India in 1915. His South African years had instilled in him a sense of civilizational worth and confidence. He had experienced what it was to be 'Indian', learned to live and work with diverse individuals and groups. He was, at the same time, painfully conscious of being a subject of Empire, sensitive to the bonds that held him in fealty to his rulers, yet determined to wear them down through deliberate civil suffering. He had learned too that delicate and subtle links hold together everyday life and civic work, personal relationships and public responsibility. Life on the Phoenix and Tolstoy farms and resistance in the Transvaal streets had shown him that ethics and politics, compassion and justice were inextricably linked. He had no doubt that the way of peace and non-violence was the way of truth.*

*In his first year in India, Gandhi travelled, observed and tested his arguments in different social contexts. He toured the country by train and on foot, and addressed meetings, outlining his faith in civil resistance, and upheld the claims of soul force over brute violence. During this time, he did other things too: set up an ashram, on the model of his South African farms and gathered disciples and friends to his cause of simple living in the pursuit of truth. Later on, he began to publish his own newspapers, in English and Gujarati.* Young India *and* Navajivan *became the carriers of his opinions.*

*His year of watching acquainted him with the important strands within nationalist thought and action. There were the Moderates, men of cautious optimism, who believed in Empire's goodwill and were biding their time for Britain to answer Indian demands for self-rule.*

*These were men who held it a virtue to share power, in however humble a fashion, with their colonial rulers and who did not wish to spoil their chances by acting unwisely. The there were the Militants, nationalists who desired to —and often did—confront their rulers with vociferous demands and sometimes violent protests.*

*Gandhi was not impressed with the Moderates. Their vision of the common good appeared too narrow, soulless and derivative. It did not take into account the spoliation of everyday life, the loss of national self-confidence, and the restlessness in the cities. But neither was he moved by the passion of the Militants. In the Punjab and Bengal, where militant nationalism had its largest number of adherents, the air was tight with militant quasi-socialist demands whose potentially violent character worried Gandhi. He was determined to strike his own path and did not lose time in marking his presence in Indian political life. Through his marvellous rhetoric of truth, sacrifice and self-worth he challenged those who were willing to wait upon Empire to deliver them, without examining their consciences with respect to what they owed themselves and their fellow human beings. He also addressed the supporters of political violence and denounced their creed.*

*More generally, he urged Indians to commit themselves to a fight against colonial rule that did not merely blame Empire, but also sought a regulation of what he considered a nation's moral life. To be truly non-violent and courageous in the face of political evil, to endure in the patient exercise of soul force, an individual had to look deep within himself and cleanse his heart of fear, prejudice and hatred. In the context of caste-ridden India, he had to learn to abjure untouchability, undertake a vow of poverty, which, for Gandhi meant living simply and practising a craft, preferably the craft of spinning. He or she also had to learn to love and, paradoxically, to die. Gandhi exhorted his countrymen and women to include in their hearts' trust those they feared and were being taught to hate, for instance, the Muslims.*

*Gandhi also addressed national well-being in terms of the relationships between men and women. He argued that women would have to be schooled differently if they were to step out of the confines of their existing domestic lives and take their place in the new world that he wished to open to them. During this period, Gandhi tested his precepts in the context of three well-defined struggles, two of which involved peasant unrest and one which had to do with labour militancy. Gandhi's novel initiatives in non-violent action drew criticism from well-established political leaders, as well as those who were fascinated but bewildered by his experiments. He answered his critics patiently, almost as if he was defining for himself the coordinates of that ineffable truth he was pursuing. History proved a mentor for he soon found himself in a situation—not of his own choosing—that required him to prove the worth of his argument. In 1919, the colonial government announced its decision to enact a set of repressive laws. The Rowlatt Bills, as they were called, were drafted to contain political dissent and action. Gandhi launched a satyagraha against these laws, which set him on a path that proved both perilous and exciting—and it earned him an important place within India's premier nationalist party, the Indian National Congress.*

*Soon, he found himself coordinating a campaign that involved hundreds of people across a large geographical area. His earlier campaigns had been restricted to specific locations and were focused in their demands. But the Rowlatt satyagraha was different. Here, his message of non-violent resistance was eagerly accepted, but understood widely as an incitement to angry rebellion. Chronic food shortages, rising prices and restrictive wartime legislation—especially in urban Punjab—had stirred sections of the public into a state of inchoate turmoil. Gandhi's call answered to their sense of felt injustice and in spite of his best intentions, righteous anger and mob fury bloodied the streets.*

*Though dismayed and shocked, Gandhi refused to be outdone by the turn of events. He immediately suspended his campaign, which, after all, was spontaneous rather than planned, and spoke out against the brute anger of those who had given in to arson, looting and murder. He spoke against government terror as well, but insisted that satyagrahis learn the value of restraint. He retreated from public action and turned to writing and lecturing on non-violence. But he was not spent. His almost immediate re-emergence with a different set of issues pointed to an inner faith and resilience that appeared limitless. He argued—as he had done in South Africa in the context of 'voluntary registration'— there was no dishonour in accepting defeat. Defeat, he held, was an index of a failure in learning—his followers had misunderstood his message of non-violence. The important thing, therefore, was to learn better. Thus, strengthened in his resolve and fortified in his creed, he went on to launch a massive non-violent struggle that brought nationalist politics out of its elitist closet and catapulted it onto the streets.*

# Vowing Truth

---

*On his arrival in India, Gandhi lost very little time in setting up an ashram. On the banks of the Sabarmati river in the city of Ahmedabad, he found a home that became, as it were, a school for non-violence. He delineated for his listeners and supporters the salient features of a highly experiential world view that encompassed and held together through subtle arguments, both private living and public duty, everyday practices and political action. Soon, satyagraha acquired a distinctive Indian character, as he pleaded for its acceptance as a valuable precept in civic life. He had his critics, and did not shy away from addressing their concerns, but he held fast to his convictions, and expounded them with great moral certainty. There was at least one occasion, though, when his actions appeared to belie his principles—this was when he decided to support British attempts to recruit for World War I. Though he argued his decision with candour, his campaign for enlistment raised more questions than it answered.*

*This set of extracts from his speeches and writings presents his arguments for satyagraha as they unfolded during these momentous years (1915-1919).*

---

*Maganlal Gandhi was related to him and an associate from the Phoenix and Tolstoy farms.*

## Letter to Maganlal Gandhi
### [After March 14, 1915]

BHAISHRI 5M,

You are right in what you think about non-violence. Its essentials are *daya (compassion - ed.), krodha (freedom from anger - ed.) aman (freedom from the desire to be respected - ed.)*, etc. Satyagraha is based on non-violence.

... In observing the vow of non-hoarding, the main thing to be borne in mind is not to store up anything which we do not require. For agriculture, we may keep bullocks, if we use them, and the equipment required for them. Where there is a recurring danger of famine, we shall no doubt store food-grains. But we shall always ask ourselves whether bullocks and food-grains are in fact needed. We are to observe all the *yamas* in thought as well, so that we shall grow more secure in them from day to day and come to think of fresh things to renounce. Renunciation has no limit to it. The more we renounce, the more shall we grow in the knowledge of the *atman*. If the mind continues to move towards renunciation of the desire for hoarding and if in practice we give up hoarding as far as it is physically possible to do, we shall have kept the vow of non-hoarding.

The same is true about non-stealing. Non-hoarding refers to stocking of things not needed. Non-stealing refers to the use of such things. If I need only one shirt to cover myself with but use two, I am guilty of stealing one from another. For, a shirt which could have been of use to someone else does not belong to me. If five bananas are enough to keep me going, my eating a sixth one is a form of theft. Suppose we have a stock of 50 limes, thinking that among us all we would need them. I need only two, but take three because there are so many. This is theft. Such unnecessary consumption is also a violation of the vow of non-violence. If, with the ideal of non-stealing in view, we reduce our consumption of things, we would grow more generous. If we do so, actuated by the ideal of non-violence, we would grow more compassionate. In assuring, as it were, every animal or living thing that it need have no fear on our account, we entertain compassion—love— for it. A man who entertains such love will not find any living being inimical to him, not even in thought ...

The principle underlying all these vows is truth. By deceiving oneself, one may refuse to recognize an act of stealing or hoarding as such. Hence, by taking careful thought we can ensure at every step that truth prevails. Whenever we are in doubt whether a particular thing should be stored or not, the simple rule is not to store it. There is no violation of truth in renunciation. When in doubt about the wisdom of speaking, it is the duty of a man who has taken the vow of truth not to speak.

I want all of you to take only such vows as each one feels inclined to, of his own free will. I always feel that vows are necessary. But anyone may take them only when he himself feels the need and take only such as he wants to ...

*Gandhijini Sadhana*; also *Mahatma Gandhijina Patro* (from Gujarati) (14: 383-5)

---

*Gandhi's Ahmedabad ashram was set up with support from local philanthropists. The ashram provided a concrete context for Gandhi to refine his highly personal experiments in living into a formal set of rules, which was to be binding on all ashram-dwellers. The salient features of this constitution are extracted below.*

## Draft Constitution for the Ashram
## [Before May 20, 1915]

... VOW OF TRUTH

It is not enough for a person under this vow that he does not ordinarily resort to untruth; such a person ought to know that no deception may be practised even for the good of the country. ...

VOW OF NON-VIOLENCE

It is not enough to refrain from taking the life of any living being. He who has pledged himself to this vow may not kill even those whom he believes to be unjust; he may not be angry with them, he must love them; thus, he would oppose the tyranny whether of parents, governments or others, but will never kill or hurt the tyrant. The follower of truth and non-violence will offer satyagraha against tyranny and win over the tyrant by love; he will not carry out the tyrant's will but he will suffer punishment even unto death for disobeying his will until the tyrant himself is won over.

VOW OF CELIBACY

It is well-nigh impossible to observe these two vows unless celibacy too is observed; and for this vow it is not enough that one does not look upon another woman with a lustful eye, one has so to control the animal passions that they will not be moved even in thought; if one is married, one will not have sexual intercourse even with one's wife, but, regarding her as a friend, will establish with her a relationship of perfect purity.

CONTROL OF THE PALATE

Until one has overcome the palate, it is difficult to observe the foregoing vows, more especially that of celibacy. Control of the palate should therefore be treated as a separate observance by one desirous of serving the country and, believing that eating is only for sustaining the body, one should regulate and purify one's diet day by day. Such a person will immediately, or gradually, as he can, leave off such articles of food as may tend to stimulate animal passions.

## VOW OF NON-STEALING

It is not enough not to steal what is commonly considered as other men's property. One who has pledged himself to this vow should realize that Nature provides from day to day just enough and no more for one's daily needs by way of food and so hold it theft to use articles of food, dress, etc., which one does not really need and live accordingly.

## VOW OF NON-POSSESSION

It is not enough not to possess and keep much, but it is necessary not to keep anything which may not be absolutely necessary for the nourishment and protection of our body: thus, if one can do without chairs, one should do so. He who has taken this vow will always bear this in mind and endeavour to simplify his life more and more.

## SUBSIDIARY OBSERVANCES

### ... VOW OF SWADESHI

The person who has taken the vow of *Swadeshi* will never use articles which conceivably involve violation of truth in their manufacture or on the part of their manufacturers. It follows, for instance, that a votary of truth will not use articles manufactured in the mills of Manchester, Germany or India, for he cannot be sure that they involve no such violation of truth. Moreover, labourers suffer much in the mills. The generation of tremendous heat causes enormous destruction of life. Besides, the loss of workers' lives in the manufacture of machines and of other creatures through excessive heat is something impossible to describe. Foreign cloth and cloth made by means of machinery are, therefore, tabooed to a votary of non-violence as they involve triple violence ...

## VOW OF FEARLESSNESS

He who is acted upon by fear can hardly observe the vows of truth, etc. The Controllers will, therefore, constantly endeavour to be free from the fear of kings or society, one's caste or family, thieves, robbers, ferocious animals such as tigers, and even of death. One who observes the vow of fearlessness will defend himself or others by truth-force or soul force.

## VOW AGAINST UNTOUCHABILITY

According to Hindu religion ... traditionally, communities such as *Dhed, Bhangi (names of so-called untouchables castes - ed.)*, etc., known by the names of *Antyaj (or, literally the last caste - ed.)*, *Pancham (the fifth caste, that is, outside the four-fold order of brahmins, kshatriyas, vaishyas and shudras - ed.) Achhut (literally, unclean - ed.)* and so on, are looked upon as untouchable, Hindus belonging to other communities believe that they will be defiled it they touch a member of any of the said communities and, if anyone does so accidentally, he thinks that he has committed a sin. The founders of the Ashram believe that this practice is a blot on Hindu religion. Themselves staunch Hindus, they believe that the Hindu race will continue to add to its load of sin so long as it regards a single community as untouchable. Some of the consequences of this practice have been terrible. In order to be free from this sin, the Ashram inmates are under a vow to regard the untouchable communities as touchable ...

## ... MOTHER TONGUE

It is the belief of the Controllers that no nation or any group thereof can make real progress by abandoning its own language, they will, therefore, use their own language. As they desire to be on terms of intimacy with their brethren from all parts of India, they will also learn the chief Indian languages; as Sanskrit is a key to Indian languages, they will learn that too.

## MANUAL WORK

The Controllers believe that body labour is a duty imposed by nature upon mankind. Such labour is the only means by which man may sustain himself; his mental and spiritual powers should be used for the common good only. As the vast majority in the world live on agriculture, the Controllers will always devote some part of their time to working on the land; when that is not possible, they will perform some other bodily labour.

## WEAVING

The Controllers believe that one of the chief causes of poverty in the land is the virtual disappearance of spinning-wheels and handlooms. They will, therefore, make every effort to revive this industry by themselves weaving cloth on handlooms.

## POLITICS

Politics, economic progress, etc., are not unconnected matters; knowing that they are all rooted in religion, the Controllers will make an effort to learn and teach politics, economics, social reform, etc., in a religious spirit and work in these fields with all the zeal that they can command ...

From printed leaflets (from Gujarati) (14: 453-57)

---

*Gandhi toured the Indian subcontinent widely in the years 1915-16. In the various meetings that he addressed, he expounded on his distinctive political and social ethics, explaining the significance of non-violence. He clearly saw his experiments in this context as constituting a fit antidote to the current culture of political militancy that fascinated the young.*

## Speech at YMCA, Madras
## April 27, 1915

MR CHAIRMAN AND DEAR FRIENDS,

... As you have heard me say perhaps, or as you have read, I am and I have been a determined opponent of modern civilization. I want you to turn your eyes today upon what is going on in Europe and if you have come to the conclusion that Europe is today groaning under the heels of the modern civilization, then you and your elders will have to think twice before you can emulate that civilization in our Motherland. But I have been told: "How can we help it, seeing that our rulers bring that culture to our Motherland?"

Do not make any mistake about it at all. I do not for one moment believe that it is for any rulers to bring that culture to you unless you are prepared to accept it, and if it be that the rulers bring that culture before us, I think that we have forces within ourselves to enable us to reject that culture without having to reject the rulers themselves. [Applause.] ... it is possible for India if she would but live up to the tradition of the sages ... to transmit a message through this great race, a message not of physical might, but a message of love. And then, it will be your privilege to conquer the conquerors not by shedding blood but by sheer force of spiritual predominance.

When I consider what is going on today in India, I think it is necessary for us to say what our opinion is in connection with the political assassinations and political dacoities. I feel that these are purely a foreign importation which cannot take root in this land. ... I, as a passive resister, will give you another thing very substantial for it. Terrorise yourself; search within; by all means resist tyranny wherever you find it; by all means resist encroachment upon your liberty, but not by shedding the blood of the tyrant. ...Our religion is based upon *ahimsa*, which in its active form is nothing but love, love not only to your neighbours, not only to your friends but love even to those who may be your enemies.

One word more in connection with the same thing. I think that if we were to practise truth, to practise *ahimsa*, we must immediately see that we also practise fearlessness. If our rulers are doing what in our opinion is wrong, and if we feel it our duty to let them hear our advice even though it may be considered sedition, I urge you to speak sedition but at your peril. You must be prepared to suffer the consequences. And when you are ready to suffer the consequences and not hit below the belt, then I think you will have made good your right to have your advice heard even by the Government. ...

*Speeches and Writings of Mahatma Gandhi* (14: 423-25)

---

*This early speech on wealth and welfare, also addressed to young people, contains, in a nutshell, Gandhi's arguments against material progress for its own sake.*

**Speech at Muir College Economic Society, Allahabad
December 22, 1916**

..."Take no thought for the morrow" is an injunction which finds
an echo in almost all the religious scriptures of the world. In well-
ordered society, the securing of one's livelihood should be and is
found to be the easiest thing in the world. Indeed, the test of
orderliness in a country is not the number of millionaires it owns,
but the absence of starvation among its masses. The only statement
that has to be examined is whether it can be laid down as a law of
universal application that material advancement means moral
progress. ... We do not deny to the Rockefellers and the Carnegies
possession of an ordinary measure of morality but we gladly judge
them indulgently. I mean that we do not even expect them to satisfy
the highest standard of morality. With them material gain has not
necessarily meant moral gain. If I were not afraid of treading on
dangerous ground, I would even come nearer home and show you
that possession of riches has been a hindrance to real growth. I
venture to think that the scriptures of the world are far safer and
sounder treatises on laws of economics than many of the modern
text-books. The question we are asking ourselves this evening is
not a new one. It was addressed to Jesus two thousand years ago.
St. Mark has vividly described the scene. Jesus is in his solemn
mood; he is earnest. He talks of eternity. He knows the world about
him. He is himself the greatest economist of his time. ... It is to
him at his best that one comes running, kneels down, and asks:
"Good Master, what shall I do that I may inherit eternal life?" And
Jesus said unto him: "Why callest thou me good? There is none
good but one, that is God. Thou knowest the commandments. Do
not commit adultery, Do not kill, Do not steal, Do not bear false
witness, Defraud not, Honour thy father and mother."

And he answered and said unto him: "Master, all these have I
observed from my youth." Then Jesus beholding him, loved him
and said unto him: "One thing thou lackest. Go thy way, sell
whatever thou hast and give to the poor, and thou shalt have
treasure in heaven—come take up the cross and follow me." And
he was sad at that saying and went away grieved—for he had great
possessions. And Jesus looked round about and said unto his

disciples: "How hardly shall they that have riches enter into the kingdom of God." And the disciples were astonished at his words. But Jesus answereth again and saith unto them: "Children, how hard it is for them that trust in riches to enter into the kingdom of God. It is easier for a camel to go through the eye of a needle than for a rich man to enter into the kingdom of God !" Here you have an eternal rule of life stated in the noblest words the English language is capable of producing ... that you cannot serve God and Mammon is an economic truth of the highest value. We have to make our choice. Western nations today are groaning under the heel of the monster-god of materialism. Their moral growth has become stunted. They measure their progress in £. s.d. American wealth has become the standard. She [sic] is the envy of the other nations. I have heard many of our countrymen say that we will gain American wealth but avoid its methods. I venture to suggest that such an attempt if it were made is foredoomed to failure.

... I would have our leaders to teach us to be morally supreme in the world. This land of ours was once, we are told, the abode of the gods. It is not possible to conceive gods inhabiting a land which is made hideous by the smoke and the din of ... chimneys and factories and whose roadways are traversed by rushing engines dragging numerous cars crowded with men mostly who know not what they are after, who are often absent-minded, and whose tempers do not improve by being uncomfortably packed like sardines in boxes and finding themselves in the midst of utter strangers who would oust them if they could and whom they would in their turn oust similarly.

I refer to these things because they are held to be symbolical of material progress. But they add not an atom to our happiness. ... Under the British aegis, we have learnt much, but it is my firm belief that there is little to gain from Britain in intrinsic morality, that if we are not careful, we shall introduce all the vices that she has been a prey to, owing to the disease of materialism. We can profit by that connection only if we keep our civilization, and our morals, straight, i.e., if instead of boasting of the glorious past, we express the ancient moral glory in our own lives and let our lives bear witness to our past. ... If we will but clean town houses, our palaces and temples of the attributes of wealth and show in them the attributes of morality, we can offer battle to any combinations of hostile forces without having to carry the burden of a heavy militia ...

*The Leader,* 25-12-1916 (15: 274-279)

---

*Gandhi's praise of non-violence was greeted with scepticism and disbelief by those nationalists who believed that the Indian nation had become enslaved because it had not learned the manly virtue of virile aggression. Lala Lajpat Rai, a celebrated militant nationalist wrote scathingly of Gandhi's non-violent creed and earned this reply.*

## On Ahimsa: Reply to Lala Lajpat Rai
## October, 1916

... With due deference to Lalaji, I must join issue with him when he says that the elevation of the doctrine of *ahimsa* to the highest position contributed to the downfall of India. There seems to be no historical warrant for the belief that an exaggerated practice of *ahimsa* synchronised with our becoming bereft of many virtues. During the past fifteen hundred years, we have as a nation given ample proof of physical courage, but we have been torn by internal dissensions and have been dominated by love of self instead of love of country ...

... If we are unmanly today, we are so, not because we do not know how to strike, but because we fear to die. He is no follower of Mahavira, the apostle of Jainism, or of Buddha or of the Vedas, who being afraid to die, takes flight before any danger, real or imaginary all the while wishing that some body else would remove the danger by destroying the person causing it. He is no follower of *ahimsa* ... who does not care a straw if he kills a man by inches by deceiving him in trade, or who will protect by force of arms a few cows and make away with the butcher, or who in order to do a supposed good to his country does not mind killing off a few officials. All these are actuated by hatred, cowardice and fear. ... *Ahimsa* does not displace the practice of other virtues, but renders their practice imperatively necessary before it can be practised even in its rudiments. ... Mahavira and Buddha were soldiers, and so was Tolstoy. Only they saw deeper and truer in their profession, and found the secret of a true, happy, honourable and godly life. Let us be joint sharers with these teachers and this land of ours will once more be the abode of gods ...

M. K. GANDHI

*The Modern Review,* October, 1916 (15: 251-54)

---

*Esther Faering, an earnest Christian, was one of Gandhi's earliest women friends. Gandhi adopted her as his daughter and carried on an intensive correspondence with her throughout his life. She admired him for his faith in non-violence, but also questioned him closely, often demanding explanations.*

## Letter to Esther Faering
## Nadiad, August 3, 1917

MY DEAR ESTHER,

You have raised big questions. I think the command of Jesus is unequivocal. All killing is bad for one who is filled with love. He will not need to kill. He will not kill. He who is filled with pity for the snake and does not fear him will not kill him and the snake will not hurt him. This state of innocence is the one we must reach. But only a few can reach it. It seems to me to be impossible for nations to reach it. Equal progress in all is an inconceivable situation. Nations will therefore always fight. One of them will be less wrong than the other. A nation to be in the right can only fight with soul force. Such a nation has still to be born. I had hoped that India was that nation. I fear I was wrong. The utmost I expect of India is that she may become a great restraining force. But she must acquire the ability to fight and suffer before she can speak to the world with any degree of effect.

The pertinent question for you and me is what is our duty as individuals. I have come to this workable decision for myself, "I will not kill anyone for any cause whatsoever but be killed by him if resistance or his will render my being killed necessary." I would give similar advice to everybody. But where I know that there is want of will altogether, I would advise him to exert his will and fight. There is no love where there is no will. In India there is not only no love but hatred due to emasculation. There is the strongest desire to fight and kill side by side with utter helplessness. This desire must be satisfied by restoring the capacity for fighting. Then comes the choice. Yes, the very act of forgiving and loving shows superiority in the doer. But that way of putting the proposition begs the question, who can love? A mouse as mouse cannot love a cat. A mouse cannot be commonly said to refrain from hurting a cat. You do not love him whom you fear. Immediately you cease to fear, you are ready for your choice—to strike or to refrain. To refrain is proof of awakening of the soul in man; to strike is proof of body-force. The ability to strike must be present when the power of the soul is demonstrated.

This does not mean that we must be bodily superior to the adversary. This is not a satisfactory letter but I think you will follow my argument. But in matters such, as these, prayer is the thing.

With love,

*My Dear Child*, pp.18-9 (15: 484-5)

---

*This was Gandhi's presidential address at a political conference, organized by nationalist enthusiasts in Gujarat. The conference lasted three days and was largely attended by cultivators, petty traders and small land-holders—his future constituency. His speech dwelt on a range of themes, including the nature of the fight against the British, and was startlingly novel in the manner in which it enlarged the sphere of political discussion, by bringing into its ambit, matters of the soul and heart.*

### Speech at Gujarati Political Conference, Godhra I
### November 3, 1917

... We may petition the Government, we may agitate in the Imperial Council for our rights; but for a real awakening of the people, the more important thing is activities directed inwards. There is a possibility of hypocrisy and selfishness tainting activities directed outwards. There is very much less danger of this in activities of the other kind. Not only will the former not be justified unless balanced by the latter, they may even be barren of results. It is not my contention that we have no activities at all directed inward, but I submit that we do not lay enough stress upon them.

If we admit that our progress has not been what it might have been, we should also admit two reasons for this. We have kept our women away from these activities of ours and have thus become victims of a kind of paralysis. The nation walks with one leg only. All its work appears to be only half or incompletely done. Moreover, the educated section, having received its education through a foreign tongue, has become enervated and is unable to give the nation the benefit of such ability as it acquires. ...The educated class, lovers of *swaraj* (*self-rule or freedom - ed.*), must freely mix with the masses. We dare not turn away from a single section of the community or disown any. We shall make progress only if we carry all with us ...

... There are two methods of attaining one's goal. Satyagraha and *duragraha*. In our scriptures, they have been described, respectively, as divine and devilish modes of action. ... A satyagrahi does not abandon his path, even though at times it seems impenetrable and beset with difficulties and dangers, and a slight departure from that straight path may appear full of promise. ... Even an inveterate enemy he conquers by the force of the soul, which is love. Love for a friend is not put to the test. There is nothing surprising in a friend loving a friend; there is no merit in it and it costs no effort. When love is bestowed on the so-called enemy, it is tested, it becomes a virtue and requires an effort, and hence it is an act of manliness and real bravery. We can cultivate such an attitude even towards the Government. ... Love does not act through fear. Looking at everything with love, we shall not regard the Government with suspicion, nor believe that all their actions are inspired with bad motives. And our examination of their actions, being directed by love, will be unerring and is bound, therefore, to carry conviction with them.

Love can fight; often, it is obliged to. In the intoxication of power, man fails to see his error. When that happens, a satyagrahi does not sit still. He suffers. He disobeys the ruler's orders and his laws in a civil manner, and willingly submits to the penalties of such disobedience, for instance, imprisonment and gallows. Thus is the soul disciplined. In this, one never finds that one's time has been wasted and, if it is subsequently realized that such respectful disobedience was an error, the consequences are suffered merely by the satyagrahi and his co-workers. In the event, no bitterness develops between the satyagrahi and those in power; the latter, on the contrary, willingly yield to him. *They discover that they cannot command the satyagrahi's obedience. They cannot make him do anything against his will. And this is the consummation of swaraj, because it means complete independence (emphasis as in the original - ed.).* It need not be assumed that such resistance is possible only against civilized rulers. Even a heart of flint will melt in the fire kindled by the power of the soul ...

... But *duragraha* is a force with the opposite attributes. ... The terrible War going on in Europe is a case in point. Why should a nation's cause be considered right and another's wrong because it overpowers the latter by sheer brute force? The strong are often seen preying upon the weak. The wrongness of the latter's cause is not to be inferred from their defeat in a trial of brute strength, nor is the rightness of the strong to be inferred from their success in such a trial. The wielder of brute force does not scruple about the means to be used. He does not question the propriety of means, if he can somehow achieve his purpose. ... The man who follows the path of *duragraha* becomes impatient and wants to kill the so-called enemy. There can be but one result of this. Hatred increases. The defeated party vows vengeance and simply bides its time. The spirit of revenge thus descends from father to son. It is much to be wished that India never gives predominance to this spirit of *duragraha*. ... The *duragrahi*, like the oilman's ox, moves in a circle. His movement is only motion but it is not progress. The satyagrahi is ever moving forward ...

*Mahatma Gandhini Vicharsrishti* (from Gujarati) (16: 123-28)

---

*Just around the time he was expounding the virtues of non-violence, Gandhi's faith in his creed went into a state of crisis. He decided to support war-time recruitment. On his arrival in India, he had remonstrated against World War I and its horrors. But in 1918, when it appeared the British would grant substantial political reforms, he decided to repay their good faith with his own brand of goodwill—and campaigned for recruitment amongst the peasants of Kheda in Gujarat.*

## Speech at Nadiad
## June 21, 1918

SISTERS AND BROTHERS,

... We occupy the position of the *Bhangi* (*name of an untouchable caste from northern and western India, associated with sanitary labour - ed.*) in the Empire. Now we have an opportunity to emancipate ourselves from such a state and we can use it in either of two ways—in a spirit of friendliness or that of hostility. If we would follow the latter course, we should not help them with a single man or with a single pie; we should even stop others from helping. We should hope for a defeat of the Allies and fight the British and drive them out. All this, even if desirable, is impossible. Though we, advocates of *swaraj*, may not help the Government, other sections of the country have been helping it. We have no strength to fight the Government, or anyone else for that matter. It has succeeded in securing help from India to the tune of a million men and crores of rupees. Evidently, therefore, if we now propose to push the British out of India in a spirit of hostility and be *Bhangis* no more, it does not seem likely that we shall in the foreseeable future succeed in breaking off the British connection through physical force.

We can, therefore, free ourselves only through a friendly approach. This is not possible unless we render all possible help to the Government at the present juncture. We want to be partners in the Empire. If there were no Empire, with whom would we be partners? Our hopes lie in the survival of the Empire. By all means, let us fight its evils. A brother fights the wrongs done by a brother. If one brother seeks to deprive another of his right, the latter will resist, but will go all out to help the former in time of difficulty and so prove the fact of their being brothers, wiping out, sometimes, even old animosities.

There is no reason to believe that we cannot bring about such a result by dealing with the British in the right manner. To be sure, we may fight the iniquities of the Empire. Even today we may do so, if they were to inflict anything afresh. At the same time, we should spare no effort in helping it to meet the danger which threatens it.

Besides, we shall learn military discipline as we help the Empire, gain military experience and acquire the strength to defend ourselves. With that strength, we may even fight the Empire, should it play foul with us. It knows this, and, therefore, it will prove the *bona fides* of the British Government if they permit us to enlist. By raising an army now, we shall be insuring against future eventualities. If the British people have the ability to rule, they do not owe it merely to their physical strength. They have the art [of government], they have skill and foresight, shrewdness and wisdom. They know how to deal with people according to their deserts. They know that, if we help, it will be in expectation of getting *swaraj*. The difference between their point of view and that of some of us is this: we say we will have *swaraj* first and then fight; they say they will not be coerced, that *swaraj* will be ours if we help ...

*Gujarati* (from Gujarati) 7-7-1918 (17: 79)

---

*Gandhi's decision to canvass for enlistment dismayed his friends and admirers and he had to clarify for himself and them, the meaning of non-violence.*

**Letter to Esther Faering**
**Nadiad, June 30, 1918**

MY DEAR ESTHER,

I had no time to write to you ere this. I wonder if you have read all I have been writing and saying just now. What am I to advise a man to do who wants to kill but is unable owing to his being maimed? Before I can make him feel the virtue of not killing, I must restore to him the arm he has lost. I have always advised young Indians to join the army, but have hitherto refrained from actively asking them to do so, because I did not feel sufficiently interested in the purely political life of the country or in the war itself. But a different and difficult situation faced me in Delhi. I felt at once that I was playing with the greatest problem of life in not tackling the question of joining the army seriously. Either we must renounce the benefits of the State or help it to the best of our ability to prosecute the war. We are not ready to renounce. Indians have a double duty to perform. If they are to preach the mission of peace, they must first prove their ability in war.

This is a terrible discovery but it is true. A nation that is unfit to fight cannot from experience prove the virtue of not fighting. I do not infer from this that India must fight. But I do say that India must know how to fight. *Ahimsa* is the eradication of the desire to injure or to kill. ... It is enough if we can face the world without flinching. It is personal courage that is an absolute necessity. And some will acquire that courage only after they have been trained to fight. I know I have put the argument most clumsily. I am passing through new experiences. I am struggling to express myself. Some things are still obscure to me.

And I am trying to find words for others which are plain to me. I am praying for light and guidance and am acting with the greatest deliberation. Do please write and fight every inch of the ground that to you may appear untenable. That will enable me to find the way.

With love,
Yours,
BAPU

*My Dear Child*, pp. 28-9 (17: 109-10)

---

*Charlie Andrews, Christian missionary and social worker, was known to Gandhi from his South African days. Gandhi valued his friendship and love greatly. Andrews was astonished by Gandhi's recruitment campaign and demanded an explanation.*

**Letter to C. F. Andrews**
**Nadiad, July 6, 1918**

MY DEAR CHARLIE,

I have your letters. I prize them. They give me only partial consolation. My difficulties are deeper than you have put them. All you raise I can answer. I must attempt in this letter to reduce my own to writing.

... You say: "Indians as a race did repudiate it, bloodlust, with full consciousness in days gone by and deliberately took their choice to stand on the side of humanity." Is this historically true? I see no sign of it either in the *Mahabharata* or the *Ramayana*, not even in my favourite Tulsidas which is much superior in spirituality to Valmiki. I am not now thinking of these works in their spiritual meanings. The incarnations are described as certainly bloodthirsty, revengeful and merciless to the enemy. They have been credited with having resorted to tricks also for the sake of overcoming the enemy. The battles are described with no less zest than now, and the warriors are equipped with weapons of destruction such as could be possibly conceived by the human imagination. The finest hymn composed by Tulsidas in praise of Rama gives the first place to his ability to strike down the enemy. Then take the Mohamedan period. The Hindus were not less eager than the Mahomedans to fight. They were simply disorganized, physically weakened and torn by internal dissensions. The code of Manu prescribes no such renunciation that you impute to the race.

Buddhism, conceived as a doctrine of universal forbearance, signally failed, and, if the legends are true, the great Shankaracharya did not hesitate to use unspeakable cruelty in banishing Buddhism out of India. And he succeeded ! Then the English period. There has been compulsory renunciation of arms but not the desire to kill. Even among the Jains the doctrine has signally failed. They have a superstitious horror of blood (shed), but they have as little regard for the life of the enemy as an European. What I mean to say is that they would rejoice equally with anybody on earth over the destruction of the enemy. All then that can be said of India is that individuals have made serious attempts, with greater success than elsewhere, to popularize the doctrine. But there is no warrant for the belief that it has taken deep root among the people.

You say further: "My point is that it has become an unconscious instinct, which can be awakened any time as you yourself have shown." I wish it was true. But I see that I have shown nothing of the kind. When friends told me here that passive resistance was taken up by the people as a weapon of the weak, I laughed at the libel, as I called it then. But they were right and I was wrong. With me alone and a few other co-workers it came out of our strength and was described as satyagraha, but with the majority it was purely and simply passive resistance what they resorted to, because they were too weak to undertake methods of violence. This discovery was forced on me repeatedly in Kaira (*during the Kheda satyagraha - ed.*) The people here, being comparatively freer, talked to me without reserve, and told me plainly that they took up my remedy because they were not strong enough to take up the other, which they undoubtedly held to be far more manly than mine. I fear that the people ... would not fearlessly walk to the gallows, or stand a shower of bullets and yet say, in one case, "we will not pay the revenue", and in the other, "we will not work for you". They have it not in them. And I contend that they will not regain the fearless spirit until they have received the training to defend themselves.

*Ahimsa* was preached to man when he was in full vigour of life and able to look his adversaries straight in the face. It seems to me that full development of body-force is a *sine qua non* of full appreciation and assimilation of *ahimsa*. I do agree with you that India with her moral force could hold back from her shores any combination of armies from the West or the East or the North or the South. The question is, how can she cultivate this moral force? Will she have to be strong in body before she can understand even the first principles of this moral force? This is how millions blaspheme the Lord of the Universe every morning before sunrise.

"I am changeless Brahma, not a collection of the five elements—earth, etc.—I am that Brahma whom I recall every morning as the spirit residing in the innermost sanctuary of my heart, by whose grace the whole speech is adorned, and whom the Vedas have described as "neti, neti".

I say we blaspheme the Lord of the Universe in reciting the above verse because it is a parrot recitation without any consideration of its grand significance. One Indian realizing in himself all that the verse means is enough to repel the mightiest army that can approach the shores of India. But it is not in us today and it will not come until there is an atmosphere of freedom and fearlessness on the soil. How to produce that atmosphere? Not without the majority of the inhabitants feeling that they are well able to protect themselves from the violence of man or beast. … I wait for instilling into any mind the doctrine of *ahimsa*, i.e., perfect love, when it has grown to maturity by having its full play through a vigorous body. My difficulty now arises in the practical application of the idea.

What is the meaning of having a vigorous body? How far should India have to go in for a training in arms-bearing? Must every individual go through the practice or is it enough that a free atmosphere is created and the people will, without having to bear arms, etc., imbibe the necessary personal courage from their surroundings? I believe that the last is the correct view, and, therefore, I am absolutely right as things are in calling upon every Indian to join the army, always telling him at the same time that he is doing so not for the lust of blood, but for the sake of learning not to fear death. …

… If the motive is right, it may be turned to the profit of mankind and that an *ahimsaist* may not stand aside and look on with indifference but must make his choice and actively co-operate or actively resist. … You can't complain of my having given you only a scrap of a letter. Instead of a letter, I have inflicted upon you what may almost read like an essay. But it was necessary that you should know what is passing in my mind at the present moment. You may now pronounce your judgement and mercilessly tear my ideas to pieces where you find them to be wrong. I hope you are getting better and stronger. I need hardly say that we shall all welcome you when you are quite able to undertake a journey.

With love,
MOHAN

From the manuscript of *Mahadev Desai's Diary*. Courtesy: Narayan Desai (17:120-24)

---

*In later years, Gandhi recalled his support for the Empire's wars and explained his past decisions and his present disenchantment. This essay helps us understand Gandhi's engagement with war in 1918.*

## Why Did I Assist in War

Not only did I offer my services at the time of the Zulu revolt but before that at the time of the Boer War and not only did I raise recruits in India during the late War, but I raised an ambulance corps in 1914 in London . If therefore I have sinned, the cup of my sins is full to the brim. I lost no occasion of serving the Government at all times. ... But on those four occasions I did honestly believe that in spite of the many disabilities that my country was labouring under, it was making its way towards freedom, and that on the whole the Government from the popular standpoint was not wholly bad and that the British administrators were honest though insular and dense.

Holding that view, I set about doing what an ordinary Englishman would do in the circumstances. I was not wise or important enough to take independent action. I had no business to judge or scrutinize ministerial decisions with the solemnity of a tribunal. I did not impute malice to the ministers either at the time of the Boer War, the Zulu revolt or the late War. I did not consider Englishmen nor do I now consider them as particularly bad or worse than other human beings. I considered and still consider them to be as capable of high motives and actions as any other body of men and equally capable of making mistakes. I therefore felt, that I sufficiently discharged my duty as a man and a citizen by offering my humble services to the empire in the hour of its need whether local or general. ...

... The whole situation is now changed for me. My eyes, I fancy, are opened. Experience has made me wiser. I consider the existing system of Government to be wholly bad and requiring special national effort to end or mend it. It does not possess within itself any capacity for self-improvement. That I still believe many English administrators to be honest does not assist me, because I consider them to be as blind and deluded as I was myself. Therefore I can take no pride in calling the empire mine or describing myself as a citizen.

On the contrary, I fully realize that I am a pariah untouchable of the empire. I must therefore constantly pray for its radical reconstruction or total destruction, even as a Hindu pariah would be fully justified in so praying about Hinduism or Hindu society. The next point, that of *ahimsa*, is more abstruse. My conception of *ahimsa* impels me always to dissociate myself from almost every one of the activities I am engaged in. My soul refuses to be satisfied so long as it is a helpless witness of a single wrong or a single misery. But it is not possible for me, a weak, frail, miserable being, to mend every wrong or to hold myself free of blame for all the wrong I see. The spirit in me pulls one way, the flesh in me pulls in the opposite direction. There is freedom from the action of these two forces, but that freedom is attainable only by slow and painful stages. I cannot attain freedom by a mechanical refusal to act, but only by intelligent action in a detached manner. This struggle resolves itself into an incessant crucifixion of the flesh so that the spirit may become entirely free.

*Young India*, 17-11-1921 (25: 101-102)

## Self-Cleansing

---

*Gandhi's satyagraha was not merely an ethic to be argued, it had to be lived. Apart from following a strict regimen of diet, work and cooperation in the ashram, satyagraha called for a re-charging of the self. He required those who accepted his world view to look deep into their hearts and root out age-old prejudices and, importantly, cultivate active love.*

*As with public acts of non-violent resistance, self-cleansing was to be undertaken in specific contexts: against the practice of untouchability; in the cause of unity between Muslims and Hindus and for the regeneration of a craft-based economy. Gandhi held that India's artisanal and craft traditions, especially the production of cloth, had been destroyed by the demands of colonial rule. Along with satyagraha, swadeshi or economic self-reliance, became a keyword in Gandhi's lexicon. This was no mere economic imperative though—it was to be understood and accepted as a moral duty that a person owed to India's poor. Spinning became, thus, the visible form of non-violent resistance to colonial economics. These years also witnessed his deep interest in issues of female autonomy and equality—his understanding and resolution of these issues were unique and, importantly, shaped by his attitudes to sexual desire and its implications.*

*The extracts in this section allow us to look at the making of a non-violent consciousness—the necessary struggles within and without that a person had to wage to be a fit agent of satyagraha.*

---

*Gandhi's creed of non-violence was tested in his own backyard, when his wife Kasturba and a few other associates protested his insistence that families be brought into the ashram. In separate letters to friends he explained his actions.*

**Letter to V. S . Srinivasa Shastri**
**September 23, 1915**

*( V. S. Srinivasa Shastri, was a liberal politician from South India, who, like Gandhi, was deeply influenced by the Ramayana - ed.)*

DEAR MR SHASTRIAR

When I took in Naiker (*an untouchable child from Madras, whom Gandhi 'adopted' - ed.*), Mrs. Gandhi did not 'kick'. Now I had to decide whether I was to take in a grown-up Gujarati *Dhed* with his wife. I decided to take him and she rebelled against it and so did another lady at the Ashram. There was quite a flutter in the Ashram. There is a flutter even in Ahmedabad. I have told Mrs. Gandhi she could leave me and we should part good friends. The step is momentous because it so links me with the suppressed classes mission that I might have at no distant time to carry out the idea of shifting to some *Dhed* quarters and sharing their life with the *Dheds*. It would mean much even for my staunchest co-workers. I have now given you the outline of the story. There is nothing grand about it. It is of importance to me because it enables me to demonstrate the efficacy of passive resistance in social questions and when I take the final step, it will embrace *swaraj*, etc ...

Yours sincerely,
M. K. GANDHI

From a photostat of the original in Gandhiji's hand (15: 46)

---

**Letter to Hermann Kallenbach**
**Ahmedabad, September 24, 1915**

MY DEAR FRIEND,

... You know what a Pariah is. He is what is called an untouchable. The widow's son whom I have taken is a Pariah but that did not shock Mrs. Gandhi so much. Now I have taken one from our own parts and Mrs.Gandhi as also Maganlal's wife were up in arms against me. They made my life miserable so far as they could. I told them they were not bound to stay with me. This irritated them the more. The storm has not yet subsided. I am however unmoved and comparatively calm.

The step I have taken means a great deal. It may alter my life a bit, i.e., I may have to completely take up Pariah work, i.e., I might have to become a Pariah myself. We shall see. Anyway let my troubles brace you up if they can ...

From the original *Gandhi-Kallenbach Correspondence* (15: 47)

---

## A Stain on India's Forehead
[After November 5, 1917]

... Why does God permit this atrocity? ... Even the slavery of the Negroes is better than this. This religion, if it can be called such, stinks in my nostrils. This certainly cannot be the Hindu religion, It was through the Hindu religion that I learnt to respect Christianity and Islam. How then can this sin be a part of the Hindu religion? But then what is to be done?

I shall put up a lone fight, if need be, against this hypocrisy. Alone I shall undergo penance and die with His name on my lips. It is possible that I may go mad and say that I was mistaken in my views on the question of untouchability, that I was guilty of a sin in calling untouchability a sin of Hinduism. Then you should take it that I am frightened, that I cannot face the challenge and that I change my views out of cowardice. You should take it, in that event, that I am in delirium.

In my humble opinion, the dirt that soils the scavenger is physical and can be easily removed. But there are those who have become soiled with untruth and hypocrisy, and this dirt is so subtle that it is very difficult to remove it. If there are any untouchables, they are the people who are filled with untruth and hypocrisy. ... I can think of no epithet to describe those who deny the feeling of hatred which underlies untouchability. If a *Bhangi* by mistake finds his way into our compartment, he will hardly escape a beating and, as for abuse, this will fall on him in a shower. The tea-seller will not hand him tea nor the shopkeeper sell him goods. We will not care to touch him even if he be dying. We give him our leavings to eat and our torn and soiled garments to wear. No Hindu is willing to teach him. He cannot dwell in a proper house. On the road, out of fear of our wrath, he has to proclaim his untouchability repeatedly. What treatment can be more indicative of hatred than this ? What does this condition of his show ? Just as in Europe, at one time, slavery was upheld under cover of religion, so now in our society hatred for the untouchables is fostered in the name of religion. Till the very end there were some people in Europe who quoted the Bible in defence of slavery. I include our present supporters of orthodoxy in this category. We shall have to free religion of the sin of untouchability which is imputed to it. Unless we do this, diseases like plague, cholera, etc., cannot be rooted out. There is nothing lowly in the occupations of the untouchables. Doctors as well as our mothers perform similar duties. It may be argued that they cleanse themselves afterwards. Yes, but if *Bhangis,* etc., do not do so, the fault is wholly ours and not theirs. It is clear that the moment we begin lovingly to hug them, they will begin to learn to be clean.

... While this country is venerated for its *tapasya*, purity, compassion and other virtues, it is also a playground of licence, sin, barbarity and other vices. At such a juncture it will be becoming for our fraternity of writers to gird up their loins to oppose and root out hypocrisy. I appeal to you to share in the sacred work that was taken up at Godhra greeting it as such and participate in the effort that may be undertaken in this cause, so that sixty million people may not break away from us in despair. Before joining this campaign, I have thoroughly reflected on my religious responsibility. A critic has made the prophecy that, in course of time, my views will change. On this I shall only say that, before such a tune comes, I shall have forsaken not only Hinduism but all religion. But it is my firm conviction that if, in the attempt to free Hinduism of this blot, I have to lay down my life, it will be no great matter ...

*Bapu aur Harijan* (from Hindi) (16: 137-141)

---

*Among the many things that occupied Gandhi's attention, the problem of Hindu-Muslim unity and its essentially fragile nature were predominant. His calls for openness and peace between communities were of a part with his larger faith in non-violence and satyagraha.*

### Speech at Gujarati Social Conference

... What shall we do to bridge the gulf that exists between Hindus and Muslims and bring together hearts that have become estranged? It is my life's mission to bring about amity between the two communities. For 25 years I have been thinking how this may be done and have been mixing with Muslim friends. What I hear about Shahabad (*Hindu-Muslim riots had taken place here in September-October - ed.*) pierces my heart and makes it bleed. If I could, I would have run up to the place and had a heart-to-heart talk with our Muslim brethren there. But I know my limitations. ... But I have been thinking about the problem, and should like to tell my Hindu brethren that we have grievously erred on this occasion, that we are more to blame. It is the duty of the wiser among the Hindus to heal the Muslims' wounds and compensate them for the losses we have inflicted on them in Arrah. I would even go to the extent of saying that, if Shahabad Hindus cannot do this, Hindus all over the country should combine to do it. The lawyer friends who have been fighting in the courts, on the two sides, should withdraw the cases and inform the Government that they do not now want them to be proceeded with.

To Muslim friends, I shall say that the fighting between the two communities in one district need not be made an excuse for fighting all over India. Even two brothers sometimes fight, but they should not be allowed to disrupt the family as a whole. In like manner, the two communities here need not take their quarrel outside the Province.

... The differences between Hindus and Muslims are over the cow. If we want cows to be protected, the thing to do is to save them from slaughter-houses. Not less than 30,000 cows and calves are killed for the British every day. While we have not succeeded in stopping this slaughter, we have no right to raise our hand against Muslims. I should like to tell the Hindus that it is no religious act to kill Muslims in order to save cows. ... I also want cows to be protected but, for that purpose, I would ask the Muslim friends to apply the knife to my neck and kill me rather than the cow. I am sure they will respond to this prayerful request. If we cherish our own freedom, we have no right to deprive others of theirs. Interference with one another's freedom leads to strained relations. If a Muslim arrogantly asks Hindus not to play on drums [near a mosque], the latter will never agree. If, however, the Muslims were to say in all humility, "Please do not play on drums and disturb us in the performance of our religious duty, in our devotions; if you do, we will lay down our lives," I am sure there is no Hindu so thoughtless as to act against their wishes.

The truth is that in this matter neither the Hindu nor the Muslim is being honest. If we want harmony, we can have it through love; never through intimidation, [for] the other party will not speak out frankly what it really feels ...

*Mahatma Gandhini Vicharsrishti* (from Gujarati) 16: 142-43)

---

*Gandhi's pleas for Hindu-Muslim unity grew more intense and sustained when he started satyagraha against the repressive Rowlatt Bills. Satyagraha appeared a fit context for Hindus and Muslims to pledge love and brotherhood towards each other.*

### The Vow of Hindu-Muslim Unity
### April 8, 1919

... A vow is a purely religious act which cannot be taken in a fit of passion. It can be taken only with a mind purified and composed and with God as witness. ... Acts which are not possible by ordinary self-denial become possible with the aid of vows which require extraordinary self-denial. It is hence believed that vows can only uplift us. If the Hindu and Muslim communities could be united in one bond of mutual friendship, and if each could act towards the other even as children of the same mother, it would be a consummation devoutly to be wished.

But before this unity becomes a reality, both the communities will have to give up a good deal, and will have to make radical changes in ideas held heretofore. Members of one community when talking about those of the other at times indulge in terms so vulgar that they but exacerbate the relations between the two. In Hindu society we do not hesitate to indulge in unbecoming language when talking of the Mahomedans and vice versa. Many believe that an ingrained and ineradicable animosity exists between the Hindus and Mahomedans. In many places we see that each community harbours distrust against the other. Each fears the other. It is an undoubted fact that this anomalous and wretched state of things is improving day by day. The Time-Spirit is ceaselessly working on unchecked, and willy-nilly we have to live together. But the object of taking a vow is speedily to bring about, by the power of self-denial, a state of things which can only be expected to come in the fullness of time. How is this possible?

Meetings should be called of Hindus—I mean the orthodox Hindus—where this question should be seriously considered. The standing complaint of the Hindus against the Mussulmans is that the latter are beef-eaters and that they purposely sacrifice cows on the Bakr-i-ld day. Now it is impossible to unite the Hindus and Mahomedans so long as the Hindus do not hesitate to kill their Mahomedan brethren in order to protect a cow. For I think it is futile to expect that our violence will ever compel the Mahomedans to refrain from cow-slaughter. I do not believe the efforts of our cow-protection societies have availed in the least to lessen the number of cows killed every day. I have had no reason to believe so. I believe myself to be an orthodox Hindu and it is my conviction that no one who scrupulously practices the Hindu religion may kill a cow-killer to protect a cow. There is one and only one means open to a Hindu to protect a cow and that is that he should offer himself as sacrifice if he cannot stand its slaughter.

Even if a very few enlightened Hindus thus sacrificed themselves, I have no doubt that our Mussulman brethren would abandon cow-slaughter. But this is satyagraha; this is equity; even as, if I want my brother to redress a grievance, I must do so by taking upon my head a certain amount of sacrifice and not by inflicting injury on him. I may not demand it as of right. My only right against my brother is that I can offer myself as sacrifice.

It is only when the Hindus are inspired with a feeling of pure love of this type that Hindu-Muslim unity can be expected. As with the Hindus, so with the Musssulmans. The leaders among the latter should meet together and consider their duty towards the Hindus.

When both are inspired by a spirit of sacrifice, when both try to do their duty towards one another instead of pressing their rights, then and then only would the long-standing differences between the two communities cease. Each must respect the other's religion, must refrain from even secretly thinking ill of the other. We must politely dissuade members of both the communities from indulging in bad language against one another. Only a serious endeavour in this direction can remove the estrangement between us ...

*Young India,* 7-5-1919 (17: 400-02)

---

*Gandhi was convinced that spinning—which he considered an old and hoary artisanal craft which had helped poor Indians tide over poverty in troubled times—was central to any programme of national re-generation. Though Gandhi's advocacy of spinning as a national vocation would be pronounced in the decade to come (in the mid and late 1920s), its beginnings may be found in these early years that shaped his understanding of national duties and responsibilities.*

## Speech on Swadeshi, Bombay
## June 28, 1919

... If a man is born in India, there must be some reason behind the fact; that being so, we need to consider what is our especial duty. That duty is *swadeshi* and is included in *dharma*. Jainism teaches compassion towards living creatures and the duty of non-violence; it even teaches the protection of violent animals against small creatures. This, however, is no justification for our neglecting the duty of compassion and non-violence towards human beings. If our neighbours are in pain or misfortune, it is our duty to share their suffering and help them.

All over the world, the religious life has lost importance to such an extent that irreligion is spreading in the name of religion and men everywhere are deceiving themselves. We claim to be men of *dharma*, whereas all our actions are tainted with *adharma*. We cannot claim to have followed *dharma* by earning money through *adharma*, and giving it in charity for promoting pious causes. Most of the people assembled here are traders by profession. We are told that trade cannot be carried on without some admixture of dishonesty. I shall be plain and tell you that, if that is so, you had better give up trade. One's *dharma* lies in refusing to forsake truth even if that means starving, and, unless we live in this manner, *dharma* will not be the central purpose of our lives.

There is a painful thing I am obliged to mention, and it is that our religious leaders, whose duty it is to enlighten people, have forgotten that duty. This is true, however much it may hurt us. Religious leaders have it in them to set an example to their followers by their conduct. Mere preaching will have no effect on those who assemble to listen to their discourses. Religious leaders, too, should follow the rule of *swadeshi*. They have plenty of time on hand. They should take to the spinning-wheel and spin and thus set an example to their followers. More than in the repetition of Rama as they tell the beads, in the music of the spinning-wheel will they hear the voice of the *atman* with a beauty all its own.

*Swadeshi* is our primary obligation because natural to us. We have forsaken this natural obligation. Because of its neglect of *swadeshi*, the nation has been ruined. Three crores in India, that is, a tenth of the total population of the country, get only one meal a day, just plain bread and no more. Crores of rupees are annually lost to foreign countries. If this wealth of crores could remain in the country, we would be able to save our starving countrymen. Thus, our economic well-being is also bound up with *swadeshi*, and in its observance there lies compassion for living beings. Moreover, *swadeshi* cloth is likely to be cheaper than English cloth. I submit to you that you should make your own cloth or get it made. The vow of *swadeshi* is not a difficult one to keep. Through it, we shall remove the hardships of our countrymen. If we work at the spinning-wheel for eight hours, we can spin one pound of yarn. The cloth being produced in India today can meet the needs of only 25 per cent of the population; we should therefore produce enough to meet the needs of the remaining 75 per cent. If, thus, people take to turning the spinning-wheel, not only shall we succeed in keeping the vow of *swadeshi* but shall also ensure production of cloth in plenty.

*Gujarati*, (from Gujarati) 6-7-1919 (18: 142-44)

---

*Gandhi seldom discussed the issue of women's rights in isolation. He viewed their rights to equality in the context of the new national life that he desired to build. This early argument for women's education linked together themes that would emerge with greater force in the years to come: celibacy, the conquest of desire, and female dignity and autonomy.*

## A Foreword

(To *Striyon ane Samajseva*, written by Bhogindrarao Divetia)

... We desire girls' education. But we have yet to discover what type of education it should be. For the present, we are only experimenting. But we are not going to bring about women's education merely through girls' schools. Thousands of girls disappear from before our eyes by becoming victims to child marriage as early as at the age of twelve. They become housewives! So long as this sinful custom does not disappear from amongst us, men will have to learn to be the teachers of women. [The fulfilment of] many of our hopes lies in their education in this respect. So long as our women do not cease to be objects of our lust and our cooks and do not become our better halves, sharing our happiness and misery, all our efforts will be futile. Some people regard their wives as animals. Some of the things in our old Sanskrit texts, as also a famous couplet of Tulsidas, are to blame for this. Tulsidas has written in one place: "drums, boors, shudras, animals and women, all are fit to be beaten." I am a devotee of Tulsidas. But my devotion is not blind. Either the above couplet is an interpolation, or if it is really by Tulsidas, he must have written it without thought, only expressing the prevalent attitude.

As for the utterances in the Sanskrit texts, the idea seems to have become fixed that every verse coined in Sanskrit is the word of the scriptures. We must get rid of this false notion and do away with this age-old attitude that regards women as inferior creatures. On the other hand, some of us, blinded by passion, worship women as a goddess or treat her as a doll and decorate her with ornaments as we decorate the idols every day. It is necessary for us to free ourselves of this wrong worship also. ... When our women, too, participate in our discussions, argue with us, understand and support our utterances, with their extraordinary intuition, understand and share our external troubles and bring to us the balm of peace, then, and not till then, will our salvation become possible. There is very little chance of bringing about such a situation merely through girls' schools. So long as we carry round our necks the millstone of child-marriage, husbands will have to act as teachers to their wives. And such education must not be confined to a knowledge of letters. Gradually they can be introduced to subjects like politics and social reform. Literacy should not be a precondition to this. Husbands will have to change their attitude towards their wives. Is it not possible for a woman to remain a student till she attains maturity and for the husband to observe *brahmacharya* till such time? Unless we were crushed with insensibility and inertia, we would certainly not subject a girl of twelve or fifteen to the great strain of child-bearing. The very thought should make us shudder. There are classes for married women and lectures are arranged for them. All this is fine. Those who are engaged in such activities are sacrificing their time and that too is a matter of credit to them. At the same time so long as men do not do their duty as stated above, we are not likely to get very good results ...

*Striyon ane Samajseva* (from Gujarati) (15: 302-04)

# Testing Authority

*Gandhi's creed of non-violence and the cluster of ideas associated with it were shaped as much by specific struggles as they were by his firm faith. In Champaran in Bihar, a long-suffering peasantry, stifled by unfair demands from European planters and Indian landlords, desired his intervention in their cause. He heeded their requests and visited Champaran. The model of action that he advocated made him an exemplar for educated middle class professionals: inspired by his moral ardour they hurried to join him in his work of rejuvenating peasant life, based on the moral edicts that he outlined. In Ahmedabad, Gandhi offered a new definition of the class struggle and economic justice, and to test the 'truth' of his position undertook a fast to secure a wage raise for the workers. In Kheda in Gujarat he urged peasants, faced with revenue demands from government, which they could not hope to fulfil in a year of bad harvest, to stand up to forced dispossession of land and property. He spoke of the virtues of strength through sacrifice and voluntary suffering.*

*In all three instances, Gandhi wrestled with his soul, indeed, with the souls of all those involved, both the oppressors and their victims and supporters. In the process, his faith in compassion and understanding, in resistance that refused to rely on hatred, anger and violence gained political form and coherence. Non-violence ceased to be a figure of speech, a moral option urged on his supporters by his obduracy, and became, instead, a public creed.*

*These struggles won for their proponents modest gains: the worst excesses of rural oppression were done away with in Champaran. In Ahmedabad, Gandhi succeeded in getting a wage raise, though this was less than what the workers had originally demanded. In Kheda, peasants did stand up to British authority, but the revenue remission desired by the peasants was not granted. In spite of these not too substantial gains, these struggles were important, for they enabled Gandhi to evolve a mode of struggle that revolutionized nationalist politics in the years to come.*

*The extracts below trace these practices of soul force and delineate a tale of non-violence in action. They also provide insights into a creed whose notions of justice were linked to compassion, rather than a restriction and re-ordering of wealth, power and authority.*

---

*Gandhi's engagement with the plight of indigo cultivators in Champaran was modest, though sustained. He petitioned government, counselled the peasants in dignified fortitude and brought together a band of satyagraha volunteers to carry out a disciplined programme of village reconstruction.*

## Instructions for Workers
## April 16, 1917

... The ryots (*peasants, in this instance, indigo cultivators - ed.*) should be instructed definitely not to use violence whether regarding their own grievances or regarding imprisonment of those who may come to assist them. But they can be and should be told that where they know they are being unjustly treated, that is, required to plant indigo when they need not, rather than go to law, they should simply refuse to plant indigo and if for so refusing they are imprisoned they should suffer imprisonment. This requires very careful explanation. Where the workers do not understand the working of this quiet resistance or do not appreciate the force of it, they may drop this point of the programme.

From a facsimile of the original given in *Mahatma*, Vol. I (15: 339-40)

---

## Letter to W. B. Heycock
## Bettiah, May 20, 1917

(*Heycock was the District Magistrate - ed.*)

DEAR MR. HEYCOCK

... It is a known fact that the desire of the planters generally is, that my friends and I should not carry on our work. I can only say that nothing but physical force from the Government or an absolute guarantee that the admitted or provable wrongs of the *raiyats* (*the same meaning as 'ryots', that is, peasants - ed.*) are to stop for ever, can possibly remove us from the District. What I have seen of the conditions of the *raiyats* is sufficient to convince me that if we withdrew at this stage, we would stand condemned before man and God and, what is most important of all, we would never be able to forgive ourselves.

But the mission is totally of peace. I cannot too often give the assurance that I bear no ill-will against the planters. I have been told that this is true of myself but that my friends are fired with an anti-English feeling and that for them this is an anti-English movement. I can only say that I do not know a body of men who have less of that feeling than my friends. I was not prepared for this pleasant revelation. I was prepared for some degree of ill-will. I would have held it excusable. I do not know that I have not been guilty of it myself under circumstances which have appeared to me most provoking. But if I found that any of my associates were, in the conduct of this mission, actuated by any ill-will at all, I should disassociate myself entirely from them and insist upon their leaving the mission. At the same time, the determination to secure a freedom for the *raiyats* from the yoke that is wearing them down is inflexible.

Cannot the Government secure that freedom? This is a natural exclamation. My answer is that they cannot, in cases like this, without such assistance as is afforded to them by my mission. The Government machinery is designedly slow. It moves, must move, along the line of least resistance. Reformers like myself, who have no other axe to grind but that of reform they are handling for the time being, specialize and create a force which the Government must reckon with. Reformers may go wrong by being overzealous, indiscreet or indolent and ignorant. The Government may go wrong by being impatient of them or over-confident of their ability to do without them. I hope, in this case, neither catastrophe will take place and the grievances, which I have already submitted and which are mostly admitted, will be effectively redressed. Then the planters will have no cause to fear or suspect the mission of which I have the honour to be in charge and they will gladly accept the assistance of volunteers who will carry on the work of education and sanitation among the villagers and act as links between them and the *raiyats* ...

From the original typewritten copy signed by Gandhiji in the National Archives of India; also *Select Documents on Mahatma Gandhi's Movement in Champaran* No. 84, pp. 144-6 (15: 388)

*War-time troubles threw the textile workers of Ahmedabad onto the streets. They demanded a rise in wages. Gandhi decided to arbitrate between the workers and the mill-owners. Meanwhile, he spent time propagating his version of class politics amongst the workers. His campaign for a wage-rise was unique. He believed in educating the striking workers, just as much he desired to awaken the mill-owners to their responsibilities. His 'education' took the form of addressing workers through leaflets that were distributed amongst them.*

## Ahmedabad Mill-Hands' Strike
## February 27, 1918

LEAFLET NO. 2

... We know that the employers have crores of rupees and the workers have nothing. If workers have no money however, they have hands and feet with which they can work, and there is no part of the world which can do without workers. Hence, if only he knows it, the worker holds the key to the situation. Wealth is unavailing without him. If he realizes this, he can be sure of success. But the worker who would wield such power must possess certain qualities of character ...

1. The worker should be truthful. There is no reason for him to tell a lie. Even if he tells a lie, he will not get the desired wage. The truthful man can be firm and a worker who is firm is never defeated.

2. He should possess courage. Many of us become permanent slaves through fear of what might happen to us if we lost our jobs.

3. He should have a sense of justice. If he asks for wages higher than his deserts, there will be hardly anyone who will employ him ...

4. He will not be angry with his employer nor bear him any grudge. After all, when everything is over, the worker is to serve under him. Every human being is liable to err. We think the employers are in the wrong in refusing the increase asked for. If

we remain straightforward till the end, the employers are sure to revise their attitude. At present they are angry. Also, they suspect that, if the present demands of the workers are granted, they will repeatedly harass them. To remove this suspicion, we should do our utmost to reassure the employers by our behaviour. The first thing to that end is to harbour no grudge against them.

5. Every worker should remember that the struggle is bound to involve suffering. But happiness follows suffering voluntarily undertaken. It is but suffering for the worker to be denied a wage sufficient to enable him to make both ends meet. ... Seeking a remedy against this suffering, we have told the employers that it is not possible for us to maintain ourselves without the wage increase demanded and that, if it is not granted to us and we are not saved from continuous starvation, we would rather starve right now ...

6. Lastly, the poor have their saviour in God. Our duty is to make the effort and then, remain fully assured that we are bound to get what He has ordained for us, remain peaceful while our request is not yet granted.

*Ek Dharmayuddha* (from Gujarati) (16: 289-90)

---

*Gandhi urged Ambalal Sarabhai, the industrialist against whom the workers were striking, to consider his duties by his employees. His mode of address and his conciliatory approach charmed Sarabhai who eventually became one of his trusted followers and supporters.*

### Letter to Ambalal Sarabhai
### Sabarmati, March 1, 1918

DEAR FRIEND,

If you succeed, the poor, already suppressed, will be suppressed still more, will be more abject than ever and the impression will have been confirmed that money can subdue everyone. If, despite your efforts, the workers succeed in securing the increase, you, and others with you, will regard the result as your failure. Can I possibly wish you success in so far as the first result is concerned? Is it your desire that the arrogance of money should increase? Or that the workers be reduced to utter submission?

Would you be so unkindly disposed to them as to see no success for you in their getting what they are entitled to, maybe even a few pice more? Do you not see that in your failure lies your success, that your success is fraught with danger for you ? ... Do you not see that your success will have serious consequences for the whole society? Your efforts are of the nature of *duragraha* ... An effort like mine is satyagraha. Kindly look deep into your heart, listen to the still small voice within and obey it, I pray you. Will you dine with me?

*Mahadevbhaini Diary,* Vol. IV (from Gujarati) (16: 300)

---

*This leaflet attempted a unique definition of economic justice.*

**March 3, 1918**

LEAFLET NO. 6

Pure justice is that which is inspired by fellow-feeling and compassion. We in India call it the Eastern or the ancient way of justice. That way of justice which has no place in it for fellow feeling or compassion is known as Satanic, Western or modern justice. Out of compassion or regard, son and father concede many things to each other to the eventual benefit of both. One takes pride in giving up a claim and thinks of one's action as proceeding from strength, not weakness. There was a time in India when servants, passing from father to son, used to serve in the same family for generations. They were regarded and treated as members of the family. They suffered with the employers in their misfortunes and the latter shared the servants' joys and sorrows. In those days, India was reputed for a social order free from friction, and this order endured for thousands of years on that basis. Even now this sense of fellow-feeling is not altogether absent in our country. Where such an arrangement exists, there is hardly any need for a third party or an arbitrator. Disputes between a master and a servant are settled between themselves amicably. There was no room in this arrangement for increase or reduction in wages according as the changing needs of the two might dictate. Servants did not ask for higher wages when there was a dearth of servants and masters did not reduce wages when servants were available in plenty. This arrangement was based primarily on considerations of mutual regard, propriety, decorum and affection.

This sense of mutual obligation was not then, as it is now, considered unpractical but ruled us in most of our affairs. ...But in most public activities of the West at present, there is no place for fellow-feeling or compassion. It is considered just that a master pays his servant what he thinks fit. It is not considered necessary to think of the servants' needs. So also the worker can make his own demand, irrespective of the employer's financial condition and this is considered just. It expects others to take these into account.

The present war in Europe (*World War I - ed.*) is fought on the same principle. No means is considered improper for defeating the enemy. Wars must have been fought even in the past, but the vast masses of the people were not involved in them. We would do well not to introduce into India this despicable idea of justice. When workers make a demand merely because they think themselves strong enough to do so, regardless of the employers' condition, they will have succumbed to the modern, Satanic idea of justice. The employers, in refusing to consider the workers' demands, have accepted this Satanic principle of justice, may be unintentionally or in ignorance ...

*Ek Dharmayuddha* (from Gujarati) (16: 302-04)

---

*The textile strike dragged on and a few dispirited workers decided to go back to work. Perturbed by their giving up on their strike pledge and determined to rouse the conscience of the mill-owners, Gandhi decided to go on a self-cleansing fast to further strengthen his and the workers' resolve.*

### Prayer Discourse in Ashram
### March 17, 1918

... I was thus forced to consider by what means the mill-hands could be made to remain firm. How could I do this without suffering myself? I saw that it was necessary to show them by example how, for the sake of one's pledge, one had to undergo suffering. So it was that I took this pledge. I am aware that it carries a taint. It is likely that, because of my vow, the mill-owners may be moved by consideration for me and come to grant the workers' [demand for] thirty-five per cent increase. My desire is that they should grant the demand only if they see its justice and not out of charity. But the natural result would be that they would do so out of charity and to that extent this pledge is one which cannot but fill me with shame. I weighed the two things, however, against each other: my sense of shame and the mill-hands' pledge. The balance tilted in favour of the latter and I resolved, for the sake of the mill-hands, to take no thought of my shame. In doing public work, a man must be prepared to put up even with such loss of face. Thus, my pledge is not at all by way of a threat to the mill-owners; on the contrary, I wish they clearly understand this and grant the 35 per cent to the mill-hands only if they think it just to do so ...

*Mahadevbhaini Diary,* Vol. IV (from Gujarati) (16: 342)

---

*In Kheda district of Gujarat, peasants waging a struggle against the colonial government for a remission of land revenue on account of a poor harvest found in Gandhi a messianic spokesman.*

### Speech at Sinhuj
### April 10, 1918

... Some will say that this struggle is merely to secure suspension of the Land revenue for a year. Yes, that is true enough; but, in reality, the struggle is for an all-important issue underlying the question of land revenue. We must become absolutely fearless. Fear is not for us, neither for men nor for women; fear is for beasts. The day before yesterday I said by way of illustration that, on seeing the frightened eyes of the bullock when a car passes by, I am moved to pity. As the car comes nearer, the bullock shakes with fear, and sometimes the car is in danger of being overturned. The bullock's fear is groundless. We are in the same condition as this bullock. It is a harsh comparison and does no credit to man, but that is the simple truth of the matter. Why should we fear without any reason? ...

... Let the Government, if it will, take away our cattle; hand over the ornaments, too, if it wants to seize them. But there is one thing we will not give up and that is our self-respect. No one who does not maintain his self-respect can be called a man of religion. He who is afraid of God is afraid of none else. He whom we have imagined as omnipotent and omniscient protects all and leads all to welfare. How can you give in, betraying all those who, in this fight for truth and *dharma*, have bound themselves by a pledge? ... A man who had yielded would feel like bringing down others and so, instead of admitting his weakness, would try to cover it up. If any of you harbours such an idea, please banish it from your mind and give courage to the satyagrahis who have taken the pledge. That is our sacred duty. If you discharge this duty, at any rate, those who have taken the pledge will stick to it unflinchingly. We want in this way to train and prepare the country, and show the right path to the Government which has chosen to disregard truth and justice; this is our aim in fighting.

... These days, the Government rules by threats. It is a wrong notion that a Government can be run on the basis of fear. We should not fall a prey to such fear. We have faith in the justice of Nature. Do not obstruct the Government when it takes away your buffaloes nor hand over anything with your own hands. We have all these years been giving and obeying in fear, resentful inside. In the result, we have come to be utterly abject. Kheda yields crops of gold and its people are brave. Despite the famine ... they have, toiling day and night, turned the land into a garden. How does it happen that the light has fled from their lands and their faces? The only reason is that the people have begun to be afraid of the Government. This fight is to emancipate ourselves from such a condition ...

... In this struggle, we shall learn another wonder-working idea, that we do not propose to fight with arms; we do not want to carry guns or spears; we shall fight with the weapon of truth. ... I hear that, in this satyagraha struggle against the Government, things are going on which are the opposite of truth. When the officer asks the farmers why they do not pay, instead of telling him that the crops have been less than four annas, they are afraid and make other excuses. We should not be rude to the *mamlatdar* (*the revenue farmer in charge of settling dues owed to the State - ed.*) or the Collector, though we need not submit to forced labour or give anything demanded as of right. Indeed, they can order nothing from us. On no account should we omit to extend to them common hospitality. We may not give them anything free, but give them what they want against its full price. We ought not to forget good manners.

... They will even tell you that I am leading you astray. It is not for me to judge whether I am leading you well or ill; I tell you only what seems right to me. If it seems so to you as well, declare with one voice that, by following my advice, you command better respect and are able to safeguard your rights. ... We have been waving the flag of *swaraj*. It is with our own efforts that we are to achieve it. We shall certainly get it if we become absolutely fearless. Whatever happens, do not pay the revenue. Let the women give courage to their husbands. If anyone has a question to ask, he may have his doubts answered. The situation demands that you act with due thought and care.

*Kheda Satyagraha* (from Gujarati) (16: 410-12)

---

*These instructions were issued to volunteers supporting the Kheda satyagraha—they reflect Gandhi's attention to detail and his organizing skills.*

### Instructions to Volunteers, Satyagraha Camp, Nadiad
### April 17, 1918

1. The volunteers must remember that, as this is a satyagraha campaign, they must abide by truth under all circumstances.

2. In satyagraha, there can be no room for rancour; which means that a satyagrahi should utter no harsh word about anyone....

3. Rudeness has no place in satyagraha. Perfect courtesy must be shown even to those who may look upon us as their enemies and the villagers must be taught to do the same. ...

4. The volunteers must remember that this is a holy war. We

embarked upon it because, had we not, we would have failed in our *dharma*. And so all the rules which are essential for living a religious life must be observed here too.

5. We are opposing the intoxication of power, that is, the blind application of law, and not authority as such. The difference must never be lost sight of. It is, therefore, our duty to help the officers in their other work.

6. We are to apply here the same principle that we follow in a domestic quarrel. We should think of the Government and the people as constituting a large family and act accordingly.

7. We are not to boycott or treat with scorn those who hold different views from ours. It must be our resolve to win them over by courteous behaviour.

8. We must not try to be clever. We must always be frank and straightforward.

9. When they stay in villages, the volunteers should demand the fewest services from the village-folk. Wherever it is possible to reach a place on foot, they should avoid using a vehicle. We must insist on being served the simplest food. Restraining them from preparing dainties will add grace to the service we render.

10. As they move about in villages, the volunteers should observe the economic condition of the people and the deficiencies in their education and try, in their spare time, to make them good.

11. If they can, they should create opportunities when they may teach the village children.

12. If they notice any violation of the rules of good health, they should draw the villagers' attention to the fact.

13. If, at any place, they find people engaged in quarrelling among themselves, the volunteers should try to save them from their quarrels.

14. They should read out to the people, when the latter are free, books which promote satyagraha. They may read out stories of Prahlad, Harishchandra and others. The people should also be made familiar with instances of pure satyagraha to be found in

the West and in Islamic literature.

15. At no time and under no circumstances is the use of arms permitted in satyagraha. It should never be forgotten that in this struggle the highest type of non-violence is to be maintained.

Satyagraha means fighting oppression through voluntary suffering. There can be no question here of making anyone else suffer. Satyagraha is always successful; it can never meet with defeat: let every volunteer understand this himself and then explain it to the people.

MOHANDAS KARAMCHAND GANDHI

*Kheda Satyagraha* (from Gujarati) (18: 436-38)

# Fearless before Terror

*Gandhi's engagement with peasant and worker issues was specific and restricted to particular locations. His adversaries were enumerable men, officials and planters in Champaran, mill-owners in Ahmedabad and government revenue officials in Kheda. Gandhi was yet to confront colonial power, in its own pitiless guise. The Rowlatt Bills proposed in 1919, provided him with an opportunity to speak the truth of non-violence to brute authority.*

The Rowlatt Bills were meant to shackle dissent and crush potential sedition against Empire in those times of war. Several leading Indians, including leaders of the Indian National Congress, the premier nationalist party of the period, were outraged at the summary powers granted to policemen and the governing authority by the terms outlined in these Bills. Initially, Gandhi decided to offer satyagraha on his own, with his band of devoted followers. Soon, however, the contagion of revolt spread and in spite of Gandhi's insistence on a non-violent struggle, acts of angry violence rocked city streets in Gujarat, the Punjab and Delhi. Government action in arresting local leaders and rumours of Gandhi being arrested and detained did not help matters. Even as widespread violence rendered the satyagraha campaign futile in its pursuit of non-violence, the Jalianwala Bagh massacre in Punjab (1919), where a British officer fired at an unarmed crowd and killed hundreds of people, mocked at the good faith that lay at the core of satyagraha.

Unlike his earlier experiments, whose limits Gandhi could regulate and even control, the Rowlatt satyagraha proved open, contingent and therefore immensely challenging. In the excitement it generated, the disappointment and shock it elicited when matters took a violent turn, and the almost impossible sufferance it demanded from its proponents, the Rowlatt satyagraha mapped a journey Gandhi would undertake several times over the next decade, as he went about preaching the virtues of non-violence. Opposition, retreat, negotiation, and a dogged commitment to a line of resistance—the various elements of Gandhi's non-violent war, familiar to his followers from South Africa, re-emerged in the Indian context with interesting implications for the future of Indian nationalism.

*The extracts below plot his remarkable journey through a political moment in time, whose violence he struggled hard to negotiate.*

---

## Speech on Satyagraha, Madras
## March 18, 1919

I regret that owing to heart-weakness, I am unable to speak to you personally. You have no doubt attended many meetings, but those that you have been attending of late are different from the others in that at the meetings to which I have referred some immediate tangible action, some immediate definite sacrifice has been demanded of you for the purpose of averting a serious calamity that has overtaken us in the shape of what are known as the Rowlatt Bills. ... The Bills require to be resisted not only because they are in themselves bad, but also because Government, who are responsible for their introduction, have seen fit practically to ignore public opinion and some of its members have made it a boast that they can so ignore that opinion. So far, it is common cause between the different schools of thought in the country. I have, however, after much prayerful consideration, and after very careful examination of the Government's standpoint, pledged myself to offer satyagraha against the Bills, and invited all men and women who think and feel with me to do likewise. Some of our countrymen, including those who are among the best of the leaders, have uttered a note of warning, and even gone so far as to say that this satyagraha movement is against the best interests of the country.

I have naturally the highest regard for them and their opinion. I have worked under some of them. ... It is not, therefore, without the greatest grief and much searching of heart that I have to place myself in opposition to their wishes. But there are times when you have to obey a call which is the highest of all, i.e., the voice of conscience, even though such obedience may cost many a bitter tear, nay, even more, separation from friends, from family, from the State to which you may belong, from all that you have held as dear as life itself. For, this obedience is the law of our being. I have no further and other defence to offer for my conduct. My regard for the signatories to the Manifesto remains undiminished, and my faith in the efficiency of satyagraha is so great that I feel that if those who have taken the Pledge will be true to it, we shall be able to show to them that they will find when we have come to the end of this struggle that there was no cause for alarm or misgivings. There is, I know, resentment felt, even by some satyagrahis over the Manifestoes. I would warn satyagrahis that such resentment is against the spirit of satyagraha. I would personally welcome an honest expression of difference of opinion from any quarter and more so from friends because it puts us on our guard. There is too much recrimination, innuendo and insinuation in our public life, and if the satyagraha movement purges it of this grave defect, as it ought to, it will be a very desirable by-product. I wish further to suggest to satyagrahis that any resentment of the two Manifestoes would be but a sign of weakness on our part. Every movement, and satyagraha most of all, must depend upon its own inherent strength, but not upon the weakness or silence of its critics ...

*Mahatma Gandhi: His Life, Writings & Speeches, pp. 343-7 (17: 336-38)*

---

*Satyagraha against the Rowlatt Bills began peacefully. But, when rumours about Gandhi's arrest reached the streets, violence broke out. Gandhi lost no time in condemning what appeared to him barbaric and unwarranted acts of terror. He argued that satyagraha implied responsible action and not merely passive resistance.*

### Satyagraha Leaflet No. 3
### Mahatma Gandhi's Warning to Satyagrahis and Sympathizers
### April 11, 1919

BROTHERS AND SISTERS,

... I have been asked whether a satyagrahi is liable for the results that follow from that movement. I have replied that they are. I therefore wish to suggest that if we cannot conduct this movement without the slightest violence from our side, the movement might have to be abandoned or it may be necessary to give it a different and still more restricted shape. *The time may come for me to offer satyagraha against ourselves (italics as in the original - ed.).* I would not deem it a disgrace that we die. I shall be pained to hear of the death of a satyagrahi. But I shall consider it to be a proper sacrifice given for the sake of the struggle. But if those who are not satyagrahis, who have not joined the movement, who are even against it, receive any injury at all, every satyagrahi will be responsible for that sinful injury. My responsibility will be a million times heavier. I have embarked upon the struggle with a due sense of such responsibility.

I have even just heard that some Englishmen have been injured. Some may have died from such injuries. If so, it would be a great blot upon satyagraha. For me Englishmen too are our brethren. We can have nothing against them. And for me sins such as I have described are simply unbearable. But I know how to offer satyagraha against ourselves as against the rulers. *What kind of satyagraha can I offer against ourselves on such occasions? What penance can I do for such sins? The satyagraha and the penance I can conceive can only be one and that is for me to fast and if need be by so doing to give up this body and thus to prove the truth of satyagraha ... (emphasis as in the original - ed.)*

From the printed original preserved in Gandhi Smarak Sangrahalaya, Delhi. Courtesy: H. S. L. Polak (17: 411-12)

---

## Speech at Mass Meeting, Ahmedabad
## April 14, 1919

BROTHERS,

I mean to address myself mainly to you. Brothers, the events that have happened in the course of the last few days have been most disgraceful to Ahmedabad, and as all these things have happened in my name, I am ashamed of them, and those who have been responsible for them have thereby not honoured me but disgraced me. A rapier run through my body could hardly have pained me more. I have said times without number that satyagraha admits of no violence, no pillage, no incendiarism; and still in the name of satyagraha, we burnt down buildings, forcibly captured weapons, extorted money, stopped trains, cut off telegraph wires, killed innocent people and plundered shops and private houses. If deeds such as these could save me from the prison-house or the scaffold, I should not like to be so saved. I do wish to say in all earnestness that violence has not secured my discharge. ...

These deeds have not benefited the people in any way. They have done nothing but harm. The buildings burnt down were public property and they will naturally be rebuilt at our expense. The loss due to the shops remaining closed is also our loss. The terrorism prevailing in the city due to martial law is also the result of this violence. It has been said that many innocent lives have been lost as a result of the operation of martial law. If this is a fact, then for that, too, the deeds described above are responsible. It will be seen that the events that have happened have done nothing but harm to us. Moreover, they have most seriously damaged the satyagraha movement. ...

... Englishmen and women have been compelled to leave their homes and confine themselves to places of protection ... A little thinking should convince us that this is a matter of humiliation for us all. The sooner this state of things stops, the better for us ...

There are two distinct duties now before us. One is that we should firmly resolve upon refraining from all violence, and the other is that we should repent and do penance for our sins. So long as we do not repent and do not realize our errors and make an open confession of them, we shall not truly change our course. The first step is that those of us who have captured weapons should surrender them. To show that we are really patient, we will contribute each of us not less than eight annas towards helping the families of those who have been killed by our acts. Though no amount of money contribution can altogether undo the results of the furious deeds of the past few days, our contribution will be a slight token of our repentance.

I hope and pray that no one will evade this contribution on the plea that he has had no part in those wicked acts. For if such as those who were no party to these deeds had all courageously and bravely gone forward to put down the lawlessness, the mob would have been checked in their career and would have immediately realized the wickedness of their doings. I venture to say that if, instead of giving money to the mob out of fear, we had rushed out to protect buildings and to save the innocent without fear of death, we could have succeeded in so doing. Unless we have this sort of courage, mischief-makers will always try to intimidate us into participating in their misdeeds. Fear of death makes us devoid both of valour and religion. For, want of valour is want of religious faith. And having done little to stop the violence, we have been all participators in the sins that have been committed. And we ought, therefore, to contribute our mite as a mark of our repentance. ... I would also advise, if it is possible for you, to observe a twenty-four hours' fast in slight expiation of these sins.

I have thus far drawn attention to what appears to be your duty. I must now consider my own. ... It is alleged that I have, without proper consideration, persuaded thousands to join the movement. That allegation is, I admit, true to a certain extent, but to a certain extent only. ... I have, therefore, decided to fast for three days, i.e., 72 hours. I hope my fast will pain no one. ... If you really feel pity for the suffering that will be caused to me, I request that that pity should always restrain you from ever again being party to the criminal acts of which I have complained. Take it from me that we are not going to win *swarajya* or benefit our country in the least by violence and terrorism. I am of opinion that if we have to wade through violence to obtain *swaraj*ya and if a redress of grievances were to be only possible by means of ill will for and slaughter of Englishmen, I, for one, would do without that *swaraj*ya and without a redress of those grievances ...

*The Bombay Chronicle*, 17-4-1919; also *Speeches and Writings of Mahatma Gandhi*, pp. 473-8 (17: 420-23)

---

### Press Statement on Suspension of Civil Disobedience
### Bombay, April 18, 1919

It is not without sorrow that I feel compelled to advise the temporary suspension of civil disobedience. I give this advice not because I have less faith now in its efficacy, but because I have, if possible, greater faith than before. It is my perception of the law of satyagraha which impels me to suggest the suspension. I am sorry, when I embarked upon a mass movement, I underrated the forces of evil and I must now pause and consider how best to meet the situation.

... I would be untrue to satyagraha, if I allowed it by any action of mine to be used as an occasion for feeding violence, for embittering relations between the English and the Indians. Our satyagraha must therefore now consist in ceaselessly helping the authorities in all the ways available to us as satyagrahis to restore order and to curb lawlessness. We can turn the tragedies going on before us to good account if we could but succeed in gaining the adherence of the masses to the fundamental principles of satyagraha. Satyagraha is like a banyan tree with innumerable branches. Civil disobedience is one such branch, *satya* (truth) and *ahimsa* (non-violence) together make the parent trunk from which all innumerable branches shoot out. We have found by bitter experience that whilst in an atmosphere of lawlessness, civil disobedience found ready acceptance. *Satya* and *ahimsa*, from which alone civil disobedience can worthily spring, have commanded little or no respect. Ours then is a Herculean task, but we may not shirk it. We must fearlessly spread the doctrine of *satya* and *ahimsa* and then, and not till then, shall we be able to undertake mass satyagraha ...

*The Hindu*, 21-4-1919 (17: 443-45)

---

*After a strategic and moral retreat into provisional quiet, Gandhi decided to renew satyagraha. This decision came in the wake of a series of actions on the part of the colonial State that showed scant disregard for the rights of citizens to express themselves freely. This included the Jalianwala Bagh massacre, when unarmed civilians were shot at by an unrepentant English officer, several arrests and incarceration and court trails that were clearly biased in favour of the rulers.*

**Satyagraha Leaflet No. 17**
**Sunday's Hartal and Fasting**
**May 7, 1919**

BROTHERS AND SISTERS,

... By hartal (*cessation of all work, akin to a general strike - ed.*), fasting and religious devotion on Sunday next, the people propose to demonstrate to the Government in terms of satyagraha that it is not possible for them to bring about true contentment by force of arms. So long as the Rowlatt legislation is not withdrawn, so long as the Government continue to suppress men like Mr. Horniman (*the English editor of the liberal Bombay Chronicle, known for its anti-imperialist stance - ed.*) who carry on innocent agitations against such acts of the Government, not only is true contentment impossible, but discontent must increase. All the world over a true peace depends not upon gunpowder but upon pure justice. When Government perpetrate injustice and fortify it by the use of arms, such acts are a sign of anger and they add injustice to injustice. If people also become angry by reason of such acts on the part of the Government, they resort to violence and the result is bad for both, mutual ill will increases. But whenever people regard particular acts of the Government as unjust and express their strong disapproval by self-suffering, the Government cannot help granting redress. This is the way of satyagraha and the people of Bombay will have an opportunity on Sunday next of giving expression in a clean manner to such disapproval.

A hartal brought about voluntarily and without pressure is a powerful means of showing popular disapproval, but fasting is even more so. When people fast in a religious spirit and thus demonstrate their grief before God, it receives a certain response. Hardest hearts are impressed by it. Fasting is regarded by all religions as a great discipline. Those who voluntarily fast become gentle and purified by it. A pure fast is a very powerful prayer. It is no small thing for lakhs of people voluntarily to abstain from food and such a fast is a satyagrahi fast. It ennobles individuals and nations. In it there should be no intention of exercising undue pressure upon the Government.

From the printed original preserved in Gandhi Smarak Sangrahalaya, Delhi. (18: 22-23)

*The violence that beat down law and authority in April-May 1919 re-focused English—and world—attention on Gandhi and his non-violence. A probing critique of satyagraha was published in* The Times of India *by an American, to which Gandhi posted this reply.*

**Letter to** *The Times of India*
**Laburnum Road, Bombay**
**August 20, 1919**

THE EDITOR
THE TIMES OF INDIA

SIR,

You will perhaps permit me to reply to "Pennsylvanian"'s well-meant advice to me. I am aware that many Englishmen honestly hold the opinion "Pennsylyanian" does, and I thank him for providing me with an opportunity for removing some of the misunderstanding that exists about satyagraha.

... The advent of satyagraha has, to my knowledge, weaned many an anarchist from his blood-thirsty doctrine. He has found that secret societies and methods of secret murder have brought nothing but a military and economic burden on this unhappy land, that it has tightened the coil of the Criminal Investigation Department, and that it has demoralized and wrecked the lives of hundreds of youths who have been led astray by it. Satyagraha has presented the rising generation with a new hope, an open road and an infallible remedy for most ills of life. It has armed that generation with an indestructible and matchless force which anyone may wield with impunity. Satyagraha tells the Youth of India, self-suffering is the only sure road to salvation . . . economic, political and spiritual (*ellipsis as in the original - ed.*).

For the most part, satyagraha *is* "evil resistance" and "civil assistance". But sometimes it *has* to be "civil resistance". Here I must call to my assistance another illustrious countryman of "Pennsylyanian", Henry Thoreau. He asks, "Must the citizen ever for a moment, or in the least degree, resign his conscience to the legislators?" He answers, "I think that we should be men first and subjects afterwards. It is not desirable to cultivate a respect for the law so much as for the right." I think that the position taken up by

Thoreau is unassailable ...

... The remedy in vogue is that of inflicting violence on those who wish to wound your conscience. Thoreau in his immortal essay shows that civil disobedience, not violence, is the true remedy. In civil disobedience, the resister suffers the consequences of disobedience. This was what Daniel did when he disobeyed the law of the Medes and Persians. That is what John Bunyan did and that is what the raiyats have done in India from time immemorial. It is the law of our being. ... Self-suffering, i.e., civil resistance, is the law of the man in us. It is rarely that the occasion for civil resistance arises in a well-ordered State. But when it does, it becomes a duty that cannot be shirked by one who counts his honour, i.e., conscience, above everything. Rowlatt Act is legislation that affects the conscience of thousands of us, and I respectfully suggest that an appeal should be addressed by Englishmen to the Government that they withdraw an Act that hurts the self-respect of the nation and that has roused such unanimous opposition, rather than that I should be asked to refrain from civil resistance in respect of it.

I am, etc.,
M. K. GANDHI

*The Times of India*, 22-8-1919 (18: 303-05)

---

*The Punjab events of 1919 created widespread hatred of all things English and led to acts of violence against individual Englishmen and women. Gandhi found this distressing and pointed out that men like Charlie Andrews, his friend from his South African days and a friend of India, were English too and that Indians ought not to give in to racial hatred.*

## Our Duty

Mr. Andrews has poured out his very life for India. He is no ordinary Englishman. He is a man of great learning, comes of an illustrious family, is a poet and a theologian. ... He has not cared for wealth or for position and, today, wanting nothing for himself, he is ever on his feet in the service of India. What is our duty towards such an Englishman? As long as there is even one Andrews among the British people, we must, for the sake of such a one, bear no hatred to them. If we hate them, we cannot bear real love for Mr. Andrews and we shall forfeit the right to accept his service. This is clear enough.

"The question is: When massacres like the one at Jallianwala Bagh take place, when British soldiers abuse us, kick us, debar us from sitting with them in trains, British officers want to keep all power to themselves and British merchants try to monopolize the principal trade of India, how can we help being angry with them? How can we ever feel affection for them?"

The difficulty is obvious. Wherever one turns, one finds hatred, anger, scorn and falsehood. When Indians do not always feel affection for one another, what can we expect from them with regard to the British? But these doubts arise from want of faith in God. An intellectual acceptance of the existence of God does not make one a believer. To believe in God but not to love people is a contradiction in terms. Faith implies truth and love. If these qualities could shine forth within us in their perfection, we would ourselves be God. ...

... But it is not only out of respect for Mr. Andrews that we must banish all hatred for the British. By doing so we shall ensure early success of our efforts for if we work on in patience. ... The British will have no occasion to visit their evil propensities on us.

# Concluding the Early Indian Years

*Gandhi's early years in India saw him delineate an ethics for living, which was at once public and private. Satyagraha constituted the core of this ethics whose objective was to persuade the world of the inherent good of a pacific existence. Non-violence was not merely an antidote to violence, but connoted an entire way of living and engaging with the self and the world.*

*Gandhi's astonishingly original ideas compelled Indians to consider their struggle for political freedom as also a struggle waged in the recesses of their hearts. Gandhi recognized the force of intractable custom and prejudice and lost no time working against the grain of popular belief, especially with respect to untouchability and Hindu-Muslim unity. Yet his solutions, if they may be regarded as such, raised for his followers and critics as many questions as they answered. To ask caste Hindus to repent and suffer for their sins towards the untouchables required them to perform a daunting moral task. But such an expiation—through service to the oppressed—did not require the caste Hindu to heed untouchable needs and demands, or confront the very real economic and social power invested in keeping untouchables subordinate and separate. During this period, this did not appear an urgent concern to either Gandhi or his critics, but would emerge as a politically contentious and morally fraught issue in the decades that followed.*

*In matters of keeping faith with British officialdom, Gandhi's actions would follow a pattern, similar to the one he charted during these early years. In subsequent struggles, his younger and more radical contemporaries sometimes felt that he erred much in this respect - to the point where he sounded placatory and content with minimal concessions from the British. They would also be troubled by his obvious disavowal of militancy of any sort, whether of labour, or the peasantry or subjugated ethnic groups.*

*The question his younger friends and comrades asked themselves in several instances was this: how does one read Gandhi's readiness to trust to the goodwill of those in power, to the remorse he believed animated even the most hardened human heart? Was it a poignant instance of moral forbearance? Or was it a moral gesture that served the objective interests of socially decisive groups that stood to lose by militancy and gain by a non-violent and gradual process of social change?*

*These questions cannot be easily answered and will haunt these pages. They are, in fact, central to any critical and serious consideration of Gandhi's ideas on non-violence.*

## Chapter 3

# 'Anguished Love': The Politics of Non-cooperation
# 1920-1924

*The year 1920 saw Gandhi experimenting again, this time with a new form of political resistance, which he christened 'Non-cooperation'. The satyagraha against the Rowlatt Bills had revealed to him the power and vulnerability of non-violence. Though he admitted failure, he was far from being exhausted. Resourceful as always, he turned his attention to an issue that had bothered him as early as 1918—the matter of the 'Khilafat'.*

*With the end of World War I, Turkey had come under British authority. There were rumours that the Caliph, as the symbolic head of the universal Islamic community, stood to be dispossessed of his authority. In India, a group of Muslim intellectuals, under the leadership of the brothers, Mohammed and Shaukat Ali, demanded that the Caliph's spiritual authority over the holy sites of Islam and the community of the faithful be re-affirmed. They were jailed for their efforts. Gandhi discovered in the support voiced by such men for the Caliph's cause, or the Khilafat, a context for protesting the general inequities of British rule in India.*

*More importantly, he was convinced that a matter that appeared of great spiritual importance to Muslims had to be endorsed and supported by Hindus. He sought to create a grand unity of purpose, which would serve as a bulwark against violence, not only between Hindus and Muslims, but in a general sense as well. Gandhi had also other things in mind: he was acutely sensitive to the general mood of discontent over the Punjab events, especially the British refusal to see justice done to*

*those who died or suffered on account of martial law in the Punjab.
Aligning two disparate causes, he called for a nation-wide campaign
against British rule—the idea was to withdraw cooperation with India's
rulers. Students and teachers were to boycott schools, lawyers were to
walk out of courts and ordinary people give up wearing foreign cloth.
This, on the one hand. On the other hand, agitating citizens were to
extend fraternal love towards each other, Hindus towards Muslims and
Muslims towards Hindus, caste Hindus towards untouchables ... They
were also to take to spinning, which Gandhi argued, had died a slow
death due to British cloth manufactures flooding the country. Spinning,
if taken up in earnest, would ameliorate rural poverty, provide poor
women with work and teach Indians the virtues of patient, concentrated
labour.*

*Gandhi took his campaign into the Indian National Congress. The
Congress was dominated by Moderate nationalists who desired to
gradually wrest power from British hands. At the moment, several in
that party were busy thinking through the implications of the political
reforms announced by the British (in 1919). These reforms were to
bring in more Indians into local legislative councils—they would be
elected on the basis of a limited franchise, comprising men of property
and university graduates, and vested with defined and extremely limited
power and authority. Gandhi's proposal with its emphasis on Non-
cooperation was initially met with hostility, but soon he won his case
and the Congress decided to endorse his campaign.*

*Non-cooperation caught the imagination of ordinary people:
householders, including women, students, hawkers, peasants and even
teachers and lawyers. It enabled everyday acts of defiance, notated
individual acts of rebellion as social protest of the highest sort and
made it known to the world that non-violence was not a weapon of the
weak and the passive, but available to the ordinary human heart,
committed to a struggle in faith and goodwill. Several hundreds of
men gave up posts in government, boycotted government institutions,
including courts of law and schools, and gave up buying foreign goods,
especially cloth (Gandhi's favourite symbol of India's economic slavery).
In short, they withdrew their links to Empire. Women who, until then,
had remained marginal to the national life were now involved in it,
persuaded by Gandhi's imprecations to them: he urged them to give up*

gold and finery, cultivate a love for khadi (handspun cloth) and, as compassionate beings, turn their attention to the nation's poor and hungry. During this period, Gandhi's ashram ethics were inflected in particular ways. For instance, the vow of celibacy, which he had defined as an important adjunct of a life of non-violence, acquired a national meaning and significance in the general context of Non-cooperation.

Rural parts were drawn into the struggle—in a way they had never been until that moment. Suffering peasants, stifled by post-war poverty and stringent revenue demands, were fired with messianic zeal and peasant struggles emerged in various parts of the north Indian countryside. Workers, fed up with war-time wage squeezes also took to the streets, and the early 1920s witnessed industrial unrest of a kind not known before. The province of Bengal alone saw 110 strikes in 1920. Clearly these were times of discontent, and Non-cooperation provided an overarching context for these various instances of anger to acquire a political resonance. Importantly, the Indian National Congress gained new adherents.

Gandhi was so enthused by the initial successes of the movement that he promised his countrymen and women that if they were disciplined in their stance and kept their vow of Hindu-Muslim unity, swaraj or self-rule would be theirs in a year's time! He became an icon, whose name and the aura associated with it inspired peasants who had never seen him.

The government remained watchful, cynical and disinclined to trust the new movement and its leaders. Gandhi was also mistrusted by those who were alarmed by mass political action, more specifically by the fact of 'disobedience' that Non-cooperation appeared to mandate and welcome. He, in turn, responded to their queries. Meanwhile, as during the Rowlatt days, violence haunted the streets. Gandhi spoke out against it but did not immediately retract his steps. He and his fellow Non-cooperators decided to intensify the momentum of their struggle and declared that they would graduate to the next stage, when they hoped to engage in a wilful civil disobedience of iniquitous laws. But history willed otherwise. A gruesome event in a northern Indian town shocked Gandhi into disbelief—an angry mob set fire to a police station, killing everyone in it. Anguished beyond measure, Gandhi called off the movement. He began a fast to cleanse his stained soul and was *subsequently arrested and arraigned. He remained in prison for two years (1922-24). '*

*On his release, he realized that the world had changed. The politics of the Khilafat had lost its moral basis. The Caliph had been dethroned by his own people, and Turkey under Mustafa Kemal had embarked on a bold experiment in modernisation. Hindu and Muslim political links, so assiduously built during the course of the campaign, had weakened considerably, in the absence of Gandhi's conciliatory healing words. There were riots everywhere. The golden moment of unity was clearly past and Gandhi had to look to other options.*

*Thus ended Non-cooperation. Tired and unwilling to commit himself to public work of the sort he had engaged in until then, and convinced that he had to school the erring national heart in non-violence, Gandhi set about doing what he called 'constructive work'. He travelled widely, spoke of the virtues of spinning, upheld the spinning wheel as a symbol of patient, gentle labour, embarked on several experiments in minimal living and spoke and wrote a lot on the need to counter untouchability. Meanwhile, he waited for that turn of the historical wheel which would enable him to experiment with non-violence, yet again.*

# Gracious Withdrawal: Non-cooperation and Its Critics

*Gandhi's Non-cooperation campaign, premised on the Khilafat and Punjab wrongs, disturbed the even progress of nationalist politics in the Indian subcontinent. Until then, the Indian National Congress had confined its activities to polite petitioning, arguing and to middle class clubs, drawing rooms and polite podiums. Now, on account of Gandhi's charisma, it suddenly found itself a party of the masses. Hundreds of people who until then had remained on the margins of history were swept into its very vortex.*

*Gandhi was at pains to explain to those critics and fellow political leaders who were obviously unsure and uneasy over this sudden outburst of political energy, that Non-cooperation was essentially pacific and in fact the most effective form of non-violent resistance to a government determined to exact legitimacy for its rule through brute force. His critics pointed to other problems: students quitting schools and lawyers walking out of courts, they held, did not augur well for an orderly civic life. Gandhi clarified his position, distinguished his creed from irresponsible anarchism and presented definitions which drew upon as many examples from daily life, as they did from history, religion and ethics. Non-cooperation appeared ready grow into a full-fledged movement of defiance, as Gandhi announced a grand satyagraha against revenue demands in Bardoli in Gujarat. He was ready to launch civil disobedience on a scale larger than anything he had done before.*

*But history fled its own promises. In Chauri Chaura, in the United Provinces, peaceful resistance turned ugly, as a mob, provoked beyond measure by police taunting, set fire to a police station, killing all those who were inside. Shocked and upset, Gandhi immediately suspended Non-cooperation, to the dismay of his supporters, many of whom were convinced that the day of reckoning for Indian's rulers was at hand. He went on a fast and subsequently was arrested on charges of sedition. He pleaded guilty to all charges and won the heart of the presiding judge who was nonplussed by his humility.*

*The extracts in this section capture the various issues at stake in the first mass struggle for Indian independence.*

*Gandhi's espousal of Non-cooperation bewildered those admirers who felt that his essentially saintly consciousness stood to be stained by an engagement with the political and called to him to leave aside politics and work for the harmony of human society as a whole. Gandhi undertook to explain his resistance to evil, as he called it.*

## Neither a Saint Nor a Politician

... The critic regrets to see in me a politician, whereas he expected me to be a saint. Now I think that the word "saint" should be ruled out of present life. It is too sacred a word to be lightly applied to anybody, much less to one like myself who claims only to be a humble searcher after truth, knows his limitations, makes mistakes, never hesitates to admit them when he makes them, and frankly confesses that he, like a scientist, is making experiments about some of "the eternal verities" of life, but cannot even claim to be a scientist because he can show no tangible proof of scientific accuracy in his methods or such tangible results of his experiments as modern science demands.

But though by disclaiming sainthood I disappoint the critic's expectations, I would have him to give up his regrets by answering him that the politician in me has never dominated a single decision of mine, and if I seem to take part in politics, it is only because politics encircle us today like the coil of a snake from which one cannot get out, no matter how much one tries. I wish therefore to wrestle with the snake, as I have been doing, with more or less success, consciously since 1894, unconsciously, as I have now discovered, ever since reaching the years of discretion. Quite selfishly, as I wish to live in peace in the midst of a bellowing storm howling round me, I have been experimenting with myself and my friends by introducing religion into politics.

Let me explain what I mean by religion. It is not the Hindu religion, which I certainly prize above all other religions, but the religion which transcends Hinduism, which changes one's very nature, which binds one indissolubly to the truth within and which ever purifies. It is the permanent element in human nature which counts no cost too great in order to find full expression and which leaves the soul utterly restless until it has found itself, known its

Maker and appreciated the true correspondence between the Maker and itself.

It was in that religious spirit that I came upon hartal. I wanted to show that it is not a knowledge of letters that would give India consciousness of herself, or that would bind the educated together. The hartal illuminated the whole of India as if by magic on the 6th of April, 1919. And had it not been for the interruption of the 10th of April, brought about by Satan whispering fear into the ears of a Government conscious of its own wrong and inciting to anger a people that were prepared for it by utter distrust of the Government, India would have risen to an unimaginable height. The hartal had not only been taken up by the great masses of people in a truly religious spirit but it was intended to be a prelude to a series of direct actions (*see above, Fearless before Terror - ed.*).

But my critic deplores direct action. For, he says, "it does not work for unity." I join issue with him. Never has anything been done on this earth without direct action. ... A meek submission when one is chafing under a disability or a grievance which one would gladly see removed, not only does not make for unity, but makes the weak party acid, angry and prepares him for an opportunity to explode. By allying myself with the weak party, by teaching him direct, firm, but harmless action, I make him feel strong and capable of defying the physical might. He feels braced for the struggle, regains confidence in himself and knowing that the remedy lies with himself, ceases to harbour the spirit of revenge and learns to be satisfied with a redress of the wrong he is seeking to remedy ...

*Young India,* 12-5-1920 (20: 304-05)

---

*Gandhi defined Non-cooperation as India's distinctive political method—the law of suffering, as he called it, was a civilizational option to the law that held it a virtue to inflict violence on those who were unjust.*

## The Law of Suffering

... We can, if we will, refrain, in our impatience, from bending the wrongdoer to our will by physical force as Sinn Feiners are doing today (*the reference here is to the Irish struggle for independence - ed.*), or from coercing our neighbours to follow our methods ... Progress is to be measured by the amount of suffering undergone by the sufferer. The purer the suffering, the greater is the progress. Hence did the sacrifice of Jesus suffice to free a sorrowing world. In his onward march he did not count the cost of suffering entailed upon his neighbours, whether it was undergone by them voluntarily or otherwise ...

... Sages of old mortified the flesh so that the spirit within might be set free, so that their trained bodies might be proof against any injury that might be inflicted on them by tyrants seeking to impose their will on them. And if India wishes to revive her ancient wisdom and to avoid the errors of Europe, if India wishes to see the Kingdom of God established on earth instead of that of Satan which has enveloped Europe, then I would urge her sons and daughters not to be deceived by fine phrases, the terrible subtleties that hedge us in, the fears of suffering that India may have to undergo, but to see what is happening today in Europe and from it understand that we *must* go through the suffering even as Europe has gone through, but not the process of making others suffer ...

... We must refuse to wait for the wrong to be righted till the wrongdoer has been roused to a sense of his inequity. We must not, for fear of ourselves or others having to suffer, remain participators in it. But we must combat the wrong by ceasing to assist the wrongdoer directly or indirectly. If a father does an injustice, it is the duty of his children to leave the parental roof. If the head master of a school conducts his institution on an immoral basis, the pupils must leave the school. If the chairman of a corporation is corrupt, the members thereof must wash their hands clean of his corruption by withdrawing from it; even so, if a government does a grave injustice, the subject must withdraw cooperation wholly or partially, sufficiently to wean the ruler from his wickedness. In each case conceived by me there is an element of suffering whether mental or physical. Without such suffering it is not possible to attain freedom.

*Young India*, 16-6-1920 (20: 397-99)

*Moving deftly between his advocacy of Non-cooperation as a moral option and his keen sense of the practical politics of withdrawing cooperation with Empire, Gandhi linked together various injustices in his description and defence of his creed.*

## Non-cooperation

... The Government has no right to occupy Mesopotamia (*after World War I - ed.*). Mandate is in fact nothing but occupation. Moreover, according to newspaper reports, the Arabs do not like even the sight of Indian soldiers there. Whether or not this is true, it is the duty of every Indian not to join such service. Those who go to Mesopotamia will be doing so merely for money. We must refuse to do this, if we do no more. Not only can it never be our duty to rule by force over the Arabs, but we, who do not wish to remain in slavery, cannot wish to make others slaves. Thus it behoves us not to ... offer ourselves as new recruits for service under the Government, especially for service which requires us to go to Mesopotamia. In addition, it is hoped that the following things will be done from August 1 onwards :

1. Titles and honorary positions will be renounced.

2. Legislatures will be boycotted.

3. Parents will withdraw their children from Government schools.

4. Lawyers will give up practice and help people to settle their civil disputes among themselves.

5. Invitations to Government functions, parties, etc., will be politely refused, Non-cooperation being given as the sole reason for doing so.

It is likely that this programme will be adopted from August 1, if the *Khilafat* question is not settled. Lala Lajpat Rai has announced Non-cooperation in the form of boycott of legislatures if justice is not done in the matter of the Punjab. So we can now take it that the Punjab too has joined the *Khilafat* agitation. Just as on this issue Muslims should take the lead, in the matter of the Punjab the Punjabis themselves should take the lead. If they do not adopt Non-cooperation, one may say that the other parts of India cannot do so either.

... Three different views on the question of [boycotting] legislatures have been expressed :

1. Not to start Non-cooperation at all;

2. to adopt Non-cooperation after election to legislatures (*these elections had been announced in the wake of the political reforms handed out by Britain in 1919, at the end of the War - ed.*);

3. to boycott legislatures from the very start.

The first position is entirely opposed to Non-cooperation. The second alone needs to be examined. I am convinced that it will be a waste of effort to try to enter legislatures and then to refrain from attending their sessions. It is a waste of money and time alike. I do not at all see the point of doing this. What if unworthy people get elected because we do not come forward? If such people enter the legislatures, the Government will not be able to run the government of an awakened people and it will be laughed at. Moreover, if we join in the elections, we shall not be able to show what real boycott can be. Our duty is so to educate public opinion—opinion of the voters—that it will be impossible for anybody to get elected to legislatures as their representatives. So long as there is lack of understanding between the king and the subject, to attend the king's council is to strengthen his hands. ... And so I hope that those who are busy trying to get elected to legislatures will give up the attempt for the present and address themselves to the more important work, that of educating public opinion on the *Khilafat* and the Punjab issues, and so serve the people that, when the time for entering legislatures comes, they will be better qualified in virtue of their service.

Now remain the other two suggestions which are likely to be severely criticized. The lawyers should, for the time being, give up practice and intending litigants or those who find themselves dragged into litigation should boycott the courts and get their disputes settled through arbitration boards. It is my confirmed belief that every Government masks its brute force and maintains its control over the people through civil and criminal courts, for it is cheaper, simpler and more honourable, for a ruler that instead of his controlling the people through naked force, they themselves, lured into slavery through courts, etc., submit to him of their own accord. If people settle their civil disputes among themselves and the lawyers, unmindful of self-interest, boycott the courts in the interest of the people, the latter can advance in no time. I have believed for many years that every State tries to perpetuate its power through lawyers. Hence, though fully aware that I will be criticized for making this suggestion, I have no hesitation in putting it forward.

What is true of lawyers is true of schools. ... I want to show the Government by rendering the schools idle that, so long as justice is not done in regard to the Punjab and the *Khilafat*, cooperation with it is distasteful. I know that this suggestion will be visited with a good deal of ridicule. But, with the passing of time, people will realize that if they refused to crowd the Government schools, it would be impossible to run the administration.

Look where we will all over the world, we shall find that the education imparted to the children is intended to facilitate smooth running of the Government. Where the Government is concerned solely with public welfare, so is the educational system; where the Government is of a mixed kind—as in India—the educational system is also calculated to confuse the intellect and is positively harmful. ...

*Navajivan*, 4-7-1920 (21: 5-7)

---

*While some doubted the efficacy of Non-cooperation, others held that its spontaneity should not be compromised or interfered with, at any cost. Gandhi did not agree: Non-cooperation, to him, was the very antithesis of secrecy and violence.*

### The Doctrine of the Sword

In this age of the rule of brute force, it is almost impossible for anyone to believe that anyone else could possibly reject the law of the final supremacy of brute force. And so I receive anonymous letters advising me that I must not interfere with the progress of Non-cooperation even though popular violence may break out. Others come to me and assuming that secretly I must be plotting violence, inquire when the happy moment for declaring open violence will arrive. They assure me that the English will never yield to anything but violence secret or open. Yet others, I am informed, believe that I am the most rascally person living in India because I never give out my real intention and that they have not a shadow of a doubt that I believe in violence just as much as most people do.

Such being the hold that the doctrine of the sword has on the majority of mankind, and as success of Non-cooperation depends principally on absence of violence ... and as my views in this matter affect the conduct of a large number of people, I am anxious to state them as clearly as possible. I do believe that where there is only a choice between cowardice and violence I would advise violence. ... I would rather have India resort to arms in order to defend her honour than that she should in a cowardly manner become or remain a helpless witness to her own dishonour.

But I believe that non-violence is infinitely superior to violence, forgiveness is more manly than punishment. Forgiveness adorns a soldier. But abstinence is forgiveness only when it proceeds from a helpless creature. ... I, therefore, appreciate the sentiment of those who cry out for the condign punishment of General Dyer (*the officer who shot at innocent civilians at Jalianwala Bagh, Punjab in 1919 - ed.*) and his like. They would tear him to pieces if they could. But I do not believe India to be helpless. I do not believe myself to be a helpless creature. Only I want to use India's and my strength for a better purpose. Let me not be misunderstood. Strength does not come from physical capacity. It comes from an indomitable will. ... We in India may in a moment realize that one hundred thousand Englishmen need not frighten three hundred million human beings. A definite forgiveness would therefore mean a definite recognition of our strength.

... It matters little to me that for the moment I do not drive my point home. We feel too downtrodden not to be angry and revengeful. But I must not refrain from saying that India can gain more by waiving the right of punishment. We have better work to do, a better mission to deliver to the world. I am not a visionary. I claim to be a practical idealist. The religion of non-violence is not meant merely for the *rishis* and saints. It is meant for the common people as well. Non-violence is the law of our species as violence is the law of the brute. The spirit lies dormant in the brute and he knows no law but that of physical might. The dignity of man requires obedience to a higher law—to the strength of the spirit.

... And so I am not pleading for India to practise non-violence because it is weak. I want her to practise non-violence being conscious of her strength and power. ... I want India to recognize that she has a soul that cannot perish and that can rise triumphant above every physical weakness and defy the physical combination of whole world. ... I invite even the school of violence to give this peaceful Non-cooperation a trial. It will not fail through its inherent weakness. It may fail because of poverty of response. Then will be the time for real danger. The high-souled men, who are unable to suffer national humiliation any longer, will want to vent their wrath. They will take to violence. So far as I know, they must perish without delivering themselves or their country from the wrong. If India takes up the doctrine of the sword, she may gain momentary victory. Then India will cease to be pride of my heart. ... India's acceptance of the doctrine of the sword will be the hour of my trial. I hope I shall not be found wanting.

My religion has no geographical limits. If I have a living faith in it, it will transcend my love for India herself. My life is dedicated to service of India through the religion of non-violence which I believe to be the root of Hinduism. Meanwhile I urge those who distrust me, not to disturb the even working of the struggle that has just commenced, by inciting to violence in the belief that I want violence. I detest secrecy as a sin. Let them give non-violent Non-cooperation a trial and they will find that I had no mental reservation whatsoever.

*Young India*, 11-8-1920 (21: 133-36)

---

*Gandhi's English admirers, even liberal men and women, were appalled by his call to not cooperate with Empire. He had to assure them that he meant no ill-will.*

## To Every Englishman in India

DEAR FRIEND,

I wish that every Englishman will see this appeal and give thoughtful attention to it. Let me introduce myself to you. In my humble opinion, no Indian has cooperated with the British government more than I have for an unbroken period of twenty-nine years of public life in the face of circumstances that might well have turned any other man into a rebel. I ask you to believe me when I tell you that my cooperation was not based on the fear of the punishments provided by your laws or any other selfish motives. It was free and voluntary cooperation based on the belief that the sum total of the activity of the British Government was for the benefit of India.

I put my life in peril four times for the sake of the Empire,—at the time of the Boer war ... at the time of the Zulu revolt in Natal ... at the time of the commencement of the late War when I raised an Ambulance corps ... and lastly, ... I threw myself in such an active recruiting ... I did all this in the full belief that acts such as mine must gain for my country an equal status in the Empire. So late as last December I pleaded hard for a trustful cooperation. I fully believed that Mr. Lloyd George (*post World War I premier of Great Britain - ed.*) would redeem his promise to the Mussulmans and that the revelations of the official atrocities in the Punjab would secure full reparation for the Punjabis. But the treachery of Mr. Lloyd George and its appreciation by you, and the condonation of the Punjab atrocities have completely shattered my faith in the good intentions of the Government and the nation which is supporting it.

But though my faith in your good intentions is gone, I recognize your bravery, and I know that what you will not yield to justice and reason, you will gladly yield to bravery. *See what this Empire means to India:* Exploitation of India's resources for the benefits of Great Britain, an ever-increasing military expenditure, and a civil service the most expensive in the world, extravagant working of every department in utter disregard of India's poverty, disarmament and consequent emasculation of a whole nation lest an armed nation might imperil the lives of a handful of you in our midst, traffic in intoxicating liquors and drugs for the purpose of sustaining a top-heavy administration, progressively repressive legislation in order to suppress an ever-growing agitation seeking to give expression to a nation's agony, degrading treatment of Indians residing in your dominions and you have shown total disregard of our feelings by glorifying the Punjab administration and flouting the Mussulman sentiment.

I know you would not mind if we could fight and wrest the sceptre from your hands. You know that we are powerless to do that, for you have ensured our incapacity to fight in open and honourable battle. Bravery on the battlefield is thus impossible for us. Bravery of the soul still remains open to us. I know you will respond to that also. I am engaged in evolving that bravery. Non-cooperation means nothing less than training in self-sacrifice. Why should we cooperate with you when we know that by your administration of this great country we are being daily enslaved in an increasing degree? ...

... My religion forbids me to bear any ill will towards you. I would not raise my hand against you even if I had the power. I expect to conquer you only by my suffering. ... You are in search of a remedy to suppress this rising ... national feeling. I venture to suggest to you that the only way to suppress it is to remove the causes. You have yet the power. You can repent of the wrong done to Indians. ... You can compel the Government to summon a conference of the recognized leaders of the people, duly elected by them and representing all shades of opinion so as to revise means for granting *swaraj* in accordance with the wishes of the people of India. But this you cannot do unless you consider every Indian to be in reality your equal and brother. I ask for no patronage, I merely point out to you, as a friend, an honourable solution of a grave problem. The other solution, namely repression, is open to you. I prophesy that it will fail ...

I am,
Your faithful friend
M. K. GANDHI

*Young India*, 27-10-1920 (21: 385-87)

---

*The poet Rabindranath Tagore, Gandhi's friend and admirer, disapproved of Non-cooperation. He was convinced it would lead to anarchy, dissuade students from educating themselves, and that withdrawal of cooperation with all things English would render Indians insular. Gandhi's riposte was affectionate and respectful.*

## The Poet's Anxiety

... Dr. Tagore ... says he has striven hard to find himself in tune with the present movement. He confesses that he is baffled. He can find nothing for his lyre in the din and the bustle of Non-cooperation. In three forceful letters he has endeavoured to give expression to his misgivings, and he has come to the conclusion that Non-cooperation is not dignified enough for the India of his vision, that it is a doctrine of negation and despair. He fears that it is a doctrine of separation, exclusiveness, narrowness and negation.

... In all humility I shall endeavour to answer the Poet's doubts. I may fail to convince him or the reader who may have been touched by his eloquence, but I would like to assure him and India that Non-cooperation in conception is not any of the things he fears, and he need have no cause to be ashamed of his country for having adopted Non-cooperation. If in actual application, it appears in the end to have failed, it will be no more the fault of the doctrine than it would be of Truth if those who claim to apply it in practice do not appear to succeed. Non-cooperation may have come in advance of its time. India and the world must then wait, but there is no choice for India save between violence and Non-cooperation.

Nor need the poet fear that Non-cooperation is intended to erect a Chinese Wall between India and the West. On the contrary, Non-cooperation is intended to pave the way to real, honourable and voluntary cooperation based on mutual respect and trust. The present struggle is being waged against compulsory cooperation, against one-sided combination, against the armed imposition of modern methods of exploitation masquerading under the name of civilization.

Non-cooperation is a protest against an unwitting and unwilling participation in evil.

The Poet's concern is largely about the students. He is of the opinion that they should not have been called upon to give up Government schools before they had others schools to go to. Here

I must differ from him. I have never been able to make a fetish of literary training. My experience has proved to my satisfaction that literary training by itself adds not an inch to one's moral height and that character-building is independent of literary training. I am firmly of the opinion that the government schools have unmanned us, rendered us helpless and godless. They have filled us with discontent, and, providing no remedy for the discontent, have made us despondent.

They have made us what we were intended to become—clerks and interpreters. A government builds its prestige upon the apparently voluntary association of the governed. And if it was wrong to cooperate with the Government in keeping us slaves, we were bound to begin with those institutions in which our association appeared to be most voluntary. The Youth of a nation are its hope. I hold that as soon as we discovered that the system of government was wholly, or mainly, evil, it became sinful for us to associate our children with it.

It is no argument against the soundness of the proposition laid down by me, that the vast majority of the students went back after the first flush of enthusiasm. Their recantation is proof rather of the extent of our degradation than of the wrongness of the step. Experience has shown that the establishment of national schools has not resulted in drawing many more students. The strongest and the truest of them came out without any national schools to fall back upon, and I am convinced that these first withdrawals are rendering service of the highest order.

But the Poet's protest against the calling out of the boys is really a corollary to his objection to the very doctrine of Non-cooperation. He has a horror of everything negative. His whole soul seems to rebel against the negative commandments of religion. ... In my humble opinion rejection is as much an ideal as the acceptance of a thing. It is an necessary to reject untruth as it is to accept truth. All religions teach that two opposite forces act upon us and that the human endeavour consists in a series of eternal rejections and acceptances.

Non-cooperation with evil is as much a duty as cooperation with good. ... We had lost the power of saying "no". It had become disloyal, almost sacrilegious, to says "no" to the government. This deliberate refusal to cooperate is like the necessary weeding process that a cultivator has to resort to before he sows. ... The nation's Non-cooperation is an invitation to the Government to cooperate with it on its own terms as is every nation's right and every good government's duty. Non-cooperation is the nation's notice that it is no longer satisfied to be in tutelage. The nation has taken to the harmless (for it), natural and religious doctrine of Non-cooperation in the place of the unnatural and irreligious doctrine of violence. And if India is ever to attain the *swaraj* of the poet's dream, she will do so only by non-violent Non-cooperation.

... An India awakened and free has a message of peace and good will to a groaning world. Non-cooperation is designed to supply her with a platform from which she will preach the message.

*Young India*, 1-6-1921 (23: 218-221)

---

*As Non-cooperation gathered momentum, enthusiastic crowds crossed the line of non-violent resistance and let loose disorder and rage. This was particularly evident during the peaceful protests organized against the visiting Prince of Wales, as he sailed into Bombay. Jews, Indian Christians and Parsis who had gathered to welcome the Prince were attacked by workers who took offence at what appeared to them a gesture of 'cooperation' on the part of the above groups of people. In some instances the 'cooperators' retaliated, with the police supporting them. Gandhi expressed his acute discomfort with this turn towards violence*

**To Co-workers**
**November 22, 1921**

COMRADES,

Past few days have been a fiery ordeal for us, and God is to be thanked that some of us have not been found wanting. The broken heads before me and the dead bodies of which I have heard on unimpeachable authority are sufficient evidence of the fact. Workers have lost their lives or limbs, or have suffered bruises in the act of preserving peace, of weaning mad countrymen from their wrath. These deaths and injuries show, that in spite of the error of many of our countrymen, some of us are prepared to die for the attainment of our goal. If all of us had imbibed the spirit of non-violence, or if some had and the others had remained passive, no blood need have been spilt. But it was not to be. Some must therefore voluntarily give their blood in order that a bloodless atmosphere may be created.

... The Parsis and the Christians sought and received the assistance of the Government such that the Government openly took sides, and armed and aided the latter in retaliatory madness, and criminally neglected to protect a single life among those, who though undoubtedly guilty in the first instance were the victims of the pardonable wrath of the Parsis, the Christians and the Jews. The Government has thus appeared in its nakedness as a party doing violence not merely to preserve peace but to sustain the aggressive violence of its injured supporters. Its police and military looked on with callous indifference whilst the Christians in their justifiable indignation deprived innocent men of their white caps (*he refers to the white-capped nationalists here - ed.*) and hammered those who would not surrender them, or whilst the Parsis assaulted or shot, not in self-defence but because the victims happened to be Hindus or Mussulmans or non-co-operators. I can excuse the aggrieved Parsis and Christians, but can find no excuse for the criminal conduct of the police and the military in taking sides.

So the task before the workers is to take the blows from the Government and our erring countrymen. This is the only way open to us of sterilizing the forces of violence. The way to immediate *swaraj* lies through our gaining control over the forces of violence, and that not by greater violence but by moral influence. We must see as clearly as daylight that it is impossible for us to be trained and armed for violence effective enough for displacing the existing Government. Some people imagine, that after all we could not have better advertised our indignation against the welcome to the Prince than by letting loose the mob frenzy on the fateful seventeenth. This reasoning betrays at once ignorance and weakness, ignorance of the fact that our goal was not injury to the welcome, and weakness because we still hanker after advertising our strength to others instead of being satisfied with the consciousness of its possession ...

But all is not lost if the workers realize and act up to their responsibility. We must secure the full cooperation of the rowdies of Bombay. We must know the mill-hands. They must either work for the Government or for us, i.e., for violence or against it. There is no middle way. They must not interfere with us. They must either be amenable to our love or helplessly submit to the bayonet. They may not seek shelter under the banner of non-violence for the purpose of doing violence. ... Similarly we must reach the rowdy element, befriend them and help them to understand the religious character of the struggle. We must neither neglect them nor pander to them. We must become their servants.

The peace that we are aiming at is not a patched up peace. We must have fair guarantees of its continuance without the aid of the Government, sometimes even in spite of its activity to the contrary. There must be a heart union between Hindus, Mussulmans, Parsis, Christians and Jews. The three latter communities may and will distrust the other two. The recent occurrences must strengthen that distrust. We must go out of our way to conquer their distrust. ... We have to make them ours by right of loving service. This is the necessity of our situation. The alternative is a civil war. And a civil war, with a third power only too happy to consolidate itself by siding now with the one and then with the other, must be held an impossibility for the near future.

And what is true of the smaller communities is also true of the cooperators. We must not be impatient with or intolerant to them. We are bound to recognize their freedom to cooperate with the Government if we claim the freedom to non-co-operate. What would we have felt if we were in a minority and the cooperators being in a majority had used violence against us? Non-cooperation *cum* non-violence is the most expeditious method known to the world of winning over opponents. And our struggle consists in winning opponents including Englishmen over to our side. We can only do so by being free from ill will against the weakest or the strongest of them. And this we can only do by being prepared to die for the faith within us and not by killing those who do not see the truth we enunciate.

1 am,

Your faithful comrade,
M. K. GANDHI

*Young India*, 24-11-1921 (25: 140-43)

---

*Non-cooperation did not keep within the bounds that Gandhi set to it. In February 1922, a police station was burnt at Chauri Chaura by a mob of angry men. This took place on the eve of the proposed satyagraha at Bardoli, which had been planned as a grand and earnest show of defiance of iniquitous laws. Gandhi was distraught with sorrow over the turn of events. He decided to forego the chance to offer satyagraha though he had served notice to the government that he would be doing so.*

### The Crime of Chauri Chaura

… It is claimed that no Non-cooperation volunteer had a hand in the brutality and that the mob had not only the immediate provocation but they had also general knowledge of the high handed tyranny of the police in that district. No provocation can possibly justify the brutal murder of men who had been rendered defenceless and who had virtually thrown themselves on the mercy of the mob. And when India claims to be non-violent and hopes to mount the throne of Liberty through non-violent means, mob-violence even in answer to grave provocation is a bad augury. Suppose the "non-violent" disobedience of Bardoli was permitted by God to succeed, the Government had abdicated in favour of the victors of Bardoli, who would control the unruly element that must be expected to perpetrate inhumanity upon due provocation? Non-violent attainment of self-government presupposes a non-violent control over the violent elements in the country. Non-violent Non-cooperators can only succeed when they have succeeded in attaining control over the hooligans of India, in other words, when the latter also have learnt patriotically or religiously to refrain from their violent activities at least whilst the campaign of Non-cooperation is going on. The tragedy at Chauri Chaura, therefore, roused me thoroughly.

"But what about your manifesto to the Viceroy and your rejoinder to his reply?" spoke the voice of Satan. It was the bitterest cup of humiliation to drink. "Surely it is cowardly to withdraw the next day after pompous threats to the government and promises to the people of Bardoli." Thus Satan's invitation was to deny Truth and therefore Religion, to deny God Himself. I put my doubts and troubles before the Working Committee and other associates whom I found near me. They did not all agree with me at first. Some of them probably do not even now agree with me. But never has a man been blessed, perhaps, with colleagues and associates so considerate and forgiving as I have. They understood my difficulty and patiently followed my argument. The result is before the public in the shape of the resolutions of the Working Committee.

The drastic reversal of practically the whole of the aggressive programme may be politically unsound and unwise, but there is no doubt that it is religiously sound, and I venture to assure the doubters that the country will have gained by my humiliation and confession of error. The only virtue I want to claim is Truth and Non-violence. I lay no claim to super human powers. I want none. I wear the same corruptible flesh that the weakest of my fellow beings wears and am therefore as liable to err as any. My services have many limitations, but God has up to now blessed them in spite of the imperfections.

For, confession of error is like a broom that sweeps away dirt and leaves the surface cleaner than before, I feel stronger for my confession. And the cause must prosper for the retracing. Never has man reached his destination by persistence in deviation from the straight path.

... Chauri Chaura is after all an aggravated symptom. I have never imagined that there has been no violence, mental or physical, in the places where repression is going on. Only I have believed, I still believe and the pages of *Young India* amply prove, that the repression is out of all proportion to the insignificant popular violence in the areas of repression. The determined holding of meetings in prohibited areas I do not call violence. The violence I am referring to is the throwing of brickbats or intimidation and coercion practised in stray cases. As a matter of fact in civil disobedience there should be no excitement. Civil disobedience is a preparation for mute suffering. Its effect is marvellous though unperceived and gentle. But I regarded a certain amount of excitement as inevitable, a certain amount of unintended violence even pardonable, i.e., I did not consider civil disobedience impossible in somewhat imperfect conditions. Under perfect conditions disobedience when civil is hardly felt. But the present movement is admittedly a dangerous experiment under fairly adverse conditions.

The tragedy of Chauri Chaura is really the index finger. It shows the way India may easily go if drastic precautions be not taken. If we are not to evolve violence out of non-violence, it is quite clear that we must hastily retrace our steps and re-establish an atmosphere of peace, re-arrange our programme and not think of starting mass civil disobedience until we are sure of peace being retained in spite of mass civil disobedience being started and in spite of Government provocation ...

*Young India*, 16-2-1922 (26: 178-80)

---

*Following the Chauri Chaura incident, Gandhi was arraigned in court for causing political confusion and for preaching against the government. He pleaded guilty and won the judge's heart.*

### The Great Trail

... I would like to state that I entirely endorse the learned Advocate-General's remarks in connection with my humble self. I think that he was entirely fair to me in all the statements that he has made, because it is very true and I have no desire whatsoever to conceal from this Court the fact that to preach disaffection towards the existing system of Government has become almost a passion with me, and the learned Advocate-General is also entirely in the right when he says that my preaching of disaffection did not commence with my connection with *Young India*, but that it commenced much earlier ...

... I wish to endorse all the blame that the learned Advocate-General has thrown on my shoulders in connection with the Bombay, the Madras and the Chauri Chaura occurrences. Thinking over these deeply and sleeping over them night after night, it is impossible to dissociate myself from the diabolical crimes of Chauri Chaura or the mad outrages in Bombay and Madras. He is quite right when he says that, as a man of responsibility, a man having received a fair share of education, having had a fair share of experience of this world, I should know the consequences of every one of my acts. I knew that I was playing with fire. I ran the risk and, if I was set free, I would still do the same. I know that I was feeling it so every day and I have felt it also this morning that I would have failed in my duty if I did not say what I said here just now.

I wanted to avoid violence. I want to avoid violence. Non-violence is the first article of my faith. It is also the last article of my creed. But I had to make my choice. I had either to submit to a system which I considered had done an irreparable harm to my country, or incur the risk of the mad fury of my people bursting forth when they understood the truth from my lips. I know that my people have sometimes gone mad; I am deeply sorry for it. I am, therefore, here to submit not to a light penalty but to the highest penalty. I do not ask for mercy. I do not ask for any extenuating act of clemency. I am here to invite and cheerfully submit to the highest penalty that can be inflicted upon me for what in law is a deliberate crime and what appears to me to be the highest duty of a citizen. The only course open to you, the Judge, is as I am just going to say in my statement, either to resign your post, or inflict on me the severest penalty, if you believe that the system and the law you are assisting to administer are good for the people of this country and that my activity is therefore injurious to the public weal. I do not expect that kind of conversion, but by the time I have finished with my statement, you will, perhaps, have a glimpse of what is raging within my breast to run this maddest risk that a sane man can run ...

*Young India*, 23-3-1922 (26: 380-1)

---

*In spite of the political and moral retreat in the wake of the Chauri Chaura incident, Non-cooperation did not entirely lose its appeal. Two major developments that began during this period came to possess a long after-life. These were: the boycott of foreign cloth and the beginning of spinning as a national activity, and the entry of women into the national movement. There was a third offshoot of Non-cooperation: Gandhi's counselling of sexual continence as an adjunct of an active public life brought the theory and practice of celibacy to public focus and linked it, irrevocably, as it were, to practices of power and control.*

## Why a Bonfire?

... If we look upon the use of foreign cloth as sinful, if we believe that its use has impoverished the country, that because of it countless numbers of our sisters have been rendered homeless, we should look upon foreign cloth as so much dirt and, just as we would not pass on to others the dirt on our person, so we should not pass on this dirt of foreign cloth to others. Had we not resolved to eschew the use of such cloth altogether, we ourselves would have continued to wear it till we had exhausted our stock. Having decided to give up its use, let us do so in fact. Giving it to someone else to use is as good as using it oneself. In giving it to others, we wish to earn the merit which accrues from a good deed. It seems to me that we cannot claim to have earned any such merit. We would throw away rotten grain; so also should we throw away foreign cloth. Hindus, Muslims, Parsis should all of them regard foreign cloth as unholy; if we do so, we would certainly not use it. To create this feeling, I think it is necessary that we discard the foreign cloth in our possession and throw it into the fire. The sentiment which will be generated by our doing this is of great value in my eyes. It is necessary, I think, to arouse so strong a feeling against foreign cloth that no one would dare try to deceive us in this matter. I shall, for this reason, regard ourselves purified if, on August 1, we burn all our garments of foreign cloth.

It is essential that we cultivate aversion to foreign cloth. Some people ask me if this would not lead to hatred of foreigners. In this movement, we should learn to condemn evil but, at the same time, love the evil-doer. Man is not as evil as his deeds. We are all full of failings; how then can we look down with contempt upon one another? All religions teach us to serve the wicked. The test whether a man is truly religious lies in his being free from the extremes of passionate attachments and hatred. He alone has known God who, having cause for anger, keeps it under control. It is the duty of every human being to know God. Keeping one's temper under control is not the *dharma* of only the sannyasi; the latter, in fact is required to keep many other difficult vows as well. We should, therefore, burn cloth but bear no ill will to those who produce it ...

*Navajivan*, 17-7-1921 (from Gujarati) (23: 439-40)

---

*Gandhi's addresses to women during this period were remarkable for their firmness and charged symbolism. Femininity represented for him the form of ideal sacrifice and he demanded women play their part in Non-cooperation.*

### Speech at Women's Meeting, Belgaum
### November 8, 1920

MY REVERED SISTERS,

In this holy temple I have been sanctified by the *darshan* of you all. What makes me especially happy is your having expressed eagerness to see my friend Shaukat Ali as well. We had all been tired and were resting for a while but, when I heard that you wanted Shaukat Ali also to be brought along, I sent for him. I see in this expression of goodwill an assurance of India's success, for I know that, so long as our Hindu women do not look upon Muslims as our brethren, the days of our misfortune will not be over. ... I have learnt from Hinduism that one should not disrespect or despise the religion of anyone else. I have also realized that, till we have learnt to cherish love for people of all other religions and for all our neighbours, we shall not succeed in our efforts for the country's welfare. I have not come here to tell you that you should change and permit people to eat in the company of Muslims or marry among them, but I have certainly come to tell you that we should bear love to every human being. I pray that you teach your children to love members of other faiths.

I also ask of you that you understand the state of national affairs in the country. For this, you do not need to be highly educated or to read any big books. I want to tell you that our Government rules like a monster. The condition is the same today as in *Ravanarajya* of old; the Government has deeply wounded the feelings of our Muslim brethren, has perpetrated terrible atrocities on men, women and children in the Punjab and, even after all this, it does not acknowledge its error, does not repent; on the contrary, it asks us to forget the cruelties. That is why I liken this Government to the rule of a monster. Our men and women should now resort to Non-cooperation with the Government, much like Sita's or Ramachandra's Non-cooperation with Ravana. The latter held out inducements to Sita, sent her various good things to eat, but she disregarded them all and practised the most rigorous *tapascharya* to be free from the clutches of Ravana. Until she was free from his hands, she would wear no fine dresses or ornaments. Ramachandra and Lakshmana practised rigid discipline of the senses, spent their days in self-denial, eating only fruits and tubers, and both the brothers practised the strictest *brahmacharya*.

I want to tell you that, while this tyrannical Government is on our back, none of you, whether man or woman, has a right to wear fine dresses or ornaments. So long as India has not become free, so long as the Muslims' wounds have not been healed, we need to live as fakirs. We should burn up our love of comfort and luxury in the fire of suffering. I entreat you, in the humblest words, to give up ways of comfort and practise severe *tapascharya*, to keep your heart and mind ever pure.

Fifty years ago, all our women—Hindu and Muslim—had the sacred spinning-wheel in their homes and every one of them wore hand-made cloth. I want to tell you, women, that our downfall began, that slavery came to be imposed on us, after we had abandoned *swadeshi-dharma*. All over the country people are dying of hunger and go naked for want of clothes. In these circumstances, every one of you should spin for at least one hour daily, in the name of India, and gift the yarn to the country. You are not likely to get fine cloth for some while, but you will get even fine cloth if you learn to produce fine yarn. However, so long as the country remains subject, we should not think of fine cloth at all, for, producing fine yarn requires much time and today in the country every minute is valuable ...

*Navajivan*, 28-11-1920 (from Gujarati) (21: 467-69)

*Even as he counselled people to support the cause of Non-cooperation,
Gandhi advocated a way of life that would incline them towards it.
This included practising sexual continence.*

### Speech to Students of Satyagraha Ashram, Ahmedabad
### [Before July 1920]

... As days pass I realize with increasing clearness that preservation
of the vital fluid is imperative if one has determined to serve the
country. Which service can I get out of you with these your lean
and lanky bodies? None of you seems to have any flesh on his
body. Bodies like yours are the result of failure to conserve the vital
fluid. All of you should conserve this fluid and build up your bodies.
As long as the body is weak, it is not possible even to acquire
knowledge, let alone putting it to any use. A hot-tempered person
can acquire knowledge, and so can a dishonest person, but one
who does not observe *brahmacharya* can never acquire knowledge.
We can gather from our Puranas that big demons, who subsequently
became embodiments of sheer lust, had to observe *brahmacharya*
for acquiring knowledge. ... That a healthy body is essential for
acquisition of knowledge needs no proof. I wish, therefore, to train
you to have bodies as strong as demons'.

... How can a person, whose body is as thin as a stick, cultivate
the virtue of forgiveness? Such a person will submit through sheer
terror. ... If I do not react in any way, it will mean that I have been
cowed down. ... I tell you, therefore, if you wish to become forgiving
and truthful heroes you must resolutely conserve your vital fluid.
If I display so much vigour at this age of 51 it is only because I have
conserved it. If I had done so from the beginning, I cannot imagine
to what heights I should have soared by now. I appeal to all parents
and guardians present here to help their boys in every way to
conserve the vital fluid. If they cannot restrain themselves any longer
and come and tell you so, requesting you to get them married,
then only should you arrange their marriage ...

*Sabarmati*, Autumn Issue, 1922 (from Gujarati) (20: 436-37)

---

### In Confidence

... I hold that a life of perfect continence in thought, speech and action is necessary for reaching spiritual perfection. And a nation that does not possess such men is the poorer for it.

But my purpose is to plead for *brahmacharya* as a temporary necessity in the present stage of national evolution. We have more than an ordinary share of disease, famines and pauperism—even starvation among millions. We are being ground down under slavery in such a subtle manner that many of us refuse even to recognize it as such, and mistake our state as one of progressive freedom in spite of the triple curse of economic, mental and moral drain. The ever-growing military expenditure, and the injurious fiscal policy purposely designed to benefit Lancashire and other British interests, and the extravagant manner of running the various departments of the State constitute a tax on India which has deepened her poverty and reduced her capacity for withstanding disease ...

... Is it right for us who know the situation to bring forth children in an atmosphere so debasing as I have described? We only multiply slaves and weaklings if we continue the process of procreation whilst we feel and remain helpless, diseased and famine-stricken. Not till India has become a free nation, able to withstand avoidable starvation, well able to feed herself in times of famine, possessing the knowledge to deal with malaria, cholera, influenza and other epidemics, have we the right to bring forth progeny. I must not conceal from the reader the sorrow I feel when I hear of births in this land. I must express that for years I have contemplated with satisfaction the prospect of suspending procreation by voluntary self-denial. India is today ill-equipped for taking care even of her present population, not because she is over-populated but because she is forced to foreign domination [sic] whose creed is progressive exploitation of her resources.

... When we are engaged in a death-grip with a powerful Government, we shall need all the strength—physical, material, moral and spiritual. We cannot gain it unless we husband the one thing which we must prize above everything else. Without this personal purity of life, we must remain a nation of slaves. Let us not deceive ourselves by imagining that because we consider the system of Government to be corrupt, Englishmen are to be despised as competitors in a race for personal virtue. Without making any spiritual parade of the fundamental virtues, they practise them at least physically in an abundant measure. Among those who are engaged in the political life of the country there are more celibates and spinsters than among us.

Spinsters among us are practically unknown except the nuns who leave no impression on the political life of the country. Whereas in Europe thousands claim celibacy as a common virtue. I now place before the reader a few simple rules which are based on the experience not only of myself but of many of my associates.

1. Boys and girls should be brought up simply and naturally in the full belief that they are and can remain innocent.

2. All should abstain from heating and stimulating foods, condiments such as chillies, fatty and concentrated foods such as fritters, sweets and fried substances.

3. Husband and wife should occupy separate rooms and avoid privacy.

4. Both body and mind should be constantly and healthily occupied.

5. "Early to bed early to rise" should be strictly observed.

6. All unclean literature should be avoided. The antidote for unclean thoughts is clean thoughts.

7. Theatres, cinemas, etc., which tend to stimulate passion should be shunned.

8. Nocturnal dreams need not cause any anxiety. A cold bath every time for a fairly strong [sic] is the finest preventive in such cases. It is wrong to say that an occasional indulgence is a safeguard against involuntary dreams.

9. Above all, one must not consider continence even as between husband and wife to be so difficult as to be practically impossible. On the contrary, self-restraint must be considered to be the ordinary and natural practice of life.

10. A heartfelt prayer every day for purity makes one progressively pure.

*Young India*, 13-10-1920 (21: 356-360)

## A Unity of Hearts

*In its early phase, Non-cooperation was almost exclusively linked to the Khilafat demand, which argued that the British re-affirm the spiritual authority of the deposed Caliph of Turkey. Khilafat appeared to Gandhi a fit context to exercise moral sentiment and compassion and thereby demonstrate the possibilities of peace and goodwill between communities who had grown to mistrust each other. During this period, Gandhi and the Ali Brothers, Mohammed Ali and Shaukat Ali, toured the country together entreating the cause of Hindu-Muslim brotherhood.*

*In spite of Hindus and Muslims uniting in the cause of Non-cooperation, the contradictions that divided rich Hindu landlords from poor Muslim peasants in Bengal, rich Hindu moneylenders from Muslim peasants in the Punjab and Hindu peasants from Muslim landlords in the United Provinces persisted. Gandhi's insistence on heart-unity appeared to flounder on the rock of class and caste interests. There were other problems as well. In the United Provinces, Muslim and Hindu intellectuals, given to rigid religious views, vilified each other in the local press—often issuing abusive pamphlets that mocked the religious views and social manners of their spiritual opponents. None of these developments deterred Gandhi from campaigning for 'heart-unity' between the two communities.*

*In 1924, Gandhi was released from prison. He found the world a changed place. The Khilafat was no more an emotive issue. The republican Turkish government of Mustafa Kemal had ended the rule of the Caliphate. Nearer home, Hindus and Muslims faced each other across stubborn and sullen lines of defence and anger. As riots broke out in several parts of the country, which saw Muslim desecration of Hindu temples and Hindu disregard for the Koran and the Prophet, an anguished Gandhi went on a life-threatening 21-day fast. He grieved for the violence, for his betrayed faith in unity, for what appeared to him Muslim ingratitude even. But history's tide had turned and he could not hope to recover the good faith of the past. Saddened and unable to understand the hatred that did not hesitate to murder, he turned away from the problem of heart-unity and looked to constructive work. The end of the 1920s thus saw him travel the country preaching sexual abstinence, arguing against untouchability and entreating people to take up spinning.*

*The extracts in this section present his troubled reflections on Hindu-Muslim unity through the decade of the 1920s, beginning with Non-cooperation and ending with the riot-ridden years that ended it. Further, they reveal his deep faith in dialogue, restraint and tolerance.*

---

### Fasting and Prayer

It is my conviction and my experience that, if fasting and prayer are done with a sincere heart and in a religious spirit, marvellous results could be obtained from them. ... A nation is born when all feel the same sort of grief at the suffering of any one among them; such a nation deserves to be immortal.

We are well aware that quite a large number of our brothers and sisters in India live in great suffering and so, truly speaking, we have occasion at every step for prayerful fasting. But our national life has not attained to this degree of intensity and purity. Even so, occasions arise when we suffer acutely. Such an occasion has arisen for our Muslim brethren. ... If the *Khilafat* disappears, Islam will lose its vitality. This the Muslims can never tolerate. ... It has been decided that on Friday, October 17, Muslims should observe a *roza,* that is, a fast of twenty-four hours; accordingly, beginning from the evening of the 16th, they should spend the whole of the 17th in prayers. This is a beautiful idea. The peace and the good that ensue from turning our thoughts to God in a time of sorrow are not to be had in any other way.

The duty of Hindus at such a time is obvious. If they regard the Muslims as their brethren, they should fully share their suffering. This is the best and the easiest method of promoting unity between Hindus and Muslims. Sharing another's sorrow is the only real sign of brotherly regard. I hope, therefore, that every man and woman in India will spend October 17 in prayer and fasting. The *Gita* is universally accepted among Hindus. They should read it through from the beginning to the end, along with a rendering of its meaning. This way the whole day will be spent in a religious spirit, and that will be the prayer of the Hindus.

I think we may, without fear, observe a hartal on that day. Those who are independent should stop their work. People in service, the labourers and those who serve in hospitals, etc., need not stop work. If people remain within doors on the day and take out no processions, there will be no cause for fear. There can be no coercion in fasting and prayer; and this should also be true about stopping work. A hartal can be effective only if it is purely voluntary. Such a hartal alone can provide the true measure of the feelings of Hindus and Muslims ...

*Navajivan*, 12-10-1919 (from Gujarati) (19: 46-8)

---

*This address was delivered in west Punjab (now in Pakistan), home to both Hindus and Muslims, and was obviously meant to wean the martial Punjabis from the gun and the sword*

### Speech at Rawalpindi

... If we are to make sacrifices in this struggle, we must match the efficiency of the Empire which we are fighting. The soldiers forget their anger and fight with discipline, with intelligence and courage. If you want to stand against them, you should be intelligent and cultivate courage and discipline.

... In Rawalpindi, Hindus and Muslims are very strong. They have the strength, too, for quarrels [among themselves]. I request them to acquire the strength to make sacrifices. The sacrifice, I repeat, is not of the kind involved in drawing the sword. Muslims are brave at it. I compliment them on this, but I should like to make them see that, if they would have the strength to employ the sword, they must also have the strength to give up their life. The Punjabis know how to draw the sword, but I call their sword mercenary. One cannot intimidate anybody with such a sword. Your sword is unavailing against anyone who can employ his more skilfully than you, and the moment you lose your grip over the sword you stand helpless.

I have found a way by which you can fight while keeping your swords sheathed. It seems to me that you will face defeat if you use your swords; not only that, but your swords will be turned against your people, men and women alike. If you want to understand the beauty of Non-cooperation, follow my advice. I do not claim to know the holy Koran, but your own Ulemas say that Non-cooperation is a strong form of jehad. One may have to die whether drawing the sword or employing Non-cooperation. Why, then, should you not sacrifice yourselves by adopting Non-cooperation which does not involve the taking of another's life?

... I shall ask the soldiers to leave the army but not to turn their arms subsequently against the enemy. I ask them, rather to become soldiers without swords, like me. I have nothing by way of physical strength; but nobody, I think, can make me do anything against my will. By and by I will also ask the peasants not to pay revenue, but I tell both the soldiers and the peasants to take no step without instructions. The beauty of our struggle lies in the discipline it requires, and so I shall ask our unarmed, swordless army not to take up their weapons without orders. They will get their orders at the opportune moment. But so long as we are not sure that we can carry the whole of India with us, we will not ask the soldiers or the peasants to do anything ...

Why do these people (*in [pre-partition] Punjab - ed.*) join the army? For money. The money which robs us of our humanity is so much dust. ... I entreat you not to allow yourselves to yield to the temptation of enlisting in the army. Earn your bread by toil, and tell them plainly that you can supply no recruits. Just think of the tremendous effect that will be produced if the Punjab declares this. Which other part has supplied as many recruits as the Punjab has? If the Punjab now refuses to supply any more, let us see who can get them from elsewhere.

I have also been a soldier of the Government, but the time has now come for me to tell it that the kingdom of God is a thousand times dearer to us than its Empire. In that kingdom, we shall be able to preserve our religion, whereas the Empire is founded on injustice and maintains itself by disobeying God. We cannot be loyal to it. The Punjab was humiliated under martial law, it lost its honour. To be even with the Government for that, tell it that you want to remain its loyal subjects, but that you can do so only if it mends its ways and does justice to the province. Tell it that, till then, you will have no love for it, will have nothing to do with it ... (*ellipsis as in the original - ed.*)

*Navajivan*, 15-8-1920 (from Gujarati) (21: 64-66)

---

*In spite of Gandhi's tireless counselling of a unity of hearts between Hindus and Muslims, several Hindus voiced doubts: they did not seem to want to trust Muslims. Gandhi tried to persuade them to see things differently.*

## To Hindus

I see that the Hindus have still mental reservations about going all out to make sacrifices on the *Khilafat* issue. I decided many years ago that India's good lay in unity of heart between Hindus and Muslims. ... I attach far more importance to Hindu-Muslim unity than to the British connection. This latter is not indispensable for the prosperity of India, whereas Hindu-Muslim unity is. Three-fourths of India can never enjoy freedom if they remain hostile to the remaining one-fourth. Extermination of seven crore Muslims is equally impossible.

Many Hindus believe that British rule serves at any rate to protect Hinduism, and, therefore, whatever other harm it may do, the protection of Hinduism is a sufficient compensation. I can think of no more humiliating idea which can occur to a Hindu. If twenty-three crore Hindus are not strong enough to defend themselves against seven crore Muslims, either the Hindu religion is false or those who believe in it are cowardly and wicked. I would rather that the Hindus and the Muslims settled their accounts by means of the sword than that the British Government maintained artificial peace between them ...

... It is wrong to believe that Muslims and Hindus can never get along together. To be sure, you will find in history cases of injustice done by Muslims. But their religion is a noble one and Muslims are a noble people. I do not believe that they have no respect for people of other faiths, or that they have no compassion in them. They know how to repay obligations. I, therefore, advise every

Hindu to place full trust in his Muslim brethren. Man by nature is pure in his heart and Muslims are no exception to this law.

So far, we have made no sincere efforts to bring about unity. Such an attempt expects no reward. Sincerity is not a matter for a shop-keeper's calculations. To help Muslims on certain conditions is as good as not helping them. ... Reward should be asked only of God. My Hindu religion teaches me not to expect a reward while doing any good deed and to trust that good always produces good. Knowing that this is an unalterable law, if we come across an instance which seems to contradict it, we should think that, with our limited understanding, we are unable to explain the contradiction. We have no ground for taking it to be an exception ...

But suppose that Muslims betray Hindus despite the latter's generous behaviour. Will Hindus, in that case, remain cowards? Are they not strong enough to protect their religion? If Hindus want to acquire strength to protect their religion, this too they will acquire by helping Muslims because, in the process, Hindus will have to display the great qualities of determination, courage, truthfulness, capacity for self-sacrifice, unity, organizing ability, etc. I do not mean that Hindus should help because of their own weakness, but rather that it has become our duty to help the Muslims as neighbours since their case is just and the means they are employing are also just. If they do not do this duty, they will strengthen their bonds of slavery and lose for ever the opportunity of winning the friendship of Muslims. Doing it, they will shake off slavery and win over Muslims.

... Bringing about so good and great a result requires a *yajna* (*sacrifice, the reference here is to Non-cooperation - ed.*)—A supreme *yajna*. Offering up, in this *yajna*, our titles, our practice and our education for material gain is, in my opinion, but a small sacrifice. Whether the Hindus make this sacrifice or not, every Hindu should try and understand the true meaning of this war.

*Navajivan,* 29-8-1920 (from Gujarati) (21 : 209-10)

---

*Gandhi was convinced that Hindu-Muslim tensions owed a lot to Hindu anger over Muslim butchers slaughtering cows for meat, and to*

*Hindus insisting on playing music outside mosques, while Muslims prayed. He returned to the cow question several times during this period, as he attempted to persuade Hindus away from the violent hatred they espoused towards Muslims on account of the cow.*

## Let Hindus Beware

... I would not kill a human being for protecting a cow, as I will not kill a cow for saving a human life, be it ever so precious. Needless to say I have authorized no one to preach vegetarianism as part of Non-cooperation. ... Hindus may not compel Mussulmans to abstain from meat or even beef-eating. Vegetarian Hindus may not compel other Hindus to abstain from fish, flesh for fowl. I would not make India sober at the point of the sword. Nothing has lowered the morale of the nation so much as violence. Fear has become the part of the national character. Non-co-operators will make a serious mistake if they seek to convert people to their creed by violence. They will play into the hands of the Government if they use the slightest coercion towards anybody in the course of their propaganda.

The cow question is a big question. The greatest for a Hindu. I yield to no one in my regard for the cow. Hindus do not fulfil their trust so long as they do not possess the ability to protect the cow. That ability can be derived either from body-force or soul force. To attempt cow-protection by violence is to reduce Hinduism to Satanism and to prostitute to a base end the grand significance of cow-protection. As a Mussalman friend writes, beef-eating, which is merely permissible in Islam, will become a duty if compulsion is resorted to by Hindus. The latter can protect the cow only by developing the faculty for dying, for suffering. The only chance Hindus have, of saving the cow in India from the butcher's knife, is by trying to save Islam from the impending peril and trusting their Mussalman countrymen to return nobility, i.e., voluntarily to protect the cow out of regard for their Hindu countrymen. The Hindus must scrupulously refrain from using any violence against Mussalmans. Suffering and trust are attributes of soul-force. I have heard that, at big fairs, if a Mussalman is found in possession of cows or even goats, he is at times forcibly dispossessed. Those, who, claiming to be Hindus, thus resort to violence are enemies of the cow and of Hinduism. The best and the only way to save the cow is to save the *Khilafat*. I hope therefore that every non-co-operator will strain himself to the utmost to prevent the slightest tendency to violence in any shape or form, whether to protect the cow or any other animal or to effect any other purpose.

*Young India*, 18-5-1921 (23: 163-64)

---

*Gandhi's efforts at heart-unity were severely challenged by events in the southern India. In 1921, Muslim peasants in north Kerala, also known as the Malabar region, were up in arms against Hindu landlords who were forcibly dispossessed of their lands. In the violence and mayhem that followed, several hundreds of Hindus were killed and some were forced to convert to Islam. Gandhi was especially concerned about the use of force in conversion. He rebuked the Hindus of Malabar for being supine and argued that Islam does not mandate forcible conversion.*

### Hindu-Muslim Unity

... Those who accept non-violence as part of *dharma* are convinced that no hatred or violence can survive in its presence. If the Hindus in Malabar had the spirit of non-violence in them, no Moplah (*Muslims of Malabar are called Moplahs - ed.*) could have forced them to do anything. But, it will be objected, every one cannot have such a spirit, and the objection has force in it. The reply is that, even if a small section of Hindus display real non-violence, others will be protected—such is the power of non-violence. What is my reply, however, if somebody argues that Hindus do not believe in non-violence ? Well if that is so, the question does not arise, for he who does not believe in non-violence will defend himself by fighting, whether he is alone or in a group. Anything which can be won through armed might can also be won through the power of non-violence.

Even the person who fights with arms is considered brave only when he opposes a powerful enemy. One who believes in non-violence faces the enemy unarmed and his strength, therefore, has no limit to it. He who cannot safeguard his *dharma* is not worthy of it. Those who were forcibly converted, why did they submit to force? Why did they not give up their lives? Or, why did they not fight and beat back the enemy, or die fighting? If it was the Englishman's protection which saved them, they have as good as accepted the Englishman's religion; if my protection had saved them, they would have accepted my *dharma*. A *dharma* of their own, they had none. One's *dharma* is a personal possession. One is oneself responsible for preserving it or losing it. What can be defended in and through a group is not *dharma*, it is dogma.

Islam does not sanction forcible conversion; it even prohibits the use of force. It is wrong to say that Islam has employed force. All those who profess a religion are not true followers of it. Does Hinduism sanction killing of Muslims for saving cows? No. Do we not know, even then, that Hindus lose their heads and fight with Muslims on this issue? If Islam recognizes the use of force it is not religion but irreligion. I am positive that Islam does not sanction the use of force. If it did, would not all Muslims openly avow so? No religion in this world has spread through the use of force. In my opinion, the history of Muslim empires which is taught to us entitles much exaggeration. Victory on the *Khilafat* issue will certainly increase the strength of Muslims and enhance their courage, but to think that they will use these against Hindus is to suggest that Muslims have no sense of honour, that it is in their nature to return evil for good, that, in other words, they have no true religion in them! All my experience is to the contrary. I have known honour and honesty in a great many Muslims.

... I should also add that every Muslim who heard the stories of Moplah atrocities was pained by them, and also that, if our people were allowed to go there at this time, the Moplahs themselves would apologize for their deeds. I am sure that they will positively apologize when we have *swaraj*. All that they know is fighting. They are our ignorant brethren. The Government of course has done nothing to reform them but neither have we done anything. Is not this the fault of the Hindus of Malabar?

*Navajivan*, 25-9-1921 (from Gujarati) (24: 325-27)

---

*From 1920-22, the Khilafat and Non-cooperation did foster a measure of fraternity amongst Hindus and Muslims, but this did not mean*

*that mistrust and prejudices had disappeared. After Gandhi's arrest*
*for sedition in 1922, the movement for heart-unity lost its most inspired*
*spokesperson and slowly retreated into quiescence. Further, in the*
*years that Gandhi was in prison (1922-24), Hindu-Muslim relations*
*worsened. On his release in 1924, Gandhi found himself having to*
*address this crisis in unity.*

## "Shudddhi" and "Tabligh"

... That ... which is keeping up the tension (*between Hindus and Muslims - ed.*) is the manner in which the *shuddhi* or conversion movement (*of the Arya Samaj, a Hindu revivalist group - ed.*) is being conducted. In my opinion, there is no such thing as proselytism in Hinduism as it is understood in Christianity or to a lesser extent in Islam. The Arya Samaj has, I think, copied the Christians in planning its propaganda. The modern method does not appeal to me. It has done more harm than good. Though regarded as a matter of the heart purely and one between the Maker and oneself, it has degenerated into an appeal to the selfish instinct. The Arya Samaj preacher is never so happy as when he is reviling other religions. My Hindu instinct tells me that all religions are more or less true. All proceed from the same God, but all are imperfect because they have come down to us through imperfect human instrumentality.

The real *shuddhi* movement should consist in each one trying to arrive at perfection in his or her own faith. In such a plan character would be the only test. What is the use of crossing from one compartment to another, if it does not mean a moral rise? What is the meaning of my trying to convert to the service of God (for that must be the implication of *shuddhi* or *tabligh*), when those who are in my fold are every day denying God by their actions? "Physician, heal thyself" is more true in matters religious than mundane. But these are my views.

If the Arya Samajists think that they have a call from the conscience, they have a perfect right to conduct the movement. Such a burning call recognizes no time limit, no checks of experience. If Hindu-Muslim unity is endangered because an Arya Samaj preacher or Mussalman preacher preaches his faith in obedience to a call from within, that unity is only skin-deep. Why should we be ruffled by such movements? Only they must be genuine. ... But no propaganda can be allowed which reviles other religions. For that would be negation of toleration. The best way of dealing with such propaganda is to publicly condemn it. Every movement attempts to put on the cloak of respectability. As soon as the public tear that cloak down, it dies for want of respectability ...

... A gentleman told me that some agents of the Aga-Khani movement (*a Muslim sect from western India - ed.*) lend money to poor illiterate Hindus and then tell them that the debt would be wiped out if the debtor would accept Islam. I would regard this as conversion by unlawful inducements. But the worst form is that preached by a gentleman of Delhi. I have read his pamphlet from cover to cover. It gives detailed instructions to preachers how to carry on propaganda. It starts with a lofty proposition that Islam is merely preaching of the unity of God. This grand truth is to be preached, according to the writer, by every Mussalman irrespective of character. ...My Mussalman friends tell me that no respectable Mussalman approves of the methods advocated. The point, however, is not what the respectable Mussalmans think. The point is whether a considerable number of Mussalman masses accept and follow them. A portion of the Punjab Press is simply scurrilous. It is at times even filthy. I have gone through the torture of reading many extracts. These sheets are conducted by Arya Samajists or Hindu and Mussalman writers. Each vies with the other in using abusive language and reviling the religion of the opponent. These papers have, I understand, a fairly large circulation. They find place even in respectable reading-rooms. I have heard it said that the Government emissaries are at the back of this campaign of calumny. I hesitate to believe it. But even assuming the truth of it, the public of the Punjab should be able to cope with the growing disgrace ...

*Young India*, 29-5-1924 (28: 56-8)

---

*During this period of acute communal tension, provoked by aggressive Hindu communal propaganda, incensed Muslim mobs took to desecrating Hindu temples in parts of the country. Gandhi was anguished but firm and unequivocal in his upholding of the virtues of tolerance and non-violence.*

## Gulbarga Gone Mad

I ... feel, perhaps more keenly than most of them, every fanatic outburst on the part of Mussulmans. I am fully aware of my responsibility in the matter. I know that many Hindus feel that I am responsible for many of these outbursts. For, they argue, I contributed the largest share to the awakening of the Mussalman masses. I appreciate the charge. Though I do not repent of my contribution, I feel the force of the objection. Therefore, if for no other reason, for this at least of greater responsibility, I must feel, more keenly than most Hindus can, these desecrations. I am both an idolater and an iconoclast in what I conceive to be the true sense of the terms. I value the spirit behind idol worship. It plays a most important part in the uplift of the human race. And I would like to possess the ability to defend with my life the thousands of holy temples which sanctify this land of ours.

My alliance with the Mussalmans presupposes their perfect tolerance for my idols and my temples. I am an iconoclast in the sense that I break down the subtle form of idolatry in the shape of fanaticism that refuses to see any virtue in any other form of worshipping the Deity save one's own. This form of idolatry is more deadly for being more fine and evasive than the tangible and gross form of worship that identifies the Deity with a little bit of a stone or a golden image. True Hindu-Muslim unity requires Mussalmans to tolerate not as a virtue of necessity, not as a policy, but as part of their religion, the religion of others so long as they, the latter, believe it to be true. Even so is it expected of Hindus to extend the same to balance as a matter of faith and religion to the religions of others, no matter how repugnant they may appear to their, the Hindus', sense of religion.

The Hindus must therefore reject the idea of retaliation. The law of retaliation we have been trying since the day of Adam and we know from experience that it has hopelessly failed. We are groaning under its poisonous effect. Above all, the Hindus may not break mosques against temples. That way lies slavery and worse. Even though a thousand temples may be reduced to bits, I would not touch a single mosque and expect thus to prove the superiority of my faith to the so-called faith of fanatics. I would love to hear of priests dying at their posts in defence of their temples and their idols. Let them learn to suffer and to die in the defence of their temples even as God allows Himself to be insulted and broken up in the insult and damage done to the idols in which being omnipresent He undoubtedly resides ...

... To the unknown Mussalmans who are undoubtedly behind these desecrations I submit: Remember that Islam is being judged by your conduct. I have not found a single Mussalman defending these outbursts not even under provocation. There seems to me to have been little if any provocation offered by the Hindus. But let us assume that it was otherwise, that Hindus played music near mosques to exasperate Mussalmans, that they even removed a stone from a minaret. Yet I venture to say that Mussalmans ought not to have desecrated Hindu temples. Even retaliation has its limits. Hindus prize their temples above their lives. It is possible to contemplate with some degree of equanimity injury to life but not to temples. Religion is more than life. Remember that his own religion is the truest to every man even if it stands low in the scales of philosophic comparison ...

*Young India*, 28-8-1924 (29: 48 – 49)

---

*Gandhi had to answer many questions during this period about what Hindus and Muslims ought to do in the face of provocation—whether they should give into fear or retaliate. He counselled another mode of response.*

### Hindu-Muslim Unity
### September 14, 1924

... Quarrels must break out so long as the Hindus continue to be seized with fear. Bullies are always to be found where there are cowards. The Hindus must understand that no one can afford them protection, if they go on hugging fear. Fear of man argues want of faith in God. Only he trusts to his physical strength who has no faith or very little faith in God's omnipresence. The Hindu must cultivate either of these two—faith in God or faith in one's physical might. If he does neither, it will spell the ruin of the community.

The first, viz., reliance on God and shaking off the fear of man is the way of non-violence and the best way. The second, viz., reliance on one's physical might is the way of violence. Both have a place in the world. It is open to us to choose either. One man cannot try both at the same time. If all the Hindus and Mussalmans both elect the way of violence, we had better cease to talk of winning *swaraj* in the immediate future. Armed peace means not a little fighting that will end with the breaking of a few heads or of a dozen temples. It must mean prolonged fighting and rivers of blood.

I am against *sangathan (military training of Hindus, organized by groups such as the Arya Samaj - ed.)* and I am not. If *sangathan* means opening *akhadas (gymnasiums - ed.)* and organizing the Hindu hooligans through them, I would regard it as a pitiable condition. You cannot defend yourself and your religion with the help of hooligans. It is substituting one peril for another, and even adding another. I would have nothing to say against *akhadas,* if they were used by the Brahmins, Banias and others for the development of their physique. *Akhadas* as *akhadas* are un-exceptionable. But I have no doubt that they are no good for giving a training to fight the Mussalmans. It will take years to acquire the physical strength to fight. The *akhada* is therefore not the way. We will have to go in for *tapasya,* for self-purification, if we want to win the hearts of Mussalmans. We shall have to cast off all the evil in us. If they attack us, we shall have to learn not to return blow for blow, but bravely to face death—not to die a craven death leaving wife and children behind, but to receive their blows and meet death cheerfully.

I would tender the same advice to the Mussalmans. But it is unnecessary, as the average Mussalman has been assumed to be a bully. The general impression is that the Mussalmans can fight and fight well. I do not, therefore, need to tell them how they should defend themselves from the attacks of the Hindus; on the contrary I have to appeal to them to forbear. I have to appeal to them to get the *goonda* element under control and to behave peaceably. The Mussalmans may regard the Hindus as a menace in other matters. They do regard them as an economic menace. They do dread the Hindus' interference with their religious rites on the *Bakri-i-Id* day. But they are in no fear of being beaten by the Hindus. I will therefore tell them only this: "You cannot protect Islam with the lathi or the sword. The age of the lathi is gone. A religion will be tested by the purity of its adherents. If you leave it to the *goondas* to defend your Faith, you will do serious harm to Islam. Islam will, in that case, no longer remain the faith of the fakirs and worshippers of Allah ..."

*Young India*, 18-9-1924 (29: 142-43)

---

*Hindu-Muslim relationships did not improve and Gandhi went on a 21-day fast. He was particularly distressed by riots that broke out in the north-west frontier town of Kohat where over 150 Hindus were killed. There were also reports of forcible conversions which saddened him. It appeared to him that he could do nothing but fast, since he had not expected Muslims to repay the good faith he had reposed in them thus. He also felt responsible for the conflagration.*

### Discussion with Mahadev Desai
### September 18, 1924

... I may be charged with having committed a breach of faith with the Hindus. I asked them to befriend Muslims. I asked them to lay their lives and their property at the disposal of the Mussalmans for the protection of their holy places. Even today I am asking them to practise *ahimsa*, to settle quarrels by dying but not by killing. And what do I find to be the result? How many temples have been desecrated? How many sisters come to me with complaints? As I was saying to Hakimji yesterday, Hindu women are in mortal terror of Mussalman *goondas*. In many places they fear to go out alone. ... How can I bear the way in which his little children were molested (*ellipsis as in the original - ed.*)? How can I now ask the Hindus to put up with everything patiently? I gave them the assurance that the friendship of Mussalmans was bound to bear good fruit. I asked them to befriend them, regardless of the result. It is not in my power today to make good that assurance, neither is it in the power of Mahomed Ali or Shaukat Ali (*the leaders of the Khilafat movement who endorsed Non-cooperation as a means of protesting British attitudes towards Turkey - ed.*) . Who listens to me? And yet I must ask the Hindus even today to die and not to kill. I can only do so by laying down my own life. I can teach them the way to die by my own example. There is no other way ... I launched no-co-operation (*ellipsis as in the original - ed.*). Today I find that people are non-co-operating against one another, without any regard for non-violence. What is the reason? Only this, that I myself am not completely non-violent. If I were practising non-violence to perfection, I should not have seen the violence I see around me today. My fast is therefore a penance. I blame no one. I blame only myself. I have lost the power wherewithal to appeal to people. Defeated and helpless I must submit my petition in His Court. Only He will listen, no one else ...

*Young India,* 23-10-1924 (29: 185)

---

*Gandhi's close comrade in the Khilafat and Non-cooperation movements, Shaukat Ali hurried to this side when he heard of the fast and urged him to not lose faith.*

### Discussion with Shaukat Ali
### September 19 1924

... Dear man, this fast is the result of several days' continued prayers. I have got up from sleep at 3 o'clock in the night and have asked Him what to do. On the 17th of September the answer came like a flash! If I have erred, He will forgive me. All I have done, all I am doing, is done in a fully godfearing spirit, and in the house of a godfearing Mussalman (*the residence of Shaukat Ali's brother, Mahomed Ali - ed.*) at that. My religion says that only he who is prepared to suffer can pray to God. Fasting and prayer are common injunctions in my religion. But I know of this sort of penance even in Islam. In the life of the Prophet I have read that the Prophet often fasted and prayed, and forbade others to copy him. Someone asked him why he did not allow others to do the thing he himself was doing. "Because I live on food divine," he said. He achieved most of his great things by fasting and prayer. I learnt from him that only he can fast who has inexhaustible faith in God. The Prophet had revelations not in moments of ease and luxurious living. He fasted and prayed, kept awake for nights together and would be on his feet at all hours of the night as he received the revelations. Even at this moment I see before me the picture of the Prophet thus fasting and praying. My dear Shaukat, I cannot bear the people accusing you and your brother of having broken your promises to me. I cannot bear the thought of such an accusation; I must die for it. This fast is but to purify myself, to strengthen myself. Let me not be misunderstood. I am speaking to you as though I was a Mussalman, because I have cultivated that respect for Islam which you have for it. After I have fasted and prayed I shall be all the stronger, with all my reverence for Islam, to appeal to both the communities. It is my own firm belief that the strength of the soul grows in proportion as you subdue the flesh. We have to fight hooliganism and we are not sufficiently spiritually strong to fight it ...

*Young India,* 23-10-1924 (29: 192-93)

---

*In spite of the fast Hindu-Muslim relationships did not improve substantially. There were many reasons for this, the chief amongst them being the very real material contradictions that divided Hindus and Muslims in various parts of the country. Gandhi's friendship with the Ali brothers, especially Shaukat Ali, came under a strain during this period (1925 onwards) after a fact-finding visit to the troubled Kohat area left each of them with different impressions of what had gone wrong. Gandhi's own status as a Hindu spokesman for Muslim interests suffered and he came to be criticized for holding opinions that he ought not to.*

## My Crime

... I have not adversely (or otherwise) criticized the teachings of the Holy Koran. But I have criticised the teachers, that is, the interpreters, in anticipation of their defending the penalty of stoning to death. I claim to understand enough of the Koran and the history of Islam to know that a multitude of interpreters have interpreted the Koran to suit their preconceived notions. My purpose was to issue a warning against the acceptance of such interpretations. But I would like to say that even the teachings themselves of the

Koran cannot be exempt from criticism. Every true scripture only gains by criticism. After all we have no other guide but our reason to tell us what may be regarded as revealed and what may not be.

The early Mussalmans accepted Islam not because they knew it to be revealed but because it appealed to their virgin reason. ... If I am at perfect liberty to express my opinion "as to whether renegades can be stoned to death under the law of Islam" why may I not express an opinion as to whether penalty of stoning to death can be imposed at all under the law of Islam? ... The Maulana (*his critic - ed.*) has betrayed intolerance of criticism by a non Muslim of anything relating to Islam. I suggest to him that intolerance of criticism even of what one may prize as dear as life itself is not conducive to the growth of public corporate life. Surely Islam has nothing to fear from criticism even if it be unreasonable.

*Young India*, 5-3-1925 (30: 336-7)

---

*Though he was increasingly prone to regard his role in mediating Hindu-Muslim tensions as redundant, Gandhi found it important to speak out against ill-founded communal arguments and put forth his defence of non-violence and his implacable opposition to hate-inducing talk of any kind.*

## My Incapacity

It would be most comfortable for my pride if I could give every applicant for help the satisfaction he may desire. But here is a sample of my hopeless incapacity.

Of what use is your leadership or Mahatmaship if you cannot stop cow-killing by asking the Mussalmans to stop it? Look at your studied silence on the Alwar atrocities (*where Hindus suffered violence at the hands of Muslims - ed.*) and your criminal silence about the affront put by the Nizam (*the Muslim ruler of Hyderabad - ed.*) upon Panditji (*Madan Mohan Malaviya, an orthodox Hindu leader and ideologue with right-wing beliefs - ed.*) whom you delight to call your respected elder brother and one of the first among the public servants and whom you have yourself acquitted of any malice against Mussalmans.

Thus have argued not the same but several persons. The first rebuke mentioned was the last to be received and it has proved the proverbial last straw. There is a telegram before me asking me to request the Mussalmans not to kill cows as sacrifice on *Bakr-Id*. I thought it was time for me at least to offer an explanation over my silence. I was prepared to live down the charge regarding Panditji, although it was a charge brought by a dear friend. He was almost apprehensive about my fame. He thought I would be accused of fear of Mussalmans and what not. But I was firm in my resolve not to take any public notice of the ban on Panditji. There was no fear of his misunderstanding me. And I knew that he stood in no need of my protection. He will survive all the bans that can be declared against him by any temporal power.

... Strange are the ways of potentates. Nothing that I could write in the pages of *Young India* would, I knew, induce H.E.H. the Nizam to recall his fiat. If I had the honour of a personal acquaintance, I would have straightway written to the ruler of Hyderabad respectfully telling him that the ban on Panditji could do no good to his State, much less to Islam. I would have even advised him to offer Panditji his hospitality when he went to Hyderabad and could have cited such example from the lives of the Prophet and his companions. But I do not possess that honour. And I knew that a public reference by me might not even reach his ears. Save, therefore, for adding to the acerbity already existing, it could have served no purpose. And as I could not add to it, even if I could not diminish it, I chose to be silent.

And my present reference I propose to use for the sake of advising such Hindus as would listen to me not to feel irritated over the incident nor to make it a cause of complaint against Islam or Mussalmans. It is not the Mussalman in the Nizam that is responsible for the ban. Arbitrary procedure is an attribute of autocracy whether it be Hindu or Mussalman. ... The remedy is cultivation of enlightened and forceful public opinion. The process must begin, as it has begun, in British India proper; because it is naturally freer, being administered directly, unlike the States (*Indian kingdoms, which were not part of British India, but effectively under British rule. Yet the rulers possessed considerable moral authority - ed.*) which are administered through the vassals of the Emperor. They, therefore, reproduce the evils of the British system without containing the few safeguards that direct British administration provides for its own sake. In the Indian States, therefore, orderliness depends more upon the personal character and whims of the chiefs for the time being than upon the constitution or rather the constitutions under which the States' government is regulated. It follows, therefore, that real reform of the States can only come when the chilling control of the British Imperial system is at least tempered by the freedom of British India secured by the disciplined power of the people.

Not that, therefore, all the journals have to observe silence. Reference to abuses in the States is undoubtedly a necessary part of journalism, and it is a means of creating public opinion. Only, my scope is strictly limited, I have taken up journalism not for its sake but merely as an aid to what I have conceived to be my mission in life. My mission is to teach by example and precept under severe restraint the use of the matchless weapon of satyagraha which is direct corollary of non-violence and truth. I am anxious, indeed I am impatient, to demonstrate that there is no remedy for the many ills of life save that of non-violence. It is a solvent strong enough to melt the stoniest heart. To be true to my faith, therefore, I may not write in anger or malice. I may not write idly. I may not write merely to excite passion.

The reader can have no idea of the restraint I have to exercise from week to week in the choice of topics and my vocabulary. It is a training for me. It enables me to peep into myself and make discoveries of my weaknesses. Often my vanity dictates a smart expression or my anger a harsh adjective. It is a terrible ordeal but a fine exercise to remove these weeds. The reader sees the pages of *Young India* fairly well dressed up and sometimes with Romain Rolland, he is inclined to say "what a fine old man this must be". Well, let the world understand that the fineness is carefully and prayerfully cultivated. And if it has proved acceptable to some whose opinion I cherish, let the reader understand that when that fineness has become perfectly natural, i.e., when I have become incapable of evil and when nothing harsh or haughty occupies, be it momentarily, my thought-world, then and not till then, my non-violence will move all the hearts of all the world. I have placed before me and the reader no impossible ideal or ordeal. It is man's prerogative and birthright ...

*Young India*, 2-7-1925 (32: 76-8)

---

*In this period of communal mistrust, C. R. Das, a popular Congress leader from Bengal attempted to address Muslim disquiet over the Congress' ambiguous silence on the question of minority rights. Das' policies, which granted conciliatory political concessions to Muslims were criticized by some Muslim political leaders. It was left to Gandhi to interpret Das' gesture.*

## "The Science Of Surrender"

Exception has been taken to my remarks at a meeting in Calcutta that Deshbandhu (*C. R. Das - ed.*), in his relations with the Mussalmans, brought "the science of surrender to perfection". The exception has been taken because my critics impute to me the implication that by surrender I mean that Deshbandhu conferred on Mussalmans favours, that is, things they were not entitled to. The critics opine that the Hindus are acting towards the Mussalmans much the same as Englishmen are acting towards us all—having first taken away everything and then offering us doles in the name of favours.

I know what I said at the meeting in question. I have not read the reports of my speech, but I desire to abide by all I said at that meeting. I make bold to say that without mutual surrender there is no hope for this distraught country. Let us not be hyper-sensitive or devoid of imagination. To surrender is not to confer favour. Justice that love gives is a surrender, justice that law gives is a punishment. What a lover gives transcends justice. And yet it is always less than he wished to give, because he is anxious to give more and frets that he has nothing left. ... Both Hindus and Mussalmans sail in the same boat. Both are fallen. And they are in the position of lovers, have to be, whether they will or no. Every act, therefore, of a Hindu towards the Mussalman and *vice versa* must be an act of surrender and not mere justice. They may not weigh their acts in golden scales and exact consideration. Each has to regard himself ever a debtor of the other. By justice, why should not a Mussalman kill a cow every day in front of me? But his love for me restrains him from so doing and he goes out of his way sometimes even to refrain from eating beef for his love of me, and yet thinks that he has done only just what is right. Justice permits me to shout my music in the ear of Maulana Mahomed Ali when he is at prayer, but I go out of my way to anticipate his feelings and make my talks whispers whilst he is praying and still consider that I have conferred no favour on the Maulana. On the other hand, I should become a loathsome creature if I exercised my just right of playing tomtom precisely at the time of his prayer. Justice might have been satisfied if Deshbandhu Das had not filled certain posts with Mussalmans, but he went out of his way to anticipate Mussalman wishes and placate Mussalman sentiment ...

Love never claims, it ever gives. Love ever suffers, never resents, never revenges itself. This talk, therefore, of justice and nothing but justice is a thoughtless, angry and ignorant outburst whether it comes from Hindus or Mussalmans. So long as Hindu and Mussalmans continue to prate about justice, they will never come together. "Might is right" is the last word of "justice and nothing but justice". Why should Englishmen surrender an inch of what they have earned by right of conquest? Or why should Indians, when they come to power, not make the English disgorge everything which their ancestors robbed them of? And yet when we come to a settlement, as we shall some day, we will not weigh in the scales of justice so called. But we shall introduce into the calculation the disturbing factor of surrender, otherwise called love or affection or fellow-feeling.

And so will it be with us Hindus and Mussalmans when we have sufficiently broken one another's heads and spilled a few gallons of innocent blood and realized our foolishness. The scales will then fall off our eyes and we shall recognize that vengeance was not the law of friendship; not justice but surrender and nothing but surrender was the law of friendship. Hindus will have to learn to bear the sight of cow-slaughter and the Mussalmans will have to discover that it was against the law of Islam to kill a cow in order to wound the susceptibilities of Hindus. When that happy day arrives, we shall know only each other's virtues. Our vices will not obtrude themselves upon our gaze. That day may be far off or it may be very near ...

*Young India*, 9-7-1925 (32: 105-07)

# Ending the Non-cooperation Years

*These years saw the maturing of Gandhi's ideas on non-violence and peaceful co-existence. He was widely viewed as a man with a mission. Even those who did not entirely agree with his ideas and some who had never even seen him were moved by his rhetoric of brave sufferance. It was as if he embodied an objective historical hunger for change.*

*The Non-cooperation campaign granted to Gandhi's creed a moral innocence and political authority—qualities that are conventionally associated with arch-revolutionary struggles that topple the social and political order of the day and empower the meek and the oppressed. This is best reflected in the manner in which the world outside India, tired of war and eager to grasp at hope of any sort, looked on his efforts. Men like Romain Rolland began to see in him a messiah for peace and began to study his method and means closely.*

*As with Gandhi's earlier struggles, both in South Africa and India, actual substantive gains were not nearly equal to the effort expended on them. The politics of boycott gradually petered out and the impetus to self-help that was present in the swadeshi argument did not really lead to a widespread regeneration of national institutions. But sporadic attempts to start national schools and craft workshops, which began during this period, remained loyal to the Gandhian creed for a long time. Peasant anger, roused by the call to not cooperate with the British, became the basis for radical peasant movements that emerged in the decade of the 1930s in parts of the country.*

*Hindu-Muslim unity proved to be both glorious and short-lived and here it must be asked if the Khilafat was indeed a durable basis on which to erect it. For one, it was supported largely by a section of the conservative Muslim clergy, and historical research into the Khilafat years has pointed out that large sections of the Muslim community in India were indifferent to this so-called crisis in Islam. Besides, Gandhi's appeal to a healing and connecting faith, while moving, did not really help constitute that heart-unity that he desired. Heart-unity floundered on the rocks of structured inequities. For instance, the Hindu-Muslim violence in Kerala was closely linked to issues of land, labour and servitude. In other parts of the country, in the Punjab, for instance,*

Muslim anger was vented largely at a class of Hindu moneylenders and traders. These contingent reasons remained intact in spite of appeals to faith and love.

Gandhi however was inclined to trust his own peculiar ecumenism : he granted to faith-induced love and generosity a social and moral authority which he refused to grant to modern versions of comradeship and justice. The latter, resting as they did, on rights and obligations that derived from the respect and equality civic persons granted each other and which were affirmed by legal arrangements, did not engage or excite his imagination. Hence he did not pay heed to the inequities which made it easy for hatred and mistrust to assume the violent forms that they did. Nor did he contemplate measures that would redress these inequities. He held that spiritual comradeship, founded on mutual respect, could transcend inequities and prejudices, however intractable these might be.

There were other inherent problems in the rhetoric of faith that Gandhi deployed. It possessed an ideological residue that stained his thought: he entreated Hindus to cultivate courage in the face of Muslim aggression, such as there was. Muslims in turn were asked to respect Hindu sentiments in certain instances, as with the cow, and to eschew their own partisanship, which Gandhi argued was inimical to the spirit of Islam. This argument assumed that Hindus were timid and that Muslims were habitually bullies. Such condescension derived from notions of Hindu and Muslim 'characters' inherited from English and nationalist historiography, and must have appeared galling to sensitive e and thinking Muslims. Yet it was also true that Gandhi's felt compassion for and interest in a faith not his own did override the claims of a received commonsense.

The years spent rousing people into non-violent Non-cooperation, however, were not wasted years. They instilled in large numbers of people the faith that the greater common good depended on them, as individuals and as moral actors whose choices could prove decisive. Significantly, Non-cooperation helped to expand the Indian National Congress' political constituency and laid the basis for its eventual emergence as the party of Indian independence.

# Chapter 4

## Truth Wars on the Seashore: Satyagraha and Salt
## 1925-1932

*In the years following Non-cooperation (1925-28), Gandhi turned his attention to less directly political matters. Khilafat lost its relevance, as Turkey became a republic. In India, Hindu-Muslim unity appeared a difficult and infinitely complex task and Gandhi, unhappy with the constant rioting of the mid-1920s, felt acutely powerless. He was also disenchanted with the political turn in the Indian National Congress. A significant section of its leadership did not wish to oppose government but, instead, desired to cooperate with it. Several leaders wished to contest elections and become members of the British-controlled legislative councils. So, from 1925-1928 Gandhi decided to experiment with constructive work: the task of re-building Indian social and economic life, through the setting up of spinning cooperatives, working at persuading people to regard untouchability as a sin and leading a simple, restrained and celibate existence.*

*The years that Gandhi spent wandering in the Indian hinterland were difficult ones for the country. Widespread peasant unrest during the Non-cooperation years had settled into a sullen restiveness. Strikes in cities, endemic in the early 1920s, led to the growth of the Indian left. Young people, attracted to socialism, as well as a disaffected proletariat came to view the communists as their natural leaders. The appeal of the left grew in the early 1930s, especially in the post-Depression years, when the links between colonial rule and economic ruin appeared all too clear.*

*Political militancy which in previous years had expressed itself with a characteristic religious ferocity, now, assumed a sharp critical edge, The Hindustan Socialist Republican Army of Bhagat Singh, a young revolutionary from the Punjab, represented the new spirit. It spoke the language of socialism and its anti-colonial anger expended itself in and through political violence directed against hated British officers and administrators. There were other developments as well. Campaigns and struggles for social justice, dignity and self-respect emerged in the south and west of India, as lower castes and untouchables formed organizations to counter the unjust hierarchies of the caste system. Determined to gain equality in all spheres, these groups did not wish to wait on upper caste goodwill to earn what was due to them. Instead, they were committed to wresting their rights through the law and a politics of persuasion and argument in civil society.*

*The Hindu-Muslim tangle acquired a further dimension during this period. The Muslim League, founded in 1907 (it had lain dormant in the Khilafat days, when the excitement of unity neutralised the appeal of partisan parties), became the premier political organization of Muslims, who were increasingly disenchanted with the Indian National Congress. While stating that it wished to make substantial concessions to Muslim political interests, the Congress did very little in practice. This angered prominent Muslims who had supported that party until then. They had other reasons to doubt the Congress' commitment to Muslim interests. Hindu conservative opinion, avowedly partisan and decidedly right-wing, was gaining favour with a section of the Congress, and Muslims were uneasy over this development.*

*This changed historical conjuncture worried Gandhi: he was truly alarmed at the rhetoric of just violence, made so attractive by the heroism of the young Bhagat Singh. He wondered what it held in store for the cause of non-violent social and political change. The growing popularity of the left challenged his mode of struggle. Their anti-capitalist reasoning and sustained opposition to the ways of Indian and English employers militated against his own notion of peaceful cooperation between the owners of capital and workers. Anti-caste ideologies and practice proved no less disquieting. For one, they demanded a complete overthrow of the existing social order. Secondly, they did not think the imperatives of the anti-colonial struggle ought to precede and determine the manner in which all other justice-related issues were transacted. Gandhi found these arguments untenable, desiring, as he did, a change of heart above all else, and reluctant, as he was, to work through the contradictions that beset Hindu caste society, before a majority of its members were ready for reform. Hindu-Muslim tensions hurt him, but he preferred not to engage with them, as he had done earlier. Instead, he chose to trust the decisions of the Congress in this instance, though he remained critical of Hindu right-wing ideologues, both within Congress and outside of it.*

*More specifically, Gandhi's responses to the historical moment were two-fold : on the one hand, he spoke out and argued against political militancy and the cult of violence, as he referred to it. On the other hand, he turned to the Congress to resolve matters of political and social concern—especially those which had caused the emergence of the Indian left. The Congress, for its part, adopted a cautious policy. Those who had opted for cooperation with the colonial government had got themselves elected to the local councils and were naturally reluctant to undertake tasks that would upset their delicate political calculations. Those who were at large in the world outside did win Gandhi a few victories, through, for example, carefully controlled peasant struggles that proved the salience of non-violent resistance.*

*In 1928 the Congress was forced to adopt a more strident anti-colonial position. This was largely due to the impetus provided to that party by the charismatic Jawaharlal Nehru and the outspoken Subash Chandra Bose. During this period, the Congress was also forced into reviewing its relationship with the government, since the latter had decided to embark on a further set of political reforms without consulting its leadership.*

*Gandhi welcomed these developments, though reluctantly. He insisted that the pace of the anti-colonial struggle ought not to follow rapid flights of political rhetoric and should instead heed controlled action. He accepted that perhaps the time had come for Indian nationalists to demand complete independence instead of dominion status (which preserved their links to Empire), but this demand could only be made after the English had been given a chance to prove their honourable intentions towards their subjects.*

*As had happened in South Africa, and more recently in the instance of Non-cooperation, Gandhi's considerate and gallant gesture to India's* rulers was ill-recompensed. Gandhi then decided that the time had come to prove to India's rulers and the world at large that Indians would stand up for their rights, but non-violently. His resolve led to one of the most spectacular political resistance campaigns in nationalist history—the salt satyagraha. The end of this campaign proved no less dramatic, for Gandhi was invited to parley with the Viceroy, Lord Irwin. The significance of this invitation lay in the fact that the colonial government had called him to confer with them, not as a subject, but as a peer. The slur of secondary citizenship was, for the time being at least, removed.

Gandhi's pact with the Viceroy required him to journey to London to participate in a round table conference on a future political constitution for India. His London visit proved tiring as well as exciting. The round table conference taxed his faith in his creed. But he found time and space to expound his beliefs in several forums in London, and elsewhere in Europe.

Eventually, the round table conference raised more problems than it addressed, and with several matters unresolved, Gandhi returned to India to find Congressmen in prison. The government had turned repressive, effectively turning its back on the promises contained in the Gandhi-Irwin pact. Gandhi protested and was himself arrested (1933). In prison, he began, what appeared to him a dogged and astonishing war against caste Hindu society—a non-violent war for their hearts.

## Answering Violence

*In the years following the suspension of Non-cooperation (1924-25), Gandhi found himself having to answer questions about the viability of satyagraha and the undeniable attractions of political militancy. Though he did not concern himself with political questions in the years that followed (1926-27), he continued to respond to events and queries that raised questions about non-violence. He returned to an active political life in 1928, a period that saw protests against the Commission, headed by Sir John Simon (or the Simon Commission as it was called) to decide on future political reforms for India. The Commission did not include Indian representatives and Indian nationalists were incensed that they should be kept out of these discussions. They decided, therefore, to boycott the Commission's hearings. The boycott was immensely successful and, further, witnessed Hindus and Muslims uniting to make it succeed.*

*Gandhi did not concern himself with either the Commission or its efforts, except to support the Congress in its decisions. He was not entirely pleased, though, with Congress developments . The tenacious anti-colonial arguments put forth by Jawaharlal Nehru and Subash Bose (in 1928) did not move him, though he was forced to concede that given the general indifference of colonial government to nationalist demands, the Congress had to define for itself a new ideal. Rather reluctantly, he came to endorse the demand for complete independence or purna swaraj, but he was insistent that independence should encompass social goals and not merely political objectives. Significantly, he endorsed the Congress' position on Hindu-Muslim matters, which did not fulfil Muslim political aspirations. The steady and creeping influence of Hindu conservative opinion on the Congress was all too visible, but Gandhi trusted it to act wisely and therefore chose to abide by its decisions.*

*In any case, his moral concerns during this period of his life were directed elsewhere—towards the problems and challenges posed by political militancy. Thus, much of his creative efforts were expended in answering the proponents of violent political action. He wrote not only of actual, physical aggression, but also of forcible dispossession of the rich, which appeared to him to lie at the heart of all socialist strategies for a new world.*

*The extracts in this section present his thoughts on political terror and its implications, his understanding of political suffering and arguments for non-violence in a conjuncture that favoured militancy.*

---

*In the wake of the Chauri Chaura violence, Gandhi had to account for the failure of satyagraha and answer the claims of those who favoured action that was more spontaneous and energetic.*

## My Friend the Revolutionary

The revolutionary whom I endeavoured to answer some time ago ... seems to me to be seeking light, even as I am, and argues fairly and without much passion. So long as he continues to reason calmly, I promise to continue the discussion.

His first question is:

... Can you be bold, nay, arrogant enough to deny it in the face of historical facts that the revolutionaries have sacrificed more for their country than any other party which professes of serve India? You are ready to make compromises with other parties, while you abhor our party and describe the[ir] sentiments as poison. Will you not tremble to use the same word of intolerance for the sentiments of any other party which is decidedly inferior in the eyes of God and men to us? What makes you shrink from calling them misguided patriots or venomous reptiles?

I do not regard the revolutionaries of India to be less sacrificing, less noble or less lovers of their country than the rest. But I respectfully contend that their sacrifice, nobility and love are not only a waste of effort, but being ignorant and misguided, do and have done more harm to the country than any other activity. For, the revolutionaries have retarded the progress of the country. Their reckless disregard of the lives of their opponents has brought on repression that has made those that do not take part in their warfare more cowardly than they were before. Repression does good only to those who are prepared for it. The masses are not prepared for the repression that follows in the trail of revolutionary activities and unwittingly strengthen the hands of the very government which the revolutionaries are seeking to destroy. It is my certain conviction that had the Chauri Chaura murders not taken place the movement attempted at Bardoli (*the satyagraha planned in 1922 - ed.*) would have resulted in the establishment of *swaraj*. Is it, therefore, any wonder that, with such opinion I call the revolutionary a misguided and therefore, dangerous patriot?

... I do make certain compromises with the other parties because, though I disagree with them, I do not regard their activities as positively harmful and dangerous as I regard the revolutionaries'. I have never called the revolutionaries "venomous reptiles". But I must refuse to fall into hysterics over their sacrifices, however great they may be. ... There is no necessary charm about death on the gallows; often such death is easier than a life of drudgery and toil in malarious tracts. ... I suggest to my friend, the revolutionary, that death on the gallows serves the country only when the victim is a "spotless lamb".

" India's path is not Europe's." Do you really believe it? Do you mean to say that warfare and organization of army was not in existence in India, before she came in contact with Europe? Warfare for fair cause—Is it against the spirit of India? *Vinashaya cha dushkritam (to destroy evil, a phrase from the Bhagavad Gita, in which Krishna declares that he as an incarnation of God is bent on destroying evil - ed.)*—Is it something imported from Europe? Granted that it is, will you be fanatic enough not to take from Europe what is good? Do you believe that nothing good is possible in Europe? ...

I do not deny that India had armies, warfare, etc., before she came in contact with Europe. But I do say that it never was the normal course of Indian life. The masses, unlike those of Europe were untouched by the warlike spirits. I have already said in these pages that I ascribe to the *Gita*, from which the writer has quoted the celebrated verse, a totally different meaning from that ordinarily given. I do not regard it as a description of, or an exhortation to, physical warfare (*During these years, Gandhi worked on an exegesis of the Bhagavad Gita which went against the grain of received opinion. He held that the book did not counsel war, only duty - ed.*) And, in any case, according to the verse quoted it is God the All Knowing

Who descends to the earth to punish the wicked. I must be pardoned if I refuse to regard every revolutionary as an all-knowing God or an avatar. I do not condemn everything European. But I condemn, for all climes and for all times, secret murders and unfair methods even for a fair cause.

... Don't you think that armed and conspired resistance against something satanic and ignoble is infinitely more befitting for any nation, especially Indian, than the prevalence of effortlessness and philosophical cowardice? I mean the cowardice which is pervading the length and breadth of Indian owing to the preaching of your theory of non-violence or more correctly the wrong interpretation and misuse of it. ... We want to produce such men in India, who will not shrink from death—whenever it may come and in whatever form—will do the good and die ...

... Armed conspiracies against something satanic is like matching satans against Satan. But since one Satan is one too many for me, I would not multiply him. ... Cowardice, whether philosophical or otherwise, I abhor. And if I could be persuaded that revolutionary activity has dispelled cowardice, it will go a long way to soften my abhorrence of the method, however much I may still oppose it on principle. But he who runs may see that owing to the non-violent movement, the villagers have assumed a boldness to which only a few years ago they were strangers. I admit that non-violence is a weapon essentially of the strong. I also admit that often cowardice is mistaken for non-violence.

My friend begs the question when he says a revolutionary is one who "does the good and dies". That is precisely what I question. In my opinion, he does the evil and dies. I do not regard killing or assassination or terrorism as good in any circumstances whatsoever. I do believe that ideas ripen quickly when nourished by the blood of martyrs. But a man who dies slowly of jungle fever in service bleeds as certainly as the one on the gallows. And if the one who dies on the gallows is not innocent of another's blood, he never had ideas that deserved to ripen.

... Last of all, I shall ask you to answer these questions: Was Guru Govind Singh (*a Sikh religious leader who took up arms - ed.*) a misguided patriot because he believed in warfare for noble cause? What will you like to say about

Washington, Garibaldi and Lenin (*men who did not rule out a role for violence in the transformation of society - ed.*)? What do you think of Kamal Pasha and De Valera (*Turkish and Irish national leaders respectively - ed.*)? Would you like to call Shivaji and Pratap (*heroic leaders from India's past - ed.*), well-meaning and sacrificing physicians who prescribed arsenic when they should have given fresh grape-juice? Will you like to call Krishna (*the God Krishna - ed.*) Europeanized because he believed also in the vinasha of dushkritas *(the destruction of evil - ed.*)?

This is a hard or rather awkward question. But I dare not shirk it. In the first instance Guru Govind Singh and the others whose names are mentioned did not believe in secret murder. These patriots knew their work and their men, whereas the modern Indian revolutionary does not know his work. He has not the men, he has not the atmosphere, that the patriots mentioned had. Though my views are derived from my theory of life I have not put them before the nation on that ground. I have based my opposition to the revolutionaries on the sole ground of expedience. Therefore, to compare their activities with those of Guru Govind Singh or Washington or Garibaldi or Lenin would be most misleading and dangerous.

But by test of the theory of non-violence, I do not hesitate to say that it is highly likely that had I lived as their contemporary and in the respective countries, I would have called everyone of them a misguided patriot, even though a successful and brave warrior. As it is, I must not judge them. I disbelieve history so far as details of acts of heroes are concerned. I accept broad facts of history and draw my own lessons or my conduct. I do not want to repeat it in so far as the broad facts contradict the highest laws of life. But I positively refuse to judge men from the scanty material furnished to us by history. ... Kamal Pasha and De Valera too I cannot judge. But for me, as a believer in non-violence out and out they cannot be my guides in life in so far as their faith in war is concerned.

I believe in Krishna perhaps more than the writer. But my Krishna is the Lord of the universe, the creator, preserver and destroyer of us all. He may destroy because He creates. But I must not be drawn into a philosophical or religious argument with my friends. I have not the qualifications for teaching my philosophy of life. I have barely qualifications for practising the philosophy I believe. I am but a poor struggling soul yearning to be wholly good—wholly truthful and wholly non-violent in thought, word and deed, but ever failing to reach the ideal which I know to be true. I admit, and assure my revolutionary friends, it is a painful climb but the pain of it is a positive pleasure for me. Each step upward makes me feel stronger and fit for the next. But all that pain and the pleasure are for me. ...

*Young India*, 9-4-1925 (31: 137-42)

---

*This address was delivered in Bengal, home to many famed political militants. Gandhi argued that those who wished to transform society ought to turn away from violence and engage in patient constructive work, such as spinning, which, in turn, would nurture and strengthen the inner life of individuals and communities. He would repeat his advice elsewhere too in the years that he travelled the length and breadth of the subcontinent.*

## Speech at Public Meeting, Chittagong
## May 12, 1925

... I could not fight my wife with violence, I could not fight my brothers with violence, I refuse to fight the Mussalmans with violence and I dare not fight the Hindus, some of whom are opposing me on the question of untouchability, with violence. I, therefore, deduce from that fund of experience that I cannot fight Englishmen with violence. You have seen in one of my writings that I have converted more Englishmen to love India than any single one of the present generation. I know it is a large claim, it is a proud claim, but it is the claim of the humble man, who has put forth that claim in all humility. I feel, if we are to fight our battle non-violently it will not be by mere words. Non-violence must be expressed in action. Action without intermission, without rest, without recreation, without the slightest pause, with continuous determination—action with the fullest faith in its efficacy is the only remedy for India and the only remedy that I can place in the hands of those little girls and boys, in the hands of the grownup people, in the hands of poets and philosophers, in the hands of sannyasins, politicians, learned professors and sweepers, in the hands of women and in the hands of robust men.

The only universal remedy I can discover today is the spinning-wheel. Multiply the force of this charkha and spin until it is done by 3 hundred millions of men and then tell me what its power will be, tell me then what it will not do. Is there nothing that we can claim to our credit? Throughout all this long, dreary forty years of political life, we have not been able to show to the world one simple action done to perfection and to fulfilment. We have placed before ourselves many programmes, I place before the nation only one programme and ask the nation to fulfil that programme before it can dare think of any other. Is it an impossible programme that you and I should wear nothing but khaddar (*handspun cloth - ed.*) , although it may be costly? It may be coarse. If it is costly, than, tear it into half and do cover your nakedness with half the cloth and it will go to your credit in the book of life. If it is coarse, then, for the sake of India, you will wear coarse cloth. Understand that the slavery of India is coarser than the coarsest khaddar, understand that the pauperism of India is infinitely coarser than the coarsest khaddar that can be produced in Chittagong. If you have heart to think for famishing millions of India, if you have heart to spin, then spin till your hands are paralysed and wear khaddar till you perspire in the coarsest khadi and then you will find that the *swaraj* of my dream—and of your dream—will break forth in the horizon and then you will dance in joy.

*Amrita Bazar Patrika,* 15-5-1925 (31:330-31)

---

*Gandhi's advocacy of non-violence at a time of great unrest appeared to some as an invitation to a quiescent life and some of his followers and critics urged him to consider what seemed to them—and were— matters of greater importance.*

### Patriot's Wail
### December 27, 1925

A friend has thus unbosomed himself:

In your weeklies you write nothing about the agriculturists, who form the bulk of the population of India. In most parts of India the agriculturist is a mere tenant, at the mercy of the zemindar, and dragging on a miserable existence. Don't you think these zemindars and talukdars are a pest in the country? Can't we solve the problem by dispossessing these zemindars and distributing their land among the poor?

I have boiled down a very long letter which, though rambling, is the cry of an agonized soul. have not been writing much about the agriculturists advisedly. For I know that it is impossible for us to do anything for them today. There are a thousand and one things that need to be done for the amelioration of the lot of the agriculturists. But so long as the reins of Government are not in the hands of the agriculturists' representatives, i.e., so long as we have no *swaraj— dharmaraj*—that amelioration is very difficult if not impossible. I know that the peasant is dragging a miserable existence and hardly gets even a scanty meal a day. That is why I have suggested the revival of the spinning-wheel.

... We may not forcibly dispossess the zemindars and talukdars, of their thousands of *bighas.* And among whom shall we distribute them? We need not dispossess them. They only need a change of the heart. When that is done, and when they learn to melt at their tenants' woe, they will hold their lands in trust for them, will give them a major part of the produce, keeping only sufficient for themselves. "We had better wait for that day until the Greek Calends," someone will say. I do not think so. I think that the world is moving towards peace, i.e., *ahimsa.* The way of violence has been tried for ages and has been found wanting. Let no one believe that the people in Russia, Italy and other countries are happy or are independent. The sword of Damocles is always hanging over their heads. Those who have the good of the Indian agriculturists at heart must pin their faith on non-violence and plod on. Those who think of other methods are vainly flattering themselves with hope of success.

What I have said above applies equally to the *sowkar* (*merchant moneylender - ed.*)and other exploiters. Nothing but their own profit appeals to them. But there too the remedy is the moral education of both. The oppressed need no other education, except in satyagraha and Non-cooperation. A slave is a slave because he consents to slavery. If training in physical resistance is possible, why should that in spiritual resistance be impossible? If we know the use of the body, why can we not know the use and power of the soul? ...

*Young India,* 4-2-1926 (33: 354-55)

---

*Gandhi was sensitive to the general mood of anger and discontent that prevailed in the mid and late 1920s, especially with regard to government repression of political prisoners. Still, he refused to counsel direct political action; instead he held that suffering for one's cause represented the highest form of protest against political Satanism.*

### Political Prisoners

... Time was when I used to analyse these cases and expose the injustice done in many of them. But that was when I had faith in the British system and when I used to take pride in its ultimate goodness. Having lost that faith, I have lost also the power of making an effective appeal to the administrators of that system. I can no longer write about British fair play and the British sense of justice. On the contrary, I feel that the administrators are precluded by their system from dealing out fair play or justice when their system is or seems to them to be in jeopardy. It is still possible, I admit, to secure justice from them when their system is not at stake in any shape or form. But when that system is or is felt by them to be in danger they lose not only their sense of justice and fair play but they lose their balance and no means appear to them to be too dishonourable or despicable for adoption to sustain it ...

... I am satisfied that the political prisoners who are held under restraint with or without trial, decorous or farcical, are so held in the interest of that system. The administrators would far rather discharge a murderer caught red-handed and found guilty of murder committed for private ends than discharge a political prisoner suspected of designs on their system, especially if he, the suspect, is believed to have violent means in view. It seems to me therefore to be waste of time and inconsistent with respect to make any appeal to the administrators in behalf of the political prisoners ...

... Let those who still have faith in the system by all means make an appeal to the British sense of justice and fair play. My course is clear. We have not yet paid anything like adequate price for the freedom we would fain breathe. I therefore regard these imprisonments as only a small part of the price we have to pay if we would have the freedom which is the birthright of man. And we shall have to march as willing victims to the slaughter-house and not helplessly like goats and sheep. We may do this violently or non-violently. The way of violence can only lead us to a blind alley and must cause endless suffering to unwilling ignorant men and women who do not know what freedom is and who have no desire to buy the valuable article. The way of non-violence is the surest and the quickest way to freedom and causes the least suffering and that only to those who are prepared for it, indeed would gladly court it. But suffering, intense, extensive and agonizing, there must be in every case. What we have gone through is but a sample of what is to come.

Therefore the task before those, who share my views about the inherent evil of the system, is to cease to appeal to the administrators, and ceaselessly and with unquenchable faith in our cause and the means to appeal to the nation. Not until the nation has developed enough strength to open the prison gates, can these prisoners be released with honour and dignity for it and them. Till then let us with becoming patience and courage submit to the imprisonment of the prisoners and ourselves prepare joyfully to share their fate. We shall certainly not hasten the advent of freedom by appealing to deaf ears for mercy and thus unconsciously inducing in the people a mentality that would dread the prisons and the gallows. Lovers of freedom have to learn to regard these as welcome friends and deliverers.

*Young India*, 29-12-1927 (41: 69-71)

---

*The Simon Commission, constituted to decide on future political reforms for India, arrived in 1927. It comprised only English members and did not include Indian representatives. Its arrival, therefore, was greeted with black flags and anger. The police had to intervene to disperse the protesting crowds and, in the course of one such intervention, Lala Lajpat Rai, the famous Punjab nationalist leader, was attacked. Gandhi held that such suffering as had been inflicted on Lajpat Rai was a victory for non-violence.*

## The Inevitable

... When ... I read the headline "Lalaji assaulted" and discovered how and why, I could not help saying: "Well done! Now we shall not be long getting *swaraj*." For whether the revolution is non-violent or violent, there is no doubt about it that before we come to our own, we shall have to learn the art of dying in the country's cause. Authority will not yield without a tremendous effort even to non-violent pressure. Under an ideal and complete non-violence, I can imagine full transformation of authority to be possible. But whilst an ideally perfect programme is possible its full execution is never possible. It is therefore the most economical thing that leaders get assaulted or shot. Hitherto obscure people have been assaulted or done to death. The assault on Lala Lajpat Rai has attracted far greater attention than even the shooting of a few men could have.

The assault on Lalaji and other leaders has set the politically-minded India athinking and it must have perturbed the Government. I am loath to think that the local Government as a body knew anything of the contemplated assault. If they did and the assault was part of a deliberate plan as in the days of yore, it is so much the worse for the Government. Then of course the Government can only pretend perturbation. I would not mention such a possibility in ordinary circumstances, but holding the view that I do about the Government—the view being based on experience —whilst I should be sorry, it would not surprise me if a discovery was made that the assault was part of a deliberate plan. I admit, that the provocation, viz., the very fact of the boycott, no matter how peaceful, was quite enough without the fraudulent story concocted by the police. I call the police version fraudulent because I would any day trust Lalaji's word against a host of interested witnesses that the police can bring to its assistance.

If I was not convinced that this system of Government is based on force and fraud, I should not have become the confirmed non-co-operator that I am. Indeed Lowes Dickinson in his essay "War,

Its Causes and Cure" has shown from sufficient evidence that a war cannot be conducted without fraud. *Pari passu* this Government of ours which professes to hold India by the sword and whose foundations were laid in fraud cannot be sustained without either, except when it undergoes transformation and is based upon popular will and confidence. Nor are we to think that the Punjab incident is to be the last of the barbarities committed during the pendency of the Statutory Commission. The boycott of the Simon Commission is a continuing sore for the Commission and the Government. Sir John Simon and his colleagues cannot be contemplating this boycott with equanimity. They have not the courage to acknowledge defeat. The boycott itself has been given additional momentum by the unprovoked assault on the Punjab leaders. The Government will therefore feel itself bound to suppress the boycott by any means that it can command. The Punjab incident therefore I regard as the first trial of strength, the strength of non-violence against violence ...

*Young India*, 8-11-1928 (43: 199-201)

---

*Lajpat Rai died a few days after being assaulted by the police. His death caused great popular anger. Bhagat Singh, of the Hindustan Socialist Republican Army, decided to avenge the death of the famed and old leader and assassinated the police officer ostensibly responsible for the attack on Lajpat Rai. Gandhi decried this and other instances of retaliatory violence.*

## Curse of Assassination

The assassination of the Assistant Superintendent Mr. Saunders of Lahore was a dastardly act apart from whether it had a political motive behind it or not. Violence being in the air, there will no doubt be silent and secret approbation of the act, especially if it is discovered to have had any connection with the assault on Lalaji and his utterly innocent comrades. The provocation was great and it became doubly great by the death of Lalaji which was certainly hastened by the nervous shock received by him from the disgraceful conduct of the police. Some will insist, not without considerable justification, on ascribing the death even to the physical effect of the injury received by the deceased in the region of the heart. The provocation received also additional strength from the Punjab Government's defence of the police conduct. I should not wonder if the assassination proves to be in revenge of the high-handed policy of the Punjab Government.

I wish however that it was possible to convince the hot youth of the utter futility of such revenge. Whatever the Assistant Superintendent did was done in obedience to instructions. No one person can be held wholly responsible for the assault and the aftermath. The fault is that of the system of Government. What requires mending is not men but the system. And when the youth of the country have the real determination they will find that it is in their power as it is in nobody else's to kill the system. English books have taught us to applaud as heroic deeds of daring, even of freebooters, villains, pirates and train-wreckers. Newspapers fill columns with exciting stories real or, in their absence, imaginary, of such deeds. Some of us have successfully learnt this art of applauding as heroic anything adventurous irrespective of the motives or contemplated results behind such deeds. This cannot be regarded as anything but a bad omen. Surely there is nothing heroic about a cold-blooded robbery accompanied by murder of an innocent wealthy pilgrim carrying treasures for distribution in well-conceived charity. There is equally none in the deliberate secret assassination of an innocent police officer who has discharged his duty however disagreeable its consequences may be for the community to which the assassin belongs.

Let us remember that the administrators of the system have held on to the system in spite of previous assassinations. After all the story of the building of the British Empire is not itself wanting in deeds of valour, adventure and sacrifice worthy, in my opinion, of a better cause. If we may regard the assassination of Mr. Saunders as a heroic deed the British people would be able to answer this one, I hope, solitary act of so-called heroism with countless such acts enough to fill a volume. But it is time we began irrespective of nationalities to regard deeds with mean motives or meaner consequences with nothing but horror, indignation and disapprobation, no matter how daring they may be. I know that this means a new valuation of such terms as heroism, patriotism, religiousness and the like.

... Islam is not better for the assassination of so many Caliphs or, to take a modern instance, for the assassination of the late Swami Shraddhanandji (*a Nationalist leader and member of the Hindu revivalist Arya Samaj was murdered by a young Muslim man - ed.*). Nor has Hinduism been ennobled by the frenzied deeds one occasionally reads about of so-called protectors of the cow. The curse of assassination and kindred crimes is not advancing the progress to humanity, religion or true civilization. Let the youth of India realize that the death of Lalaji can only be avenged by regaining her freedom. Freedom of a nation cannot be won by solitary acts of heroism even though they may be of the true type, never by heroism so-called. The temple of freedom requires the patient, intelligent, and constructive effort of tens of thousands of men and women, young and old. Acts such as we are deploring decidedly retard the progress of this quiet building. When it does nothing else, it diverts the attentions of countless builders.

*Young India*, 27-12-1928 (43: 446 –47)

---

### The Bomb and the Knife

At the back of the bomb thrown in the Assembly by men bearing Hindu names (*ostensibly followers of Bhagat Singh - ed.*) and the knife of Rajpal's (*an Arya Samaj nationalist with prejudices against Muslims - ed.*) assassin bearing a Muslim name runs the same philosophy of mad revenge and impotent rage. The bomb-throwers have discredited the cause of freedom in whose name they threw the bombs; the user of the knife has discredited Islam in whose name the perpetrator did the mad deed. The Government would be foolish if they become nervous and resort to counter madness. If they are wise, they will perceive that they are in no small measure to blame for the madness of the bomb-thrower. By their indifference to popular feeling they are exasperating the nation and the exasperation is bound to lead some astray. Congressmen whose creed is non-violence will do well not to give even secret approval to the deed but pursue their method with redoubled vigour, if they have real faith in it. Rajpal's assassination has given him a martyrdom and a name which he did not deserve. He had made full reparation in regard to his pamphlet (*against Muslims - ed.*) . He had also already suffered for it. The assassination has brought him posthumous renown.

I tender the members of the martyr's family my condolences and hope that neither they nor the Arya Samajists will harbour any ill will against the Mussalmans because of the deed of one mad man amongst them. The assassin will, I expect, in due course pay the last penalty for his deed. It is to be fervently hoped that there will not be a repetition of the sorry scenes one witnessed over the funeral of Abdul Rashid (*the man who killed the Arya Samaj leader, Swami Shraddhanand - ed.*).

Of course the bomb and the knife derive their lease of life from the world's belief in violence as a remedy for securing supposed justice. Organized destruction is no less immoral because it is not a crime in the penal code of nations. The insensate speed with which the nations of the West are hourly forging new weapons of destruction for purposes of war is suffocating the world with the spirit of violence. Little wonder if hot-heads of all nations and all faiths should overstep the limits of the penal code even at the risk of their lives. The bomb-thrower and the assassin will live on so long as public opinion of the world tolerates war. But they can always be kept under check if local opinion does not approve of or tolerate their activity.

The bomb is more easily dealt with than the knife. The bomb has no *milieu* in India. The Government can stop it today if they choose, not by frightfulness but by conceding the national demand gracefully and in time. But that is hoping against hope. For the Government to do so would be a change of heart, not merely of policy. And there is nothing on the horizon to warrant the hope that any such change is imminent. The hope therefore lies really in the nation, in the Congressmen. In my wanderings I have sensed no belief amongst national workers in methods of violence. I have however missed a living faith in the method of non-violence, I have felt even a want of faith in it. An atmosphere of despair undoubtedly pervades the air. This demoralizing uncertainty disables workers from appreciating to the full the programme prescribed by the National Congress. They do not see that if non-violence is to express itself in national activities for attainment of freedom, the Congress programme is the natural and inevitable outcome. We can to a great extent checkmate the bomb-thrower, if we would have faith in our own programme and work for it.

*Young India*, 18-4-1929 (45: 363-64)

---

*Gandhi's disquiet over violence was only matched by his willingness to explore the various implications of non-violence: the importance of dialogue, and its corollary, civil disagreement. This was most evident in the many conversations he had during this period with members of the Christian clergy, such as John Mott, who were astonished by his biblical ardour and bewildered by his resistance to conversion to a creed he obviously respected.*

### Interview to John Mott
### [Before March 1, 1929]

[DR. MOTT:] What do you consider to be the most valuable contribution that India can make to the progress of the world?

[GANDHIJI:] Non-violence, which the country is exhibiting at the present day on a scale unprecedented in history. But for it, there might have been a blaze, for provocation of the gravest kind has not been wanting on the side of the Government. There is no doubt a school in the country that believes in violence, but it is a mere excrescence on the surface and its ideals are not likely to find a congenial soil in the country.

What causes you solicitude for the future of the country?

Our apathy and hardness of heart, if I may use that Biblical phrase, as typified in the attitude towards the masses and their poverty. Our youth are full of noble feelings and impulses but these have not yet taken any definite practical shape. If our youth had a living and active faith in truth and non-violence, for instance, we should have made much greater headway by now. All our young men, however, are not apathetic. In fact without the closest cooperation of some of our educated young men and women, I should not have been able to establish contact with the masses and to serve them on a nationwide scale; and I am sustained by the hope that they will act as the leaven, and in time transform the entire mass.

From this they passed on to the distinctive contributions of Hinduism, Islam and Christianity to the upbuilding of the Indian nation.

The most distinctive and the largest contribution of Hinduism to India's culture is the doctrine of *ahimsa*. It has given a definite bias to the history of the country for the last three thousand years and over and it has not ceased to be a living force in the lives of India's millions even today. It is a growing doctrine, its message is still being delivered. Its teaching has so far permeated our people that an armed revolution has almost become an impossibility in India, not because, as some would have it, we as a race are physically weak, for it does not require much physical strength so much as a devilish will to press a trigger to shoot a person, but because the tradition of *ahimsa* has struck deep roots among the people.

Islam's distinctive contribution to India's national culture is its unadulterated belief in the oneness of God and a practical application of the truth of the brotherhood of man for those who are nominally within its fold. I call these two distinctive contributions. For in Hinduism the spirit of brotherhood has become too much philosophized. Similarly though philosophical Hinduism has no other god but God, it cannot be denied that practical Hinduism is not so emphatically uncompromising as Islam.

What then is the contribution of Christianity to the national life of India? I mean the influence of Christ as a part from Christianity, for I am afraid there is a wide gulf separating the two at present.

Aye, there's the rub. It is not possible to consider the teaching of a religious teacher apart from the lives of his followers. Unfortunately, Christianity in India has been inextricably mixed up for the last one hundred and fifty years with the British rule. It appears to us as synonymous with materialistic civilization and imperialistic exploitation by the stronger white races of the weaker races of the world. Its contribution to India has been therefore largely of a negative character. It has done some good in spite of its professors. It has shocked us into setting our own house in order. Christian missionary literature has drawn pointed attention to some of our abuses and set us a thinking.

What has interested me most is your work in connection with the removal of untouchability. Will you please tell me what is the most hopeful sign indicating that this institution is as you say on its last legs?

It is the reaction that is taking place in orthodox Hinduism and the swiftness with which it has come about. As a most illustrious example I will mention Pandit Malaviyaji. Ten years back he was as punctilious in the observance of the rules with regard to untouchability as perhaps the most orthodox Hindu of that day. Today he takes pride in administering the *mantra* of purification to the untouchables by the bank of the Ganges, sometimes even incurring the wrath of unreasoning orthodoxy. He was all but assaulted by the diehard section in Calcutta in December last for doing this very thing. In Wardha a wealthy merchant Sheth Jamnalal Bajaj recently threw open his magnificent temple to the untouchables and that without arousing any serious opposition. The most remarkable thing about it is that from the record kept in the temple of the daily visitors it was found that the attendance had gone up instead of declining since the admission of the untouchables to it. I may sum up the outlook by saying that I expect the tide against untouchability to rise still more swiftly in the near future, astonishingly swift as it has already been.

Where do you find your friends? Do you get the backing of the Mussalmans and the Christians in this work?

The Mussalmans and the Christians can from the very nature of the case render little help in this matter. The removal of untouchability is purely a question of the purification of Hinduism. This can only be effected from within.

But my impression was that Christians would be a great help to you in this connection. The Rev. Whitehead, Bishop of the Church of England Mission, made some striking statements about the effect of Christian mass movement in ameliorating the condition of the untouchables in the Madras Presidency.

I distrust mass movements of this nature. They have as their object not the upliftment of the untouchables but their ultimate conversion. This motive of mass proselytization lurking at the back in my opinion vitiates missionary effort.

There are conflicting opinions on this point. There are some who seriously believe that the untouchables would be better off if they turned Christians from conviction, and that it would transform their lives for the better.

I am sorry I have been unable to discover any tangible evidence to confirm this view. I was once taken to a Christian village. Instead of meeting among the converts with that frankness which one associates with a spiritual transformation, I found an air of evasiveness about them. They were afraid to talk. This struck me as a change not for the better but for the worse.

Do you then disbelieve in all conversion?

I disbelieve in the conversion of one person by another. My effort should never be to undermine another's faith but to make him a better follower of his own faith. This implies belief in the truth of all religions and therefore respect for them. It again implies true humility, a recognition of the fact that the divine light having been vouchsafed to all religions through an imperfect medium of flesh, they must share in more or less degree the imperfection of the vehicle.

Is it not our duty to help our fellow-beings to the maximum of truth that we may possess, to share with them our deepest spiritual experiences?

I am sorry I must again differ from you, for the simple reason that the deepest spiritual truths are always unutterable. That light to which you refer transcends speech. It can be felt only through the inner experience. And then the highest truth needs no communicating, for it is by its very nature self-propelling. It radiates its influence silently as the rose its fragrance without the intervention of medium.

But even God sometimes speaks through His prophets.

Yes, but the prophets speak not through the tongue but through their lives. I have however known that in this matter I am up against a solid wall of Christian opinion.

Oh, no, even among Christians there is a school of thought-and it is growing—which holds that the authoritarian method should not be employed but that each individual should be left to discover the deepest truths of life for himself. The argument advanced is that the process of spiritual discovery is bound to vary in the case of different individuals according to their varying needs and temperaments. In other words they feel that propaganda in the accepted sense of the term is not the most effective method.

I am glad to hear you say this. That is what Hinduism certainly inculcates.

What counsel do you give to the young men who are fighting a losing battle with their lower selves and come to you for advice?

Simply prayer. One must humble oneself utterly and look beyond oneself for strength.

But what if the young men complain that their prayer is not heard, that they feel like speaking to brass heavens as it were?

To want an answer to one's prayer is to tempt God. If prayer fails to bring relief it is only lip prayer. If prayer does not help nothing else will. One must go on ceaselessly. This then is my message to the youth. In spite of themselves the youth must believe in the all-conquering power of love and truth. The difficulty with our youth is that the study of science and modern philosophy has demolished their faith and so they are burnt up by the fire of disbelief. That is due to the fact that with them faith is an effort of the intellect, not an experience of the soul. Intellect takes us along in the battle of life to a certain limit but at the crucial moment it fails us. Faith transcends reason. It is when the horizon is the darkest and human reason is beaten down to the ground that faith shines brightest and comes to our rescue. It is such faith that our youth require and this comes when one has shed all pride of intellect and surrendered oneself entirely to His will.

*Young India*, 21-3-1929 (46: 142-50)

*The problem of violence and the way it compromised an individual's search for truth haunted Gandhi in an existential sense as well and he tried hard to wrest meaning out of his agony.*

## Letter to Narandas Gandhi
## July 28/31, 1930

CHI NARANDAS,

... The path of Truth is as narrow as it is straight. Even so is that of *ahimsa*. It is like balancing oneself on the edge of a sword. By concentration an acrobat can walk on a rope. But the concentration required to tread the path of Truth and *ahimsa* is far greater. The slightest inattention brings one tumbling to the ground. One can realize Truth and *ahimsa* only by ceaseless striving. But it is impossible for us to realize perfect truth so long as we are imprisoned in this mortal frame. We can only visualize it in our imagination. We cannot, through the instrumentality of this ephemeral body, see face to face truth which is eternal. That is why in the last resort we must depend on faith.

It appears that the impossibility of full realization of truth in this mortal body led some ancient seeker after truth to the appreciation of *ahimsa*. The question which confronted him was: "Shall I bear with those who create difficulties for me, or shall I destroy them?" The seeker realized that he who went on destroying others did not make headway but simply stayed where he was, while the man who suffered those who created difficulties marched ahead and at times even took the others with him. The first act of destruction taught him that the truth which was the object of his quest was not outside himself but within. Hence the more he took to violence, the more he receded from truth. For in fighting the imagined enemy without, he neglected the enemy within.

We punish thieves because we think they harass us. They may leave us alone; but they will only transfer their attentions to another victim. This other victim, however, is also a human being, ourselves in a different form, and so we are caught in a vicious circle. The trouble from thieves continues to increase, as they think it is their business to steal. In the end we see that it is better to tolerate the thieves than to punish them. The forbearance may even bring them to their senses. By tolerating them we realize that thieves are not different from ourselves, they are our brethren, our friends, and may not be punished. But whilst we may bear with the thieves, we may not endure the infliction. That would only induce cowardice. So we realize a further duty. Since we regard the thieves as our kith and kin, they must be made to realize the kinship. And so we must take pains to devise ways and means of winning them over. This is the path of *ahimsa*. It may entail continuous suffering and the cultivating of endless patience. Given these two conditions, the thief is bound in the end to turn away from his evil ways and we shall get a clearer vision of truth. Thus step by step we learn how to make friends with all the world; we realize the greatness of God, of Truth ...

... *Ahimsa* is not the crude thing it has been made to appear. Not to hurt any living thing is no doubt a part of *ahimsa*. But it is its least expression. The principle of *ahimsa* is hurt by every evil thought, by undue haste, by lying, by hatred, by wishing ill of anybody. It is also violated by our holding on to what the world needs. But the world needs even what we eat day by day. In the place where we stand there are millions of micro-organisms to whom the place belongs and who are hurt by our presence there. What should we do then? Should we commit suicide ? Even that is no solution, if we believe, as we do, that so long as the spirit is attached to the flesh, on every destruction of the body it weaves for itself another. The body will cease to be only when we give up all attachment to it. This freedom from all attachment is the realization of God as Truth. Such realization cannot be attained in a hurry. Realizing that this body does not belong to us, that it is a trust handed over to our charge, we should make the right use of it and progress towards our goal. I wished to write something which would be easy for all to understand, but I find that I have written a difficult discourse. However, no one who has thought even a little about *ahimsa* should find any difficulty in understanding what I have written.

It is perhaps clear from the foregoing that without *ahimsa* it is not possible to seek and find Truth. *Ahimsa* and Truth are so intertwined that it is practically impossible to disentangle and separate them. They are like the two sides of a coin, or rather of a smooth unstamped metallic disc. Who can say which is the obverse and which is the reverse? Nevertheless, *ahimsa* is the means and Truth is the end. Means to be means must always be within our reach, and so *ahimsa* becomes our supreme duty and Truth becomes God for us. If we take care of the means, we are bound to reach the end sooner or later. If we resolve to do this, we shall have won the battle. Whatever difficulties we encounter, whatever apparent reverses we sustain, we should not lose faith but should ever repeat one *mantra:* "Truth exists, it alone exists. It is the only God and there is but one way of realizing it; there is but one means and that is *ahimsa.* I will never give it up. May the God that is Truth, in whose name I have taken this pledge, give me the strength to keep it."

Blessings from
BAPU

From a microfilm of the Gujarati (49: 407-09)

# A Matter of Salt

*Political militancy refused to bow out gracefully from the historical stage, in spite of Gandhi's sustained criticism of its methods and objectives. Labour took to the streets and braved police truncheons and closed factory gates. State repression outgrew opposition to it, and in a generally calamitous decade, this added to the miseries of the poor. The colonial government was obdurate and refused to heed nationalist demands.*

*Looking about for an adequate form of struggle that would focus government ills into a fine and intense point, Gandhi decided to launch satyagraha against what was admittedly a minor ill amongst an entire category of major offences by government—its salt laws. Gandhi, however, had his reasons. For one he had waited for his 'inner voice' to speak to him and it had spoken thus. Secondly, he wanted a movement that would ignite thousands of hearts into fervent and spontaneous action. The call to defy the salt laws was bound to achieve this, for these laws, however minor, affected every man and woman. Salt was not only an item of diet in the Indian kitchen but a symbol of worth and honour.*

*There was yet another dimension to this struggle. Gandhi implored women to step out in hundreds, to test the truth of his campaign. He appealed to their qualities of tolerance, patience and fortitude in the face of suffering and insisted that these were the virtues demanded of every satyagrahi in the present moment. (He also knew that if women were to participate in large numbers, the possibility of violent confrontations with the police, and the proclivity to violent acts would be far less.)*

*Gandhi managed to distil the wrongs experienced by his country men and women into this one small, significant act, as if a fistful of salt showed to the world the infinite and patient suffering of his people. The government had initially been dismissive of what appeared to them an eccentric act. But they had underestimated the moral aura that surrounded Gandhi's public demonstrations of non-violence. The whole world came to know about it, due to the very large presence of foreign newsmen and women at Dandi, the town along the west coast of*

*India that he had chosen as the place where he and his followers would stop and pick up a handful of salt.*

*Along with thousands of others, Gandhi was arrested and interred. Months later, he was called for talks by the Viceroy who had to concede that he had to parley with a peer, and not seek to dictate to a subject. Gandhi, in turn, agreed graciously to open talks with a government whose satanic vices he had denounced with much feeling only a few months earlier. The outcome of the tasks did not satisfy all those who had suffered his cause (and theirs), and once again he found himself explaining, arguing and demanding that people learn not to mistrust their adversary's goodwill.*

*These extracts help us understand the manner in which a momentous historical event in the cause of non-violence was staged and carried through to its triumphant conclusion.*

---

*In 1928-29, the Congress came to adopt a trenchant critique of colonial rule. Advanced by Jawaharlal Nehru, this resulted in a demand for complete independence. The Congress served notice to Empire, demanding that it grant the legitimacy of this goal by the end of 1929, or be prepared to face another round of organized resistance to its rule. Gandhi was asked to take the lead in this struggle-to-be. After much critical thought, he agreed, convinced that civil resistance would not only force the government to act, but also serve as an antidote to violence, which appeared to hold hundreds of militant nationalists in its thrall.*

### To The Indian Critics

... There is undoubtedly a party of violence in the country. It is growing in strength. It is as patriotic as the best among us. What is more, it has much sacrifice to its credit. In daring it is not to be surpassed by any of us. It is easy enough to fling unkind adjectives at its members, but it will not carry conviction with them. I am not now referring to the frothy eloquence that passes muster for patriotism. I have in mind that secret, silent persevering band of young men and even women who want to see their country free at any cost. But whilst I admire and adore their patriotism, I have no faith whatsoever in their method. They and I are as poles asunder. India's salvation does not lie through violence. I am convinced that their methods have cost the country much more than they know or will care to admit. ... But they will listen to no argument however reasonable it may be, unless they are convinced that there is a programme before the country which requires at least as much sacrifice as the tallest among them is prepared to make. They will not be allured by our speeches, resolutions or even conferences. Action alone has any appeal for them. This appeal can only come from non-violent action which is no other than civil resistance. In my opinion it and it alone can save the country from impending lawlessness and secret crime.

That even civil resistance may fail and may also hasten the lawlessness is no doubt a possibility. But if it fails in its purpose, it will not be civil resistance that will have failed. It will fail, if it does, for want of faith and consequent incapacity in the civil resisters. This argument may not appeal to the critic. I shall be sorry, if it does not. Even so, he will perhaps admit the purity of my motive. We must cease to dread violence, if we will have the country to be free. Can we not see that we are tightly pressed in the coil of violence? The peace we seem to prize is a mere makeshift, and it is bought with the blood of the starving millions. If the critics could only realize the torture of their slow and lingering death brought about by forced starvation, they would risk anarchy and worse in order to end that agony. The agony will not end till the existing rule of spoliation has ended.

I would have waited if I could have been convinced that the condition of the masses has undergone progressive amelioration under British rule. Alas, he who runs may see that it has progressively deteriorated under that rule. It is a sin, with that knowledge, to sit supine, and for fear of imaginary anarchy or worse, to stop action that may prevent anarchy, and is bound, if successful, to end the heartless spoliation of a people who have deserved a better fate.

*Young India*, 23-1-1930 (48: 257-58)

---

*In order to persuade public opinion and moderate nationalists to accept his indictment of Empire and the necessity of satyagraha, and to convince militant nationalists that his non-violent resistance actually meant to challenge and provoke British authority, Gandhi adopted a range of arguments.*

## Some Implications

It is clear, that the riches derived from the tillers of the soil are not a voluntary contribution (*to the government - ed.*) or a contribution compelled for their benefit. ... In order that this enormous contribution may be exacted without resistance, violence has been organized by the British Government on a scale unknown before and manipulated in so insidious a manner as not to be easily seen or felt as such. British rule has appeared to me to be a perfect personification of violence. There are snakes that by thievery appearance paralyse their victims. They do not need to make any further demonstration of their power.

... Let us, too, understand how organized violence works and is on that account far more harmful than sporadic, thoughtless, sudden outburst. Ordered violence hides itself often behind camouflage and hypocrisy as we see them working through the declarations of good intentions, commissions, conferences and the like, or even through measures conceived as tending to the public benefit but in reality to the benefit of the wrongdoer. Greed and deceit are often the offspring as they are equally often the parents of violence. Naked violence repels like the naked skeleton shorn of flesh, blood and the velvety skin. It cannot last long. But it persists fairly long when it wears the mask of peace and progress so-called. Such awe-inspiring violence concealed under a "golden lid" begets the violence of the weak which in its turn works secretly and sometimes openly. Non-violence has to work in the midst of this double violence. But if it is the supreme law governing mankind, it must be able to make its way in the face of the heaviest odds.

Violence such as we have to face may well make us cowards utterly unable to discover the method of working non-violence. If therefore the forces of violence arrayed against us cannot be checkmated during our time, it would be no proof of the futility of non-violence, it would certainly be proof of the pervading cowardice. The greatest obstacle in the path of non-violence is the presence in our midst of the indigenous interests that have sprung up from British rule, the interests of monied men, speculators, scrip holders, land-holders, factory owners and the like. All these do not always realize that they are living on the blood of the masses, and when they do, they become as callous as the British principals whose tools and agents they are. If like the Japanese samurai they could but realize that they must give up their blood-stained gains, the battle is won for non-violence. It must not be difficult for them to see that the holding of millions is a crime when millions of their own kith and kin are starving and that therefore they must give up their agency.

No principal has yet been found able to work without faithful agents. But non-violence has to be patient with these as with the British principals. The aim of the non-violent worker must ever be to convert. He may not however wait endlessly. When therefore the limit is reached, he takes risks and conceives plans of active satyagraha which may mean civil disobedience and the like. His patience is never exhausted to the point of giving up his creed. But working in a hostile atmosphere, he runs the risk of forces of violence, which till then were held under check from mutual fear, being let loose through the restraint of such fear being removed. The Government will spread out its red paws in what it will call self-defence, the party of violence may commit the mistake of seeing its chance of coming out in the open.

The non-violent party must then prove its creed by being ground to powder between the two millstones. If there is such a party, all is well for India and the world. My hope and plans are built upon an ever-increasing faith in the existence of that party of true non-violence.

*Young India,* 6-2-1930 (48: 294-96)

---

*Even as he indicted the violence of Empire, Gandhi affirmed his creed, that he would never depart from his chosen path.*

### Never Faileth

... The responsibility devolving on me is the greatest I have ever undertaken. It was irresistible. But all will be well, if it is *ahimsa* that is guiding me. For the seer who knew what he gave to the world has said, "Hate dissolves in the presence of *ahimsa*." The true rendering of the word in English is love or charity. And does not the Bible say:

Love worketh no ill to his neighbour,
Believeth all things,
Hopeth all things,
Never faileth.

Civil disobedience is sometimes a peremptory demand of love. Dangerous it undoubtedly is, but no more than the encircling violence. Civil disobedience is the only non-violent escape from its soul-destroying heat. The danger lies only in one direction, in the outbreak of violence side by the side with civil disobedience. ... The struggle, in freedom's battle, of non-violence against violence, no matter from what quarter the latter comes, must continue till a single representative is left alive. More no man can do, to do less would be tantamount to want of faith.

*Young India*, 20-2-1930 (48: 328)

---

*Before he prepared himself and his followers to defy Empire, Gandhi wrote to the Viceroy, Lord Irwin, urging him to act on the wrongs inflicted on India.*

**Letter to Lord Irwin**
**Satyagraha Ashram, Sabarmati**
**March 2, 1930**

DEAR FRIEND,

... Though I hold the British rule in India to be a curse, I do not, therefore, consider Englishmen in general to be worse than any other people on earth I have the privilege of claiming many Englishmen as dearest friends. Indeed much that I have learnt of the evil of British rule is due to the writings of frank and courageous Englishmen who have not hesitated to tell the unpalatable truth about that rule. And why do I regard the British rule as a curse?

It has impoverished the dumb millions by a system of progressive exploitation and by a ruinously expensive military and civil administration which the country can never afford. It has reduced us politically to serfdom. It has sapped the foundations of our culture. And, by the policy of cruel disarmament, it has degraded us spiritually. Lacking the inward strength, we have been reduced, by all but universal disarmament, to a state bordering on cowardly helplessness ...

...Nevertheless, if India is to live as a nation, if the slow death by starvation of her people is to stop, some remedy must be found for immediate relief. The proposed Conference (*the round table conference which the officials of Empire wished to convene - ed.*) is certainly not the remedy. It is not a matter of carrying conviction by argument. The matter resolves itself into one of matching forces. Conviction or no conviction, Great Britain would defend her Indian commerce and interests by all the forces at her command. ... India must consequently evolve force enough to free herself from that embrace of death. It is common cause that, however disorganized and, for the time being, insignificant it may be, the party of violence is gaining ground and making itself felt. Its end is the same as mine. But I am convinced that it cannot bring the desired relief to the dumb millions. And the conviction is growing deeper and deeper in me that nothing but unadulterated non-violence can check the organized violence of the British Government. Many think that non-violence is not an active force. My experience, limited though it undoubtedly is, shows that non-violence can be an intensely active force. It is my purpose to set in motion that force as well against the organized violent force of the British rule as [against] the unorganized violent force of the growing party of violence. To sit still would be to give rein to both the forces above mentioned. Having an unquestioning and immovable faith in the efficacy of non-violence as I know it, it would be sinful on my part to wait any longer.

This non-violence will be expressed through civil disobedience, for the moment confined to the inmates of the satyagraha Ashram, but ultimately designed to cover all those who choose to join the movement with its obvious limitations. I know that in embarking on non-violence I shall be running what might fairly be termed a mad risk. The victories of truth have never been won without risks, often of the gravest character. Conversion of a nation that has consciously or unconsciously preyed I have deliberately used the word "conversion". For my ambition is no less than to convert the British people through non-violence, and thus make them see the wrong they have done to India. I do not seek to harm your people. I want to serve them even as I want to serve my own. I believe that I have always served them. I served them up to 1919 blindly. But when my eyes were opened and I conceived Non-cooperation, the object still was to serve them. I employed the same weapon that I have in all humility successfully used against the dearest members of my family. If I have equal love for your people with mine it will not long remain hidden. It will be acknowledged by them even as the members of my family acknowledged it after they had tried me for several years. If the people join me as I expect they will, the sufferings they will undergo, unless the British nation sooner retraces its steps, will be enough to melt the stoniest hearts ...

*Young India*, 12-3-1930 (48: 365-66)

---

*The breaking of the salt laws began as a modest enough campaign. Gandhi and his loyal band of followers marched along the seashore and picked up salt, in defiance of the laws. Meetings were organized in villages along the way, in which Gandhi spoke of the importance of resisting political power that was blind to its own exercises of authority but added that on no account should people resort to violence.*

## Speech at Borsad
## March 18, 1930

At one time I was wholly loyal to the Empire and taught others to be loyal. I sang "God Save the King" with zest and taught my friends and relations to do so. Finally, however, the scales fell from my eyes, and the spell broke. I realized that the Empire did not deserve loyalty. I felt that it deserved sedition. Hence I have made sedition my *dharma*. I try to explain it to others that while sedition is our *dharma*, to be loyal is a sin. To be loyal to this Government, that is to say to wish it well, is as good as wishing ill of the crores of people of India. We get nothing in return for the crores of rupees that are squeezed out of the country; if we get anything, it is the rags from Lancashire. To approve the policy of this Government is to commit treason against the poor. You should free yourselves from this latter offence. I believe I have done so. Hence I have become ready to wage a peaceful war against this Government. I am commencing it by violating the salt law. It is for this purpose that I am undertaking this march. At every place, thousands of men and women have conferred their blessings upon it. These blessings are not showered on me but on the struggle.

Our patience has been severely tried. We must free ourselves from the yoke of this Government and we are prepared to undergo any hardships that we may have to suffer in order to secure *swaraj*. It is our duty as well as our right to secure *swaraj*. I regard this as a religious movement since sedition is our *dharma*. Every moment I desire the end of the policies of this Government. I have no desire to touch even a single hair of our rulers. But we certainly shall not bow down to them. Kindly, therefore, become conscious of your responsibilities and wash away your sins against India. Today we are defying the salt law. Tomorrow we shall have to consign other laws to the waste-paper basket. Doing so we shall practise such severe Non-cooperation that finally it will not be possible for the administration to be carried on at all. Let the Government then, to carry on its rule, use guns against us, send us to prison, hang us. But how many can be given such punishment? Try and calculate how much time it will take a lakh of Britishers to hang thirty crores of persons. But they are not so cruel. They are human beings like us and perhaps we would be doing the same things that they are doing if we had been in their position. Man does not have the strength to fight circumstances; the latter mould his actions. Hence I do not feel that they are to be blamed for this.

But I find their policy so bitter, that I would destroy it today if I could. It will be destroyed regardless of whether I am put behind the bars or allowed to remain free. I breathe here before you and with every breath that I take, I desire this very thing. I am fully convinced that there is nothing base in it. I act exactly as I believe.

No one has been able to reply to the complaint I have registered before God and mentioned in my letter to the Viceroy. No one says that the salt tax is just. No one says that the expenditure on the army and the administration is justified. No one holds that the policy of collecting land revenue is justifiable, nor indeed that it is proper to extort 20 to 25 crores of rupees from the people after making drunkards and opium-addicts of them and breaking up their homes. Both foreigners and British officers testify to the fact that all this is true. However, what can be done about it? ...

... My prostrating myself on the ground for the sake of removing the hardships of crores of people was of no avail. I have spared no efforts in drafting appeals. Everyone knows that I know how to use polite language. However, I have become a revolutionary when politeness and persuasion proved infructuous. I find peace in describing myself as a revolutionary and I practise my *dharma* to some extent. In a revolution which is calm, peaceful and truthful, you should get yourselves enrolled regardless of the religion to which you belong. If you enlist yourselves with sincerity and if you can keep up your courage, the salt tax will have been abolished, this administration will have come to an end and all the hardships enumerated in the letter to the Viceroy as well as those which have not been so enumerated will have to cease. Then when new administrative policies are to be formulated, the time will be ripe for solving communal disputes and satisfying everyone. I invite you all in the name of God. Even the Britishers will join in this movement. Will they perpetrate many injustices in order to justify one? And will they put innocent men behind the bars, whip them and hang them?

God can never be identified with that which is untruth, that which is injustice. It is as plain as I am speaking to you here and now. I see equally clearly that the days of this administration are numbered and total *swaraj* is in sight. The Goddess of Independence is peeping in and wishes to garland us. If at such a time we run away, who will be as unworthy as we?

*Navajivan*, 23-3-1930 (from Gujarati) (48: 453-56)

---

*The salt satyagraha appeared a startling act of defiance to Gandhi's English friends. He explained his position to them lucidly.*

## "Render Unto Caesar"

An unknown English friend has thought it worth while cabling to me that in launching upon civil disobedience I am going against the teaching of Jesus: "Render unto Caesar that which is Caesar's." Another, an Indian Christian, writes from the Punjab somewhat in the same fashion and, forsaking charity, pours abuse upon my devoted head for my action. He says further that whereas he considered me to be a good man formerly, he is now utterly undeceived. I can reassure this friend that civil disobedience is no new thing with me. I began to preach and practise it in 1906. His regard for me therefore was evidently from ignorance, if his present dislike of me is wise.

But I have learnt from the New Testament, as also from other sources, that if one wishes to walk in the fear of God, one should be indifferent about popular praise or blame. Now for the question. As I hold my conduct to be in utter agreement with universal religion and as I hold the New Testament teaching in great esteem, I should not like it to be justly said of me that I was going against the teaching of Jesus. "Render unto Caesar" was quoted against me before too. I have not read into the celebrated verse the meaning that my critics have sought to put into it. Jesus evaded the direct question put to him because it was a trap. He was in no way bound to answer it. He therefore asked to see the coin for taxes. And then said with withering scorn, "How can you who traffic in Caesar's coins and thus receive what to you are benefits of Caesar's rule refuse to pay taxes?" Jesus's whole preaching and practice point unmistakably to Non-cooperation, which necessarily includes non-payment of taxes. Jesus never recognized man's authority as against God's. He who disregarded the whole host of priesthood, which was in those days superior to kinghood, would not have hesitated to defy the might of emperors had he found it necessary.

And did he not treat with supreme disdain the whole of the farcical trial through which he was made to pass? Lastly, let me warn honest friends against running into the trap of literalism. The "letter" surely "killeth", it is the "spirit" that "giveth life". In the present case I find no difficulty in reading into the text a satisfactory meaning. But it would matter little to me that some text should confound me, if there was no mistaking the spirit of the whole teaching of a book respected as among the world's religious scriptures.

*Young India*, 27-3-1930 (48: 483)

---

*Gandhi was arrested and interned for breaking the salt laws and for causing popular disaffection. At the end of his internment, the Viceroy, Lord Irwin invited Gandhi for talks (1931). The meeting was not entirely conclusive. Some concessions were granted, including the remission of the salt tax. Irwin promised to release some of the jailed satyagrahis, but remained obdurately silent on the Congress' request that the death sentence against Bhagat Singh and his comrades be revoked. On the question of complete independence, which Congress had declared to be its goal, the Viceroy refused to relent. Gandhi, however, felt the talks were productive, though limited in the gains they procured. He was even hopeful that Bhagat Singh would be released.*

## Statement to the Press
## Delhi, March 5, 1931

... For a settlement of this character, it is not possible nor wise to say which is the victorious party. If there is any victory, I should say it belongs to both. The Congress has never made any bid for victory. In the very nature of things the Congress has a definite goal to reach and there can be no question of victory without reaching the goal. I would, therefore, urge all my countrymen and all my sisters instead of feeling elated, if they find in the terms any cause for elation, to humble themselves before God and ask Him to give them strength and wisdom to pursue the course that their mission demands for the time being, whether it is by way of suffering or by way of patient negotiation, consultation and conference.

I hope, therefore, that the millions who have taken part in this struggle of suffering during the past twelve months will now, during the period of conference and construction, show the same willingness, the same cohesion, the same effort and the same wisdom that they have in an eminent degree shown during what I would describe as a heroic period in the modern history of India. But I know that, if there would be men and women who will feel elated by the settlement, there are, also those who will be, and are, keenly disappointed. Heroic suffering is like the breath of their nostrils. They rejoice in it as in nothing else. They will endure unendurable sufferings, be they ever so prolonged, but when suffering ceases they feel their occupation gone and feel also that the goal has receded from the view. To them I would only say, "Wait, watch, pray and hope." Suffering has its well-defined limits. Suffering can be both wise and unwise, and when the limit is reached, to prolong it would be not unwise but the height of folly. It would be folly to go on suffering when the opponent makes it easy for you to enter into a discussion with him upon your longings. If a real opening is made, it is one's duty to take advantage of it and, in my humble opinion, the settlement has made a real opening. Such a settlement has necessarily to be provisional as this is. ...

... I owe a word to hundreds, if not thousands, of my erstwhile fellow-prisoners on whose behalf I have been receiving wires and who will still be languishing in jails when satyagrahi prisoners who were jailed during the past 12 months will have been discharged. Personally, I do not believe in imprisoning, by way of punishment, even those who commit violence. I know that those who have done violence through political motives are entitled to claim, if not the same wisdom, certainly the same spirit of love and self-sacrifice that I would claim for myself. And, therefore, if I could have justly secured their liberty in preference to my own or that of fellow-satyagrahis I should truthfully have secured it. But I trust they will realize that I could not in justice ask for their discharge. But that does not mean that I or the members of the Working Committee have not them in mind.

The Congress has embarked deliberately, though provisionally, on a career of cooperation. If congressmen honourably and fully implement the conditions applicable to them of the settlement, the Congress will obtain an irresistible prestige and would have inspired Government with confidence in its ability to ensure peace, as I think it has proved its ability to conduct disobedience. And if the people in general will clothe the Congress with that power and prestige, I promise that it will not be long before every one of these political prisoners is discharged including the detenus, the Meerut prisoners (*Bhagat Singh and his comrades - ed.*) and all the rest.

*Young India*, 12-3-1931 (51: 207-11)

*Gandhi's talks with the Viceroy—the Gandhi-Irwin Pact—had brought him and the Congress back to negotiating with the British. The Congress agreed to participate in the round table conference and work at a comprehensive political settlement which, among other things, would safeguard minority interests. Gandhi discovered in the proposed conference an opportunity to return to one of his salient concerns: that generous heart-unity, in addition to political concessions and justice claims, could alone successfully resolve the antagonisms which were woven into the Hindu-Muslim tangle.*

## Speech at Public Meeting, Delhi
### March 7, 1931

... The settlement that has been just arrived at will fail of effect without a real heart-unity between Hindus and Mussalmans. Without that unity our going to the Conference will be of no avail. No one will pretend that the Conference can help us to achieve that unity. A heart-unity can be achieved between pure hearts purged of distrust and that can be achieved only outside the Conference. In this I seek your cooperation and ask you to count on my doing my utmost. In a letter I received yesterday the correspondent asks me why I should not make the same advances to the Mussalmans as I did to the Viceroy. Why, he asks, should I not wait on esteemed Mussalman friends who are desirous of unity and beg on bended knees for their cooperation? I like the suggestion and the correspondent may be sure that I shall leave nothing undone to plead with my Mussalman friends. But you must understand that there are limits to the capacity of an individual, and the moment he flatters himself that he can undertake all tasks, God is there to humble his pride. For myself, I am gifted with enough humility to look even to babes and sucklings for help.

And that reminds me that in this mission of mine I can count on the hearty and active cooperation of my sisters who beat all previous records of suffering and sacrifice during the last heroic campaign. To them I say : If you are convinced that Hindu-Muslim unity is a *sine qua non* I ask you to use against your own countrymen the same weapon of satyagraha that you used so effectively against Government. Tell your men that you will non-co-operate with them, you will not cook for them, you will starve yourselves and them so long as they do not wash their hands of these dirty communal squabbles. Assure me of your cooperation, and you will add tremendously to my strength and to my power of pleading.

We Hindus are described, to a certain extent rightly, as the majority community. Well, to them I would say the same thing as I used to do in 1921 (*during the Khilafat struggle - ed.*), viz., that voluntary surrender on the part of either community—preferably by the majority community—of all rights and privileges would immediately effect this unity. It would be a great thing, a brave thing, for the Hindus to achieve this act of self-denial. Let them say to the Mussalmans: "Have as big a share of the spoils as you want; we will be content to serve you." What after all are the things you are quarrelling for? Not indeed for air and water. It is for seats on legislatures and local bodies. What has the vast majority of you got to do with them? How many of you can go there? And what can you do there? Outside the legislatures you did wonderful things; you defied the ordinances, you defied lathi-charges and "firing" orders, because you were conscious of your strength. If you retain the same consciousness, what would it matter to you if your Parliament had all Mussalmans in it and no Hindu? I am sick of these squabbles for seats, this scramble for the shadow of power. How I wish I could bring home to all Congressmen that they should have nothing to do with these legislatures? The very act of voluntary surrender will clothe you with a power undreamt of before ...

*Young India*, 12-3-1931 (51: 226-227)

---

*The revolutionary Bhagat Singh was hanged by the colonial government. His hanging cast a cloud over the Gandhi-Irwin pact, and Gandhi had to explain himself.*

## Bhagat Singh

Brave Bhagat Singh and his two associates have been hanged. Many attempts were made to save their lives and even some hopes were entertained, but all was in vain. Bhagat Singh did not wish to live. He refused to apologize; declined to file an appeal. If at all he would agree to live, he would do so for the sake of others; if at all he would agree to it, it would be in order that his death might not provoke anyone to indiscriminate murder. Bhagat Singh was not a devotee of non-violence, but he did not subscribe to the religion of violence; he was prepared to commit murder out of a sense of helplessness.

His last letter was as follows: "I have been arrested while waging a war. For me there can be no gallows. Put me into the mouth of a cannon and blow me off." These heroes had conquered the fear of death. Let us bow to them a thousand times for their heroism. But we should not imitate their act. I am not prepared to believe that the country has benefited by their action. I can see only the harm that has been done. We could have won *swaraj* long ago if that line of action had not been pursued and we could have waged a purely non-violent struggle. There may well be two opinions on this conjecture of mine.

However, no one can deny the fact that if the practice of seeking justice through murders is established amongst us, we shall start murdering one another for what we believe to be justice. In a land of crores of destitutes and crippled persons, this will be a terrifying situation. These poor people are bound to become victims of our atrocities. It is desirable that everyone should consider the consequences of this. Further, we want a *swaraj* which is theirs and for them. By making a *dharma* of violence, we shall be reaping the fruit of our own actions. Hence, though we praise the courage of these brave men, we should never countenance their activities. By hanging these men, the Government has demonstrated its own brute nature, it has provided fresh proof of its arrogance resulting from its power by ignoring public opinion. From this hanging it may be concluded that it is not the intention of the government to part with any real power to the people. The Government certainly had the right to hang these men. However, there are some rights which do credit to those who possess them only if they are enjoyed in name only. If a person exercises all his rights on all occasions, in the end they are destroyed. On this occasion, the Government would have brought credit to itself if it had not exercised its rights and this would have been highly useful in maintaining peace. However, it is obvious that the Government has not to date developed such discretion ...

*Navajivan*, 29-3-1931 (from Gujarati) (51: 316-17)

---

*The Gandhi-Irwin pact was greeted less than warmly by those who felt that the British had conceded very little to Gandhi and the Congress. Hundreds of satyagrahis were still in jail, peasant resisters who had braved violence and hardship before and during the salt satyagraha felt let down, because their grievances were not entirely addressed, and everywhere the young felt dismayed by Bhagat Singh's death. Besides, the Muslim League and several prominent Muslim leaders who were neither with the Congress nor the League were unhappy with the Congress' reluctance to address the question of Muslim rights with the seriousness it deserved. They were gearing themselves to raise the issue in London. Gandhi was not to be daunted by this or any other task and journeyed to London (1932) to participate in the round table conference. Once there, he was feted, honoured and made to speak in diverse forums, interviewed, and drew a varied crowd. The extract below, taken from an interview he granted an American journalist, is a sample of the views he expounded in London—on the themes of capitalist greed, human need and production.*

### Interview to Callender, London
### [October 16, 1931]

Q. Do you feel, Gandhiji, that mass production will raise the standard of living of the people?

A. I do not believe in it at all. There is a tremendous fallacy behind Mr Ford's (*Henry Ford - ed.*) reasoning. Without simultaneous distribution on an equally mass scale, the production can result only in a great world tragedy. Take Mr. Ford's cars. The saturation point is bound to be reached soon or later. Beyond that point the production of cars cannot be pushed. What will happen then? Mass production takes no note of the real requirement of the consumer. If mass production were in itself a virtue, it should be capable of indefinite multiplication. But it can be definitely shown that mass production carries within it its own limitations.

If all countries adopted the system of mass production, there would not be a big enough market for their products. Mass production must then come to a stop.

Q. I wonder whether you feel that this saturation point has already arrived in the Western world. Mr. Ford says that there never can be too many articles of quality, that the needs of the world are constantly increasingly that, therefore, while there might be saturation in the market for a given commodity, the general saturation would never be reached.

A. Without entering upon an elaborate argument, I would categorically state my conviction that the mania for mass production is responsible for the world crisis. Granting for the moment that machinery may supply all the needs of humanity, still, it would concentrate production in particular areas, so that you would have to go in a round-about way to regulate distribution, whereas, if there is production and distribution both in the respective areas where things are required, it is automatically regulated, and there is less chance for fraud, none for speculation.

The interviewer had earlier met Ford in America, who had put forward the view that demand for cheaper things would stimulate mass production. The American friend mentioned Mr. Ford's favourite plan of decentralization of industry by the use of electric power conveyed on wires to the remotest corner, instead of coal and steam, as a possible remedy, and drew up the picture of hundreds and thousands of small, neat, smokeless villages, dotted with factories, run by village communities. "Assuming all that to be possible", he finally asked Gandhiji, "how far will it meet your objection?"

A. My objection won't be met by that, because, while it is true that you will be producing things in innumerable areas, the power will come from one selected centre. That, in the end, I think, would be found to be disastrous. It would place such a limitless power in one human agency that I dread to think of it. The consequence, for instance, of such a control of power would be that I would be dependent on that power for light, water, even air, and so on. That, I think, would be terrible.

Q. Have you any idea as to what Europe and America should do to solve the problem presented by too much machinery?

A. You see that these nations are able to exploit the so-called weaker or unorganized races of the world. Once those races gain this elementary knowledge and decide that they are no more going to be exploited, they will simply be satisfied with what they can provide themselves. Mass production, then, at least where the vital necessities are concerned, will disappear.

Q. But even these races will require more and more goods as their needs multiply.

A. They will then produce for themselves. And when that happens, mass production, in the technical sense in which it is understood in the West, ceases.

Q. You mean to say it becomes local.

A. When production and consumption both become localized, the temptation to speed up production, indefinitely and at any price, disappears. All the endless difficulties and problems that our present-day economic system presents, too, would then come to an end. Take a concrete instance. England today is the cloth shop of the world. It, therefore, needs to hold a world in bondage to secure its market. But under the change that I have envisaged, she would limit her production to the actual needs of her 45 millions of population. When that need is satisfied, the production will necessarily stop. It won't be continued for the sake of bringing in more gold irrespective of the needs of a people and at the risk of their impoverishment. There would be no unnatural accumulation of hoards in the pockets of the few, and want in the midst of plenty in regard to the rest, as is happening today, for instance, in America. America is today able to hold the world in fee by selling all kinds of trinkets, or by selling her unrivalled skill, which she has a right to do. She has reached the acme of mass production, and yet she has not been able to abolish unemployment or want. There are still thousands, perhaps millions of people in America who live in misery, in site of the phenomenal riches of the few. The whole of the American nation is not benefited by the mass production.

Q. There the fault lies in distribution. It means that, whilst our system of production has reached a high pitch of perfection, the distribution is still defective. If distribution could be equalized, would not mass production be sterilized of its evils?

A. No, the evil is inherent in the system. Distribution can be equalized when production is localized; in other words, when the distribution is simultaneous with production. Distribution will never be equal so long as you want to tap other markets of the world to dispose of your goods. That does not mean that the world has not use for the marvellous advances in science and organization that the Western nations have made. It only means that the Western nations have to use their skill. If they want to use their skill abroad, from philanthropic motives, America would say, "Well, we know how make bridges, we won't keep it a secret, but we say to the whole world, we will teach you how to make bridges and we will charge you nothing." America says, "Where other nations can grow one blade of wheat, we can grow two thousand." Then, America should teach that art free of charge to those who will learn it, but not aspire to grow wheat for the whole world, which would spell a sorry day for the world indeed.

The American friend next asked Gandhiji, referring to Russia, whether it was not a country that had developed mass production without exploiting, in Gandhiji's sense, the less industrialized nations, or without falling into the pit of unequal distribution.

A. In other words, you want me to express opinion on State-controlled industry, i.e., an economic order in which both production and distribution are controlled and regulated by the State as is being today done in Soviet Russia. Well, it is a new experiment. How far it will ultimately succeed, I do not know. If it were not based on force, I would dote on it. But today, since it is based on force, I do not know how far and where it will take us.

Q. Then, you do not envisage mass production as an ideal future of India?

A. Oh yes, mass production, certainly, but not based on force. After all, the message of the spinning-wheel is that. It is mass production, but mass production in people's own homes. If you multiply individual production to millions of times, would it not give you mass production on a tremendous scale? But I quite understand that your "mass production" is a technical term for production by the fewest possible number through the aid of highly complicated machinery. I have said to myself that that is wrong.

My machinery must be of the most elementary type which I can put in the homes of the millions. Under my system, again, it is labour which is the current coin, not metal. Any person who can use his labour has that coin, has wealth. He converts his labour into cloth, he converts his labour into grain. If he wants paraffin oil, which he cannot himself produce, he uses his surplus grain for getting the oil. It is exchange of labour on free, fair and equal terms—hence it is no robbery. You may object that this is a reversion to the primitive system of barter. But is not all international trade based on the barter system? Look, again, at another advantage, that this system affords. You can multiply it to any extent. But concentration of production *ad infinitum* can only lead to unemployment. You may say that workers thrown out of work by the introduction of improved machinery will find occupation in other jobs. But in an organized country where there are only fixed and limited avenues of employment, where the worker has become highly skilled in the use of one particular kind of machinery, you know from your own experience that this is hardly possible. Are there not over three millions unemployed in England today? A question was put to me only the other day: "What are we doing today with these three million unemployed?" They cannot shift from factory to field in a day. It is a tremendous problem.

Q. ... Some people have the impression that you are opposed to machinery in general. This is not true, I believe.

A. That is quite wrong. The spinning-wheel is also machinery. It is a beautiful work of art. It typifies the use of machinery on a universal scale. It is machinery reduced to the terms of the masses.

Q. So, you are opposed to machinery, only because and when it concentrates production and distribution in the hands of the few?

A. You are right. I hate privilege and monopoly. Whatever cannot be shared with the masses is taboo to me. That is all.

*Harija*n, 2-11-1934 (54: 21-25)

# Ending the Years of the Truth Wars

*This period of Gandhi's political life is remarkable for two reasons: firstly, his views on non-violence acquired a distinctive resonance, as he argued them out with those who obviously believed in a different creed. His conversations with political militants were open and frank, and his manner of answering their queries, ingenuous. But, significantly, he preferred to engage with the problems of their method, rather than their understanding of justice. His antipathy to their ostensible militancy prevented him from actively enquiring into their ideals. His relationship to Bhagat Singh is suggestive in this respect. While mindful of his idealism and courage, Gandhi could not bring himself to admire the young man. Though he tried to convince the Viceroy to commute the death sentence awarded to Bhagat Singh and his associates, he did not hold out a counter-plan of action, should his plea be overlooked. In other words, he did not wish to undertake a struggle for their release.*

*Secondly, these years witnessed not merely one of the most dramatic representations of satyagraha, but also signalled a new phase of Gandhian politics: from being a creed and an instance of ethical method, non-violence graduated to a spectacular performance, and one that brought together the moral and political aspects of satyagraha. Contemporary historians revising the past see in the salt march an adroit attempt to deflect the revolutionary energies of the time and, therefore, a measure that served Indian's socially decisive classes, whose power would otherwise have been challenged by political and labour militancy. They argue that Gandhi's non-violence, while morally credible, was also strategically deployed. They also point out that, unlike Non-cooperation, these truth wars on the sea-shore were sustained by a moral and cultural rhetoric that was recognizably Hindu (such a criticism was advanced during the salt march by the radical anti-caste Self-respect movement from the southern India, which protested and satirized the 'epic' character of the struggle to draw attention to its internal political logic). In any case, given their steady alienation from the Congress since the late 1920s, Muslim participation in the stirring events of the time remained marginal.*

*We also see, during this period, Gandhi the leader of the Congress coming into his own in an authoritative, public sense. The Congress* became a forum he nurtured and commanded, chiefly through the power of his conscience and the enormous goodwill he enjoyed with different sections of the party and its public. In turn, Gandhi's political counter to militancy, embodied in the salt march, served that party well. It helped it gain legitimacy in the eyes of protesting Indians, a section of whom had begun to look to other—more radical—political options. In his negotiations with the Viceroy and through his participation in the round table conference, he represented Congress concerns, often seeing himself as its chief moral arbiter, who alone had the power to explain, interpret and grant absolution to its politics.

In the years that followed the salt march, an uneasy fit came to exist between his moral choices and the strategic needs of Congress and its socially powerful leadership. The suspension of satyagraha in the wake of the Gandhi-Irwin pact, for instance, coincided with the demands of Indian big business, whose proponents were guardedly sympathetic to the nationalist cause, that normalcy be resumed in civic life. In another instance, with respect to the Hindu-Muslim tangle, his moral helplessness resulted in his accepting—and often rationalising— the Congress' problematic position on Muslim rights, which was not acceptable to the Muslim League.

The Congress tested and troubled Gandhi too, but, bound as a pietist is to his Church, however impossible its actions, he felt linked in fealty and would not let go of it. Nor did he seek to reform it through fiat. He believed then and always in setting an ethical standard that he embodied, hoping that others would emulate his example. A few did, but to many he served as a useful icon, whose radiating presence protected them from their own sins. For his part, he retained his personal moral credibility but his political judgement raised as many uncomfortable questions as it answered, as we shall see in his responses to the Hindu-Muslim question.

## Chapter 5

## The Violence Within: Responding to Untouchability
## 1933-1937

*Gandhi's time in England was marked by both elation and anxiety. He was widely feted, questioned and welcomed as the conscience of a world that was turning increasingly materialistic and his views were publicised in various forums. However, at the round table conference he had come to attend, matters unfolded differently. He had to confront two intertwined developments: Muslim and untouchable representatives, invited by the rulers of Empire to articulate their communities' points of view, belied the representative claims of both Gandhi and the Congress. Further, Dr. Ambedkar, the radical untouchable leader from Maharashtra challenged Gandhi's faith in the ability of caste Hindu society to reform itself and for the Congress to preside over these reforms.*

*Dr. Ambedkar, educated in Columbia University and the University of London, had emerged as a popular anti-caste and labour leader in Maharashtra and was recognized in the rest of India too as a man whose intellectual and political commitment to his cause were beyond reproach. He understood untouchability to be linked to economic oppression and inequality and desired more just and equal economic and social arrangements for the untouchables. A child of the Enlightenment, Dr. Ambedkar preferred to trust to the objective authority of the law and the justice invested in rights claims, than in the penitential Hindu heart.*

*At the round table conference convened in 1932 in London, the differences between Dr. Ambedkar and Gandhi were pronounced and would not admit of an amicable resolution. The British, for their part, were sympathetic to Dr. Ambedkar's claims and wily enough to exploit them to render the Congress' authority vulnerable. They offered, therefore, what Dr. Ambedkar desired: separate electorates to the untouchables. Gandhi was opposed to this, chiefly because he did not view untouchables as a distinct social entity, with interests that were separable and distinct from those of other Hindus.*

*These differences were not resolved at the round table conference and pursued the two men, even on their return to India. Gandhi returned to India in 1933 where his pact with the Viceroy, the Gandhi-Irwin pact, was being systematically dishonoured. Political repression against nationalists continued and soon Gandhi found himself in prison. In August 1933, Prime Minister Ramsay Macdonald announced what has since come to be known as the 'communal award', which granted separate electorates to Muslims and the untouchables. While Gandhi was unhappy about the award as such, he had long reconciled himself to not being able to convince or carry Muslim opinion, outside of the Congress, with him in the matter of electoral representation. But the question of the untouchables rested on an altogether different footing with him—so he decided to protest the offer as well as caste Hindu reluctance to grant untouchables their due. Gandhi thus began his 'epic' fast unto death.*

*Then began a series of negotiations between Dr. Ambedkar and Gandhi which culminated in a pact, the Poona pact, that recognized the principle of reserved seats, rather than separate electorates. Gandhi thereafter turned to a struggle for the soul of India, as he later referred to it. He spent the better part of the decade protesting untouchability, imploring caste Hindu society to heed the darkness they harboured in their hearts and minds and cast out the violence and hatred that informed their attitudes towards untouchables. This proved to be a novel non-violent campaign—one that every Hindu had to wage with himself or herself. Gandhi's imprecations to caste Hindus persisted almost till the end of his life. Meanwhile, he held out a redemptive moral promise to the untouchables, assuring them that repentant caste Hindus would honour it, even if this took several years.*

# The Strength to Love: Some Early Arguments

---

*To understand better the nature of the differences between Gandhi and Ambedkar it is important to trace the development of Gandhi's views on untouchability from the time he started protesting against it. The intense moral anger, sometimes bordering on despair, that characterised his strictures against untouchability in the 1930s grew out of his complex engagements with the theories and practices of social discrimination, especially untouchability.*

*The extracts below plot and define for the reader the coordinates that held in place Gandhi's moral universe during those momentous years (1920-28) and indicate his point of arrival in the mid-1930s, when he began to respond to Dr. Ambedkar. They also reveal his unique style of exhorting social change. On the one hand he implored caste Hindus to treat untouchables fairly and with compassion. On the other hand, he argued that untouchables had to reform themselves. As always, Gandhi was focused in his objectives: he made it clear that he was not asking for a reform or transformation of the Hindu social organization, the caste system, but only desired to see the excrescence of untouchability removed. Yet he was not entirely at peace with himself and continued to define and re-define his understanding of the caste system and untouchability.*

---

*Gandhi was often audacious in his use of symbols and the manner in which he provoked moral horror. In the extract below, he compares those who practise untouchability to General Dyer who shot at a helpless crowd of civilians in Punjab in 1919 and to Michael O'Dwyer, the governor of the Punjab, whose rule of terror was one of the reasons for Gandhi launching the Non-cooperation movement.*

### The Sins of Untouchability

... Has not a just Nemesis overtaken us for the crime of untouchability? Have we not reaped as we have sown? Have we not practised Dyerism and O'Dwyerism on our own kith and kin? We have segregated the "pariah" and we are in turn segregated in the British Colonies. We deny him the use of public wells; we throw the leavings of our plates at him. His very shadow pollutes us. Indeed there is no charge that the "pariah" cannot fling in our faces and which we do not fling in the faces of Englishmen.

How is this blot on Hinduism to be removed? "Do unto others as you would that others should do unto you." I have often told English officials that, if they are friends and servants of India, they should come down from their pedestal, cease to be patrons, demonstrate by their loving deeds that they are in every respect our friends, and believe us to be equals in the same sense they believe fellow-Englishmen to be their equals. After the experiences of the Punjab and the *Khilafat*, I have gone a step further and asked them to repent and to change their hearts. Even so it is necessary for us Hindus to repent of the wrong we have done, to alter our behaviour towards those whom we have "suppressed" by a system as devilish as we believe the English system of the Government of India to be.

We must not throw a few miserable schools at them: we must not adopt the air of superiority towards them. We must treat them as our blood-brothers as they are in fact. We must return to them the inheritance of which we have robbed them. And this must not be the act of a few English-knowing reformers merely, but it must be a conscious voluntary effort on the part of the masses. We may not wait till eternity for this much belated reformation. We must aim at bringing it about within this year of grace, probation, preparation, and *tapasya*. It is a reform not to follow *swaraj* but to precede it.

*Young India*, 19-1-1921 (22: 225)

---

*Gandhi's friend and interlocutor, Charlie Andrews, wondered if Gandhi had lost sight of the untouchability issue, now that he was advocating Non-cooperation. Gandhi assured him that he had not forgotten his vows in this respect and noted that he held them with a seriousness that need not be doubted.*

**Letter to Charlie Andrews**
**Calcutta, January 29, 1921**

MY DEAREST CHARLIE,

... I look at the problem as an Indian and a Hindu, you as an Englishman and a Christian. You look at it with the eye of an observer, I as an affected and afflicted party. You can be patient, and I cannot. Or you as a disinterested reformer can afford to be impatient whereas I as a sinner must be patient if I would get rid of the sin. I may talk glibly of the Englishman's sin in Jallianwala. But as a Hindu, I may not talk about the sin of Hinduism against the untouchables. ... I must act and have ever acted. You act, you do not speak, when you feel most ...

... I am attacking the sacredotalism of Hinduism. That Hindus consider it a "sin" to touch a portion of human beings because they are born in a particular environment! I am engaged as a Hindu in showing that it is not a sin and that it is sin to consider that touch a sin. It is a bigger problem than that of gaining Indian independence but I can tackle it better if I gain the latter on the way. It is not impossible that India may free herself from English domination before India has become free of the curse of untouchability. Freedom from English domination is one of the essentials of *swaraj* and the absence of it is blocking the way to all progress.

... I began this work in S[outh] A[frica]—before I ever heard of you and I was conscious of the sin of untouchability before I came under other Christian influences in S[outh] A[frica]. The truth came to me when I was yet a child. I used to laugh at my dear mother for making us bathe if we brothers touched any pariah. It was in 1897 that I was prepared in Durban to turn Mrs. Gandhi away from the house because she would not treat on a footing of equality Lawrence who she knew belonged to the pariah class and whom I had invited to stay with me. It has been a passion of my life to serve the untouchables because I have felt that I could not remain a Hindu if it was true that untouchability was a part of Hinduism.

I have only told you half the truth. I feel as keenly about the Kalighat as I do about the untouchables. Whenever I am in Calcutta the thought of the goats being sacrificed haunts me and makes me uneasy. ... The pariah can voice his own grief. He can petition. He can even rise against Hindus. But the poor dumb goats? I sometimes writhe in agony when I think of it. But I do not speak or write about it. All the same I am qualifying myself for the service of these fellow creatures of mine who are slaughtered in the name of my faith. I may not finish the work in this incarnation. I shall be born again to finish that work or someone who has realized my agony will finish it ...

Yours truly,
MOHAN

From a photostat (22: 272-74)

---

*Passionate though Gandhi was in his condemnation of untouchability, he refused to apportion blame to any one section of Hindu society. Thus he disagreed with those who held that untouchability was mandated and upheld chiefly by the so-called highest caste in the Hindu social order, the brahmins.*

## Speech at Satara
## November 7, 1920

... Maybe you do not look upon Brahmins with reverence, but all the same they deserve to be respected for their *tapascharya,* their knowledge, their self-sacrifice and holiness. I would certainly hesitate to attribute any errors to the Brahmins who composed the Upanishads and other holy books, but I said, and I say it again, that even they, by sanctioning the practice of untouchability, have some share in Satan's work. You will not be able to save your own religion by abusing Brahmins and burning down their houses. If at all you claim to be Hindus, know that your conduct is un-Hindu. If you say you are not Hindus, I tell you that you have still another *dharma* to respect. I wish you well in your non-Hinduism. [I tell you this] just as I would tell Jains that they were welcome to think of themselves as non-Hindus but that, if they looked upon India as their country, they had another *dharma* to abide by—the *swaraj-dharma.* This *dharma* teaches you, if you wish to have *swaraj*, to be on good terms with Hindus. Who were Tilak, Gokhale, Ranade and Agarkar (*social reformers and nationalists - ed.*)? Though Brahmins, they served the cause of non-Brahmins at the greatest cost to themselves. Tilak Maharaj bore sincere love to me, though

I am a non-Brahmin.

By indulging in violent contempt of a community which has produced men like Ramdas, Tulsidas (*brahmin poets - ed.*) , Ranade, Tilak and others, it is impossible that you can rise. ...You talk of resorting to Non-cooperation against Brahmins but one must be pure in heart to be fit to employ the sacred term "non-co- operation". I speak of the British Empire as Satanic, but I can do so because I wish ill to no Englishman. If you demand justice from the Brahmins, you must practise *tapascharya* like theirs. If you take up the sword, you yourselves will perish ...

*Navajivan,* 14-11-1920 (from Gujarati) (21: 462 -63)

---

*Gandhi's views on brahmins were of a part with his overall belief structure: unlike radical social dissenters who held that untouchability was integral to the Hindu caste order, and therefore cannot be destroyed without a transformation of caste society, Gandhi argued that untouchability was distinct from the caste order. It was an excrescence, whereas the caste order, with its hierarchy of professions appeared to him perfectly rational. His views were challenged in western and southern India, where the opinion of anti-caste radicals held sway.*

### The Caste System

I have received several angry letters about my remarks during my Deccan tour (*western Indian tour - ed.*) on the caste system. I am not publishing these letters because there is nothing but vituperation in them, and when there is no vituperation, there is little argument about them. I am anxious to open the columns of *Young India* to opinion expressing dissent from its views, but the writers must be brief and interesting. Acrimony is no argument. I am obliged to make these remarks because two writers at least would have gained publicity for their letters if they had not been prolix and unintelligible in their expression. The question, however, that my correspondents have raised commands attention and deserves an answer. They argue that the retention of the caste system spells ruin for India and that it is caste which has reduced India to slavery.

In my opinion it is not caste that has made us what we are. It was our greed and disregard of essential virtues which enslaved us. I believe that caste has saved Hinduism from disintegration. But like every other institution it has suffered from excrescences. I consider the four divisions (*brahmin, kshatriya, vaishya and shudra, also known as varna divisions - ed.*) alone to be fundamental, natural, and essential. The innumerable sub-castes are sometimes a convenience, often a hindrance. The sooner there is fusion the better. The silent destruction and reconstruction of sub-castes have ever gone on and are bound to continue. Social pressure and public opinion can be trusted to deal with the problem. But I am certainly against any attempt at destroying the fundamental divisions.

The caste system is not based on inequality, there is no question of inferiority, and so far as there is any such question arising, as in Madras, Maharashtra or elsewhere, the tendency should undoubtedly be checked. But there appears to be no valid reason for ending the system because of its abuse. It lends itself easily to reformation. The spirit of democracy, which is fast spreading throughout India and the rest of the world, will, without a shadow of doubt, purge the institution of the idea of predominance and subordination.

The spirit of democracy is not a mechanical thing to be adjusted by abolition of forms. It requires change of the heart. If caste is a bar to the spread of that spirit, the existence of five religions in India—Hinduism, Islam, Christianity, Zoroastrianism and Judaism—is equally a bar. The spirit of democracy requires the inculcation of the spirit of brotherhood, and I can find no difficulty in considering a Christian or a Mohammedan to be my brother in absolutely the same sense as a blood brother, and Hinduism that is responsible for the doctrine of the caste is also responsible for the inculcation of the essential brotherhood, not merely of man but even of all that lives.

One of my correspondents suggests that we should abolish the caste [system] but adopt the class system of Europe—meaning thereby I suppose that the idea of heredity in caste should be rejected. I am inclined to think that the law of heredity is an eternal law and any attempt to alter that law must lead us, as it has before led, to utter confusion. I can see very great use in considering a Brahmin to be always a Brahmin throughout his life. If he does not behave himself like a Brahmin, he will naturally cease to command the respect that is due to the real Brahmin. It is easy to imagine the innumerable difficulties if one were to set up a court of punishments and rewards, degradation and promotion. If Hindus believe, as they must believe, in reincarnation, transmigration, they must know that nature will, without any possibility of mistake, adjust the balance by degrading a Brahmin, if he misbehaves himself, by reincarnating him in a lower division, and translating one who lives the life of a Brahmin in his present incarnation to Brahminhood in his next.

Interdrinking, interdining, intermarrying (*not all castes could freely interdine or marry amongst each other and untouchables could never do either with caste Hindus - ed.*), I hold, are not essential for the promotion of the spirit of democracy. I do not contemplate under a most democratic constitution a universality of manners and customs about eating, drinking and marrying. We shall ever have to seek unity in diversity, and I decline to consider it a sin for a man not to drink or eat with anybody and everybody. In Hinduism, children of brothers may not intermarry. The prohibition does not interfere with cordiality of relations; probably it promotes healthiness of relationships. ... Carried to ridiculous extremes they (*such prohibitions as the above - ed.*) may become harmful, and if the motive is one of arrogation, of superiority, the restraint becomes an indulgence, therefore hurtful. But as time goes forward and new necessities and occasions arise, the custom regarding interdrinking, interdining and intermarrying will require cautious modifications or rearrangement.

Thus whilst I am prepared to defend, as I have always done, the division of Hindus into four castes as I have so often said in these columns, I consider untouchability to be a heinous crime against humanity. It is not a sign of self-restraint but an arrogant assumption of superiority. It has served no useful purpose and it has suppressed, as nothing else in Hinduism has, vast numbers of the human race who are not only every bit as good as ourselves, but are rendering in many walks of life an essential service to the country. It is a sin of which the sooner Hinduism purges itself the better it is for itself, if it is to be recognized as an honourable and elevating religion. I know no argument in favour of its retention and I have no hesitation in rejecting scriptural authority of a doubtful character in order to support a sinful institution. Indeed I would reject all authority if it is in conflict with sober reason or the dictates of the heart. Authority sustains and ennobles the weak when it is the handiwork of reason but it degrades them when it supplants reason sanctified by the still small voice within.

*Young India*, 8-12-1920 (22: 66-69)

---

*Gandhi was convinced that untouchability had no sanction in Hinduism. Yet both conservative Hindus and radical reformers disagreed with him. For the former, untouchability was a part of their faith, for the latter, the faith itself had to be abjured. Gandhi did not consider either of these arguments tenable.*

## Speech at *Antyaj* Conference, Nagpur
## December 25, 1920

... Hindus are convinced that it is a sin to touch the *Antyajas* (*literally the last caste - ed.*). It is a difficult task to make them see reason. We are so much in the grip of lethargy and inertia, so deeply sunk in misery, that we can't even think. Our religious heads, too, are so deeply sunk in ignorance that it is impossible to explain things to them. Eradicating the evil of untouchability means in fact persuading Hindu society of its need. It will be impossible for the *Antyajas* to destroy the crores of Hindus and end the evil of untouchability. If the practice is enjoined in the Vedas or the *Manusmriti*, they ought to be replaced. But where are the men who will write new scriptures? I am a man of the world and lay no claim to being a religious leader. With many shortcomings myself, how can I lay down a moral and ethical code for the Hindus? I may only persuade them to do what I want by making myself worthy of their compassion.

The task is full of difficulties. However, if our reformers only realize that to seek to eradicate this evil by destroying Hindu society is a futile attempt, they will be convinced that they will achieve their purpose only by being patient. I tell you, my *Antyaj* friends, you are as much Hindus as I am, as much entitled to the privileges of Hinduism as I am. If you understand it properly, you have in your own hands the weapons you need, much as we have in our own hands the weapons we need to see an end of the Empire. Just as begging will not avail us for this purpose, so also the means of ending the practice of untouchability is in the hands of the *Antyajas* themselves. If they ask me to teach them Non-cooperation, I am ready to start this very evening. Non-cooperation is a process of self-purification.

... Hindus say that the *Antyajas* drink, that they eat anything and everything, that they do not observe rules of personal cleanliness, that they kill cows. I do not believe that all this is true. No one who claims to be a Hindu can eat beef. If the *Antyajas* want to employ Non-cooperation, they should give up drinking and eating beef or, at any rate, killing cows. I do not ask the tanners to give up their work. Englishmen do this work but we don't mind saluting them. These days even Brahmins do it. I see no uncleanliness in doing sanitary work. I have myself done that work for a long time, and I like doing it. My mother taught me that it is holy work. Though it means handling unclean things, the work itself is holy. Anyone who does it and looks upon it as holy work will go to heaven. You can remain in the Hindu fold without giving it up. If anyone offers you left-over food or cooked food, you should refuse to accept it and ask him to give you grains instead. Be clean in your habits. When you have finished your work of cleaning latrines, change your dress. Though doing this work, you should observe as much cleanliness as my mother did.

You will ask me how you are to get clothes into which you may change; you should, in that case, tell the Hindus that you will not work unless you get Rs. 15 or 20 or 30, whatever you think you need, you can tell them that you perform an essential service for society, in the same way that carpenters and blacksmiths do. Make yourselves fearless. I know the *Antyajas* of Gujarat, know their nature. I teach them this same thing, that they should end the evil of untouchability by their own strength, that they should live as thorough-going Hindus so that other Hindus may honour them instead of despising them. I want to get the thing done through you or through Hindu society itself. I ask you to make yourselves fit for the rights which you demand. By saying so, I do not wish to suggest that you are not already fit. When I ask the country to be fit for *swaraj*, I do not imply that it is unfit. I only ask it to be fitter than it is. I tell the *Antyajas*, likewise, that they have a right to be free, to be the equals of any other Hindu; I ask them, however, to do *tapascharya* and be fitter for these things ...

*Navajivan*, 2-1-1921 (from Gujarati) (22: 132-34)

---

*Recognising the force of the criticisms levelled against the caste system in southern India, especially in the Tamil country, Gandhi came to modify his opinions on the subject. However, he continued to maintain, in one form or another, that the division of society into four varnas or estates, which were not really caste divisions but divisions of labour, was not to be reviled.*

### Speech at Public meeting, Rajapalayam
### October 4, 1927

... I draw the sharpest distinction between *varnashrama* (*the division of society into four estates and four stages of life - ed.*) and caste. Untouchability I hold to be an unpardonable sin and a great blot upon Hinduism. Caste I hold to be an obstacle to our progress and an arrogant assumption of superiority by one group over another. And untouchability is its extreme bad example. It is really high time that we got rid of the taint of untouchability and the taint of caste. Let us not degrade *varnashrama* by mixing it up with untouchability or with caste.

My conception of *varnashrama* has nothing in common with its present distinction of untouchability and caste. *Varna* has nothing to do with superiority or inferiority. *Varna* is the recognition of a definite law that governs human happiness. And it simply means that we must treasure and conserve all the good qualities that we inherit from our ancestors, and that therefore each one should follow the profession of his father so long as the profession is not immoral. And anyone who believes that man is born in order that he might worship his Maker must recognize that he will be able to fulfil his purpose of life if he does not waste his time in finding new professions. You will therefore see that this conception of *varna* has nothing in common with caste.

And, therefore, I would ask you to gird up your loins in order to fight this curse of untouchability and caste, and all the influence that you might have at your command in order to see that every temple is thrown open to all irrespective of caste. In closing our temples against anyone at all we forget that we are making God Himself "untouchable" ...

*The Hindu*, 6-10-1927 (40: 205-06)

---

*Gandhi's views on the varna order and the ethics associated with it underwent even subtler modifications, as he struggled to answer the arguments put forth by Dr. Ambedkar.*

### Dr. Ambedkar and Caste

The following has just been received from Dr. Ambedkar:

The outcaste is a bye-product of the caste system. There will be outcastes as long as there are castes. Nothing can emancipate the outcaste except the destruction of the caste system. Nothing can help to save Hindus and ensure their survival in the coming struggle except the purging of the Hindu faith of this odious and vicious dogma.

Dr. Ambedkar is bitter. He has every reason to feel so. He has received a liberal education. He has more than the talents of the average educated Indian. Outside India he is received with honour and affection, but, in India, among Hindus, at every step he is reminded that he is one of the outcastes of Hindu society ...

As to the burden of his message, the opinion he holds about the caste system is shared by many educated Hindus. I have not, however, been able to share that opinion. I do not believe the caste system, even as distinguished from *varnashrama*, to be an "odious and vicious dogma". It has its limitations and its defects, but there is nothing sinful about it, as there is about untouchability, and, if it is a bye-product of the caste system it is only in the same sense that an ugly growth is of a body, or weeds of a crop. It is as wrong to destroy caste because of the outcastes as it would be to destroy a body because of an ugly growth in it, or a crop because of the weeds. The outcasteness, in the sense we understand it, has, therefore, to be destroyed altogether. It is an excess to be removed, if the whole system is not to perish. Untouchability is the product, therefore, not of the caste system, but of the distinction of high and low that has crept into Hinduism and is corroding it. The attack on untouchability is thus an attack upon this "high-and-low"ness. The moment untouchability goes, the caste system itself will be purified, that is to say, according to my dream, it will resolve itself into the true *varnadharma*, the four divisions of society, each complementary of the other and none inferior or superior to any other, each as necessary for the whole body of Hinduism as any other.

*Harijan,* 11-2-1933 (59: 227-28)

---

**Interview to Associated Press**
**February 14, 1933**

... I should go the whole length with Dr. Ambedkar in fighting the arrogation of superiority on the part of any individual or class over any other. My fight against untouchability is a fight against this horrid doctrine. If untouchability goes from the heart of Hindus, superiority and inferiority are also gone.

But when Dr. Ambedkar wants to fight *varnashrama* itself I cannot be in his camp, because I believe *varnashrama* to be an integral part of Hinduism. It is quite evident that the *varnashrama* of Dr. Ambedkar's conception is being practised today, but that is not my conception of *varnashrama*. In my opinion, at present both *varnadharma* (*the duties mandated for the four varnas - ed.*) and *ashramadharma* (*the duties mandated for the four stages of a person's life - ed.*) are in abeyance, and if I were asked what *varna* is in operation at present, I would say Shudra *varna*, not because it is the lowest, but because it is the only thing that remains, for the divine knowledge, the power behind it and wealth for the support of this knowledge and power are gone.

Knowledge, power and wealth there certainly are in a way. But in the religious conception of *varnadharma*, these three have to be used not for personal ends, but for spiritual and social advance. The only thing that remains open for all today is service, also included in the scheme of *varnashramadharma*, for a spiritual end. Out of that spirit of service, it is possible to revive spiritual knowledge, the power to defend it and the wealth to sustain both. Then, those who are in possession of that knowledge, and will use it for society will be Brahmins, those who use that power for the benefit of society will be Kshatriyas, and those who gain wealth and use wealth, also for society, are Vaishyas. They will all depend for their very existence on Shudras, the embodiments of real service. For me that is true *varnashrama*, and there is no question of superiority or inferiority in this conception ...

*The Hindu*, 15-2-1933; also *The Hindustan Times*, 15-2-1933 (59: 275-76)

## Proposing Solutions: A Question of Faith

*The decade of the 1920s, which saw Gandhi exhorting social change through recognition and repentance, also saw the rise to prominence of Dr. Ambedkar, who challenged Gandhi's manner of resolving the untouchable question. He called upon untouchables to assert their rights and stake their claims for whatever was owed to them as equal human beings and as subjects of an Empire, which, whatever else it did, did not heed caste differences. Dr. Ambedkar also desired legal and constitutional guarantees for the rights he claimed, since he did not believe that Hindu society would live up to whatever promises it made to itself with respect to the untouchables.*

*Gandhi was greatly troubled by this manner of addressing an issue that was dear to him. At the round table conference (1932), and later on, he opposed Dr. Ambedkar's separate political solution to the problem of untouchable representation in the legislature and argued with him in a most unusual way: by going on a fast unto death. The brief extracts in this section present Gandhi's responses to Dr. Ambedkar—both politically and ethically.*

---

*These questions were posed to Gandhi by newsmen and English observers of the Indian scene, when he was in England, representing the Congress at the round table conference convened to outline a new scheme of political reform for India.*

### Answers to Questions, London
[Before October 16, 1931]

... Q. What about the untouchables? Dr. Ambedkar was very severe on you and said that the Congress had no right to claim to represent the untouchables.

Ans. I am glad you have asked the question. I do not mind Dr. Ambedkar. He has a right even to spit upon me, as every untouchable has, and I would keep on smiling if they did so. But I may inform you that Dr. Ambedkar speaks for that particular part of the country where he comes from. He cannot speak for the rest of India and I have numerous telegrams from the so-called "untouchables" in various parts of India assuring me that they have the fullest faith in the Congress and disowning Dr. Ambedkar. And this confidence has a reason. They know the work that the Congress is doing for them and they know that, if they cannot succeed in making their voice felt, I would be prepared to lead a campaign of civil resistance on their behalf and paralyse the Hindu orthodox opposition, if there were such an opposition against them. On the other hand, if they were to be given special electorates, as Dr. Ambedkar persists in demanding, it would do that very community immense harm. It would divide the Hindu community into armed camps and provoke needless opposition.

Q. I see your point, and I have no doubt that you can legitimately speak for the untouchables. But you seem to ignore the fact that communities all the world over insist on being represented by their own people. ... The great stubborn fact against you is that you are not an untouchable.

Ans. I know it very well. But the fact that I claim to represent them does not mean that I should think of representing them on the legislatures. By no means. I should have their own representatives drawn from their own class on the legislatures, and if they are left out, I should provide for their statutory co-option by the elected members. But when I am talking of representing them, I am talking of the representation on the Round Table Conference and I can assure you that, if anyone in India challenged our claim, I should gladly face a referendum and successfully ...

*Young India*, 29-10-1931 (54: 18-19 )

---

*The following is extracted from Gandhi's response to Dr. Ambedkar's demand for separate electorates for the untouchables. This was addressed to both the Indian and British delegates at the round table conference.*

## Speech at Minorities Committee Meeting, London
## November 13, 1931

PRIME MINISTER AND FELLOW DELEGATES,

... I can understand the claims advanced by other minorities but the claims advanced on behalf of the untouchables, that to me is the "unkindest cut of all". It means the perpetual bar-sinister. I would not sell the vital interests of the untouchables even for the sake of winning the freedom of India. I claim myself in my own person to represent the vast mass of untouchables. Here I speak not merely on behalf of the Congress, but I speak on my own behalf, and I claim that I would get, if there was a referendum of the untouchables, their vote, and that I would top the poll. And I would work from one end of India to the other to tell the untouchables that separate electorates and separate reservation is not the way to remove this bar-sinister, which is the shame, not of them, but of orthodox Hinduism.

Let this Committee and let the whole world know that today there is a body of Hindu reformers who are pledged to remove this blot of untouchability. We do not want on our register and on our census untouchables classified as a separate class. Sikhs may remain as such in perpetuity, so may Mohammedans, so may Europeans. Will untouchables remain untouchables in perpetuity? I would far rather that Hinduism died than that Untouchability lived. Therefore, with all my regard for Dr. Ambedkar, and for his desire to see the untouchables uplifted, with all my regard for his ability, I must say in all humility that here the great wrong under which he has laboured and perhaps the bitter experiences that he has undergone have for the moment warped his judgment. It hurts me to have to say this, but I would be untrue to the cause of the untouchables, which is as dear to me as life itself, if I did not say it. I will not bargain away their rights for the kingdom of the whole world. I am speaking with a due sense of responsibility, and I say that it is not a proper claim which is registered by Dr. Ambedkar when he seeks to speak for the whole of the untouchables of India. It will create a division in Hinduism which I cannot possibly look forward to with any satisfaction whatsoever.

I do not mind untouchables, if they so desire, being converted to Islam or Christianity. I should tolerate that, but I cannot possibly tolerate what is in store for Hinduism if there are two divisions set forth in the villages. Those who speak of the political rights of untouchables do not know their India, do not know how Indian society is today constructed, and therefore I want to say with all the emphasis that I can command that, if I was the only person to resist this thing, I would resist it with my life.

Indian Round Table Conference (Second Session): *Proceedings of Federal Structure Committee and Minorities Committee*, Vol. I, pp. 543-4 (54: 158-59)

---

*Gandhi's mission in London was not successful. The government announced that it was willing to grant separate electorates for Muslims and the untouchables. When this announcement was made, Gandhi was in India, and in prison. He responded to this new British offering by writing to the British Premier, Ramsay Macdonald.*

## Letter to Ramsay Macdonald
## August 18, 1932

DEAR FRIEND,

... I have read the British Government's decision on the representation of minorities and have slept over it. In pursuance of my ... declaration at the meeting of the Minorities Committee of the Round Table Conference on 13th November, 1931, at St. James' Palace (*see above - ed.*), I have to resist your decision with my life. The only way I can do so is by declaring a perpetual fast unto death from food of any kind save water with or without salt and soda.

This fast will cease if during its progress the British Government, of its own motion or under pressure of public opinion, revise their decision and withdraw their scheme of communal electorates for the "depressed" classes, whose representatives should be elected by the general electorate under the common franchise no matter how wide it is.

The proposed fast will come into operation in the ordinary course from the noon of 20th September next, unless the said decision is meanwhile revised in the manner suggested above.

... As a man of religion that I hold myself to be, I have no other course left open to me. ... It may be that my judgment is warped and that I am wholly in error in regarding separate electorates for the "depressed" classes as harmful to them or to Hinduism. If so, I am not likely to be in the right with reference to other parts of my philosophy of life. In that case my death by fasting will be at once a penance for my error and a lifting of a weight from off those numberless men and women who have childlike faith in my wisdom. Whereas if my judgment is right, as I have little doubt it is, the contemplated step is but the due fulfilment of the scheme of life, which I have tried for more than a quarter of a century, apparently not without considerable success.

I remain,
Your faithful friend,
M. K. GANDHI

*The Bombay Chronicle*, 13-9-1932 (56: 347-48)

---

## Letter to Ramsay Macdonald
## September 9, 1932

DEAR FRIEND,

I have to thank you for your frank and full letter telegraphed and received this day. I am sorry, however, that you put upon the contemplated step an interpretation that never crossed my mind. I have claimed to speak on behalf of the very class to sacrifice whose interests you impute to me a desire to fast myself to death. I had hoped that extreme step itself would effectively prevent any such selfish interpretation. Without arguing I affirm that for me this matter is one of pure religion. The mere fact of "Depressed" classes having double votes does not protect them or Hindu society in general from being disrupted. In establishment of a separate electorate at all for "Depressed" classes I sense the injection of a poison that is calculated to destroy Hinduism and do no good whatsoever to "Depressed" classes. You will please permit me to say that no matter how sympathetic you may be you cannot come to a correct decision on a matter of such vital and religious importance to the parties concerned.

I should not be against even over-representation of "Depressed" Classes. What I am against is their statutory separation, even in a limited form, from Hindu fold, so long as they choose to belong to it. Do you not realize that if your decision stands and constitution comes into being, you arrest the marvellous growth of work of Hindu reformers who have dedicated themselves to the uplift of their suppressed brethren in every walk of life?

I have therefore been compelled reluctantly to adhere to the decision conveyed to you. As your letter may give rise to a misunderstanding, I wish to state that the fact of my having isolated for special treatment the "Depressed" Classes question from other parts of your decision does not in any way mean I approve of or am reconciled to other parts of decision. In my opinion many other parts are open to very grave objection. Only I do not consider them to be any warrant for calling from me such self-immolation as my conscience has prompted me to in the matter of "Depressed" Classes ...

I remain,
Your faithful friend,
M. K. GANDHI

Government of India, *Home Department, Political, File No. 31/113/32 Pol.* Courtesy: National Archives of India (57: 8)

## Being Penitential: Gandhi Responds to Ambedkar

*Gandhi's fast worried the Congress, whose leaders thought it to be a needless distraction from the real business of politics. Dr. Ambedkar however realized its significance and met Gandhi in prison. He urged him to re-think his stance, but Gandhi would not give up on his resolve—he was fasting so that caste Hindus would mend their ways and demonstrate to the world that untouchables were their brethren, as Hindu as any of them. Dr. Ambedkar was equally unwilling to barter the electoral gains for the untouchables, which he had worked very hard to realize into law. But he knew that he was up against an iron will and had been drawn into a drama whose resolution rested entirely with him. The great responsibility that history had chosen to invest him with framed his responses to Gandhi.*

*After a series of long talks Gandhi and Dr. Ambedkar agreed to settle for reserved seats instead of separate electorates. Untouchables would 'remain with' the caste Hindus and vote together with them to choose untouchable candidates. A grateful Gandhi immediately embarked on a programme of reform, which included the setting up of an institution, the Harijan Sevak Sangh that would address untouchable needs. Gandhi also started a newspaper, Harijan, devoted to the cause of abolishing untouchability. He endorsed and supported efforts to legislate laws that would enable untouchables to enter temples, a right denied to them in the name of custom and scripture. Ultimately the laws did not get passed. Congress leaders who were initially behind these legislative efforts discreetly withdrew their support when a further set of political reforms was announced (in 1935). Elections were to be held soon and the party did not want to risk angering conservative opinion. The franchise was as yet a limited one and linked to education, property and land ownership—that is, most of the several thousand voters were men from the upper castes, who did not look kindly upon attempts at social change.*

*For Gandhi this did not matter. He had never awaited legal fiat to validate his efforts and for him temple entry was important, as much for symbolic and ethical reasons, as any other (as the extracts here reveal). The extracts in this section reveal Gandhi at his moral best—they are fine examples of persuasive non-violent rhetoric in the cause of social change. He unravelled the various discourses that meshed together to constitute commonsensical prejudices with respect to untouchability to show how hollow and insubstantial these arguments were. He also spoke to and debated with untouchable leaders and groups who were sceptical of the Harijan Sevak Sangh and the intentions of caste Hindu reformers.*

---

*Soon after ending his fast, Gandhi began to address the question of untouchability with a marked fervour. He chose to speak to caste Hindus, adopting, at times, an unforgiving and stern moral tone that expressed his resolve of the moment.*

### Statement on Untouchability II
### November 5, 1932

... It is well to remind ourselves of what wrongs we have heaped upon the devoted heads of the Harijans (*children of God, Gandhi's name for untouchables, which he uses often from this period onwards - ed.*). Socially they are lepers. Economically they are worse than slaves. Religiously they are denied entrance to places we miscall "houses of God". They are denied the use, on the same terms as the caste men, of public roads, public hospitals, public wells, public taps, public parks and the like, and in some cases their approach within a measured distance is a social crime, and in some other rare enough cases their very sight is an offence.

They are relegated for their residence to the worst quarters of cities or villages where they practically get no social services. Caste Hindu lawyers and doctors will not serve them as they do other members of society. Brahmins will not officiate at their religious functions. The wonder is that they are at all able to eke out an existence or that they still remain within the Hindu fold. They are too downtrodden to rise in revolt against their suppressors. I have recalled these tragic and shameful facts in order to make the workers vividly realize the implications of the Yeravda Pact (*the pact between Gandhi and Dr. Ambedkar - ed.*). It is only ceaseless effort that can raise these downtrodden fellow beings from degradation, purify Hinduism, and raise the whole Hindu society and with it the whole of India.

Let us not be stunned by this simple recital of the wrongs. If the demonstration during the last week was a genuine expression of repentance on the part of caste Hindus, all will be well, and every Harijan will soon feel the glow of freedom. But before this much-desired end can be achieved the message of freedom will have to be carried to the remotest village. Indeed the work in the village is far more difficult than in the big cities where it is possible quickly to mobilize public opinion.

... And here I would like to recall what Dr. Ambedkar told me. He said, "Let there be no repetition of the old method when the reformer claimed to know more of the requirements of his victims than the victims themselves", and therefore, he added "tell your workers to ascertain from the representatives of the Harijans what their first need is and how they would like it to be satisfied. Joint refreshments are good enough by way of demonstration, but they may be overdone. There is a flavour of patronage about them. I would not attend them by myself. The more dignified procedure would be to invite us to ordinary social functions without any fuss. Even temple-entry, good and necessary as it is, may wait. The crying need is the raising of the economic status and decent behaviour in the daily contact."

I must not repeat here some of the harrowing details given by him from his own bitter experiences. I felt the force of his remarks. I hope every one of my readers will do likewise.

Many suggestions have been sent to me for adoption by the reformers. One is a repetition of what Swami Shraddhanandji used to repeat so often, namely, that every Hindu should have in his home a Harijan who would be for all practical purposes a member of the family. The second comes from a non-Hindu friend deeply interested in India's welfare. He says that every well-to-do Hindu should bear the expense of giving, if possible under his own observation, higher education to a Harijan young man or girl so that these after finishing their education might work for the uplift of fellow-Harijans. Both the suggestions are worthy of consideration and adoption ...

*The Epic Fast,* pp. 318-22 (57: 332-33)

*One of the most important results of the Gandhi-Ambedkar pact was the setting up of an anti-untouchability league by Gandhi, in association with others. Later called the* Harijan Sevak Sangh, *this consisted chiefly of caste Hindu servitors—and their wealthy patrons—who looked to cleanse themselves and society of the stain of untouchability through serving its victims.*

## Statement on Untouchability X
## December 9, 1932

... I have repeatedly declared in unequivocal terms that caste Hindus are sinners who have sinned against those who are called untouchables. Caste Hindus are responsible for the present condition of the untouchables. Immediately, therefore, they repent for the sin and purify themselves by removing the load of untouchability from off the backs of untouchables, we shall discover perfect transformation among the latter. Not that they will at once shed the habits of a lifetime, but there would be conscious effort on their part to shed those habits and everywhere the multitude of caste Hindus will be helping them to give up those habits.

It would be like the suppressed members of a family rejoining the suppressors, feeling the warmth of reunion and suppressors receiving them as if they were never separated. Even among the liberal-minded workers, I have often heard the opinion expressed that untouchability should be removed only when the Harijans give up their bad habits, educate themselves and live clean lives utterly forgetting that Harijans cannot do these things whilst they remain untouchables. Even if they would, they forget also that individual Harijans who are living decently are not received on terms of equality by caste Hindus and the very best amongst them are denied the ordinary amenities of life every day and contact with caste Hindus. Their birth constitutes the automatic cause for the penal servitude for life which cannot be commuted by any change in manners or any other consideration. Hence there is and can be no incentive to better their mode of life. The idea has taken deep root in their minds that they may hope for no redemption at least during their present lifetime.

The only way therefore is to undo the mischief and make them realize the dignity of their status as men. Caste Hindus should first unconditionally take them up as their very own and then and then only can a change in their condition on a vast scale take place. Therefore the first and foremost items in the programme of work should be a whirlwind propaganda for educating and canvassing opinion among caste Hindus. This work can be done by personal visits on a most intensive scale and by flooding the country with literature on the subject.

In my opinion untouchability is as self-demonstrated a sin as untruth. The proposition does not need the support of Shastras (*prescriptive scripture - ed.*). Nevertheless, as there is a body of learned men who invoke the aid of Shastras in order to justify untouchability by reason of mere birth, it would be well for workers to arm themselves with pro-reform literature. There is a growing body of learned men in Shastras who emphatically hold that untouchability as it is believed and practised today, has no support whatsoever in the Shastras. This propaganda can only be entrusted to workers who have character to lose, those who will not be easily ruffled by insults, who have patience to listen to counter argument and wit enough to combat it.

In a movement of religious reform, there is no room whatsoever for coercion in any shape or form. Reformers will have to submit to their fate if as a result of this personal canvassing it is discovered that a vast majority of Hindus have no sense of sin about untouchability or even otherwise are averse to its removal and the consequent raising of the Harijans' status. They will have then without being irritated against the majority shown by personal suffering that they are in the right and the majority in the wrong and this they can best do by making common cause with Harijans and voluntarily denying themselves those rights and conveniences which are today denied to Harijans. Such an act of self-denial by a large body of men and women will by itself fill the Harijans with hope and raise them in their own estimation and encourage them to an effort for self-improvement.

The most effective work that can be done among caste men is to induce them to take one Harijan at least per family either as member or at least as domestic servant. ... If untouchability of Harijans is removed, there can be no objection to their sharing the family meal precisely on the same terms as other castes. There are again innumerable social functions and ceremonies to which Harijans are never invited by caste men. Their cattle and other domestic animals may share their joys and sorrows but not Harijans or, if they do, these are occasions when they are pointedly reminded that they are not the same sort of human beings as caste Hindus.

I have pointed out only a few illustrations of the kind of propaganda and work that can be and should be done amongst caste men to purge themselves of the sin but, even as special treatment and care are bestowed upon a banished member of the family when he is recalled, so will caste men do the work amongst Harijans themselves when the sense of sin has really dawned upon them. They will then go to the Harijans not as teachers or donors but as debtors going to their creditors to discharge their obligations and in that humble spirit they will offer to teach them, their children and otherwise help them in every way possible for them.

... It is, therefore, not enough for them to be able to say that they have touched half a dozen Harijans during the day or even that they have fed a Harijan but their newly born affection for them should make them impatient to render this neglected portion of humanity every help that it is in their power to render.

After all, Harijans themselves have to feel the effect of the new awakening in Hinduism and they cannot do so unless caste men come in contact with them in every walk of life and every activity ...

*The Bombay Chronicle*, 10-12-1932 (58: 156-158)

---

*Even as he entreated reform, Gandhi was acutely aware of the dangers that beset the reformer's task: how was the reformer to be sure that he or she had achieved or persuaded a genuine change of heart, and not a superficial, paternalistic change in attitudes?*

## Civil Resistance and Harijan Service

... The *savarna* (*upper caste - ed.*) Hindus are at one end, Harijans at the other, and the evil custom of ages, which has assumed the dignity of religious tenet, will not be uprooted without penance and purification. Whilst it gladdens my heart that thousands of people flock to the meetings that are being held in towns and villages and that they willingly give their pices as a token of their approval of the movement, I am painfully conscious of the fact that, if the thousands were suddenly called upon to enforce in their own lives what they seem to approve by their attendance at these meetings, they would fail to respond, not from want of will, but from sheer inability. I have discovered this again and again amongst my closest associates who have frankly confessed their inability to enforce immediately in their conduct what they knew was the right thing and what they knew had to be done immediately. They had to put up a brave fight against their traditional repugnance.

The mere intellectual grasp that untouchability is an evil, corroding Hinduism, and that belief in it is tantamount to disbelief in God, His goodness and His Fatherhood, is not enough to destroy the monster. The vicarious penance of the comparatively pure is needed to bring about a change in the hearts of both *savarnas* and Harijans ...

*Harijan*, 1-12-1933 (62: 215)

---

## Speech at Pubic Meeting, Vizagapatnam
## December 28, 1933

You drove me today, on my alighting at the station, through a row of Harijans who were being fed at that time through the charity of some townsman. Whilst he may be entitled to thanks for his liberality, I must confess that it was not a soul-stirring scene. I hung my head in shame as the car was driven through the road along which Harijan men and women were feeding. Just imagine how you and I would feel if some insolent person drove his car through the road where we were taking our meals. I know the custom under which caste dinners are given. All traffic along the road on which dinners are given is entirely prohibited, so that it is possible for diners to have their meals and to be served in perfect peace.

As I have said repeatedly, this movement of purification goes down to the roots of our hearts. I have not asked *savarna* Hindus to appear as patrons before Harijans and throw the leavings of their dishes to them. But I have invited them to open out their hearts to Harijans and to find there a sanctuary for them. But what I saw today was like the act of a patron towards his dependents. And do you know, not only my car was driven through the rows of people taking meals, but other cars followed and the crowd also followed these cars. And I noticed that it was a hard thing for those poor people to protect their food from dust blowing on it. It was not, to say the least, a becoming performance. And you can now understand my grief at having been obliged to witness it.

I know there was no evil intention behind this act. I know also that there was not a single person who had any desire to insult these Harijans who were given free meals. I understand also that those who took me through that road thought it would please me to drive through the rows of Harijans taking meals. I know it was nothing but simple thoughtlessness. As we have been told by Shastras, to live a religious life is like walking on the edge of a sword. And in a worldwide movement like this of self-purification among millions of human beings, a single thoughtless act takes the shape of sin. Every act of ours, therefore, in connection with this Harijan movement has to be dictated and dominated by punctiliousness, extreme caution and inward searching. Having witnessed this scene, I thought it would be wrong on my part not to make a public reference to it. By drawing your attention to it, I have endeavoured to warn the public taking part in this movement of self-purification against a repetition of the scene of this morning.

This brings me to what we are doing today through the length and breadth of India. I have not the shadow of a doubt that untouchability is an unmitigated curse on Hinduism. If the Shastras represent the will and wish of God, there can be no warrant whatsoever in them for untouchability, for which you find no parallel in any part of the world save India. It is bad enough when dictated by selfish motives to consider ourselves high and other people low. But it is not only worse but a double wrong when we tack religion to an evil like untouchability. It, therefore, grieves me when learned pundits come forward and invoke the authority of the Shastras for a patent evil like untouchability. I have said, and I repeat today, that we, Hindus, are undergoing a period of probation. Whether we desire it or not, untouchability is going. But if during this period of probation we repent for the sin, if we reform and purify ourselves, history will record that one act as a supreme act of purification on the part of the Hindus. But if, through the working of the time spirit, we are compelled to do things against our will and Harijans come to their own, it will be no credit to the Hindus or to Hinduism. But I go a step further and say that if we fail in this trial, Hinduism and Hindus will perish.

*Harijan,* 5-1-1934 (62: 357-58)

---

*Gandhi's almost messianic zeal in addressing the 'sin' of untouchability touched new heights in 1934. That year, a massive earthquake killed hundreds of people in Bihar in northern India. Gandhi considered the earthquake a punishment meted out for society's sins against the untouchables.*

### Speech at Reception by Merchants, Madura
### January 26, 1934

... I want you to believe with me that for this absolutely unthinkable affliction in Bihar your sins and my sins are responsible. And then when I ask myself what can be that atrocious sin that we must have committed to deserve such a calamity which staggers us and which today probably has staggered the whole world,— within living memory there is no record of an earthquake of this magnitude in India—I tell you the conviction is growing on me that this affliction has come to us because of this atrocious sin of untouchability. I beseech you not to laugh within yourself and think I want to appeal to your instinct of superstition. I don't. I am not given to making any appeal to the superstitious fears of people. I may be called superstitious, but I cannot help telling you what I feel deep down in me. I do not propose to take up your time and my time by elaborating this. You are free to believe it or to reject it. If you believe with me, then you will be quick and think there is no such thing as untouchability as we practise it today in the Hindu Shastras. You will think with me that it is a diabolical sin to think of any human being as an untouchable. It is man's insolence that tells him that he is higher than any other ...

*The Hindu,* 27-1-1934 (63: 45)

---

## Speech at Public Meeting, Monghyr
## April 3, 1934

... After so many lives were lost and so many houses destroyed, God has roused us from our slumber. All the religions say that when sin accumulates upon the earth, a total cataclysm follows. Untouchability is a great sin. Are we prepared to get rid of it or not is the great question.

Someone has said that that sin is not confined only to the fifteen millions of Biharis. Nothing can be more absurd than to suppose that the Biharis were specially marked by nature for its attention because they are more wicked than the rest. Misfortune is not a proof of an individual's wickedness. All the same, there is an indissoluble connection between natural calamities and man's sin. You cannot have an interruption of the moral law in one part without producing a reaction in the entire system. When one limb is afflicted, through it the entire body is punished. Every calamity should, therefore, lead to a thorough cleansing of individual as well as social life.

What sin have the Muslims committed? Shall I tell you their sin? Their sin is that they have kept up the relationship with us in spite of the fact that we observe untouchability. Can it be a divine law that some persons are born untouchables and remain so for generations? Even men do not have such a law. It does not exist anywhere in this world. The plight of Negroes in America is very bad. They are untouchables but they are not considered to have been born so. Treating them as untouchables is not considered a *dharma*. There are a vast number of people who treat Negroes as untouchables but such behaviour is not considered a part of religion.

It is not that Bihar has incurred this punishment because it is more wicked. Bihar is a part of India. It is a part of the world. God alone knows His ways. We only know that God is full of compassion, love and kindness, so the punishment he metes out must have been based on justice. It is beyond my power to comprehend how. It is beyond the power of anyone. We should consider the calamity as an outcome of our sins—not your sins but mine. Everyone should consider Bihar's calamity as his own and should feel as sad for those who died there as he might have felt at the death of his own relatives. One would be called a human being only if he did that and only then could he claim to know God. We should try to wash off our sins—individual and social—while this tragedy is fresh in our minds ...

*Harijanbandhu,* 29-4-1934 (from Gujarati) and *Harijan,* 20-4-1934 (63 : 351-52)

---

*Gandhi counselled that Hindu temples be thrown open to Harijans, as a gesture of goodwill and justice. During this time, a temple entry bill was awaiting legislative sanction in the councils of British India. Gandhi's views lent strength to the bill, but more important, attempted to secure civic consensus for it.*

### Temple-Entry v. Economic Uplift

One sees sometimes in the public Press criticism on the temple-entry question. It is double-barrelled, being directed on the one hand by Harijans and on the other by sanatanists. Some of the Harijans say, "We do not want temple-entry; do not build temples, but use all you receive for economic uplift." Some sanatanists say, "Give up the temple-entry question altogether. You are hurting our feelings by forcing Harijans into temples." Both are wrong in substance. Not one single pice out of the purse has been or will be spent for building temples.

Attempt is being made only to have public temples opened to Harijans on the same terms on which they are open to the other Hindus. It is a matter of choice for the Harijans to visit or not to visit them; *savarna* Hindus have to lift the bar against Harijans. For those millions who regard temples as treasure-chests of spiritual wealth, they are living realities which they hold dear as life itself. If they are truly repentant towards Harijans, they must share these treasures with the latter. I know what the opening of temples means to Harijans. Only last week, between Dharwar and Belgaum, I opened three temples to Harijans in the presence of crowds of *savarna* Hindus and Harijans. If critics had been present at the opening and noticed the pleasure on the countenances of the Harijans present as they bowed before the image and received the prasad, their criticism would have been silenced. Harijan critics would have realized that, apart from themselves, Harijans at large did desire temple-entry. Sanatanist critics would have realized that temples, wherever they were opened, were being opened with the fullest concurrence of the temple-goers concerned and in the presence of crowds of them.

No hole-and-corner opening can do any good whatsoever to Hinduism. To be of spiritual or any value at all, the opening has to be performed with due publicity, solemnity and the willing consent of the existing temple-goers, and not of such self-styled reformers as have no faith or interest in temples and for whom temples may even be a superstition.

... As for the economic uplift, it is altogether wrong to put it in opposition to temple-entry. Temple-entry can only help such uplift. For, when Harijans are freely admitted to temples, all the avenues to economic betterment must be automatically open to Harijans as to others. So far as the moneys received are concerned, they will all be used only for economic uplift, if it is admitted that educational uplift also means economic, in that it makes the educated Harijan fitter for running life's race. I am aware that education among the *savarnas* has often rendered them less fit for the race. But that has been so, because their education has meant contempt for labour. There is not much danger of such a mishap with the general body of Harijans for some time to come at least. And the danger can be averted altogether, if those who are in charge of the movement will take care to purge Harijan education of the evils of the current method, which ignores the technical side for the most part, if not altogether.

*Harijan*, 16-3-1934 (63: 287-88)

## Temple-Entry

Even though not a single Harijan enters Hindu temples, it is the duty of caste Hindus to throw them open to their brethren the Harijans. It is the truest sign of removal of untouchability from the caste Hindu heart. The other disabilities have undoubtedly to go, but if this one remains untouchability does not die. The civil disabilities will go in course of time, whether caste Hindus wish it or not, but the temples cannot be opened without their free will. There is nothing to prevent a Harijan from drawing water from a public well or demanding at a public school equal treatment with the other pupils. He does not do so today in a vast majority of cases, only because he is yet too timid to assert his legal right. He has reason to be afraid of physical hurt and worse from the caste Hindus. But as he grows from strength to strength, he will certainly assert himself and exercise the right which, owing to his helplessness, he has been hitherto unable to exercise. Not so, however, about temple-entry. If Harijans in a body marched to a temple, they would be prevented by law from entering that temple. Hence the necessity for agitation by caste Hindu reformers for opening their temples to Harijans.

As to temples designed specially for Harijans, I have always opposed such projects. But there have always been reservations. I would not oppose a movement among Harijans themselves for building a temple accessible to both themselves and the caste Hindus. Nor would I oppose the building of such temples by caste Hindus. In other words I do not always oppose the building of temples as such. I think that they play an important and useful part in the lives of millions of people.

That I do not go to the orthodox temples is irrelevant to the issue before us. In order to prove my belief in temples, I need not be a visitor myself. Surely it is enough that I believe in God and offer daily worship not as a mere formality but as an integral part of my spiritual food. Of course I go out of my way to invite Harijans to attend the daily open-air worship. I do so, however, not to wean them from the desire to visit orthodox temples.

Corruption in the temples there undoubtedly is. The illiteracy and cruel ignorance of the priests in charge of most temples is deplorable. But that is a reason for their reformation, not condemnation to destruction. Nor need Harijans pay anything to the priests. Thousands visit temples without paying even a pie. I verily believe that the movement for the opening of temples to Harijans, when it succeeds, as it must some day not far distant, will sweep the temples clean of any of their glaring abuses.

*Harijan*, 14-11-1936 (70: 73-4)

---

*At the height of the anti-untouchability campaigns, orthodox Hindu opinion was extremely unhappy with Gandhi. There was an attempt on his life to which he responded with his usual grace and courage.*

### Statement on Bomb Incident
### Poona, June 25, 1934

I have had so many narrow escapes in my life that this newest one does not surprise me. God be thanked that no one was fatally injured by the bomb, and I hope that those who were more or less seriously injured, will be soon discharged from hospital.

I cannot believe that any sane sanatanist could ever encourage the insane act that was perpetrated this evening. But I would like sanatanist friends to control the language that is being used by speakers and writers claiming to speak on their behalf. The sorrowful incident has undoubtedly advanced the Harijan cause. It is easy to see that causes prosper by the martyrdom of those who stand for them. I am not aching for martyrdom, but if it comes in my way in the prosecution of what I consider to be the supreme duty in defence of the faith I hold in common with millions of Hindus, I shall have well earned it, and it will be possible for the historian of the future to say that the vow I had taken before Harijans that I would, if need be, die in the attempt to remove untouchability was literally fulfilled. Let those who grudge me what yet remains to me of this earthly existence know that it is the easiest thing to do away with my body. Why then put in jeopardy many innocent lives in order to take mine which they hold to be sinful? What would the world have said of us if the bomb had dropped on me and the party, which included my wife and three girls, who are as dear to me as daughters and are entrusted to me by their parents? I am sure that no harm to them could have been intended by the bomb-thrower.

I have nothing but deep pity for the unknown thrower of the bomb. If I had my way and if the bomb-thrower was known, I should certainly ask for his discharge, even as I did in South Africa in the case of those who successfully assaulted me.

Let the reformers not be incensed against the bomb-thrower or those who may be behind him ...

*Harijan*, 29-6-1934 (64: 94-95)

---

*In the course of the tour he undertook throughout the country (1933-36) to gather support for the activities of the Harijan Sevak Sangh, Gandhi had occasion to discuss his work with several untouchable groups and their representatives, many of whom asked him tellingly difficult questions.*

## Discussions with Harijans, Delhi
## December 10, 1933

Q. Do you consider temple-entry as the only way to solve our troubles?

A. It is my firm belief that caste Hindus will not have fulfilled their obligations till they have opened all their temples to Harijans. It is immaterial to me whether Harijans come to worship in those temples or not. It is a matter of sheer justice and penance for caste Hindus. It is repugnant to my sense of justice that Harijans should be excluded from places of worship which are open to other Hindus. I would not consider untouchability as having been eradicated, unless and until the bar against Harijans' entry into temples is removed altogether.

Q. Will you not help us in our economic distress ? To us economic uplift is the chief thing.

A. The economic uplift has not been overlooked. But I should not be satisfied if you were given crores of rupees and yet were still considered untouchables, or if palaces were built for you and you were still kept out of the pale of Hindu society. I should be satisfied only when you are put on a par with caste Hindus in every respect. Thus economic uplift is only one of the many items in our programme.

Q. We should not conceal from you our misgivings about the money collected by you being properly used for our welfare. It depends upon your getting honest workers to work out the scheme, of whom there are very few at present. Would you not then put the funds into our hands to be used according to our discretion? We must tell you frankly we do not trust the present workers.

A. I do not mean to say that no Harijans can take part in the disbursement of the funds. But as the whole reform is conceived as a matter of penance and reparation on the part of caste Hindus, they have to find the best way of using them. They must be guided by the advice of Harijans, but the actual administration of the funds has to rest with them. I may assure you that the least part of these funds will be spent for propaganda. By far the greater part will go directly into the pockets of Harijans. ... They are voiceless. They consider themselves sub-human. In Orissa, some years back, an old man came to me with a straw in his mouth. I tried to awaken in him the sense that he was my equal as a human being. Another Harijan came to me in Cochin all trembling with fear. He was considered invisible in those parts and was afraid of coming into the world of touchables. These people are a standing reproach to us. In the work I am doing, I have these in mind. This service, then, has been taken up, not so much to please Harijans as to discharge a peremptory obligation. We want to wipe out our shame and to die in that effort if need be. We are striving to the best of our ability to render you selfless service, but if Harijans do not accept it, I shall know that we are too late. But the month's experience convinces me that the vast majority gladly accept this service. We do not wish to leave a single phase of your life untouched. We approach you as servants and not as patrons.

Q. You have only added a new name "Harijan" to the many names we already had. Even this new name is significant of our separateness from the others. Unless this sense of separateness goes, in fact as well as in name, how are we to be satisfied?

A. The name "Harijan" was suggested by one of your own class. Thousands have welcomed the name as a good substitute for the offensive names "untouchable" and "avarna". So long as untouchability is not completely removed, a name to distinguish you from others will be required, and an inoffensive name is any day better than one that stinks in the nostrils. When untouchability is gone and Harijans are merged into the Hindus, I do not know by what name—Harijan or Hindu—the whole community will choose to call itself, but till that day comes, distinguishing names will have to be used. You should know that I have become a Harijan by choice and am trying to serve you as one of yourselves; and I am sure that the service will, in the end, be accepted by all Harijans, if I have offered it in a selfless spirit. I would plead with you for a little more patience to see what is being done. The Harijan Sevak Sangh has no other end in view but your good.

*Harijan*, 22-12-1933 (62: 265-67)

---

*The Adi-Karnataka Sangh was an organization of untouchables in the state of Mysore.*

### Interview to Adi-Karnataka Sangh
### June 10, 1936

... D'Souza: You may call yourselves debtors but the Harijans cannot help suspecting a superiority complex in all that you do, and you will lend yourselves to the suspicion that instead of devising means to help them you are devising new means to keep them down.

Gandhiji: If there is suspicion for which there is no ground, I do not mind the suspicion. The *savarnas'* action if it is honest will dispel it. I do not blame the Harijans because they have known nothing better.

A Harijan: There is no suspicion. We simply wanted to narrate our hardships.

Gandhiji: Need you narrate them to me? Don't I know them? Don't I proclaim from the house-tops that you have to rise all along the line? ... We are all debtors; we know that we can pay nothing more than small instalments, and that our creditors may be so enraged as to fling those instalments in our faces and kick us out. But we have to tolerate even this if such is to be our lot. For our goal is to pay the principal with interest. When Dr. Ambedkar abuses us, I say that it serves us right. Then sometimes the creditor becomes so great that he does not care for the debt of the debtors. We, however, have to forget everything else and concentrate on repaying the debt. ... Hinduism is a dying cult if it will not purge itself of untouchability and will perish, Ambedkar or no Ambedkar. If our attempt is sincere, I assume you will see no superiority complex among the reformers. I admit that as I see Hinduism, darkness envelops many *savarnas*. They call irreligion religion. Now it is out of this darkness that a very imperfect class of sinners are trying to come out. As regards the condition of some Harijans, I am reminding the *savarnas* day in and day out that it is they the *savarnas* who are responsible for the filthy habits of some of the Harijans. I tell them it is wrong of them to insist on Harijans getting clean before they receive the same status as other Hindus. We have to admit them first and then make them clean. ...

... D'Souza: We thank you for having given us the assurance you have given. We want you to extend to the Harijans the hand of fellowship. A sinner should not behave as though in expressing penitence he was doing some service to God ...

*Harijan,* 27-6-1936, and *The Hindu,* 11-6-1936 (69: 101-02)

---

*In spite of his oft-stated faith that untouchability was slowly fading out, Gandhi had to repeat his arguments often to obtain a fair hearing.*

### Speech at Harijan Workers Conference, Kengeri
### June 10, 1936

... And why do I say that untouchability is a curse, a blot and a powerful poison that will destroy Hinduism? It is repugnant to our sense of humanity to consider a single human being as untouchable by birth. If you were to examine the scriptures of the world and the conduct of peoples other than Hindus, you would not find any parallel to the untouchability I have brought to your attention just now. I can well understand a person being untouchable whilst he is performing a task which he himself would feel makes him untouchable. For instance, a nurse, who is nursing a patient who is helpless and bleeding and soiling his clothes and suffering from a disease giving out from his body a foul smell, such a nurse whilst she is nursing such a patient is untouchable. But when she has washed herself, she becomes as touchable as ourselves. Not only that. She is not only just as fit to move in society as any of us, but she is also adorable for the profession which she follows. She is worthy of our respect and, so long as we have ranks in our society, she must occupy a very high place amongst us.

Now look at the other side of the picture. Take, for instance, Dr. Ambedkar. He is pronounced as belonging to the Depressed Classes and as being untouchable. Intellectually he is superior to thousands of intelligent and educated caste Hindus. His personal cleanliness is as high as that of any of us. Today he is an eminent lecturer in Law. Tomorrow you may find him a Judge of the High Court. In other words, there is no position in the Government of this country to which he may not aspire and rise, and to which an orthodox Brahmin can rise. But that orthodox Brahmin will be defiled by the touch of Dr. Ambedkar and that because of his unpardonable sin that he was born a Mahar (Untouchable)!

If we had not been habituated to think that untouchability by birth is an integral part of Hinduism, we would not conduct ourselves towards our fellow human beings as many of us conduct ourselves even today. I know that I have told you nothing new in this my talk to you today. I know I have said this same thing in a much more burning language than I have done today. Yet what I say is not, and will not be, superfluous so long as this simple fact of the need for the removal of untouchability does not affect your understanding or conduct.

... What will you do to remove it? If all of you will say that you have done your duty by declaring that untouchability is a blot on Hinduism, it will be a mockery. It will not be enough even if you in a flush of enthusiasm go to a Harijan and touch him and embrace him, and then forget all about him. It will not do even if you go to the Harijan quarters every day and make it a point to touch a number of Harijans as a token of your conviction. What is required of you is that you should regulate your day-to-day conduct in such a manner that you make it absolutely evident to the Harijans whom you come across that a better day has dawned for them all ...

*Harijan*, 20-6-1936 (69: 104-5)

---

*In 1935, Gandhi's counselling of a reform of the caste Hindu heart faced an unexpected challenge. Dr. Ambedkar made a dramatic announcement, that though he was born a Hindu, he would not die as one, implying that he was looking to convert to another faith. Gandhi's responses were characteristic, as is evident from this note he wrote Vallabhbhai Patel, his close associate and independent India's first Home Minister.*

## Letter to Vallabhbhai Patel
## November 14, 1935

BHAI VALLABHBHAI ,

You must be strong enough now to talk and shout [in your usual manner]. I went through your letter to Ambedkar. It is apt but is not likely to have any effect on him at present. He cannot help abusing me how can he spare you, than? Here, as in London, there are several influences acting on him from behind. The pity of it is that the problem has been given exaggerated importance because of his threats. Even that wouldn't matter, were it not that instead of exploiting the situation for constructive work people are going about the wrong way to solve it. Instead of making a determined effort for the eradication of untouchability, they are trying to win over Ambedkar with appeals and entreaties. But let it be; this is the atmosphere in which we have to work. Look where you will, you find nothing but an exhibition of fear and weakness ...

Blessing from
BAPU

*Bapuna Patro-2: Sardar Vallabhbhaine*, pp. 192-3 (68: 147)

## Speech at Gandhi Seva Sangh Meeting IV
### March 4, 1936

Q. ... What is your view about the position Dr. Ambedkar has taken?

A. Had I been in Dr. Ambedkar's place, I would have been as angry. In his position, may be, I would not have been a believer in non-violence. When overcome by anger, a person does whatever comes to his mind. Whatever Dr. Ambedkar does, we must bear it in all humility. Not only that, it would be a service to Harijans. If he really hits us with shoes, we must bear even that. But we should not be afraid of him. There is no need to kiss Dr. Ambedkar's feet to convince him. That would be a disservice. If he and the other Harijans who have no faith in Hinduism embrace another religion, that too would make for our expiation. We deserve such treatment. Our task [now] is to wake up to the situation and purify ourselves. There is no need for flattery. That is why I expressed my sorrow at his announcement and suggested self-purification. I did nothing more ...

*Gandhi Seva Sanghke Dwitiya Adhiveshan (Savli) Ka Vivaran*, pp. 59-63 (from Hindi) (68: 267)

---

### A Dangerous Proposal

... Dr. Ambedkar wants to scourge the *savarna* Hindus as he has every right to do, but he may not expect the latter to be party to it. He has every right to be impatient. But prejudices and superstitions centuries old do not die in a moment. No one who has at all cared to study the reform movement will deny that every attempt humanly possible has been and is being made to bring home to the *savarna* Hindus the message of the anti-untouchability movement. If Dr. Ambedkar's proposal were accepted, the reform movement would receive a setback which might mean death to it in the end. For it contemplates a paper but legal transfer of Harijans from the Hindu fold to some other, no matter by what name the latter is called. It must mean fratricide. Harijans themselves will be cut up into two rival sections, and if they are both classified as Harijans within the meaning of the Pact their state then will be worse than it is today, and it will be an evil day for unhappy India if such a calamity descends on her. It is futile to argue that although there will be nominal change of religion, there won't be a real one, and if there is any, it would not be so bad as if Harijans were called Christians or Muslims. If it is a change of religion, it matters little under what label they are classified.

Only if they are said to belong to another religion and still remain Harijans, an additional cause of internecine quarrel would be created; and all this to satisfy the desire to punish savarna Hindus. And who are we, the self-constituted leaders, to barter away the religious freedom of Harijans? Has not every Harijan, however dull or stupid he may be, the right to make his own choice? It is one thing for Dr. Ambedkar and those who wish to change over to some other religion to do so, and wholly another for political or other parties (*Gandhi has in mind parties such as the revivalist and right-wing Hindu Mahasabha which were competing for Dr. Ambedkar's attention - ed.*) to assume such change for the mass of Harijans and to base thereon legal and other consequences of a far-reaching character. If the leaders of different religions in India ceased to compete with one another for enticing Harijans into their fold, it would be well for this unfortunate country. I have the profound conviction that those who are engaged in the competition are not serving the cause of religion. By looking at it in terms of politics or economics they reduce the religious values, whereas the proper thing would be to estimate politics and every other thing in terms of religion.

Great as the other forces of the world are, if there is such a thing as God soul-force is the greatest of all. ... No instrument devised by man has been able to know anything positive of soul force or spiritual force. It is on that force that the true religious reformer has hitherto relied and never without hope fulfilled. It is that force which will finally govern the welfare of Harijans and everyone else and confound the calculations of men however gifted they may be intellectually. The reformer who has entered upon the duty of ridding Hinduism of the disease of untouchability has to depend in everything he does on that force and nothing else.

*Harijan*, 22-8-1936 (69: 314-16)

# Concluding the "Harijan" Years

*Gandhi's long and resilient struggle with untouchability—the violence within—came to be re-shaped in the 1930s. His early moral reasoning for the abolition of untouchability, which he developed and re-defined during the years of Non-cooperation, faced a severe political challenge with the rise to political and social prominence of Dr. Ambedkar. The latter's determined resistance to what he considered Gandhi's dubious moralising lead him to seek solutions within a recognisably modern framework—of the law, rights and the State. Gandhi responded to this challenge by re-working his ideas and by raising the pitch of moral intensity with which he had always attended to the problem. Rather than combat Dr. Ambedkar on the terrain of rights and politics, he chose to field his opposition on the ambiguous terrain of religious faith and duty.*

*Gandhi's complex and at times convoluted reasoning on the subject of untouchability owed a great deal to the culture that he was most familiar with —the paternalistic mercantile culture of Gujarat, which looked to Jainism on one hand and devotional Hinduism centred on the worship of Krishna, on the other, for its spiritual sustenance. This culture was modest in its opposition to social oppression and unlike its radical Marathi counterpart, did not countenance a destruction of social inequities. Modern developments—the spread of education, the institution of a uniform system of justice—did not produce in Gujarat those far-reaching changes that transformed western and southern Indian societies and propelled lower caste and untouchable Hindus to challenge the caste hierarchy. In this sense, Gandhi's efforts were both pioneering and radical. It is not accidental that most of his heartfelt admonitions of untouchability were addressed to his Gujarati interlocutors.*

*In the event, efforts to turn the caste Hindu heart to admit remorse and penitence—in the post-Poona Pact 1930s—did achieve results. For one, there emerged a concerted attempt to help untouchables in dire straits, through the welfare and ameliorative activities of the Harijan Sevak Sangh. The actual nature of the Sangh's work was disputed by untouchable leaders, including Dr. Ambedkar, who argued that they were unable to commend its efforts, which were found wanting, when compared with the high moral rhetoric that sustained* those efforts. More generally too Dr. Ambedkar felt that Gandhi's attempts to seek a religious solution to a social and political problem only served to reify the status of untouchables, rendering them permanent objects of the caste Hindus' pietistic paternalism. Besides, rather than encourage untouchables to assert their rights to a common justice and humanity, caste Hindu initiatives, however well-meaning, only served to stymie the untouchables' political progress.

Dr. Ambedkar's most severe critique, though, was of the Indian National Congress and the manner in which Gandhi's views lent it a moral aura, which belied that party's deep-grained social conservatism and disinterest in social reform. He was particularly hard on the Congress' attempts to legislate temple entry, which, he held, were cosmetic and calculated to win it favour with the untouchables. He also observed that in this instance Gandhi's initial support of the temple entry bills and his disavowal of their significance, when they failed to be passed, appeared an exercise in moral sophistry. Too often, Gandhi brought his distinctive moral reasoning to explain away and legitimize Congress' failures and wrongs. Later, Dr. Ambedkar wrote up his views on Gandhi and untouchability into a volume of essays, titled, What Congress and Gandhi did to the Untouchables. It was published in 1945.

Dr. Ambedkar's indictment of Gandhi has grown in its meanings and significance since the time it was advanced. For one, Gandhi's reliance on a reform of the caste Hindu heart has not caused a fundamental convulsion of the social conscience, though, it did move individuals to re-examine their lives. Secondly, it has become increasingly clear—from a growing political and historical scholarship of the period—that Gandhi's insistence on separating untouchability from its constituent location in the caste system prevented him from considering seriously those powerful critiques of the social order that had emerged during his lifetime in southern and western India. These critiques addressed untouchability within the overall logic of the caste system—described by Dr. Ambedkar and the southern anti-caste radical, E V Ramasamy, as a system of graded inequality, which mandated exclusion and difference at every level of a complex and layered social hierarchy. In contrast to these views, Gandhi argued that the divisions of the caste order were really horizontal divisions of labour which helped to minimise competition, enabled restraint and made for stability.

*Significantly, Dr. Ambedkar pointed out that the system divided workers vertically and not only horizontally, and that some were deemed high and others low.*

*Yet, as we have seen, Gandhi's understanding of caste and untouchability was not static. Though he held on to his faith in an idealised social system where a division of labour and labourers did not connote inequality and instead implied horizontal comradeship, his sense of this system altered. In the late 1940s he argued that the only valid role left to citizens was that of the shudra or the man of service or the ati-shudra, the untouchable, who took on social dirt to keep society clean: for in the dutiful performance of this role alone lay the practise of deep spiritual knowledge.*

*In spite of his active engagement with the problems of untouchability until almost the end of his life, Gandhi today has more critics than admirers, as far as this subject is concerned. Anti-caste radicals, taking their cue from Dr. Ambedkar, observe that Gandhi's intent is not really what matters to posterity, as much as the fact that he did not view untouchables as active historical beings, or engage with them as sentient persons, capable of exercising moral and political choices on their own. They further note: untouchable existence appeared to embody for Gandhi a state of human wretchedness; untouchables were living effects of an evil we seem to be capable of in our dealings with fellow human beings. So, fighting untouchability was, for him, a measure of self-cleansing, and has to be understood as such, and not as an initiative to end untouchability.*

*Gandhi's fight against the darkness within, then, was limited by its premises. But at the same time, the moral edge that he brought to his reasoning on privilege and power, and his recognition of the public and civic importance of remorse and reconciliation are matters that cannot be ignored. Caste Hindus in India have not had such a sympathetic yet determined interlocutor since his time, and the caste Hindu conscience has been left to its own moral indolence. There does not exist today, amongst a majority of caste Hindus, that burning sincerity or ethical sorrow, which Gandhi held was necessary for real social change to occur. Whatever social change has taken place has been due to the force of law in some instances, and because deprived communities have relentlessly asserted their rights to a decent civic existence.*

# Chapter 6

## Uneasy Times: When Nations Stood Divided
## 1938-1944

*The late 1930s were uneasy years. Hindu-Muslim relationships attained a new low during this time. Political reforms, announced in 1935 by the colonial government led to elections in 1937. The franchise was widened though it was still nowhere close to universal suffrage. Indians elected to local government—to provincial legislative councils—acquired fairly substantial powers, but British authority continued to remain decisive. The elections divided the polity unevenly. There were Hindu majority provinces, where the Congress mandate was accepted, and a smaller number of Muslim majority provinces, where Muslim parties, including the Muslim League, won the largest number of seats in the newly elected councils. (According to the decisions made a the round table conference of 1932, Muslims constituted a separate electorate). Though this division in itself did not lead to violence, it proved to be an enabling context for Hindus and Muslims to confront each other acrimoniously, both in the Councils and on the streets.*

*Gandhi remained detached from these events, though he was disturbed by reports of Congress misrule and distressed by growing Hindu-Muslim tension, including instances of rioting. There were other reasons for his dejection. The rise of the left, both within and outside the Congress, had led to the formation of a socialist bloc within the party. These were also years when India's capitalist class shifted their support decisively to the Congress right wing, comprising Hindu revivalists in the main. Earlier, in the manner of older mercantile communities, Indian big business had responded to Gandhi's call to them to act as trustees of their wealth and serve worthy social causes: some amongst them underwrote Gandhi's spinning experiments and later on, in the 1930s, the activities of the Harijan Sevak Sangh. However by the late 1930s, when it became increasingly clear that Gandhi was firm in his opposition to modern capitalist growth, India's capitalists were willing to even look to the left-wing Nehru who was excited by modern technological progress.*

*Gandhi did not appear to grant this development any measure of importance and in some ways even encouraged it—he was responsible for limiting Nehru's socialist leanings. To him the problems posed by socialism were essentially problems of political militancy. He read in the socialists' incitements to class war an invitation to violence and a defiance of the Congress' political authority. He was also disturbed by the growing demands made on Congress by a restive people—political prisoners languishing in gaols, peasants wanting an amelioration of their plight, striking workers, citizens who wanted greater liberty to criticize their rulers ...*

*There was revolt in the princely states, so-called because they were ruled by pre-modern kings. These kingdoms were not part of the administrative territory of British India but were effectively under British political control. The Congress had to take a position on the demands for greater democracy in princely India. Gandhi accepted the wisdom of Congress intervention, but was uneasy with the anger that appeared to rule the streets in these old kingdoms.*

*Gandhi's responses to the dilemmas of the period were three-fold: though defending its fledgling ministries, he criticized Congressmen in no uncertain terms and urged them to adopt a credo of patient and humble service, especially in resolving matters of Hindu-Muslim tension. Secondly, he argued with the left bloc in the Congress, justifying the use of discipline in regulating popular protest. Lastly, he attempted to work out a model for satyagraha in the despotic princely states. Meanwhile, he was also watchful of the international situation. Global political developments around this time—the rise of Hitler and a growing Nazi belligerence—mocked his faith in non-violence and peace (see Chapter 7). Further, Britain dragged India into an expensive, prolonged and destructive conflict without really consulting the opinion of India's leaders. Gandhi—and the Congress—both felt the injustice of this imperial decision and were determined to confront Britain with her own avowed concerns for democracy, which animated her war aims in Europe. This confrontation proved to be dramatic and tedious in turn, with the Congress unable to act beyond what was allowed it within the terms of wartime regulations.*

*Gandhi however was vastly inventive and the years 1939-1942 saw him experiment with non-violence in diverse ways, ranging from the expansive to the tortuous. The deep-seated discontent and unhappiness of the period erupted with particular force when, with an imminent Japanese invasion in the offing, Gandhi and the Congress called on the British to 'Quit India'. To Gandhi, who had striven hard not to embarrass Britain in her moment of crisis, there appeared no choice but to serve notice to Empire: Hindu-Muslim mistrust had reached an apogee during the war years, with the Muslim League demanding a separate Islamic state, to be carved out of the subcontinent's Muslim majority areas. It was clear that the colonial government was sympathetic to this demand. It was determined to wilfully build on communal hatred and dissension to render nationalist claims vulnerable, and to prolong its own rule in one way or another in the subcontinent. Gandhi felt that a grand show of nationalist anger was necessary: to demonstrate to Empire that independence could not be further delayed and to insist, in the face of the Muslim League's cry for Pakistan, that India could offer an united front to colonial rule.*

## To Serve and Suffer: Satyagraha in Power

*In 1937 elections to legislative councils were held. The Congress was returned to power in eight provinces in British India, and Muslim parties to five provinces. The Muslim League was, as yet, nowhere as powerful as it would be in the early 1940s. It had not done as well as other Muslim groups, such as those in Bengal and the Punjab, and was perceived even by Muslim politicians as an unnecessarily troublesome organization defending narrow, partisan interests. In the United Provinces of the northern Indian plains, the League had attempted to work with the Congress before the elections but once the latter attained a majority and came to power, the two parties broke faith with each other.*

*The reasons for this were various: liberal Congressmen were afraid that the League would stand in the way of land reforms, since its constituency comprised rich landlords. Muslims in the Congress found the League's insistence on a separate Muslim political identity untenable, while conservative Hindu Congressmen actively resented it. In the event, the break when it happened proved irreversible, for the moment at least, and left the League feeling unfairly outwitted and bitter. The fact that the Congress had adopted, from early 1937 onwards, a 'Muslim mass contact' programme that attempted to mobilise Muslims on economic issues did not help matters, as the League saw in this gesture a move to divide the Muslim community. These conditions proved ripe for discord and the late 1930s witnessed Hindu-Muslim rioting in several parts of northern India.*

*Gandhi was unhappy with Congress responses to Hindu-Muslim dissensions and unusually despondent. He was particularly troubled by the manner in which the Congress ministries functioned and dismayed by what he called 'their corruption, their selfishness and petty bickerings' as well as their easy willingness to use force, even as the British had, to quell popular protests. More specifically, the rise of various interest groups in the Congress worried Gandhi: there was a socialist bloc, a group that was wished to support popular protests in the autocratic princely states, conservative Hindu fringe groups that were obstinate in their mistrust of Muslims … The socialists worried him in particular and he held them responsible for fomenting discontent amongst the masses. His responses to the situation were varied. On the one hand, he refused to countenance impatient denunciations of the Congress ministries; on the other hand, he was extremely critical of the average Congressman's will to power. He counselled non-violence and tolerance yet he asserted the need for the Congress to speak with one voice, calling for restraint and discipline and warning against an abuse of freedom.*

*The extracts in this section show a troubled Gandhi, as he responded to disparate concerns, impelled, in each instance, to account for the resilience of satyagraha.*

---

*As Hindu-Muslim tension grew, conservative opinion in both communities hardened, leading to the rise of demagogic leaders in either camp. Fiery rhetoric inflamed popular passion and in the northern Indian United Provinces where demagogues of both sorts were active, a series of riots took place. Gandhi was both anguished and ashamed by the manner in which Congressmen conducted themselves during the riots.*

## Our Failure
### [Before March 22, 1938]

The communal riots in Allahabad—the headquarters of the Congress—and the necessity of summoning the assistance of the police and even the military show that the Congress has not yet become fit to substitute the British authority. It is best to face this naked truth, however unpleasant it may be. The Congress claims to represent the whole of India, not merely those few who are on the Congress register. It should represent even those who are hostile to it and who will even crush it, if they could. Not until we make good that claim, shall we be in a position to displace the British Government and function as an independent nation. This proposition holds good whether we seek to displace British rule by violent action or non-violent.

Most probably by the time these lines appear in print, peace would have been established in Allahabad and the other parts. That, however, will not take us further in our examination of the fitness of the Congress as an organization ready to displace British authority in its entirety.

... The riots and certain other things I can mention should make us pause and ask ourselves whether the Congress is really growing from strength to strength. I must own that I have been guilty of laying that claim. Have I been overhasty in doing so? It is my conviction that the phenomenal growth of the Congress is due to its acceptance and enforcement, however imperfect, of the policy of non-violence. Time has arrived to consider the nature of Congress non-violence. Is it non-violence of the weak and the helpless or of the strong and the powerful? If it is the former, it will never take us to our goal and, if long practised, may even render us for ever unfit for self-government. The weak and helpless are non-violent in action because they must be. But in reality they harbour violence in their breasts and simply await opportunity for its display. It is necessary for Congressmen individually and collectively to examine the quality of their non-violence. If it does not come out of real strength, it would be best and honest for the Congress to make such a declaration and make the necessary changes in its behaviour.

By this time, i. e., after seventeen years' practice of non-violence, the Congress should be able to put forth a non-violent army of volunteers numbering not a few thousands but lacs who would be equal to every occasion where the police and the military are required. ... A non-violent army acts unlike armed men, as well in times of peace as of disturbances. They would be constantly engaged in constructive activities that make riots impossible. Theirs will be the duty of seeking occasions for bringing warring communities together, carrying on peace propaganda, engaging in activities that would bring and keep them in touch with every single person, male and female, adult and child, in their parish or division. Such an army should be ready to cope with any emergency, and in order to still the frenzy of mobs, should risk their lives in numbers sufficient for the purpose. A few hundred, maybe a few thousand, such spotless deaths will once for all put an end to the riots. Surely a few hundred young men and women giving themselves deliberately to mob fury will be any day a cheap and braver method of dealing with such madness than the display and use of the police and the military.

It has been suggested that when we have our independence riots and the like will not occur. This seems to me to be an empty hope, if in the course of the struggle for freedom we do not understand and use the technique of non-violent action in every conceivable circumstance. To the extent that the Congress Ministers have been obliged to make use of the police and the military, to that extent, in my opinion, we must admit our failure. That the Ministers could not have done otherwise is unfortunately only too true. I should like every Congressman, I should like the Working Committee, to ask themselves why we have failed, if they think with me that we have.

*Harijan,* 26-3-1938 (73: 23-5)

---

### The Choice

My remarks arising out of the recent riots in U.P. have attracted much attention. Friends have sent me cuttings from the Press. This is some of the criticism printed or spoken:

(1) My writing betrayed hysteria.

(2) I wrote without sufficient data.

(3) I had recanted my views on Non-cooperation and civil resistance.

(4) I had been driven to the policy of the Liberals (*those who had always opposed direct action against the British - ed.*).

(5) Congressmen had never adopted non-violence as between themselves.

(6) I was expecting the impossible from human nature.

(7) If my position was accepted *swaraj* would never be obtained, for all India could never become non-violent.

There is much more I could cull from the criticism. I have only taken the relevant parts.

1. If my article betrayed hysteria, the symptoms still persist, for in spite of the criticism which I have studied with the care it demanded, I see nothing to change the position I have taken up. The critics should remember that my proposition was specific and

narrow. *Swaraj* could not be obtained through non-violent means unless our non-violence was of the brave and such as to be able to deal effectively with violence. I have not maintained that it could not be obtained by other means. But if it could be so obtained we were not ready to deliver the goods, for we were not ready for matching our force against the British.

2. All the data required were that there were riots, no matter on how small a scale, that Congressmen were not able to deal with them non-violently, and that the aid of the police and the military had to be summoned. There was no dispute about these three broad facts. They were enough to enable me to draw the conclusion I did. In this there was no reflection on the Ministers. I have admitted that they could not have acted otherwise. The fact, however, remains that the Congress non-violence was not able to cope with the emergency.

3. There is nothing in my article to warrant the inference that I had lost my faith in Non-cooperation and civil resistance. All I need say is that it is brighter than ever. The two are quite enough to bring *swaraj*, provided that non-violence practised is of the bravest.

4. I wish I could be drawn towards the policy of the Liberals. I have many personal friends among them. But they have no sanction. I claim that I have an infallible sanction. My article was written to show that during the riots it was not the sanction that had failed, the failure was of the organization which had accepted the sanction, namely, active, constructive non-violence.

5. I can only refer the critics to the many resolutions of the Congress which do not confine the use of non-violence only towards Englishmen. Indeed I remember having many discussions at the Working Committee meetings at which the necessity of non-violence among ourselves was emphasized.

6. Well, human nature has hitherto responded nobly to the call of non-violence. But I am concerned with the Congress nature. Congressmen have to sign a pledge which commits them to non-violence. My question was and is—have they non-violence in them? If they have, is it of the brave? My thesis is that if it is of the brave, it should be enough for dealing with the riots and for delivering

the goods.

7. This is answered in the foregoing. But I have the fear that our non-violence is not of the kind required. Congressmen may not treat my warning lightly. After all I am supposed to be the Congress expert, however inefficient, on non-violence. I have confidence in my readings and my remedies...

Here are some of the remedies :

1. We must discover a solution for the Hindu-Muslim tension. I use that expression deliberately instead of "communal"—for if we find this, the other will follow as a matter of course.

2. There must be a purging of the Congress registers so as to make them proof against bogus voters. From all accounts I receive, our registers contain too many bogus names to be called at all accurate.

3. Congressmen must not be afraid to find themselves in a minority.

4. Without delay every Provincial Congress Committee should raise a proper corps of volunteers pledged to non-violence in thought, word and deed. And there should be a manual of instructions as to training, etc., prepared for universal use.

There is nothing heroic or impracticable in these suggestions. But they are impracticable if those who lead have no living faith in non-violence. If they have not, the sooner non-violence is removed from the Congress vocabulary the better it is for the Congress and the nation. The alternative is certainly not unadulterated violence. The Congress is the only political organization in the world which has, at my instance, adopted unadulterated non-violence for the attainment of *swaraj*. It is its only sanction. I dare say that if its quality is not what it should be, it will do great harm to the nation. In the last heat we may be found to be cowards instead of brave men and women. And there is no disgrace greater than cowardice for fighters for freedom. Surely there is nothing to be ashamed of in retracing our steps. If we feel that we shall not be able to displace the British power without a violent struggle, the Congress must say so to the nation and prepare accordingly. We must do what is being done all the world over—"forbear when we can, hit when we must".

If that is to be our creed or policy, we have lost precious seventeen years. But it is never too late to learn and mend. Seventeen years in the life of a nation is nothing. It will go hard with Congressmen if having received the warning they do not make the choice.

*Harijan*, 9-4-1938 (73: 86-9)

---

*The socialist bloc within the Congress had grown in numbers and popularity in the mid and late 1930s. Socialists were dismayed by the rank conservatism of certain Congress leaders and incensed by the manner in which they tried to rein in their own partymen. Gandhi had to mediate and explain the Congress' stance.*

## Discussion with Communists
## [Before November 11, 1938]

COMMUNISTS: We confess, we do not understand what it is exactly you stand for. We oppose you, not necessarily because we always differ from you but because we do not know your mind and so regard your actions with vague fear and distrust. Faith would become easier if we understand you. ... We have again and again made it clear that we do not want any condonation of violence or incitement to violence. What distresses us is this. Whereas there was enlargement of civil liberty on Congress taking office, ... civil liberty has actually suffered curtailment under the Congress ministries. We are driven to feel that this cry about abuse of civil liberty has been raised merely as a convenient pretext to shield the Ministers, some of whom have been behaving exactly like the old bureaucrats.

GANDHIJI: I am more than glad that you have come to me, because you have come to the real culprit. I must confess that I am the sole author of that resolution (*passed by the Congress, warning Congressmen against a misuse of freedom and civil liberty - ed.*). It is based upon unimpeachable evidence in my possession. But you should have known from my writings that they were meant to help Ministers to avoid action against those who have incited to violence and even actually committed it. Instead of Ministers taking action against them my purpose was to create public opinion against violent speeches, writings or acts. The resolution was a substitute for legal action. I want you to accept my assurance that I would not screen a single Minister who interferes with civil liberty or acts contrary to Congress resolutions ...

C. We feel puzzled. You have said that coercive measures should be used to put down incitement to violence. Is it right to use Government violence to check the so-called incitement to violence by Congressmen?

G. The question is badly put. But my answer is there. There should be no Government violence. But if a man kills a little child and robs it of its ornaments and if I deprive him of the liberty to repeat the performance, I would not call my act violence. It would be violence if my act was meant to be a punishment. I would like to make my position clearer still. You cannot have the cake and eat it. Assuming that there has been violence of speech, it has to be noticed by the Congress or the Congress Ministers. I have suggested the former course. The resolution was in pursuance of that course. Of course you may question the validity or sufficiency of proof in the possession of the Working Committee. In that case, you could have called for proofs and accepted the resolution subject to the production by the Working Committee of the proof in its possession. If you admit that violent speech or writing does not come under the protection of civil liberty, there should have been no walk-out. Surely he who runs may see that in the Congress provinces latitude of speech and writing is allowed such as has never before been enjoyed.

C. All the same, we cannot reconcile ourselves to the bias which the High Command has persistently shown against us. We have put ourselves under Congress discipline. We have joined the Congress because it is the only body that can raise a popular movement. If we misbehave, we may be put out and should lose caste with the people. As a people's party we must move with the people or go out. These Ministers, on the other hand, are seeking to set themselves above the people to make themselves immune to democratic influence. We are wedded to no dogma. Tell us what we can do together in immediate practice. Our motives may differ but practice will count.

G. You should also admit that neither the resolution nor, I think, my article makes mention of socialists or communists. Violence is no monopoly of any one party. I know Congressmen who are neither socialists nor communists but who are frankly devotees of the cult of violence. Contrariwise, I know socialists and communists who will not hurt a fly but who believe in the universal ownership of instruments of production. I rank myself as one among them. But here I am not thinking of myself but of others whom I have the good fortune to know. What you have said, however, makes it clear to me that you do not put the same stress as I do on the means. But I understand your argument. Our minds are working at cross purposes. I want to occupy a corner in your hearts, if I can. But some of you have told me frankly that it is impossible, for they look at things from opposite poles. The utmost they can do is to tolerate me because they credit me with some capacity for sacrifice and influence over the masses. Now I make a sporting offer. One of you or all of you can come to me at Segaon when I return there, study me, see all my papers, look at the correspondence, ask me questions, and decide upon the course you would adopt in your dealings with me. There is no secrecy with me. My mission is to convert every single Indian to my view of the means of liberation. If only that happens, complete independence is ours for the having.

They next questioned Gandhiji as to the possibility of the Communist Party being legalized. "We do not *want* violence," they explained. "It is true that we have not made non-violence our creed. We are not pledged to non-violence at all cost and for all time to come, but for the time being and in the immediate future we see no necessity for violence. Our method is thus, just now, the same as that of the Congress. We are forced at present to function as a secret organization because we are under ban. If the ban is removed, the necessity for secrecy should cease. For the rest we can only give the assurance that should we in the future find it necessary to drop non-violence, we shall make a clear and open declaration about it."

G. If you mean that you do not as a party believe in violence, then you should make that statement. All your literature that I have studied clearly says that there is no independence without resort to force. I know that there is a body of communists that is slowly veering round to non-violence. I would like you to make your position absolutely plain and above board. I have it from some of the literature that passes under the name of communist literature that secrecy, camouflage and the like are enjoined as necessary for the accomplishment of the communist end, especially as communism has to engage in an unequal battle against capitalism which has organized violence at its beck and call. I would, therefore, like you, if you can, to make it plain that you do not believe in these things I have mentioned.

The communist friends promised to send Gandhiji an authoritative statement setting forth the position of their party.

G. You may think over what I have said, keep yourself in touch with me, correct me when you think I go astray, and try to understand me. Do not distrust me. When you have doubts express them fearlessly. And I suggest that we leave the discussion at that. But I should be glad to think that we part with the determination to understand one another and but to meet again.

*Harijan*, 10-12-1938 (74: 211-14)

---

*The princely states ruled by 'native' kings lay nominally outside the administrative authority of British India, yet British arms and support kept the despotism of their rulers alive. Popular discontent against princely rule grew during this period. Initially Gandhi counselled the Congress to desist intervening in the internal affairs of the States, but he realized that since the protesters looked up to the Congress and were, anyway, being advised by them, non-intervention was not a viable political option anymore.*

## States and the People

The almost simultaneous awakening in the various States is a very significant event in the national struggle for independence. It will be wrong to think that such awakening can be due to the instigation of one person or a body of persons or any organization. It is just possible that the Haripura resolution of the Congress put the people of the States on their mettle and they realized as never before that their salvation depended upon their own labours. But above all it is the time spirit that has brought about the awakening. It is to be hoped that the Princes and their advisers will recognize it and meet the legitimate aspirations of the people. There is no half-way house between total extinction of the States and the Princes making their people responsible for the administration of their States and themselves becoming trustees for the people, taking an earned commission for their labours.

... Even as the British Government, as the Paramount Power, are bound to protect the Princes against harm from outside or within, they are equally or *a fortiori* bound to ensure just rule on the part of the Princes. Hence it is their bounden duty, when they supply the police or the military to any State, to see that there is a proper emergency justifying the request and that the military or the police will be used with becoming restraint. From Dhenkanal ( *a princely state in eastern India, in what is now Orissa - ed.*) have come to me stories of fiendish cruelty exercised by the State myrmidons under the shadow of the police supplied by the Paramount Power. I asked for evidence in support of some of the unnamable cruelties. And I have enough to inspire belief. Indeed, it is a question whether responsible Ministers in the provinces (*that is, Congress ministers of the British Indian provinces - ed.*) have not a moral responsibility in respect of the people of the States in their respective provinces. ... So long as the States and the people are satisfied, Ministers have no worry. But have they none if there is, say, a virulent epidemic in the States which, if neglected, may easily overtake the province in which they are situated? Have they none when there is a moral epidemic which seems to be raging in Dhenkanal?

... I feel that the Ministers in the provinces are morally bound to take notice of gross misrule in the States within their borders and to tender advice to the Paramount Power as to what, in their opinion, should be done. The Paramount Power, if it is to enjoy friendly relations with the provincial Ministers, is bound to give sympathetic ear to their advice.

There is one other matter which demands the urgent attention of the States and their advisers. They fight shy of the very name Congress. They regard Congressmen as outsiders, foreigners and what not. They may be all that in law. But man-made law, if it is in conflict with the natural law, becomes a dead letter when the latter operates in full force. The people of the States look up to the Congress in all matters affecting their interest. Many of them are members of the Congress.

… In the eyes of the Congress there is no distinction between members from the States and from India called British. It is surely detrimental to the interests of the States to ignore the Congress or Congressmen, especially when it or they seek to render friendly assistance. They must recognize the fact that the people in the States are in many cases guided by the Congress. They know that I am responsible for the policy of non-interference hitherto followed by the Congress. But with the growing influence of the Congress it is impossible for me to defend it in the face of injustice perpetrated in the States. If the Congress feels that it has the power to offer effective interference, it will be bound to do so when the call comes. And if the Princes believe that the good of the people is also their good, they would gratefully seek and accept the Congress assistance. It is surely in their interest to cultivate friendly relations with an organization which bids fair in the future, not very distant, to replace the Paramount Power, let me hope, by friendly arrangement. Will they not read the handwriting on the wall?

*Harijan*, 3-12-1938 (74: 254-56)

---

*As was his wont, Gandhi decided to support and carry out his own version of a struggle against princely rule. He chose to do so in the tiny state of Rajkot, in Gujarat. But in spite of his presence and entreaties, the rulers of the State, especially its dewan, or presiding minister, Virawala, reneged on an original promise of conceding to the people's demands. Gandhi found this unacceptable and frustrating and wrote this frank note to Virawala.*

**Letter to Virawala**

## March 2, 1939

What am I to do? I am writing this after having remained awake half the night. During the last three days, you have made me pass through a very bitter experience. I could see no desire on your part to adhere to any statement you made. All the time you appeared anxious to get out of every commitment. Last night's talk was the culmination, and I am now able to understand why it is that the citizens of Rajkot stand in terror of you.

You have invited me to study your whole career. I accepted that invitation. But you have really not left very much for me to investigate. God has not given me that much strength, that much purity and that much non-violence for, otherwise I would have been able to enter your heart. I feel ashamed and sad that I have been unable to win you over. I believe that the influence you have over the Thakore Saheb (*the ruler of the State - ed.*) is not an influence for his good. My heart wept night before last when I saw his mental helplessness and I hold you responsible for it. I have just addressed a letter to the Thakore Saheb and am sending this at the same time to you. You will no doubt see that letter and, therefore, I am not sending you a copy of it. Although you had given me your final decision, I would still request you to advise the Thakore Saheb to accept my suggestions. May God enter your heart.

*Sardar Vallabhbhai Patel.* Vol II, p. 346 (75: 132-33)

---

*Gandhian satyagraha suffered in Rajkot. Once the dewan reneged on his promises, Gandhi did not see a way out, except to appeal to the British to use their influence with him. The British agreed, but insisted that in any future political reform in Rajkot, Muslim and untouchable interests must be secured. Gandhi was amenable to this suggestion, but when the arrangements were being worked out, he found that the latter had been pitted against him and the Congress. He was both startled and unhappy and felt his satyagraha to be a failure: he had lost faith in his own abilities to persuade through suffering and sought British help, which, in this instance, proved the undoing of the struggle. This is an extract from his conversations with a Rajkot citizens' group (or Praja Parishad), supported by the Congress. .*

## Talk with Praja Parishad Workers
## May 15, 1939

... What is it that prevents me from throwing the Award (*the British-mediated Award - ed.*) overboard? It is not only faint-heartedness but it smacks of diplomacy. ... I am talking so much of *ahimsa*, but I am not walking fearlessly into the mouth of *himsa*. A satyagrahi seeks no adventitious aid—not of worldly forces, not of the Paramount Power. He deals directly wih his opponent and wins him by love and utter self-surrender to God. The very difficulty of implementing the Award, the very fact that it has proved a Pandora's box shows that God wants me to throw it away, however seemingly fruitful of future good it may be. God seems to be speaking to me in strident tones; "Your victory was no victory. Throw it away !" You want me to go on with the work of the Award, because it belongs to you. But how can I go on with it when my courage fails me, my hands are shaking and I am faltering? It is a moral issue with me. The consciousness of the wrong of the initial step I took oppresses me and I cannot go on with it, however much you may want me to go on with it. What will you do with such a halting, faltering general? I must throw the Award overboard and you in your turn may throw the general overboard.

*Harijan*, 27-5-1939 (75: 393-94)

---

*The unease experienced by Gandhi in the late 1930s was compounded by the outbreak of World War II. Gandhi was apprehensive and disheartened about the global situation. He distinguished, though, between fascist Germany and Britain and urged the Congress to offer 'unconditional support' for British war efforts, but in a non-violent manner. The Congress did not agree to this, and insisted that they could offer support, only if Britain made known its war aims. The Congress wanted a guarantee that in the Allied fight for democracy, India would count. Gandhi found himself alone in not wanting to embarrass Britain in her time of crisis.*

## Statement to the Press
## Segaon, August 23, 1939

... On the war resolution I had a conclusive defeat. ... I saw that I could not carry my resolution unless I argued and pressed for it. But I had no such desire. ... If the Congress heartily believed in non-violence in its fullness even as a policy, this was its testing time. But Congressmen, barring individual exceptions, do not believe in such non-violence. Those who do, believe that it is the right thing only for a fight against the Government for wresting power. But the Congress has no non-violent message for the world. ... In the face of the violence going on in India itself and in the face of the fact that Congress Governments have been obliged to fall back upon military and police assistance, a declaration to the world of non-violence would have seemed a mockery. It would have carried no weight in India or with the world. Yet, to be true to myself, I could not draft any other resolution than I did. The fate, to which I was party, of my resolution proved the wisdom of my withdrawal of official connection with the Congress.

... We pursue the same goal. They all of them would go the whole length with me if they could, but they want to be true to themselves and to the country which they represent for the time being, even as I want to be true to myself. I know that the progress of non-violence is seemingly a terribly slow process. But experience has taught me that it is the surest way to the common goal. There is deliverance neither for India nor for the world through clash of arms. Violence, even for vindication of justice, is almost played out. With that belief I am content to plough a lonely furrow, if it is to be my lot that I have no co-sharer in the out-and-out belief in non-violence.

*Harijan*, 26-8-1939 (76: 259-260)

---

*The colonial government did not respond to the Congress' insistence that it make a political offer to the nationalists. The Congress had no option but to negotiate. It now said that it would help with the military defence of India if only the government would, in principle, accept the Congress' demand for independence towards the conclusion of the war, and allow Indians to participate in decisions pertaining to the prosecution of the war. To Gandhi, this appeared a travesty of non-violence, but his word did not prevail.*

## Both Happy and Unhappy

... I pleaded hard with the Committee: "If you have faith in non-violence of the strong, now is the time to act up to it. It does not matter that many parties do not believe in non-violence whether of the strong or of the weak. Probably that is all the greater reason for Congressmen to meet the emergency by non-violent action. For if all were non-violent, there could be no anarchy and there would be no question of anybody arming for meeting aggression from without. It is because Congressmen represent a party of non-violence, in the midst of parties who do not believe in it, that it becomes imperative for Congressmen to show that they are well able to act up to their faith."

But the members of the Working Committee felt that Congressmen would not be able to act up to it. It would be a new experience for them. They were never before called upon to deal with such a crisis. The attempt made by me to form peace brigades to deal with communal riots and the like had wholly failed. Therefore they could not hope for the action contemplated.

My position was different. With the Congress non-violence was always a policy. It was open to it to reject it if it failed. If it could not bring political and economic independence, it was of no use. For me non-violence is a creed. I must act up to it whether I am alone or have companions. Since propagation of non-violence is the mission of my life, I must pursue it in all weathers.

... I am both happy and unhappy over the result. Happy because I have been able to bear the strain of the break and have been given the strength to stand alone. Unhappy because my word seemed to lose the power to carry with me those whom it was my proud privilege to carry all these many years which seem like yesterday. But I know that, if God shows me the way to demonstrate the efficacy of non-violence of the strong, the break will prove to have been temporary. If there is no way, they will have justified their wisdom in bearing the wrench of letting me go my way alone. If that tragic discovery of my impotence is in store for me, I hope still to retain the faith that has sustained me all these years and to have humility enough to realize that I was not a fit enough instrument to carry the torch of non-violence any further.

*Harijan*, 29-6-1940 (78: 351-2)

---

## Discussion at Congress Working Committee Meeting
## July, 3/7, 1940

GANDHIJI: I have been oppressed all the time by the fact that I now represent a totally different mentality from that of the Working Committee. When I asked for absolution it was not a formal thing. ... Granting the implications that I have drawn from the last resolution you cannot possibly escape its logical conclusion. You will want to seize power. You will have to surrender certain things in order to get it. You will have to be like other parties. You will be driven into their ways. Maybe you will be an advanced party. This picture repels me. I don't believe in the expression "seizure of power". There is no such thing as "seizure of power". I have no power save what resides in the people. I am a mere representative of the power in the people.

... The Viceroy is here to serve his country, its interests and therefore he must use all resources that India has mercilessly. If we participate in war effort, we shall have learnt some lesson in the art of violence, even if the Britishers are defeated. This will gives us some experience, some power such as a soldier has but all this at cost of independence, this seems to me the logical consequence of your resolution. This does not appeal to me.

... I regret the Congress took what I considered as a backward step, but it is a perfectly honourable step. It has taken the only step that it could. I will still try to wean it and the rank and file from this mistake. If the rank and file feel with me the Working Committee will retract the step. A larger issue of internal anarchy was before us. What contribution shall we make if anarchy overtakes us? Will the masses cooperate in the non-violent effort? I will test the masses and if I find that they will desert me I will shape my policy accordingly, but I won't collapse before they collapse. The terrible things that are going on in Europe fill me with anguish. I do not know where I could come in there ...

C. RAJAGOPALACHARI (*Congressman from the southern Indian state of Tamil Nadu and Gandhi's ardent friend and admirer - ed.*): I cannot go with Gandhiji in his conception of the State. Ours is a political organization not working for non-violence but for the political ideal. We are working in competition with other political parties.

JAWAHARLAL NEHRU (*Free India's first Prime Minister, Gandhi's protégé in politics - ed.*): I agree with Rajaji (*that is Rajagopalachari - ed.*) in his understanding of violence and non-violence ; else we cannot function on the political plane.

GANDHIJI: Very difficult questions have arisen in the course of the discussion. Rajaji has summarily rejected the idea that we can retain power by non-violent means. This was illustrated even when we attained it by non-violent means while the Congress was in office. To the extent they used violence the ministries failed. Their action showed bankruptcy of our non-violence. Perhaps we could not have done otherwise. I advised giving up of office. Rajaji however does not accept what I have said, that it is possible to hold office without the use of more than police violence.

... I say again with experience and conviction that it is possible to touch power through non-violence, but we may not take it. A non-violent organization may not accept office but it can get things done its way. Thus alone can we have power if we have not non-violent control over people. Jawaharlal has done less than justice to those who believe in non-violence. He means that they want to be superior men leaving the dirty work of violence to be done by others. I hold, on the other hand, that we don't take power at all. It involves emoluments, glory and things which people prize. Those in power consider that they are superior and others subordinate.

When a non-violent man refuses to take over power he says, "I decline because if I accept I shall make a mess of it. I am not built that way. Let credit go to others." I never felt that I was superior to those who took power nor did they feel that they were inferior or called upon to do a dirty job. Now suppose you at this critical moment hold fast to non-violence in the midst of other parties who swear by violence, you will be in a minority. Why should a small non-violent group immediately expect to win power before they convert others? Let others hold power. A group of non-violent men wishing to convert the country to non-violence will not bother about power. In holding fast to the creed you will have converted a majority of the people. A man who has self-confidence will convert the country. But you say millions will never arrive at that stage. I feel practically certain they can ...

... I think impatience has seized us. If we do not take office others will take office. If you think that you can serve the people by entering into competition with others you are mistaken. We are democrats. We would be presumed to be ruling by the will of the people. We must dismount if people rebel. We have not given that trial to non-violence which we might have. All of us did our best. Let us do better. If we do better, if we have got the proper courage we shall have left something for India to be proud of. I would like you to feel with me that it is perfectly possible to hold the State without an army. If anybody comes I will square accounts with him along non-violent lines. Why should we fear that they will swallow us? Violent people fight violent people. They do not touch non-violent people. We build up huge armaments in order to ward off an attack in some distant future. The divisions in the country also provide us with reason for our keeping to non-violence. We can hold our people peacefully against the whole world.

*Wardha Office Satyagraha File, 1940-41.* Courtesy: Nehru Memorial Museum and Library (78: 393-97)

---

*Britain rejected the Congress' demands for a statement on Indian independence and offered vague promises of greater Indian participation in the Viceroy's Council (a sort of war cabinet). Rebuffed, the Congress hurried back to Gandhi, who decided that perhaps it was time that the party protested: Congress must insist on its right to preach against the War.*

### Speech at All-India Congress Committee Meeting, Bombay II September 15, 1940

... I do not want England to be defeated or humiliated. It hurts me to find St. Paul's Cathedral damaged. It hurts me as much as I would be hurt if I heard that the Kashi Vishvanath Temple or the Jama Masjid was damaged. I would like to defend both the Kashi Vishvanath Temple and the Jama Masjid and even St. Paul's with my life, but would not take a single life for their defence. That is my fundamental difference with the British people. My sympathy is there with them nevertheless.

Let there be no mistake on the part of Englishmen, Congressmen, or others whom my voice reaches, as to where my sympathy lies. It is not because I love the British nation and hate the German. I do not think that the Germans as a nation are any worse than the English or the Italians are any worse. We are all tarred with the same brush; we are all members of the vast human family. I decline to draw any distinctions. I cannot claim any superiority for Indians. We have the same virtues and the same vices. Humanity is not divided into watertight compartments so that we cannot go from one to another. They may occupy one thousand rooms, but they are all related to one another. I would not say, "India should be all in all, let the whole world perish." That is not my message. India should be all in all, consistently with the well-being of other nations of the world. I can keep India intact and its freedom also intact only if I have goodwill towards the whole of the human family and not merely for the human family which inhabits this little spot of the earth called India. It is big enough compared to other smaller nations, but what is India in the wide world or in the universe?

Let there be no mistake as to what I am about. I want my individuality to remain unimpaired. If I lose it, I would be of no service to India, much less to the British people, still less to humanity. My individual liberty is the same as the nation's, convertible with national liberty. I do not claim any greater liberty for myself. Hence my liberty is equal to the liberty of all of you and no greater. I feel that, if my liberty is at stake, yours is also at stake. I claim the liberty of going through the streets of Bombay and say that I shall have nothing to do with this war, because I do not believe in this war, and in this fratricide that is going on in Europe ...

... I may fail in my mission. But I have never approached a mission in despair. I may have approached it with the consciousness that I may be faced with a blind wall. But I have often penetrated blind walls. I shall approach the Viceroy in the confidence and hope that he will understand the great reasonableness of the request of the Congress for full liberty to preach "no war" in India. Everyone should have perfect liberty to preach by pen and tongue: "We cannot aid imperialism, we cannot help spoliation."

... There are many parties in the Congress. We are not all of the same opinion. ... Let it not be said of you that you come to the Congress although you do not believe in non-violence. How can you possibly sign the Congress pledge with violence in your breasts? I want complete obedience to the policy of non-violence. While the policy lasts, it is the same as though it was a creed, for so long as it holds good it is as good as a creed. My creed holds me for life; yours so long as you hold it. Resign from the Congress, and you are free from it. Let us be clear regarding the language we use and the thoughts we nurture. For, what is language but the expression of thought? Let your thought be accurate and truthful, and you will hasten the advent of *swaraj* even if the whole world is against you. You will have won *swaraj* without having to spend nine million pounds a day or without burning a single home. If you are true to your policy, I am sure that without doing any of these things you will build up the majestic edifice of freedom ...

*Harijan*, 29-9-1940 (79: 222-27)

---

*With Japan's entry into the war, India stood imperilled—Gandhi and the Congress were watchful of the situation. They knew that Britain was at her most vulnerable just then—Subash Chandra Bose, the Congress radical from Bengal, had already left India, to throw in his lot with the Axis powers, and had actually established contact with Japan. In the event, Britain was worried about how the Congress would respond. Gandhi's response was distinctive: he outlined an idealistic campaign, but one full of implications for the immediate present.*

**Interview to the Press, Bombay**
**May 16, 1942**

... Q. There is a report about some new scheme that you want to propound in one of your Harijan articles about non-violent Non-cooperation if any invader came to India. Could you give us an idea?

A. It is wrong. I have no plan in mind. If I had, I should give it to you. But I think nothing more need be added when I have said that there should be unadulterated non-violent Non-cooperation, and if the whole of India responded and unanimously offered it, I should show that without shedding a single drop of blood Japanese arms—or any combination of arms—can be sterilized. That involves the determination of India not to give quarter on any point whatsoever and to be ready to risk loss of several million lives ...

Q. But, unadulterated non-violent Non-cooperation has not been successful against Great Britain. How will it succeed against a new aggressor?

A. I combat the statement altogether. Nobody has yet told me that non-violent Non-cooperation, unadulterated, has not succeeded. It has not been offered, it is true. Therefore, you can say that what has not been offered hitherto is not likely to be offered suddenly when India faces the Japanese arms. I can only hope that, in the face of danger, India would be readier to offer non-violent Non-cooperation.

Perhaps India is accustomed to British rule for so many years that the Indian mind or India's masses do not feel the pinch so much as the advent of a new power would be felt. But your question is well put. It is possible that India may not be able to offer non-violent Non-cooperation. ... If India does not respond to that call, then India must respond to the call of some leader or some organization wedded to violence. For instance, the Hindu Mahasabha (*a Hindu right-wing organization - ed.*) is trying to rouse the Hindu mind for an armed conflict. It remains to be seen whether that attempt succeeds. I for one do not believe it will succeed.

Q. Would you advise non-violent Non-cooperation against scorched-earth policy? Would you resist the attempt to destroy sources of food and water?

A. Yes. A time may come when I would certainly advise it, for I think it is ruinous, suicidal, and unnecessary—whether India believes in non-violent Non-cooperation or in violence. And the

Russian and Chinese examples make no appeal to me. If some other country resorts to methods which I consider to be inhuman, I may not follow them. If the enemy comes and helps himself to crops, I may be obliged to leave, because I cannot or care not to defend them. I must resign myself to it. And there is a good example for us. A passage was quoted to me from the Islamic literature. The Caliph issued definite instructions to the armies of Islam that they should not destroy the utility services, they should not harass the aged and women and children; and I do not know that the arms of Islam suffered any disaster because the armies obeyed those instructions.

Q. But what about factories—especially factories for the manufacture of munitions?

A. Suppose there are factories for grinding wheat or pressing oil-seeds. I should not destroy them. But munitions factories, yes; for I would not tolerate munitions factories in a free India if I had my way. Textile factories I would not destroy and I would resist all such destruction. However, it is a question of prudence. I have not suggested immediate enforcement of the whole programme in pursuance of the demand for British withdrawal. It is there of course. But I am trying, if I am allowed to continue to cultivate and educate public opinion, to show that behind this demand of mine there is no ill-will, no malice. It is the most logical thing that I have suggested. It is in the interests of all, and since it is an entirely friendly act, I am moving cautiously, watching myself at every step. I will do nothing in haste, but there is the fixed determination behind every act of mine that the British must withdraw. ...

Q. Can India give her moral sympathy or support to either of the parties to the war?

A. My own personal view is well known. And if I can convert India to my view, there would be no aid to either side; but my sympathies are undoubtedly in favour of China and Russia.

Q. But what about Britain?

A. I used to say that my moral support was entirely with Britain. I am very sorry to have to confess that today my mind refuses to give that moral support. British behaviour towards India has filled me with great pain ...

Q. What about America?

A. I expressed my opinion some time ago that it was a wrong thing for America and unfortunate for the world peace that America, instead of working, as she could have worked, for world peace, identified herself with war.

Q. But was there any alternative for her?

A. I am sure she would have, if she had intended, brought about peace. But it is my firm opinion that she did not use her opportunity. I know that I have no right to criticize such a big nation. I do not know all the facts that determined America to throw herself into the cauldron. But somehow or other, opinion has forced itself upon me that America could have remained out, and even now it can do so if she divests herself of the intoxication that her immense wealth has produced. And I would like to repeat what I have said about the withdrawal of British power from India. Both America and Britain lack the moral basis for engaging in this war, unless they put their own houses in order, while making a fixed determination to withdraw their influence and power both from Africa and Asia, and remove the colour-bar. They have no right to talk about protecting democracies and protecting civilization and human freedom until the canker of white superiority is destroyed in its entirety ...

*Harijan*, 24-5-1942 (82: 286-90)

---

*In the wake of the colonial war-time government's indifference to nationalist demands and the imminent Japanese invasion of India, Gandhi and Congress decided to confront the government with a 'do-or-die' resolution. Gandhi formulated for himself reasons for the validity of this resolution that called upon the British to 'Quit India' (See also p.) .*

## Note on Letter from Horace Alexander
## August 3, 1942

... I have passed many sleepless nights to discover the various ways of ending the struggle (*to win English attention to the plight of an enslaved nation forced to confront an invader - ed.*) with the least commotion. But I saw that some form of conflict was inevitable to bring home the truth to the British mind. I have no doubt that events would show that I was right, that I acted in the spirit of pure friendship.

British authority would deal summarily with the movement (*that Gandhi contemplated - ed.*). The sufferings will be all on the side of the people. True, but in the end Britain will lose in the moral fibre. But to let her continue as she is doing is to make her bankrupt and, perhaps, lose the battle, whereas the movement, which I have advised the Congress to take up, is designed to prevent bankruptcy and enable Great Britain to acquire a moral height which must secure victory for her and her Allies. There is no claim here for philanthropy. The fact stands and nobody has ever denied it that by this movement India stands to gain her goal of independence. But this is irrelevant here. What is relevant here is the fundamental fact that the movement is designed to help Britain in spite of herself. This is a very big, almost arrogant claim. I am not ashamed to advance it because it comes from an agonized heart. Time alone will show the truth or falsehood of the claim. I have no doubt as to the verdict. For the testimony of reason may be wrong, but of the heart never.

From a photostat (83: 166-67)

# Divided Hearts: The Demand for Pakistan

*On the outbreak of World War II in 1939, the Congress ministries resigned in protest against the British dragging of an unwilling India into war. Gandhi was anguished by the war and felt that this larger violence could only do ill to the Indian situation, tense as it was and riddled with hatred between Hindus and Muslims. He was also pained by the manner in which the colonial government appeared determined to deploy Muslim disaffection to its own ends. The Congress, for its part, did not seem to have learnt its lessons in non-violence well, and this worried him too.*

*Gandhi's dismay knew no bounds when the Muslim League announced at its Lahore conference in 1940 that it would settle for nothing less than a separate Islamic state. Meanwhile the British, who were being urged by the Congress to concede the demand for independence formally, considering they were fighting in the name of freedom and independence in Europe, sent a mission to India to study the situation. Headed by Sir Stafford Cripps, this mission recommended a divisive solution that would politically partition Hindu and Muslim communities in north-western and north-eastern India. Gandhi knew then that separatism, in the name of religion, had come to stay. In a determined appeal to the British and the public, he and the Congress decided to stage a demonstration of political and nationalist fervour—they called on the British to 'Quit India'.*

*The 'Quit India' resolution was well-timed. The Japanese were on India's shores and the British were nervous—they needed Indian support in the event of an invasion, and Gandhi felt that no help could be offered, unless Indians felt assured that the British would do right by them. Further, the resolution was also meant to stir all political communities into a show of unity—to Gandhi, only a united struggle on the ground which brought together Hindus and Muslims and countless others could settle the communal problem once and for all.*

*The extracts in this section capture the tension and frustration experienced by Gandhi during this period and his manner of engaging his troubled conscience. The Rajkot events, which had shown Gandhi the 'British' hand in fomenting communal discontent, the seemingly irreconcilable dissensions in Congress, the growing distance between Muslims and Hindus, now clearly visible on the streets and in everyday contexts, and the fact that the Congress did not appear to possess an abiding faith in non-violence: all these factors wracked Gandhi's mind, as the 1930s drew to a close and the world appeared set on a cataclysmic course of violence.*

---

### Non-Violence v. Violence

... In theory, if there is sufficient non-violence developed in any single person, he should be able to discover the means of combating violence, no matter how widespread or severe, within his jurisdiction. I have repeatedly admitted my imperfections. I am no example of perfect *ahimsa*. I am evolving. Such *ahimsa* as has been developed in me has been found enough to cope with situations that have hitherto arisen. But today I feel helpless in the face of the surrounding violence ...

It seems to me that the united action of the Hindus and the Muslims blinded me to the violence that was lurking in the breasts of many. The English who are trained diplomats and administrators are accustomed to the line of least resistance, and when they found that it was more profitable to conciliate a big organization than to crush it by extensive frightfulness, they yielded to the extent that they thought was necessary.

It is, however, my conviction that our resistance was predominantly non-violent in action and will be accepted as such by the future historian. As a seeker of truth and non-violence, however, I must not be satisfied with mere action if it is not from the heart. ... Non-violent action without the cooperation of the heart and the head cannot produce the intended result. The failure of our imperfect *ahimsa* is visible to the naked eye. Look at the feud that is going on between Hindus and Muslims. Each is arming for the fight with the other. The violence that we had harboured in our breasts during the Non-cooperation days is now recoiling upon ourselves. The violent energy that was generated among the masses, but was kept under check in the pursuit of a common objective, has now been let loose and is being used among and against ourselves. The same phenomenon is discernible, though in a less crude manner, in the dissension among Congressmen themselves and the use of forcible methods that the Congress Ministers are obliged to adopt in running the administrations under their charge.

This narrative clearly shows that the atmosphere is surcharged with violence. I hope it also shows that non-violent mass movement is an impossibility unless the atmosphere is radically changed. To blind one's eyes to the events happening around us is to court disaster. It has been suggested to me that I should declare mass civil disobedience and all internal strife will cease, Hindus and Muslims will compose their differences, Congressmen will forget mutual jealousies and fights for power. My reading of the situation is wholly different. If any mass movement is undertaken at the present moment in the name of non-violence, it will resolve itself into violence largely unorganized and organized in some cases ...

... But if I cannot find an effective, purely non-violent method, outbreak of violence seems to be a certainty. The people demand self-expression. They are not satisfied with the constructive programme prescribed by me and accepted almost unanimously by the Congress. As I have said before, the imperfect response to the constructive programme is itself proof positive of the skin-deep nature of the non-violence of Congressmen.

... But if there is an outbreak of violence, it would not be without cause. We are yet far from the independence of our dream. The irresponsibility of the Centre, which eats up 80 percent of the revenue, grinds down the people and thwarts their aspirations, is daily proving more and more intolerable. It is no use saying that it is impossible to persuade persons willingly to part with their power. I have claimed that satyagraha is a new experiment. It will be time to pronounce it a failure when Congressmen have given it a genuine trial. Even a policy, if it is honestly pursued, has to be pursued with all one's heart. We have not done so.

*Harijan*, 8-7-1939 (76: 77-81)

---

*Continuing reports of Muslim anger with the Congress and insistent rumours of Muslims wanting a separate state pushed Gandhi into making a firm criticism of what he understood as a violent imperial will to divide and rule.*

## The Pity of It

The Congress has never given up the effort to solve the communal question. It is even now engaged in the difficult task. But it is wrong to use Congress inability to reach a solution for keeping India from her destined goal. British officials including Viceroys have admitted that they have ruled by following the policy of "divide and rule". The British established themselves by taking advantage of our internal quarrels and have remained by keeping them alive. It is unnecessary for my argument to prove that the policy is being followed deliberately. The British have made themselves believe that they are ruling because of our quarrels, and that they will gladly retire when we have ceased to quarrel. Thus they are moving in a vicious circle. The British rule must be permanent if the adjustment of the communal quarrel is a condition precedent to India becoming independent. It is a purely domestic problem which we are bound to solve if we are to live at peace with one another.

... (Another) English critic ... says among many other things: "British people feel that Great Britain needs to carry the Muslim world with her at this time of immense struggle." I have no difficulty in sympathizing with this position. Only let us clear the issues. Great Britain cannot afford to risk defeat for the sake of doing justice. This is just what an overwhelming number of Indians feel. The Congress, before it can offer ungrudging support to Britain, wants to feel sure that hers is an absolutely just cause. The recent events have created a grave doubt about it. Absolute protection of the rights of minorities is a greater concern of the Congress than it ever can be of Great Britain. The Congress dare not seek and cannot get justice, if it is not prepared to do it itself. To be above suspicion is the only way open to non-violent organizations. But British policy may make a just solution impossible at the present moment.

*Harijan,* 2-12-1939 (77: 137-38)

---

*Though the official demand for a separate Islamic state was not made until the Lahore conference of the Muslim League in March 1940, Mohammed Ali Jinnah, the League's foremost leader and ideologue, had referred to the fact of Muslims being a distinctive political community in several forums. Gandhi's responses to this statement were unequivocal in their opposition to it.*

## Unity v. Justice

... My belief is unshaken that without communal unity *swaraj* cannot be attained through non-violence. But unity cannot be reached without justice between communities. Muslim or any other friendship cannot be bought with bribery. Bribery would itself mean cowardice and therefore violence. But if I give more than his due to my brother, I do not bribe him nor do I do any injustice. I can disarm suspicion only by being generous. Justice without generosity may easily become Shylock's justice. I must, however, take care that the generosity is not done at the expense of the very cause for which it is sought to be done. I cannot, therefore, drop the idea of unity or the effort for it. But what is wanted is not so much justice as right action.

Quaid-e-Azam Jinnah's ... picture of India as a continent containing nations counted according to their religions, if it is realized, would undo the effort the Congress had been making for over half a century. But I hope that Quaid-e-Azam Jinnah's opinion is a temporary phase in the history of the Muslim League. Muslims of the different provinces can never cut themselves away from their Hindu or Christian brethren. Both Muslims and Christians are converts from Hinduism or are descendants of converts. They do not cease to belong to their provinces because of change of faith. Englishmen who become converts to Islam do not change their nationality. I hope Quaid-e-Azam Jinnah does not represent the considered opinion even of his colleagues.

*Harijan*, 27-1-1940 (77: 246-27)

---

## Confusion of Thought

Q. ... You will be responsible for a gross injustice if you persist in giving to India a majority Government with only "safeguards" for the minorities. The latter ought to have an effective part in the actual government of the country.

A. You have evidently confused majority rule with Hindu rule implying that the Hindu majority is irremovable. The fact is that the majority in all the provinces is a mixed majority. The parties are not Muslims and Hindus; they are Congressmen, independents, Muslim Leaguers, Muslim independents, labourites, etc. The Congress majority everywhere is a mixed majority and could be better balanced if there was no tension. The tension is a distemper. A distemper can never be a permanent feature of any growing society which India is. Whatever the outcome of the Muslim League demonstration and its claim, some day or other there will be a solution of the issues raised. The outcome will never be pure Muslim or Hindu majorities in any single province. The parties will be mixed and aligned according to different policies, unless democracy is crushed and autocracy reigns supreme in India as a whole or India is vivisected into two or more dead parts. If you have followed my argument, it must be clear to you that there will never be a denial of power to any party or group so far as the Congress is concerned. Minorities are entitled to full protection of their rights, for so long as they have to divide power with others, they run the risk of their special rights being adulterated ...

*Harijan*, 6-4-1940 (78: 106-7)

---

*In the face of the Lahore resolution on a separate Muslim state, Gandhi upheld the claims of independence for all and argued that if the British were to immediately leave India, Hindus and Muslims could settle their arguments amicably.*

## A Baffling Situation

A question has been put to me: Do you intend to start general civil disobedience although Quaid-e-Azam Jinnah has declared war against Hindus and has got the Muslim League to pass a resolution favouring vivisection of India into two ? If you do, what becomes of your formula that there is no *swaraj* without communal unity ?

I admit that the step taken by the Muslim League at Lahore

creates a baffling situation. … In the present instance there is nothing to prevent the imperial rulers from declaring their will in unequivocal terms that henceforth India will govern herself according to her own will, not that of the rulers as has happened hitherto. Neither the Muslim League nor any other party can oppose such a declaration. For the Muslims will be entitled to dictate their own terms. Unless the rest of India wishes to engage in internal fratricide, the others will have to submit to Muslim dictation if the Muslims will resort to it. I know no non-violent method of compelling the obedience of eight crores of Muslims to the will of the rest of India, however powerful a majority the rest may represent. The Muslims must have the same right of self-determination that the rest of India has. We are at present a joint family. Any member may claim a division. Thus, so far as I am concerned, my proposition that there is no *swaraj* without communal unity holds as good today as when I first enunciated it in 1919.

… But I do not believe that Muslims, when it comes to a matter of actual decision, will ever want vivisection. Their good sense will prevent them. Their self-interest will deter them. Their religion will forbid the obvious suicide which the partition would mean. The "two nations" theory is an untruth. The vast majority of Muslims of India are converts to Islam or are descendants of converts. They did not become a separate nation as soon as they became converts. A Bengali Muslim speaks the same tongue that a Bengali Hindu does, eats the same food, has the same amusements as his Hindu neighbour. They dress alike. I have often found it difficult to distinguish by outward sign between a Bengali Hindu and a Bengali Muslim. The same phenomenon is observable more or less in the South among the poor who constitute the masses of India …

… And is Islam such an exclusive religion as Quaid-e-Azam would have it ? Is there nothing in common between Islam and Hinduism or any other religion? Or is Islam merely an enemy of Hinduism? … Quaid-e-Azam has … raised a fundamental issue. … He does not say some Hindus are bad; he says Hindus as such have nothing in common with Muslims. I make bold to say that he and those who think like him are rendering no service to Islam; they are misinterpreting the message inherent in the very word Islam. I say this because I feel deeply hurt over what is now going on in the name of the Muslim League. I should be failing in my duty, if I did not warn the Muslims of India against the untruth that is being propagated amongst them. This warning is a duty because I have faithfully served them in their hour of need and because Hindu-Muslim unity has been and is my life's mission.

*Harijan*, 6-4-1940 (78: 108-110)

---

*Though the demand for a separate Islamic state appeared to Gandhi an impossibility, he conceded that if a sufficient number of Muslims desired it, it must become a reality.*

### Hindu-Muslim Tangle

The partition proposal has altered the face of the Hindu-Muslim problem. I have called it an untruth. There can be no compromise with it. At the same time I have said that, If the eight crores of Muslims desire it no power on earth can prevent it, notwithstanding opposition, violent or non-violent It cannot come by honourable agreement.

That is the political aspect of it. But what about the religious and the moral which are greater than the political? For at the bottom of the cry for partition is the belief that Islam is an exclusive brotherhood, and anti-Hindu. Whether it is against other religions it is not stated. The newspaper cuttings in which partition is preached describe Hindus as practically untouchables. Nothing good can come out of Hindus or Hinduism. To live under Hindu rule is a Sin. Even joint Hindu-Muslim rule is not to be thought of. The cuttings show that Hindu and Muslims are already at war with one another and that they must prepare for the final tussle.

Time was when Hindus thought that Muslims were the natural enemies of Hindus. But as is the case with Hinduism, ultimately it comes to terms with the enemy and makes friends with him. The process had not been completed. As if nemesis had overtaken Hinduism, the Muslim League started the same game and taught that there could be no blending of the two cultures. In this connection I have just read a booklet by Shri Atulanand Chakrabarti which shows that ever since the contact of Islam with Hinduism there has been an attempt on the part of the best minds of both to see the good points of each other, and to emphasize inherent similarities rather than seeming dissimilarities. ... If the evidence collected there reflects the true evolution of Islam in India, then the partition propaganda is anti-Islamic.

Religion binds man to God and man to man. Does Islam bind Muslim only to Muslim and antagonize the Hindu? Was the message of the Prophet peace only for and between Muslims and war against Hindus or non-Muslims? Are eight crores of Muslims to be fed with this which I can only describe as poison? Those who are instilling this poison into the Muslim mind are rendering the greatest disservice to Islam. I know that it is not Islam. I have lived with and among Muslims not for one day but closely and almost uninterruptedly for twenty years. Not one Muslim taught me that Islam was an anti-Hindu religion.

*Harijan*, 4-5-1940 (78: 178-79)

---

*In 1941, Hindu-Muslim riots broke out in western India, which showed Congressmen in a rather poor light and lent credence to Jinnah's charges against that party. Gandhi exhorted Congressmen to mend their ways and be true to the creed of non-violence in situations where it was most called for.*

### Communal Riots
### Sevagram, May 4, 1941

Hindu-Muslim riots that have broken out in many important places in the country must have saddened all sane people. My grief however is special. The Congress influence seems to have been practically unfelt during the dark days. We have proved ourselves barbarians and cowards in these places. Arson, looting and killing of innocent people including children, have been common in almost all the places. Thousands have run away from their homes for fear of their lives. Congress influence was not to be measured by the number of members on the Congress register but by its leavening quality. It has been shown clearly that the influence is negligible in riots and the like. Individual cases apart, the Congress produced little or no influence over either the Muslims or the Hindus in the affected areas. From the accounts received it seems that Muslim fanatics in Dacca and Ahmedabad did their worst in inflicting damage on Hindu property by looting and burning with a deliberation that showed premeditation.

Hindus, instead of boldly standing up and facing the mischief-makers, fled in their thousands from the danger zone. And where they did not, they were as barbarous as the assailants. These were all untouched by the Congress non-violence. And yet these are the men who form the bulk of the Congress meetings. If the Congress has no control over the masses on such occasions, there is not much value in Congress non-violence as a positive force. The Congress cannot take charge of the Government if the British suddenly withdraw ...

... Congressmen's course is clear. They must examine the contents of their non-violence. If it does not go as far as the regulation of inter-communal and such other relations, it is of no use for the acquisition of independence. I prophesy that without pervasive non-violence of the brave, when the question of real transfer of power comes, it won't be the Congress who will have the privilege and the responsibility of delivering the goods. The power will descend to those who are able to make effective use of violence.

In Europe two forces, equally matched in destructive skill and bravery, are ranged against one another. The goal before both is domination. In spite of all the will in the world, I have found no difference in kind between the two. The difference in degree does not interest me. The British heel is bad enough for me. As a man wedded to independence and non-violence, I must fight Nazism and Fascism equally with the enslaving British Imperialism. But has the Congress really the non-violent strength even to fight this imperialism which we know through and through?

We have to fight for it either violently or non-violently, whether it is the Congress or the League or the Hindu Mahasabha that fights for it. I am satisfied that the two sectional organizations will never win independence for the masses, Hindu, Muslim, Christian,

Sikh, Parsi, Jew. The Congress is the only organization that has laboured for national solidarity from the beginning. But that labour will be vain if the Congress does not prove true to its trust. I do not mind Congressmen changing their creed in spite of many leaders being in jail or openly leaving the Congress. I can see my way to rebuilding the Congress with five true men with whom there is neither Hindu nor Muslim nor any other.

Religion is a personal matter. It ought not to affect the political field. Then what should a Congressman do? He must resolutely refuse to take sides and defend with his life and without the use of violence the person who is in distress. ... What is required is a brave heart—a possession which is in nobody's giving and which therefore can never be taken away. He must instil into his neighbours the lesson that even violence can be both decent and indecent. It is no bravery to kill unawares an innocent person because he does not belong to one's religion or to burn his property. Those who do so disgrace their religion and themselves and positively mar the effort for independence ...

*Congress Bulletin*, No. 6, 1942, *File No. 3/42/41,Home Department, Pol.(I)*. Courtesy: National Archives of India. Also A.I.C.C. File, 1941. Courtesy: Nehru Memorial Museum and Library (80: 211-14)

---

*Sir Stafford Cripps was sent to India as an ambassador of Empire. He held talks with both Congressmen and members of the Muslim League. Personally, he appeared to favour a liberal political settlement, but he had to heed the orders of Winston Churchill, Britain's war-time conservative Prime Minister, who clearly indicated that he wished to 'play the Muslim card' to defer independence. Gandhi felt confirmed in his belief that the British had a stake in keeping alive communal hatred and granting it political credence.*

### Unity is Vital in India
### [After April 12, 1942]

The proposals that Sir Stafford Cripps advanced for settling the political deadlock in India contemplated splitting the country into three parts, each part o have a different system of government. These proposals, it would seem, would be to the liking of many of

India's Muslim leaders, since they have for long advocated dividing the country between Hindus and Muslims. Yet Sir Stafford's plan differed in many respects from the Muslim League's plan, and so it received no more enthusiastic a reception from them than it received from the Indian National Congress. The Muslim League represents Muslims; the Indian National Congress purports to represent Hindus and Muslims alike. Can the Congress claim be supported? ... I believe that the Congress embodies the hopes and aspirations of all India. Its traditions unfit it to represent Hindus as against Muslims or vice versa. It is fit only to represent the common interest of all sons of Hindustan ...

I myself could never subscribe to the partitioning of the country. I would fight it with every means at my disposal and yet I must declare that national independence is an impossibility until Indians have solved this communal problem. There are two ways of solving it. One is the way of non-violence, the other the way of violence. ... If peace is ever to come in that manner, through both parties being equally matched in violent weapons, I know that it will not come in my lifetime, and if it came, I should not care to be a witness of it. For it will be an armed peace, to be broken at any moment.

Whether those who believe in the two-nation theory can live as friends with those who believe in one nation, I do not know. If the vast majority of Muslims regard themselves as a separate nation having nothing in common with the Hindus and others, no power on earth can compel them to think otherwise. If they want partition of India on that basis, they must have partition, unless the Hindus want to fight against such a division. So far as I can see, preparation for such a fight is going on now on behalf of both parties. I dread to see it. That way lies national suicide. One party or the other will call in outside help (*that is, of government - ed.*). In that case, good-bye to independence.

The only true and just way is the way of unity and non-violence of regarding one another not as members of hostile cultures but as sons of the same great motherland. Hindus and Muslims have worked and do work together in peace; they lived together in peace in the past; they can live together in peace in the future. Our task is to assure each son of the motherland that whatever his beliefs, his rights and religious and cultural interests will be protected by the laws of the land, formulated by a national assembly democratically elected.

Now, with the aggressor at the gates (*the Japanese - ed.*), more than ever unity is vital in India. I desire above all things to see a joint struggle against him and to achieve independence. In the very process of doing this, it is highly likely that we shall have forgotten our quarrels in the same common goal. But if we find that we have not forgotten them, then will be the time to quarrel among ourselves, if quarrel we must. Not now. Now India herself stands in the balance.

*The Bombay Chronicle*, 25-4-1942 (82: 188-90)

---

*The failure of the Cripps Mission, the colonial government's indifference to the demands for independence, and the anger and discontent that lay hidden in street corners and in many a nationalist heart impelled Gandhi to think of a satyagraha that would communicate to India's rulers their subjects' anguished cry for justice. But he still had to engage with the Hindu-Muslim tangle.*

## To Muslim Correspondents

"How can you think of a mass movement for liberation without first closing with Muslims?", ask Muslim correspondents whose letters fill my file. I used at one time to think like my correspondents. But I see that for the moment I cannot reach the Muslim mind. The Muslim League blocks my way. I try to read the League newspapers. They give me a peep into the League mind in so far as they represent it. In their opinion I am thoroughly untrustworthy. Even my services during the *Khilafat* days wear for them a sinister meaning. I am quite clear in my mind that this is a passing phase. I am not aware of having done a single disservice to any Muslim cause or a Muslim person. Thank God, even today I claim numerous Muslim friends. I do not know how to get rid of the distrust. "Give Pakistan," say my critics. I answer, "It is not in my giving." If I felt convinced of the rightness of the demand, I should certainly work for it side by side with the League. But I do not. I would like to be convinced.

Nobody has yet told me all its implications. Those that are described in the anti-Pakistan Press are too terrible to contemplate. But I cannot take them from the opposition. Only the protagonists know what they want and mean. I plead for such an exposition. Surely Pakistanis want to convert the opposition, not to force them? Has an attempt ever been made to meet the opposition in a friendly manner and to convert them? I am sure the Congress is willing to be converted, let alone me. But what am I to do meanwhile? I feel that now is the time for India to play an effective part in the fortunes of the war, if she becomes free from British servitude. I am convinced too that nothing stands in the way of that freedom except British unwillingness to give up India as the happy hunting-ground for the British that she has been for three centuries. ... Thinking Indians cannot idle away their time. I think that if even a large number, if not all of us, are prepared to undergo any sacrifice that may fall to our lot, would impress the British rulers that they can no longer hold India as a British possession. I believe too that such a number is available. Needless to say, their action must be non-violent, irrespective of their belief, as even a military man's has often to be, on behalf of his cause. The fight has been conceived in the interest of the whole of India. The fighters will gain no more than the poorest Indian. They will fight, not to seize power but to end the foreign domination, cost what it may.

What will happen after, if ever we reach that stage, will depend upon how we act when the all-powerful British hand is withdrawn. We may quarrel among ourselves or we may adjust our quarrels and agree to set up ordered rule on behalf of the people. It may be a democratic constitution or unadulterated autocracy or oligarchy. ... Militarily the most powerful party may set up its rule and impose it on India if the people submit. Muslims may declare Pakistan and nobody may resist them. Hindus may do likewise, Sikhs may set up their rule in territories inhabited by them. There is no end to the possibilities.

And to all this idle speculation let me suggest one more addition. The Congress and the League being best organized parties in the country may come to terms and set up a provisional government acceptable to all. And this may be followed by a duly elected

Constituent Assembly.

The movement has only one aim—that is, of displacing the British Power. If that happy event comes about and if it is followed by a stable government, it will most assuredly decide the fate of the war— I shall hope in a non-violent manner. India can show no other strength during this war at any rate. Why should not Muslims who believe in Pakistan but also believe in independent India join such a struggle? If on the other hand they believe in Pakistan through British aid and under British aegis, it is a different story. I have no place in it.

*Harijan,* 2-7-1942 (83: 79-81)

---

*The fact that even Congressmen such as his trusted friend, C. Rajagopalachari, favoured a settlement with the Muslim League that would recognize the principle of separation of peoples, and his growing belief that until the British left India, the Hindu-Muslim problem would know of no solution, propelled Gandhi to advance his 'Quit India' resolution.*

## Speech at All-India Congress Committee Meeting, Bombay August 8, 1942

... The Qaid-e-Azam says that he is compelled to say bitter things (*about the Congress and Gandhi - ed.*) but that he cannot help giving expression to his thoughts and his feelings. Similarly I would say: I consider myself a friend of the Mussalmans. Why should I then not give expression to the things nearest to my heart, even at the cost of displeasing them? How can I conceal my innermost thoughts from them ...There is neither fair play nor justice in saying that the Congress must accept a thing even if it does not believe in it and even if it goes counter to principles it holds dear.

Rajaji said: "I do not believe in Pakistan. But Mussalmans ask for it, Mr. Jinnah asks for it, and it has become an obsession with them. Why not then say 'yes' to them just now? The same Mr. Jinnah will later on realize the disadvantages of Pakistan and will forgo the demand." I said: "It is not fair to accept as true a thing which I hold to be untrue and ask others to do so in the belief that the demand will not be pressed when the time comes for settling it finally. If I hold the demand to be just, I should concede it this very day. I should not agree to it merely in order to placate Jinnah Saheb. Many friends have come and asked me to agree to it for the time being to placate Mr. Jinnah, disarm his suspicions and to see how he reacts to it. But I cannot be party to a course of action with a false promise. At any rate, it is not my method."

The Congress has no sanction but the moral one for enforcing its decisions. It believes that true democracy can only be the outcome of non-violence. The structure of a world federation can be raised only on a foundation of non-violence, and violence will have to be totally abjured from world affairs. If this is true, the solution of the Hindu-Muslim question, too, cannot be achieved by resort to violence. If the Hindus tyrannize over the Mussalmans, with what face will they talk of a world federation? ... The Congress has agreed to submitting all the differences to an impartial international tribunal and to abide by its decisions. If even this fairest of proposals is unacceptable, the only course that remains open is that of the sword, of violence. How can I persuade myself to agree to an impossibility? To demand the vivisection of a living organism is to ask for its very life. It is a call to war. The Congress cannot be party to such a fratricidal war. Those Hindus who, like Dr. Moonje and Shri Savarkar, believe in the doctrine of the sword may seek to keep the Mussalmans under Hindu domination. I do not represent that section. I represent the Congress. You want to kill the Congress which is the goose that lays golden eggs. If you distrust the Congress, you may rest assured that there is to be a perpetual war between the Hindus and the Mussalmans, and the country will be doomed to continue warfare and bloodshed. If such warfare is to be our lot, I shall not live to witness it.

... There is much in my heart that I would like to pour out before this assembly. One thing which was uppermost in my heart I have already dealt with. You may take it from me that it is with me a matter of life and death. If we Hindus and Mussalmans mean to achieve a heart unity, without the slightest mental reservation on the part of either, we must first unite in the effort to be free from the shackles of this Empire. If Pakistan after all is to be a portion of

India, what objection can there be for Mussalmans against joining this struggle for India's freedom? The Hindus and Mussalmans must, therefore, unite in the first instance on the issue of fighting for freedom ...

... The Qaid-e-Azam has said that the Muslim League is prepared to take over the rule from the Britishers if they are prepared to hand it over to the Muslim League, for the British took over the Empire from the hands of the Muslims. This, however, will be Muslim raj. The offer made by Maulana Saheb and by me does not imply establishment of Muslim raj or Muslim domination. The Congress does not believe in the domination of any group or any community. It believes in democracy which includes in its orbit Muslims, Hindus, Christians, Parsis, Jews—every one of the communities inhabiting this vast country ...

... The Congress does not belong to any one class or community; it belongs to the whole nation. It is open to Mussalmans to take possession of the Congress. They can, if they like, swamp the Congress by their numbers, and can steer it along the course which appeals to them. The Congress is fighting not on behalf of the Hindus but on behalf of the whole nation, including the minorities. It would hurt me to hear of a single instance of a Mussalman being killed by a Congressman. In the coming revolution, Congressmen will sacrifice their lives in order to protect the Mussalman against a Hindu's attack and vice versa. It is a part of their creed, and is one of the essentials of non-violence. You will be expected on occasions like these not to lose your heads. Every Congressman, whether a Hindu or a Mussalman, owes this duty to the organization to which he belongs. The Mussalman who will act in this manner will render a service to Islam. Mutual trust is essential for success in the final nation-wide struggle that is to come. I have said that much greater sacrifices will have to be made this time in the wake of our struggle because of the opposition from the Muslim League and from Englishmen ...

... Every one of you should, from this moment onwards, consider yourself a free man or woman, and act as if you are free and are no longer under the heel of this imperialism. It is not a make-believe that I am suggesting to you. It is the very essence of freedom. ...

Here is a mantra, a short one, that I give you. You may imprint it on your hearts and let every breath of yours give expression to it. The mantra is: "Do or Die." We shall either free India or die in the attempt; we shall not live to see the perpetuation of our slavery. Every true Congressman or [Congress] woman will join the struggle with an inflexible determination not to remain alive to see the country in bondage and slavery. Let that be your pledge. ... Let every man and woman live every moment of his or her life hereafter in the consciousness that he or she eats or lives for achieving freedom and will die, if need be, to attain that goal. Take a pledge with God and your own conscience as witness, that you will no longer rest till freedom is achieved and will be prepared to lay down your lives in the attempt to achieve it. He who loses his life will gain it; he who will seek to save it shall lose it. Freedom is not for the coward or the faint-hearted ...

*Mahatma*, Vol. VI, pp. 154-64 (83: 191-195)

---

*The 'Quit India' call was persuasive rhetoric, but neither the Congress nor Gandhi had worked out a coherent plan of action to back it: they expected the colonial government to respond to their call to action and invite them for discussions, and so had not planned a campaign like they did during the salt satyagraha. In the event the British not only did not heed their call, but arrested the entire leadership of the Congress. However, the protests that had begun in the wake of the 'Quit India' call grew spontaneously and in some instances turned violent. The government accused Gandhi and the Congress of pursuing a hypocritical policy of verbal non-violence and strategic violence. Gandhi was pained by the criticism but refused to accept the blame.*

**Letter to Lord Linlithgow**
**Personal**
**January 19, 1943**

DEAR LORD LINLITHGOW,

... Of course, I deplore the happenings which have taken place since 9th August last. But have I not laid the whole blame for them at the door of the Government of India? Moreover I could not express any opinion on events which I cannot influence or control, and of which I have but a one-sided account. You are bound *prima facie* to accept the accuracy of reports that may be placed before you by your departmental heads. But you will not expect me to do so. Such reports have before now often proved fallible. It was for that reason that, in my letter of 31st December, I pleaded with you to convince me of the correctness of the information on which your conviction was based. You will perhaps appreciate my fundamental difficulty in making the statement you have expected me to make. This, however, I can say from the house-top, that I am as confirmed a believer in non-violence as I have ever been. You may not know that any violence on the part of Congress workers I have condemned openly and unequivocally. I have even done public penance more than once. I must not weary you with examples. The point I wish to make is that on every such occasion I was a free man. This time the retracing, as I have submitted, lies with the Government. You will forgive me for expressing an opinion challenging yours. I am certain that nothing but good would have resulted, if you had stayed your hand and granted me the interview, which I had announced on the night of the 8th August, I was to seek ...

I am ,

Your sincere friend,

M. K. GANDHI

*Gandhiji's Correspondence with the Government*, pp. 21-2; also *Correspondence with Mr. Gandhi*, pp. 6-7 (83: 276-78)

---

*Gandhi's impassioned letter to the Viceroy did not help to clarify matters. The latter continued to accuse Gandhi of harbouring secret political motives and fomenting violence. Gandhi decided to go on a fast to purify himself. The fast ended well but the political stalemate continued. Gandhi and others remained in prison until 1944, as violent anger reigned in the streets and hundreds were arrested and interned.*

## Letter to Lord Linlithgow
## Detention Camp, February 7, 1943

DEAR LORD LINLITHGOW,

... You say that there is evidence that I—I leave my friends out for the moment—"expected this policy to lead to violence", that I was "prepared to condone it", and that "the violence that ensued formed part of a concerted plan, conceived long before the arrest of Congress leaders". I have seen no evidence in support of such a serious charge. … You have condemned men and women before trying them and hearing their defence. Surely there is nothing wrong in my asking you to show me the evidence on which you hold them guilty. What you say in your letter carries no conviction. Proof should correspond to the canons of English jurisprudence.

If the wife of a member of the Working Committee (*of the Congress - ed.*) is actively engaged in "planning the bomb outrages and other acts of terrorism", she should be tried before a court of law and punished, if found guilty. The lady you refer to could only have done the things attributed to her after the wholesale arrests of 9th August last, which I have dared to describe as leonine violence. You say that the time is not yet ripe to publish the charges against the Congress. Have you ever thought of the possibility of their being found baseless when they are put before an impartial tribunal? Or that some of the condemned persons might have died in the meanwhile or that some of the evidence that the living can produce might become unavailable? …

Lastly, you read into my letters a meaning which is wholly inconsistent with my declaration, in one of them, of adherence to unadulterated non-violence. For, you say in your letter under reply that "acceptance of my point of view would be to concede that the authorized Government of the country on which lies the responsibility for maintaining peace and good order, should allow movements to take place that would admit preparations for violence, interruption of communications, for attacks on innocent persons, for murders of police officers and others to proceed unchecked". I must be a strange friend of yours whom you believe to be capable of asking for recognition of such things as lawful.

I have not attempted an exhaustive reply to the views and statements attributed to me. This is not the place nor the time for such a reply. I have only picked out those things which in my opinion demanded an immediate answer. You have left me no loophole for escaping the ordeal ( *a purifying fast which eventually lasted 21 days - ed.*) I have set before myself. I begin it on the 9th instant with the clearest possible conscience. Despite your description of it as "a form of political blackmail", it is on my part meant to be an appeal to the Highest Tribunal for justice which I have failed to secure from you ...

From a photostat. Courtesy: India Office Library. Also *Gandhiji's Correspondence with the Government*, pp. 30-2, and *Correspondence with Mr. Gandhi*, pp. 11-2 (83: 283-84)

## Concluding Uneasy Times

---

*The late 1930s reveal an adroit, though increasingly tired, Gandhi, as he attempted to keep step with the march of the times. He had to account for the Congress' political authority, now that it was a party of rule. He legitimized and chastised it in turn. At the same time, he had to remind the Congress of its essentially combative role. Imperialism, after all, had not dislodged itself and had to be confronted and overcome. Gandhi was however uneasy with those who wished to be combative—the impatient socialists within Congress—and was determined to limit their influence. His responses were framed, during this period, by World War II on one hand, and by the growing dissension and distance between the Congress and the Muslim League on the other.*

*As far as the war was concerned, he moved from a state of unconditional support to one where he enjoined action against Empire— as he remarked with reference to the 'Quit India' satyagraha, 'a do or die' action. Meanwhile, he argued that his moral logic remained the same in both instances. He was not calling for violence; earlier he had counselled non-violent support, now he merely wished to withdraw that support, or rather did not wish to offer it, instead he would resist British presence as such non-violently, by demanding that it leave India. His confrontation with Empire was determined by other considerations as well. The Muslim League had earned the goodwill of the colonial government and its demand for Pakistan had fallen on willing ears. The British, Gandhi held, were determined to divide Indians in order to continue their own rule. Therefore, it was imperative that nationalists demonstrate their strength, through non-violent resistance and defiance.*

*However, Gandhi's call to the British to 'Quit India' appeared to his English and American detractors an instance of moral casuistry. He denied that the imminent Japanese invasion had anything to do with his change of stance, and held that he was offering Britain a chance to acquit herself honourably in the eyes of India and the world. But the fact remained that the British were embarrassed and frustrated and responded by promptly imprisoning him and the entire working committee of the Congress party.*

*Jinnah, leader of the Muslim League, felt that Gandhi's call to resist British presence and for the British to quit India was a call to Hindus to mobilise themselves for a transfer of power and authority. After all Gandhi had been worried to death about Hindu-Muslim violence, and rather than seek a democratic, contractual solution, had opted for the dramatic.*

*Gandhi went on to answer Jinnah's criticisms, but it is clear, from his explanations of the notice he served the British, that he granted Jinnah's accusations, their ground. He did see the 'Quit India' struggle as a last-ditch attempt to unify warring Congress factions, re-interest them in the cause of non-violence, and to embody a glorious nationalist moment in history. What he failed to see, or would not see, was the manner in which sections of Muslims in the country had grown steadily alienated from the national movement. He also did not recognize the force of Hindu right-wing opinion within the Congress.*

*Significantly, his complicated experiments with truth during this period in time did not prove conclusive, as is evident from the failure of the Rajkot satyagraha,. Likewise, his serving of notice to the British did not yield the desired results. It rebound on him, as Lord Linlithgow went on to accuse him of planning for violence and disaffection, following the 'Quit India' call. The reasons for his time-tested moral strategies failing him are diverse and complex: for one, his deft coupling of the moral and the pragmatic did not possess the convincing resonance it had had in the 1930s, whether this had to do with the salt laws, or with the pact he eventually signed with Dr. Ambedkar. Secondly, his usually keen sensitivity to the slightest variation of the political and moral tenor of his times was compromised by his distance from the developments of the day: growing anger between Muslims and Hindus on the streets in parts of the subcontinent, the manner in which the Muslim League gained in popularity in the early 1940s, and the will to power so avidly held and exercised by Congressmen.*

*These years reveal to us, as past years of struggle have, a Gandhi whose ideas, especially ideas about non-violence, assume their characteristic resonance only in concrete contexts. Non-violence as a creed emerged stained by the times allowing itself, as it did, to be leavened by the demands of the here and now.*

# Chapter 7

## Telling the Truth About War
## 1939-1945

*Global political developments in the 1930s—the rise of Hitler and a growing Nazi belligerence— appeared to mock Gandhi's faith in non-violence and peace. He felt the burden of his times with a particular acuity but it was not his wont to remain passive, or allow his pessimism to paralyse him: he was determined to argue and act his way out of it.*

*In India, he did not want to impede British war efforts, but neither would he support them. Instead he urged non-violence as a viable political option, and one that could be pursued both by individuals and nations on the one hand and by aggressor nations and their victims, on the other. As the war dragged on and Indian national opinion against Britain dragging India into a choiceless war without conceding Indian rights to freedom and self-rule grew, Gandhi decided to act, but insisted that protests remain focused, non-violent and decorous.*

*More generally, and significantly, Gandhi refused to demonise fascism to the extent that it prevented a rational analysis of the links that bound together fascism, imperialism and colonial exploitation. In other words, he was convinced that British imperialism compromised the allied nations' professed moral horror of fascism and their commitment to democracy and freedom. Likewise, he was unmoved by those pleas which urged him to suspend faith in the possibilities of moral renewal even in those who appeared incapable of it, such as the Nazis. His arguments in this context were advanced in the course of a dialogue with Jewish admirers who were baffled by his suggestion that the Jews suffer satyagraha in Germany to persuade Hitler to change his mind.*

*These years also witnessed Gandhi arguing with pacifist friends, amplifying and deepening the message of the New Testament, which, to Gandhi, provided a model of pacifist faith and action. Determined to practise his distinctive pacifist ethics in perfect good faith, he addressed personal letters of goodwill to Hitler, the colonial war government, the people of Britain, the people of Japan and to the suffering Jews. He attempted to mediate, in his characteristic manner, the question of Palestine.*

*The dropping of the atom bomb confirmed Gandhi's sense of the irreversibility of violence: the bomb in fact embodied this fact and its presence and destructive potential served to further hone his commitment to non-violence.*

# Touching the Heart of Evil: Gandhi's War

*World War II did not frighten Gandhi, it filled him with despair instead. But at the same time he experienced a new and determined resolve to uphold the claims of non-violence. It became clear from the late 1930s, at least from 1938, that Hitler was serious in his ruthlessly aggressive intent. Initially Gandhi thought him to be a political dictator who was just mildly truculent in observing the norms required by international political decorum. Soon it became apparent that this was not the case. As German aggression expanded, Gandhi felt more than ever the need to counsel a helpless and frightened world, the virtue of resisting evil in calm faith, and to compel good through appropriate political or just acts.*

*Once he was seized of this idea, he acted on it: he wrote letters to Hitler (which were never delivered, since the British did not think it wise or politic to deliver them to their arch enemy), attempted to engage English public opinion and later on, requested the Japanese not to advance further in their march towards a fascist future.*

*The extracts below offer fascinating readings in his creed of non-violence, which, as always proved itself entirely apposite to the times.*

**Letter to Adolf Hitler**
**As At Wardha, C. P., India, July 23, 1939**

DEAR FRIEND,

Friends have been urging me to write to you for the sake of humanity. But I have resisted their request, because of the feeling that any letter from me would be an impertinence. Something tells me that I must not calculate and that I must make my appeal for whatever it may be worth.

It is quite clear that you are today the one person in the world who can prevent a war, which may reduce humanity to the savage state. Must you pay that price for an object however worthy it may appear to you to be? Will you listen to the appeal of one who has deliberately shunned the method of war not without considerable success? Anyway I anticipate your forgiveness, if I have erred in writing to you.

I remain,

Your sincere friend,

From a photostat (76: 156-57)

---

*Hitler's rise to power and the imminence of war saddened Gandhi, and we find this sorrow inflecting all his pronouncements during this period.*

## Statement to the Press
## Segaon, August 27, 1939

... I have been hesitating to say anything on the impending world crisis which affects the welfare not of a few nations but of the whole of mankind. I have felt that my word can have no effect on those on whom depends the decision whether there is to be war or peace. I know that many in the West believe that my word does carry weight. I wish I shared their belief. Not having such belief I have been praying in secret that God may spare us the calamity of war. But I have no hesitation in redeclaring my faith in reason, which is another word for non-violence, rather than the arbitrament of war for the settlement of disputes or redress of wrongs. I cannot emphasize my belief more forcibly than by saying that I personally would not purchase my own country's freedom by violence even if such a thing were a possibility. My faith in the wise saying that what is gained by the sword will also be lost by the sword is imperishable. How I wish Herr Hitler would respond to the appeal of the President of the United Sates and allow his claim to be investigated by arbitrators in whose choice he will have as effective a voice as the disputants.

*Harijan*, 2-9-1939 (76: 273)

---

*As the war touched English shores, Gandhi visited the Viceroy, Lord Linlithgow, to offer his services in the cause of peace and to plead against the madness of war. He did not have the Congress' support or endorsement, because that party wished to bargain with government—offering support in return for greater political power to Indian representatives. Gandhi's stance baffled his supporters who were alternatively annoyed and frustrated by his attitude.*

## Statement to the Press
## Simla, September 5, 1939

At Delhi, as I was entraining for Kalka, a big crowd sang in perfect good humour, to the worn-out refrain of "*Mahatma Gandhiki jai*". "We do not want any understanding". I had then my weekly silence. Therefore I merely smiled. And those who were standing on the footboard returned the smile with their smile, whilst they were admonishing me not to have any understanding with the Viceroy. I had also a letter from a Congress Committee giving me similar warning.

I knew that I had no authority to speak for any person except myself. ... I had answered a telegraphic invitation (*from Viceroy Linlithgow - ed.*) and taken the first train I could catch. And what is more, with my irrepressible and out-and-out non-violence, I knew that I could not represent the national mind and I should cut a sorry figure if I tried to do so. I told His Excellency as much. Therefore there could be no question of any understanding or negotiation with me. Nor, I saw, had he sent for me to negotiate. I have returned from the Viceregal Lodge empty-handed and without any understanding, open or secret. If there is to be any understanding, it would be between the Congress and the Government.

Having, therefore, made my position vis-a-vis the Congress quite clear, I told His Excellency that my own sympathies were with England and France from the purely humanitarian standpoint. I told him that I could not contemplate without being stirred to the very depth the destruction of London which had hitherto been regarded as impregnable. And as I was picturing before him the Houses of Parliament and the Westminster Abbey and their possible destruction, I broke down. I have become disconsolate. In the secret of my heart I am in perpetual quarrel with God that He should allow such things to go on. My non-violence seems almost impotent.

But the answer comes at the end of the daily quarrel that neither God nor non-violence is impotent. Impotence is in men. I must try on without losing faith even though I may break in the attempt.

... I must refuse to believe that Germans contemplate with equanimity the evacuation of big cities like London for fear of destruction to be wrought by man's inhuman ingenuity. They cannot contemplate with equanimity such destruction of themselves and their own monuments. I am not therefore just now thinking of India's deliverance. It will come, but what will it be worth if England and France fall, or if they come out victorious over Germany ruined and humbled ?

... It is in the midst of this catastrophe without parallel that Congressmen and all other responsible Indians individually and collectively have to decide what part India is to play in this terrible drama.

*Harijan*, 9-9-1939 (76: 311-312)

---

### Source of My Sympathy

The statement made by me just after my interview with H. E. the Viceroy has had a mixed reception. It has been described as sentimental twaddle by one critic and as a statesman-like pronouncement by another ...

I have a spirited protest from a correspondent. It calls for a reply. I do not reproduce the letter as parts of it I do not understand myself. But there is no difficulty in catching its drift. The main argument is this :

... I suggest to you that there is no difference between Chamberlain and Hitler. Is England's record in India any better than Hitler's in another part of the world in similar circumstances? Hitler is but an infant pupil of the old imperialist England and France. I fancy that your emotion at the Viceregal Lodge had the better of your judgment.

No one perhaps has described English misdeeds more forcibly, subject to truth, than I have. No one has resisted England more effectively, perhaps, than I have. And my desire for and power of resistance remain unabated. But there are seasons for speech and action, as there are seasons for silence and inaction. In the dictionary of satyagraha there is no enemy. But as I have no desire to prepare a new dictionary for satyagrahis, I use the old words giving them a new meaning. A satyagrahi loves his so-called enemy even as his friend. He owns no enemy. As a satyagrahi, i.e., votary of *ahimsa*, I must wish well to England. My wishes regarding Germany were, and they still are, irrelevant for the moment. But I have said in a few words in my statement that I would not care to erect the freedom of my country on the remains of despoiled Germany, I should be as much moved by a contemplation of the possible destruction of Germany's monuments. Herr Hitler stands in no need of my sympathy. In assessing the present merits, the past misdeeds of England and the good deeds of Germany are irrelevant. Rightly or wrongly, and irrespective of what the other Powers have done before under similar circumstances, I have come to the conclusion that Herr Hitler is responsible for the war. I do not judge his claim ...

... I think I am right in saying that the whole world was anxious that Herr Hitler should allow his demand to be examined by an impartial tribunal. If he succeeds in his design, his success will be no proof of the justness of his claim. It will be proof that the Law of the Jungle is still a great force in human affairs. It will be one more proof that though we humans have changed the form we have not changed the manners of the beast.

I hope it is now clear to my critics that my sympathy for England and France is not a result of momentary emotion or, in cruder language, of hysteria. It is derived from the never-drying fountain of non-violence which my breast has nursed for fifty years. I claim no infallibility for my judgment. All I claim is that my sympathy for England and France is reasoned. I invite those who accept the premises on which my sympathy is based to join me. What shape it should take is another matter. Alone I can but pray. And so I told His Excellency that my sympathy had no concrete value in the face of the concrete destruction that is facing those who are directly engaged in the war.

*Harijan*, 30-9-1939 (76: 320-22)

*After Hitler's victorious march across German borders into a greater part of Europe, the reality of Nazi power could not be denied. Gandhi visited the Viceroy yet another time and counselled him to re-examine the virtues of non-violence. This letter recapitulates his conversations with the Viceroy.*

## Letter to Lord Linlithgow
## Birla House, Albequerque Road
## New Delhi, June 30, 1940

DEAR LORD LINLITHGOW,

... Assuming that Nazis were as bad as they were said to be, victory must be unattainable without copying the Nazi methods. That would mean no deliverance from Nazism. Sufficient had happened to prove the utter futility of armaments for the protection of small nations no matter how brave they were.

Britain's victory after the slaughter and ruthlessness which it must involve could never make the world safe for democracy, nor bring it peace. Such a victory must mean another preparation for a war more inhuman than the present, as this one had proved more inhuman than the last. For this and similar reasons I urged with all the earnestness and force at my command that if Britain could accept the non-violent method, it would redound to her eternal glory and would count for much greater bravery than her proverbial bravery in war. I hoped too that it would not be retorted that I had no warrant for appealing to Britain suddenly to accept the non-violent method when I had failed in persuading my colleagues and co-workers to accept it when the time had come for its enforcement in its fullness.

I said in anticipation of the possibility of such a retort that my colleagues and I represented a weak and subject people wholly unarmed and untrained in the use of arms. The non-violence of my conception was essentially for those who were conscious of their ability to wield them with effect. Therefore I suggested that if Britain could be convinced of the superiority of non-violence over violence, now was the psychological moment for the full adoption of the non-violent method. Britain with all her intentions could not protect Abyssinia, Czechoslovakia, Poland, Finland, Norway,

Denmark, Holland, Belgium and France. If Britain could accept the method presented by me, it would point to all these countries the way of deliverance and ensure the peace of the world as no other method ever would or could. It would confound Nazi wisdom and put all the Nazi armaments out of use.

Lastly, I said that my proposal was based on a practical experience of non-violence extending over half a century of ceaseless striving, experiment, research and prayer. I therefore requested you to present my proposal to His Majesty's Government for acceptance as coming from a life-long friend and well-wisher of the British people ...

From a printed copy: *Lord Linlithgow Papers*. Courtesy: National Archives of India (78: 371-72)

---

*The first of Gandhi's two letters to the 'ordinary Briton', this one was written on the eve of the impending Nazi attack on the British Isles. Deploying arguments, similar to the ones he had suggested to Linlithgow, Gandhi urged 'every Briton' to offer non-violent resistance to Britain.*

## To Every Briton

... I appeal to every Briton, wherever he may be now, to accept the method of non-violence instead of that of war for the adjustment of relations between nations and other matters. Your statesmen have declared that this is a war on behalf of democracy. There are many other reasons given in justification. You know them all by heart. I suggest that at the end of the war, whichever way it ends, there will be no democracy left to represent democracy.

This war has descended upon mankind as a curse and a warning. It is a curse inasmuch as it is brutalizing man on a scale hitherto unknown. All distinctions between combatants and non-combatants have been abolished. No one and nothing is to be spared. Lying has been reduced to an art. Britain was to defend small nationalities. One by one they have vanished, at least for the time being. It is also a warning. It is a warning that, if nobody reads the writing on the wall, man will be reduced to the state of the beast, whom he is shaming by his manners. I read the writing when the hostilities broke out. But I had not the courage to say the word. God has given me the courage to say it before it is too late.

I appeal for cessation of hostilities, not because you are too exhausted to fight, but because war is bad in essence. You want to kill Nazism. You will never kill it by its indifferent adoption. Your soldiers are doing the same work of destruction as the Germans. The only difference is that perhaps yours are not as thorough as the Germans. If that be so, yours will soon acquire the same thoroughness as theirs, if not much greater. On no other condition can you win the war. In other words, you will have to be more ruthless than the Nazis. No cause, however just, can warrant the indiscriminate slaughter that is going on minute by minute. I suggest that a cause that demands the inhumanities that are being perpetrated today cannot be called just.

I do not want Britain to be defeated, nor do I want her to be victorious in a trial of brute strength, whether expressed through the muscle or the brain. Your muscular bravery is an established fact. Need you demonstrate that your brain is also as unrivalled in destructive power as your muscle? I hope you do not wish to enter into such an undignified competition with the Nazis. I venture to present you with a nobler and a braver way, worthy of the bravest soldier. I want you to fight Nazism without arms, or, if I am to retain the military terminology, with non-violent arms. I would like you to lay down the arms you have as being useless for saving you or humanity. You will invite Herr Hitler and Signor Mussolini to take what they want of the countries you call your possessions. Let them take possession of your beautiful island, with your many beautiful buildings. You will give all these, but neither your souls, nor your minds. If these gentlemen choose to occupy your homes, you will vacate them. If they do not give you free passage out, you will allow yourself, man, woman and child, to be slaughtered, but you will refuse to owe allegiance to them.

This process or method, which I have called non-violent Non-cooperation, is not without considerable success in its use in India. … I make bold to say that you who are India's masters would have become her pupils and, with much greater skill than we have, perfected this matchless weapon and met the German and Italian friends' menace with it. Indeed the history of Europe during the past few months would then have been written differently.

Europe would have been spared seas of innocent blood, the rape of so many small nations, and the orgy of hatred.

This is no appeal made by a man who does not know his business. I have been practising with scientific precision non-violence and its possibilities for an unbroken period of over fifty years. I have applied it in every walk of life, domestic, institutional, economic and political. I know of no single case in which it has failed. Where it has seemed sometimes to have failed, I have ascribed it to my imperfections ...

I claim to have been a lifelong and wholly disinterested friend of the British people. At one time I used to be also a lover of your empire. I thought that it was doing good to India. When I saw that in the nature of things it could do no good. I used, and am still using, the non-violent method to fight imperialism. Whatever the ultimate fate of my country, my love for you remains, and will remain, undiminished. My non-violence demands universal love, and you are not a small part of it. It is that love which has prompted my appeal to you.

May God give power to every word of mine. In His name I began to write this, and in His name I close it. May your statesmen have the wisdom and courage to respond to my appeal ...

*Harijan*, 6-7-1940 (78: 386-88)

---

*Gandhi's second letter to Hitler took the form of a Christmas Eve appeal for peace.*

## Letter to Adolf Hitler
## Wardha, December 24, 1940

DEAR FRIEND,

That I address you as a friend is no formality. I own no foes. My business in life has been for the past 33 years to enlist the friendship of the whole of humanity by befriending mankind, irrespective of race, colour or creed.

I hope you will have the time and desire to know how a good portion of humanity ... living under the influence of that doctrine of universal friendship view your action. We have no doubt about your bravery or devotion to your fatherland, nor do we believe that you are the monster described by your opponents. But your own writings and pronouncements and those of your friends and admirers leave no room for doubt that many of your acts are monstrous and unbecoming of human dignity, especially in the estimation of men like me who believe in universal friendliness. Such are your humiliation of Czechoslovakia, the rape of Poland and the swallowing of Denmark. I am aware that your view of life regards such spoliations as virtuous acts. But we have been taught from childhood to regard them as acts degrading humanity. Hence we cannot possibly wish success to your arms.

But ours is a unique position. We resist British Imperialism no less than Nazism. If there is a difference, it is in degree. One-fifth of the human race has been brought under the British heel by means that will not bear scrutiny. Our resistance to it does not mean harm to the British people. We seek to convert them, not to defeat them on the battle-field. Ours is an unarmed revolt against the British rule. But whether we convert them or not, we are determined to make their rule impossible by non-violent Non-cooperation. It is a method in its nature indefensible. It is based on the knowledge that no spoliator can compass his end without a certain degree of cooperation, willing or compulsory, of the victim. Our rulers may have our land and bodies but not our souls. They can have the former only by complete destruction of every Indian—man, woman and child.

That all may not rise to that degree of heroism and that a fair amount of frightfulness can bend the back of revolt is true but the argument would be beside the point. For, if a fair number of men and women be found in India who would be prepared without any ill will against the spoliators to lay down their lives rather than bend the knee to them, they would have shown the way to freedom from the tyranny of violence. I ask you to believe me when I say that you will find an unexpected number of such men and women in India. They have been having that training for the past 20 years.

We have been trying for the past half a century to throw off the British rule. The movement of independence has been never so strong as now. The most powerful political organization, I mean the Indian National Congress, is trying to achieve this end. We have attained a very fair measure of success through non-violent effort. We were groping for the right means to combat the most organized violence in the world which the British power represents. You have challenged it.

It remains to be seen which is the better organized, the German or the British. We know what the British heel means for us and the non-European races of the world. But we would never wish to end the British rule with German aid. We have found in non-violence a force which, if organized, can without doubt match itself against a combination of all the most violent forces in the world.

In non-violent technique, as I have said, there is no such thing as defeat. It is all "do or die" without killing or hurting. It can be used practically without money and obviously without the aid of science of destruction which you have brought to such perfection. It is a marvel to me that you do not see that it is nobody's monopoly. If not the British, some other power will certainly improve upon your method and beat you with your own weapon. You are leaving no legacy to your people of which they would feel proud. They cannot take pride in a recital of cruel deeds, however skilfully planned. I, therefore, appeal to you in the name of humanity to stop the war. You will lose nothing by referring all the matters of dispute between you and Great Britain to an international tribunal of your joint choice. If you attain success in the war, it will not prove that you were in the right. It will only prove that your power of destruction was greater. Whereas an award by an impartial tribunal will show as far as it is humanly possible which party was in the right.

You know that not long ago I made an appeal to every Briton to accept my method of non-violent resistance. I did it because the British know me as a friend though a rebel. I am a stranger to you and your people. I have not the courage to make you the appeal I made to every Briton. Not that it would not apply to you with the same force as to the British. But my present proposal is much simple [sic] because much more practical and familiar.

During this season when the hearts of the peoples of Europe yearn for peace, we have suspended even our own peaceful struggle.

Is it too much to ask you to make an effort for peace during a time which may mean nothing to you personally but which must mean much to the millions of Europeans whose dumb cry for peace I hear, for my ears are attuned to hearing the dumb millions? I had intended to address a joint appeal to you and Signor Mussolini, whom I had the privilege of meeting, when I was in Rome during my visit to England as a delegate to the Round Table Conference (*Gandhi spent time in Europe, especially in France and Italy, after the conference - ed.*). I hope that he will take this as addressed to him also with the necessary changes.

I am,

Your sincere friend,

M. K. GANDHI

From a copy. Courtesy: G. D. Birla (79: 453-56)

---

*Gandhi's second letter to 'every Briton' was written after Japan entered the war (1941) and a Japanese invasion of British India seemed certain.*

## To Every Briton

... I ask every Briton to support me in my appeal to the British at this very hour to retire from every Asiatic and African possession and at least from India. That step is essential for the safety of the world and for the destruction of Nazism and Fascism. In this I include Japan's "ism" also. It is a good copy of the two. Acceptance of my appeal will confound all the military plans of all the Axis Powers and even of the military advisers of Great Britain.

... British statesmen talk glibly of India's participation in the war. Now India was never even formally consulted on the declaration of war. Why should it be? India does not belong to Indians. It belongs to the British. It has been even called a British possession. The British practically do with it as they like. They make me—an all-war resister—pay a war tax in a variety of ways.

... If I was a student of economics, I could produce startling figures as to what India has been made to pay towards the war apart from what are miscalled voluntary contributions. No contribution made to a conqueror can be truly described as voluntary ...

... Before the Japanese menace overtakes India, India's homesteads are being occupied by British troops—Indian and non-Indian. The dwellers are summarily ejected and expected to shift for themselves. They are paid a paltry vacating expense which carries them nowhere. Their occupation is gone. They have to build their cottages and search for their livelihood ...

... People in East Bengal may almost be regarded as amphibious. They live partly on land and partly on the waters of the rivers. They have light canoes which enable them to go from place to place. For fear of the Japanese using the canoes the people have been called upon to surrender them. For a Bengali to part with his canoe is almost like parting with his life. So those who take away his canoe he regards as his enemy.

Great Britain has to win the war. Need she do so at India's expense? Should she do so? But I have something more to add to this sad chapter. The falsity that envelopes Indian life is suffocating. Almost every Indian you meet is discontented. But he will not own it publicly. The Government employees, high and low, are no exception. ... This all-pervading distrust and falsity make life worthless unless one resists it with one's whole soul.

You may refuse to believe all I say. ... I have stated what I believe to be the truth, the whole truth and nothing but the truth. My people may or may not approve of this loud thinking. I have consulted nobody. This appeal is being written during my silence day. I am just now concerned with Britain's action. When slavery was abolished in America many slaves protested, some even wept. But protests and tears notwithstanding, slavery was abolished in law. But the abolition was the result of a bloody war between the South and the North; and so though the Negro's lot is considerably better than before, he still remains the outcaste of high society. I am asking for something much higher. I ask for a bloodless end of an unnatural domination and for a new era, even though there may be protests and wailings from some of us.

*Harijan*, 17-5-1942 (82: 271-73)

---

*With the Japanese pressing against India's borders, Gandhi addressed this note to the people of Japan. It was carried in three Japanese papers.*

## To Every Japanese

I must confess at the outset that though I have no ill-will against you, I intensely dislike your attack upon China. From your lofty height you have descended to imperial ambition. You will fail to realize that ambition and may become the authors of the dismemberment of Asia, thus unwittingly preventing World Federation and brotherhood without which there can be no hope for humanity.

Ever since I was a lad of eighteen studying in London, over fifty years ago, I learnt, through the writings of the late Sir Edwin Arnold, to prize the many excellent qualities of your nation. I was thrilled when in South Africa I learnt of your brilliant victory over Russian arms. After my return to India from South Africa in 1915, I came in close touch with Japanese monks who lived as members of our Ashram from time to time. One of them became a valuable member of the Ashram in Sevagram, and his application to duty, his dignified bearing, his unfailing devotion to daily worship, affability, unruffledness under varying circumstances and his natural smile, which was positive evidence of his inner peace, had endeared him to all of us.

And now that owing to your declaration of war against Great Britain he has been taken away from us, we miss him as a dear co-worker. He has left behind him as a memory his daily prayer and his little drum, to the accompaniment of which we open our morning and evening prayers. In the background of these pleasant recollections I grieve deeply as I contemplate what appears to me to be your unprovoked attack against China and, if reports are to be believed, your merciless devastation of that great and ancient land.

It was a worthy ambition of yours to take equal rank with the great powers of the world. Your aggression against China and your alliance with the Axis powers was surely an unwarranted excess of the ambition. I should have thought that you would be proud of the fact that that great and ancient people, whose old classical literature you have adopted as your own, are your neighbours. Your understanding of one another's history, tradition, literature should bind you as friends rather than make you the enemies you are today.

If I was a free man, and if you allowed me to come to your country, frail though I am, I would not mind risking my health, maybe my life, to come to your country to plead with you to desist from the wrong you are doing to China and the world and therefore to yourself. But I enjoy no such freedom. And we are in the unique position of having to resist an imperialism that we detest no less than yours and Nazism. Our resistance to it does not mean harm to the British people.

We seek to convert them. Ours is an unarmed revolt against British rule. An important party in the country is engaged in a deadly but friendly quarrel with the foreign rulers. But in this they need no aid from foreign powers. You have been gravely misinformed, as I know you are, that we have chosen this particular moment to embarrass the Allies when your attack against India is imminent. If we wanted to turn Britain's difficulty into our opportunity we should have done it as soon as the war broke out nearly three years ago.

Our movement demanding the withdrawal of the British power from India should in no way be misunderstood. In fact if we are to believe your reported anxiety for the independence of India, a recognition of that independence by Britain should leave you no excuse for any attack on India. Moreover the reported profession sorts ill with your ruthless aggression against China. I would ask you to make no mistake about the fact that you will be sadly disillusioned if you believe that you will receive a willing welcome from India. The end and aim of the movement for British withdrawal is to prepare India, by making her free for resisting all militarist and imperialist ambition, whether it is called British Imperialism, German Nazism, or your pattern. If we do not, we shall have been ignoble spectators of the militarization of the world in spite of our belief that in non-violence we have the only solvent of the militarist spirit and ambition.

Personally I fear that without declaring the independence of India the Allied powers will not be able to beat the Axis combination which has raised violence to the dignity of a religion. The Allies cannot beat you and your partners unless they beat you in your ruthless and skilled warfare. If they copy it their declaration that they will save the world for democracy and individual freedom must come to naught. I feel that they can only gain strength to avoid copying your ruthlessness by declaring and recognizing now the freedom of India, and turning sullen India's forced cooperation into freed India's voluntary cooperation.

To Britain and the Allies we have appealed in the name of justice, in proof of their professions, and in their own self-interest. To you I appeal in the name of humanity. It is a marvel to me that you do not see that ruthless warfare is nobody's monopoly. If not the Allies some other power will certainly improve upon your method and beat you with your own weapon. Even if you win you will leave no legacy to your people of which they would feel proud. They cannot take pride in a recital of cruel deeds however skilfully achieved. Even if you win it will not prove that you were in the right; it will only prove that your power of destruction was greater. This applies obviously to the Allies too, unless they perform now the just and righteous act of freeing India as an earnest and promise of similarly freeing all other subject peoples in Asia and Africa.

Our appeal to Britain is coupled with the offer of free India's willingness to let the Allies retain their troops in India. The offer is made in order to prove that we do not in any way mean to harm the Allied cause, and in order to prevent you from being misled into feeling that you have but to step into the country that Britain has vacated. Needless to repeat that if you cherish any such idea and will carry it out, we will not fail in resisting you with all the might that our country can muster. I address this appeal to you in the hope that our movement may even influence you and your partners in the right direction and deflect you and them from the course which is bound to end in your moral ruin and the reduction of human beings to robots.

The hope of your response to my appeal is much fainter than that of response from Britain. I know that the British are not devoid of a sense of justice and they know me. I do not know you enough to be able to judge. All I have read tells me that you listen to no appeal but to the sword. How I wish that you are cruelly misrepresented and that I shall touch the right chord in your heart! Anyway I have an undying faith in the responsiveness of human nature. On the strength of that faith I have conceived the impending movement in India, and it is that faith which has prompted this appeal to you.

I am ,

Your friend and well-wisher,

M. K. GANDHI

*Harijan*, 26-7-1942 (83: 114-117)

---

*This was Gandhi's first major statement on the use of the bomb—he did not respond immediately to the catastrophe but waited to gather his sense of what it meant for the cause of non-violence.*

## Atom Bomb and Ahimsa

It has been suggested by American friends that the atom bomb will bring in *ahimsa* (non-violence) as nothing else can. It will, if it is meant that its destructive power will so disgust the world that it will turn it away from violence for the time being. This is very like a man glutting himself with dainties to the point of nausea and turning away from them only to return with redoubled zeal after the effect of nausea is well over. Precisely in the same manner will the world return to violence with renewed zeal after the effect of disgust is worn out. Often does good come out of evil. But that is God's, not man's plan. Man knows that only evil can come out of evil, as good out of good.

That atomic energy, though harnessed by American scientists and army men for destructive purposes, may be utilized by other scientists for humanitarian purposes is undoubtedly within the realm of possibility. But that is not what was meant by my American friends. They were not so simple as to put a question which connoted an obvious truth. An incendiary uses fire for his destructive and nefarious purpose, a housewife makes daily use of it in preparing nourishing food for mankind. So far as I can see, the atomic bomb has deadened the finest feeling that has sustained mankind for ages.

There used to be the so-called laws of war which made it tolerable. Now we know the naked truth. War knows no law except that of might. The atom bomb brought an empty victory to the Allied arms but it resulted for the time being in destroying the soul of Japan. What has happened to the soul of the destroying nation is yet too early to see.

Forces of nature act in a mysterious manner. We can but solve the mystery by deducing the unknown result from the known results of similar events. A slaveholder cannot hold a slave without putting himself or his deputy in the cage holding the slave. Let no one run away with the idea that I wish to put in a defence of Japanese misdeeds in pursuance of Japan's unworthy ambition. The difference was only one of degree. I assume that Japan's greed was more unworthy. But the greater unworthiness conferred no right on the less unworthy of destroying without mercy men, women and children of Japan in a particular area.

The moral to be legitimately drawn from the supreme tragedy of the bomb is that it will not be destroyed by counter-bombs even as violence cannot be by counter-violence. Mankind has to get out of violence only through non-violence. Hatred can be overcome only by love. Counter-hatred only increases the surface as well as the depth of hatred. I am aware that I am repeating what I have many times stated before and practised to the best of my ability and capacity. What I first stated was itself nothing new. It was old as the hills. Only I recited no copy-book maxim but definitely announced what I believed in every fibre of my being. Sixty years of practice in various walks of life has only enriched the belief which experience of friends had fortified. It is however the central truth by which one can stand alone without flinching. I believe in what Max Muller said years ago, namely, that truth needed to be repeated as long as there were men who disbelieved it.

*Harijan*, 7-7-1946 (91: 220-22)

---

*The following is a fragment from an interview given to an English journalist.*

## Talk with an English Journalist, New Delhi
[Before September 24, 1946]

Q. ... And the atom bomb?

A. Oh, on that point you can proclaim to the whole world without hesitation that I am beyond repair. I regard the employment of the atom bomb for the wholesale destruction of men, women and children as the most diabolical use of science.

Q. What is the antidote? Has it antiquated non-violence?

A. No. It is the only thing the atom bomb cannot destroy. I did not move a muscle when I first heard that the atom bomb had wiped out Hiroshima. On the contrary, I said to myself, "Unless now the world adopts non-violence, it will spell certain suicide for mankind."

*Harijan*, 29-9-1946 92: 234

---

*The end of World War II saw the allied powers meeting in a peace conference in San Francisco. Gandhi was not sure if the conference could guarantee peace for all time, as he told Ralph Coniston of the Collier's Weekly.*

## Interview to Ralph Coniston
[Before April 25, 1945]

RALPH CONISTON: Why do you feel so sceptical about the possibility of a lasting peace emerging from the defeat of the Axis Powers?

GANDHIJI: The reason is patent. Violence is bound sooner or later to exhaust itself but peace cannot issue out of such exhaustion. I am uttering God's truth when I say that unless there is a return to sanity, violent people will be swept off the face of the earth ... (*ellipsis as in the original - ed.*) Those who have their hands dyed deep in blood cannot build a non-violent order for the world.

R. C. While the representatives of the big powers who would be meeting at San Francisco were what they were, the people at large, after the experience of the horrors of war, would force the hands of their respective Governments.

G. I know the European mind well enough to know that when it has to choose between abstract justice and self-interest, it will plump for the latter. The man in the street even in America does not think much for himself. He will put faith in what Roosevelt says. Roosevelt gives him market, credit and all that. Similarly Churchill can say to the English working class that he has kept the Empire intact and preserved for them the foreign markets. The people will, as they do, follow him.

R. C. So, you don't think that the average man in Europe or America cares much for the high ideals for which the war is professed to be fought?

G. I am afraid, I do not. If you hold the contrary view, I shall honour you for your belief but I cannot share it.

R. C. Then, you don't think the Big Five or the Big Three can guarantee peace?

G. I am positive. If they are so arrogant as to think that they can have lasting peace while the exploitation of the coloured and the so-called backward races goes on, they are living in a fool's paradise.

R. C. You think they will fall out among themselves before long?

G. There you are stealing my language. The quarrel with Russia has already started. It is only a question when the other two—England and America—will start quarrelling with each other. Maybe, pure self-interest will dictate a wiser course and those who will be meeting at San Francisco will say: "Let us not fall out over a fallen carcass." The man in the street will gain nothing by it. Freedom of India along non-violent lines, on the other hand, will mean the biggest thing for the exploited races of the earth. I am, therefore, trying to concentrate on it. If India acts on the square when her turn comes, it will not dictate terms at the Peace Conference but peace and freedom will descend upon it, not as a terrifying torrent, but as "gentle rain from heaven". Liberty won non-violently will belong to the least. That is why I swear by non-violence. Only when the least can say, "I have got my liberty" have

I got mine.

The conversation then turned to the issue of the treatment of the aggressor nations after the war.

G. As a non-violent man, I do not believe in the punishment of individuals, much less can I stomach the punishment of a whole nation.

R. C. What about the war criminals?

G. What is a war criminal? Was not war itself a crime against God and humanity and, therefore, were not all those who sanctioned, engineered, and conducted wars, war criminals? War criminals are not confined to the Axis Powers alone. Roosevelt and Churchill are no less war criminals than Hitler and Mussolini. Hitler was "Great Britain's sin". Hitler is only an answer to British imperialism, and this I say in spite of the fact that I hate. Hitlerism and its anti-Semitism. England, America and Russia have all of them got their hands dyed more or less red—not merely Germany and Japan. The Japanese have only proved themselves to be apt pupils of the West. They have learnt at the feet of the West and beaten it at its own game.

R. C. What would you see accomplished at San Francisco?

G. Parity among all nations—the strongest and the weakest— the strong should be the servants of the weak not their masters or exploiters.

R. C. Is not this too idealistic?

G. Maybe. But you asked me what I would like to see accomplished. It is my belief that human nature is ever working upward. I can, therefore, never take a pessimistic view of the future of human nature. If the Big Five say, "We shall hold on to what we have", the result will be a terrible catastrophe and then Heaven help the world and the Big Five. There will be another and bloodier war and another San Francisco.

R. C. Would the results of the second San Francisco be any better than that of the first?

G. I hope so. They will be saner then. They will have gained their balance somewhat after their third experience.

R. C. Would you not go to the West to teach them the art of peace?

G. In the second World War some British pacifists, including Dick Sheppard and Maude Royden had written to me asking me to point the way. My reply in substance was: Even if one of you can become true in the right sense of the word, that one man will be able to inculcate non-violence among the European folk. I cannot today save Europe, however much I may like to. I know Europe and America. If I go there I shall be like a stranger. Probably I shall be lionized but that is all. I shall not be able to present to them the science of peace in language they can understand. But they will understand if I can make good my non-violence in India. I shall then speak through India. I, therefore, declined to accept the invitations from America and Europe. My answer would be the same today.

R. C. If you were at San Francisco, what would you be advocating there?

G. If I knew I would tell you but I am made differently. When I face a situation, the solution comes to me. I am not a man who sits down and thinks out problems syllogistically. I am a man of action. I react to a situation intuitively. Logic comes afterwards, it does not precede the event. The moment I am at the Peace Conference, I know the right word will come. But not beforehand. This much, however, I can say that whatever I say there will be in terms of peace, not war.

R. C. What kind of world organization would promote an enduring peace or preserve it?

G. Only an organization based predominantly on truth and non-violence.

R. C. With the present imperfect condition of the world and human nature, what means would in your opinion promote peace?

G. Nearest approach to the condition laid down in my answer to the previous question.

R. C. Would you have a world government?

G. Yes. I claim to be a practical idealist. I believe in compromise so long as it does not involve the sacrifice of principles. I may not get a world government that I want just now but if it is a government that would just touch my ideal, I would accept it as a compromise. Therefore, although I am not enamoured of a world federation, I shall be prepared to accept it if it is built on an essentially non-violent basis.

R. C. If the nations of the world were to consider world government as a means for preserving peace and promoting the welfare of all peoples, would you advocate the abandonment of India's aspiration for independence in order to join in the general plan?

G. If you will carefully go through the much abused Congress resolution of August 1942 (*which, among other things, demanded that the British 'Quit India' - ed.*), you will discover that independence is necessary for India becoming an efficient partner in any scheme for the preservation of lasting peace in the world.

*Mahatma Gandhi: The Last Phase*, Vol. I, Book I, pp. 113-6 (86: 222-25)

# Active Suffering: Gandhi's Call to the Jews

*Gandhi keenly followed developments in Europe in the years leading to World War II. He was aware of the crisis that had beset European Jewry and decried Hitler's intentions. He exhorted the Jews to not lose heart and counselled that they go bravely to their death. Gandhi also simultaneously followed developments in Palestine. Earlier, in the 1920s, he had written against the post-World War I mandate given to the British in the Arab world, and declared his opposition to Palestine being treated as and considered a homeland of the Jews.*

*In the late 1930s, when emigration to Palestine was proposed as a fit solution to a threatened and homeless people, he renewed his objections. Leading Jewish and Zionist intellectuals, including the philosopher Martin Buber, debated Gandhi's views on these matters. They were startled by his counselling of satyagraha to those who were being herded into Nazi death camps and did not agree with his views on Palestine.*

*The extracts below encapsulate the more important arguments of this complex and uneasy dialogue.*

### The Jews

Several letters have been received by me asking me to declare my views about the Arab-Jew question in Palestine and the persecution of the Jews in Germany. It is not without hesitation that I venture to offer my views on this very difficult question.

My sympathies are all with the Jews. I have known them intimately in South Africa. Some of them became lifelong companions. Through these friends I came to learn much of their age-long persecution. They have been the untouchables of Christianity. The parallel between their treatment by Christians and the treatment of untouchables by Hindus is very close. Religious sanction has been invoked in both cases for the justification of the inhuman treatment meted out to them. Apart from the friendships, therefore, there is the more common universal reason for my sympathy for the Jews.

But my sympathy does not blind me to the requirements of justice. The cry for the national home for the Jews does not make much appeal to me. The sanction for it is sought in the Bible and the tenacity with which the Jews have hankered after return to Palestine. Why should they not, like other peoples of the earth, make that country their home where they are born and where they earn their livelihood?

Palestine belongs to the Arabs in the same sense that England belongs to the English or France to the French. It is wrong and inhuman to impose the Jews on the Arabs. What is going on in Palestine today cannot be justified by any moral code of conduct. The mandates have no sanction but that of the last war. Surely it would be a crime against humanity to reduce the proud Arabs so that Palestine can be restored to the Jews partly or wholly as their national home.

The nobler course would be to insist on a just treatment of the Jews wherever they are born and bred. The Jews born in France are French. If the Jews have no home but Palestine, will they relish the idea of being forced to leave the other parts of the world in which they are settled? Or do they want a double home where they can remain at will? This cry for the national home affords a colourable justification for the German expulsion of the Jews.

But the German persecution of the Jews seems to have no parallel in history. The tyrants of old never went so mad as Hitler seems to have gone. And he is doing it with religious zeal. For he is propounding a new religion of exclusive and militant nationalism in the name of which any inhumanity becomes an act of humanity to be rewarded here and hereafter. The crime of an obviously mad but intrepid youth is being visited upon his whole race with unbelievable ferocity. If there ever could be a justifiable war in the name of and for humanity, a war against Germany, to prevent the wanton persecution of a whole race, would be completely justified. But I do not believe in any war. A discussion of the pros and cons of such a war is therefore outside my horizon or province.

Germany is showing to the world how efficiently violence can be worked when it is not hampered by any hypocrisy or weakness masquerading as humanitarianism. It is also showing how hideous, terrible and terrifying it looks in its nakedness.

Can the Jews resist this organised and shameless persecution? Is there a way to preserve their self-respect, and not to feel helpless, neglected and forlorn? I submit there is. No person who has faith in a living God need feel helpless or forlorn. Jehovah of the Jews is a God more personal than the God of the Christians, the Mussalmans or the Hindus, though as a matter of fact in essence, He is common to all and one without a second and beyond description. But as the Jews attribute personality to God and believe that He rules every action of theirs, they ought not to feel helpless. If I were a Jew and were born in Germany and earned my livelihood there, I would claim Germany as my home even as the tallest gentile German may, and challenge him to shoot me or cast me in the dungeon; I would refuse to be expelled or to submit to discriminating treatment. And for doing this, I should not wait for the fellow Jews to join me in civil resistance but would have confidence that in the end the rest are bound to follow my example. If one Jew or all the Jews were to accept the prescription here offered, he or they cannot be worse off than now. And suffering voluntarily undergone will bring them an inner strength and joy which no number of resolutions of sympathy passed in the world outside Germany can.

The calculated violence of Hitler may even result in a general massacre of the Jews by way of his first answer to the declaration of such hostilities. But if the Jewish mind could be prepared for voluntary suffering, even the massacre I have imagined could be turned into a day of thanksgiving and joy that Jehovah had wrought deliverance of the race even at the hands of the tyrant. For to the godfearing, death has no terror. It is a joyful sleep to be followed by a waking that would be all the more refreshing for the long sleep.

It is hardly necessary for me to point out that it is easier for the Jews than for the Czechs to follow my prescription. And they have in the Indian satyagraha campaign in South Africa an exact parallel. There the Indians occupied precisely the same place that the Jews occupy in Germany. The persecution had also a religious tinge. President Kruger used to say that the white Christians were the chosen of God and Indians were inferior beings created to serve the whites. A fundamental clause in the Transvaal constitution was that there should be no equality between the whites and coloured races including Asiatics. There too the Indians were consigned to ghettos described as locations. The other disabilities were almost of the same type as those of the Jews in Germany. The Indians, a mere handful, resorted to satyagraha without any backing from the world outside or the Indian Government. Indeed the British officials tried to dissuade the satyagrahis from their contemplated step. World opinion and the Indian Government came to their aid after eight years of fighting. And that too was by way of diplomatic pressure not of a threat of war.

But the Jews of Germany can offer satyagraha under infinitely better auspices than the Indians of South Africa. The Jews are a compact, homogeneous community in Germany. They are far more gifted than the Indians of South Africa. And they have organised world opinion behind them. I am convinced that if someone with courage and vision can arise among them to lead them in non-violent action, the winter of their despair can in the twinkling of an eye be turned into the summer of hope. And what has today become a degrading man-hunt can be turned into a calm and determined stand offered by unarmed men and women possessing the strength of suffering given to them by Jehovah. It will be then a truly religious resistance offered against the godless fury of dehumanised man. The German Jews will score a lasting victory over the German gentiles in the sense that they will have converted the latter to an appreciation of human dignity. They will have rendered service to fellow-Germans and proved their title to be the real Germans as against those who are today dragging, however unknowingly, the German name into the mire.

And now a word to the Jews in Palestine. I have no doubt that they are going about it in the wrong way. The Palestine of the Biblical conception is not a geographical tract. It is in their hearts. But if they must look to the Palestine of geography as their national home, it is wrong to enter it under the shadow of the British gun. A religious act cannot be performed with the aid of the bayonet or the bomb. They can settle in Palestine only by the goodwill of the Arabs. They should seek to convert the Arab heart. The same God rules the Arab heart who rules the Jewish heart. They can offer satyagraha in front of the Arabs and offer themselves to be shot or thrown into the Dead Sea without raising a little finger against them. They will find the world opinion in their favour in their religious aspiration. There are hundreds of ways of reasoning with the Arabs, if they will only discard the help of the British bayonet. As it is, they are co-shares with the British in despoiling a people who have done no wrong to them.

I am not defending the Arab excesses. I wish they had chosen the way of non-violence in resisting what they rightly regarded as an unwarrantable encroachment upon their country. But according to the accepted canons of right and wrong, nothing can be said against the Arab resistance in the face of overwhelming odds.

Let the Jews who claim to be the chosen race prove their title by choosing the way of non-violence for vindicating their position on earth. Every country is their home including Palestine not by aggression but by loving service. A Jewish friend has sent me a book called *The Jewish Contribution to Civilization* by Cecil Roth. It gives a record of what the Jews have done to enrich the world's literature, art, music, drama, science, medicine, agriculture, etc. Given the will, the Jew can refuse to be treated as the outcaste of the West, to be despised or patronised. He can command the attention and respect of the world by being man, the chosen creation of God, instead of being man who is fast sinking to the brute and forsaken by God. They can add to their many contributions the surpassing contribution of non-violent action.

*Harijan,* 26-11-1938 (74: 239-42)

---

### Reply to German Critics

I was not unprepared for the exhibition of wrath from Germany over my article about the German treatment of the Jews. I have myself admitted my ignorance of European politics. But in order to commend my prescription to the Jews for the removal of their many ills, I did not need to have an accurate knowledge of European politics. The main facts about the atrocities are beyond dispute.

When the anger over my writing has subsided and comparative calmness has returned, the most wrathful German will find that underlying my writing there was friendliness towards Germany, never any ill will.

Have I not repeatedly said that active non-violence is unadulterated love—fellow-feeling? And if the Jews, instead of being helplessly and of necessity non-violent, adopt active non-violence, i.e., fellow-feeling for the gentile Germans deliberately, they cannot do any harm to the Germans and I am as certain as I am dictating these lines that the stoniest German heart will melt. Great as have been the Jewish contributions to the world's progress, this supreme act of theirs will be their greatest contribution and war will be a thing of the past.

It passes comprehension why any German should be angry over my utterly innocuous writing. Of course, German critics, as others, might have ridiculed it by saying that it was a visionary's effort doomed to fail. I therefore welcome this wrath, though wholly unmerited, against my writing. Has my writing gone home? Has the writer felt that my remedy was after all not so ludicrous as it may appear, but that it was eminently practical if only the beauty of suffering without retaliation was realised?

To say that my writing has rendered neither myself, my movement, nor German-Indian relations any service, is surely irrelevant, if not also unworthy, implying as it does a threat; and I should rank myself a coward if, for fear of my country or myself or Indo-German relations being harmed, I hesitated to give what I felt in the innermost recesses of my heart to be cent percent sound advice.

The Berlin writer has surely enunciated a novel doctrine that people outside Germany may not criticise German action even from friendliest motives. For my part I would certainly welcome the interesting things that Germans or other outsiders may unearth about Indians. I do not need to speak for the British. But if I know the British people at all, they, too, welcome outside criticism, when it is well-formed and free from malice. In this age, when distances have been obliterated, no nation can afford to imitate the fabled frog in the well. Sometimes it is refreshing to see ourselves as others see us. If, therefore, the German critics happen to see this reply, I hope that they will not only revise their opinion about my writing but will also realise the value of outside criticism.

*Harijan,* 17-12-1938 (74: 295-96)

## Some Questions Answered

Friends have sent me two newspaper cuttings criticising my appeal to the Jews. The two critics suggest that in presenting non-violence to the Jews as a remedy against the wrong done to them I have suggested nothing new, and that they have been practising non-violence for the past two thousand years. Obviously, so far as these critics are concerned, I did not make my meaning clear. The Jews, so far as I know, have never practised non-violence as an article of faith or even as a deliberate policy. Indeed, it is a stigma against them that their ancestors crucified Jesus. Are they not supposed to believe in eye for an eye and tooth for a tooth? Have they no violence in their hearts for their oppressors? Do they not want the so-called democratic powers to punish Germany for her persecution and to deliver them from oppression? If they do, there is no non-violence in their hearts. Their non-violence, if it may be so called, is of the helpless and the weak.

What I have pleaded for is renunciation of violence of the heart and consequent active exercise of the force generated by the great renunciation. One of the critics says that favourable public opinion is necessary for the working of non-violence. The writer is evidently thinking of passive resistance conceived as a weapon of the weak. I have drawn a distinction between passive resistance of the weak and active non-violent resistance of the strong. The latter can and does work in the teeth of the fiercest opposition. But it ends in evoking the widest public sympathy. Sufferings of the non-violent have been known to melt the stoniest hearts. I make bold to say that if the Jews can summon to their aid the soul power that comes only from non-violence, Herr Hitler will bow before the courage which he has never yet experienced in any large measure in his dealings with men, and which, when it is exhibited, he will own is infinitely superior to that shown by his best storm troopers. The exhibition of such courage is only possible for those who have a living faith in the God of Truth and Non-violence, i.e., Love.

Of course, the critics can reasonably argue that the non-violence pictured by me is not possible for masses of mankind, it is possible only for the very few highly developed persons. I have combated that view and suggested that, given proper training and proper generalship, non-violence can be practised by masses of mankind.

I see, however, that my remarks are being misunderstood to mean that because I advise non-violent resistance by the persecuted Jews, by inference I expect or would advise non-interference by the democratic Powers on behalf of the Jews. I hardly need to answer this fear. Surely there is no danger of the great Powers refraining from action because of anything I have said. They will, they are bound to, do all they can to free the Jews from the inhuman persecution. My appeal has force in the face of the fact that the great Powers feel unable to help the Jews in an effective manner.

*Harijan,* 17-12-1938 (74: 297-99)

---

### Is Non-Violence Effective?

In dealing with my answer to the criticism that the Jews had been non-violent for 2,000 years, *The Statesman* says in the course of an editorial:

The whole world has heard of Pastor Niemoeller and the sufferings of the Lutheran Church; here many Pastors and individual Christians bore themselves bravely before People's Courts, violence and threats; without retaliation they bore noble witness to the truth. And what change of heart is there in Germany? Buried in prisons and concentration camps are today, and have been for five years, members of the Bible Searchers' Leagues who rejected Nazi militarism as conflicting with Christ's Gospel of peace. And how many Germans know of them or, if they know, do anything about it? ... It is suggested by Mr. Gandhi that Herr Hitler would bow before a courage "infinitely superior to that shown by his own Storm Trooper." ... Courage to a Nazi, however, seems a virtue only when displayed by his own supporters: elsewhere it becomes the impudent provocation of Jewish-Marxist canaille.

I do not think that the sufferings of Pastor Niemoeller and others have been in vain. They have preserved their self-respect intact. They have proved that their faith was equal to any suffering. That they have not proved sufficient for melting Herr Hitler's heart merely shows that it is made of a harder material than stone. But the hardest metal yields to sufficient heat. Even so must the hardest heart melt before sufficiency of the heat of non-violence. And there is no limit to the capacity of non-violence to generate heat.

Every action is a resultant of a multitude of forces even of a contrary nature. There is no waste of energy. So we learn in the books on mechanics. This is equally true of human actions. The difference is that in the one case we generally know the forces at work, and when we do, we can mathematically foretell the resultant. In the case of human actions, they result from a concurrence of forces of most of which we have no knowledge. But our ignorance must not be made to serve the cause of disbelief in the power of these forces. Rather is our ignorance a cause for greater faith. And non-violence being the mightiest force in the world and also the most elusive in its working, it demands the greatest exercise of faith. Even as we believe in God in faith, so have we to believe in non-violence in faith.

Herr Hitler is but one man enjoying no more than the average span of life. He would be a spent force if he had not the backing of his people. I do not despair of his responding to human suffering even though caused by him. But I must refuse to believe that the Germans as a nation have no heart or markedly less than the other nations of the earth. They will some day or other rebel against their own adored hero, if he does not wake up betimes. And when he or they do, we shall find that the sufferings of the Pastor and his fellow-workers had not a little to do with the awakening.

An armed conflict may bring disaster to German arms; it cannot change the German heart even as the last defeat did not. It produced a Hitler vowed to wreak vengeance on the victors. And what a vengeance it is! My answer, therefore, must be the answer that Stephenson gave to his fellow-workers who had despaired of ever filling the deep pit that made the first railway possible. He asked his co-workers of little faith to have more faith and go on filling the pit. It was not bottomless, it must be filled. Even so I do not despair because Herr Hitler's or the German heart has not yet melted. On the contrary I plead for more suffering and still more till the melting has become visible to the naked eye. And even as the Pastor has covered himself with glory, a single Jew bravely standing up and refusing to bow to Hitler's decrees will cover himself with glory and lead the way to the deliverance of the fellow Jews.

I hold that non-violence is not merely a personal virtue. It is also a social virtue to be cultivated like the other virtues. Surely society is largely regulated by the expression of non-violence in its mutual dealings. What I ask for is an extension of it on a larger, national and international scale ...

*Harijan,* 7-1-1939 (74: 391-93)

## The Jewish Question

The Managing Editor of *Jewish Frontier*, published at 275 Seventh Avenue, New York City, was good enough to send me a copy of the March number of the magazine with the request that I should deal with its reply to my article on the Jews in Germany and Palestine. The reply is very ably written. I wish I had space for reproducing the whole of it ...

Let me say that I did not write the article as a critic. I wrote it at the pressing request of Jewish friends and correspondents. As I decided to write, I could not do so in any other manner. But I did not entertain the hope when I wrote it that the Jews would be at once converted to my view. I should have been satisfied if even one Jew had been fully convinced and converted.

Nor did I write the article only for today. I flatter myself with the belief that some of my writings will survive me and will be of service to the causes for which they have been written. I have no sense of disappointment that my writing had not to my knowledge converted a single Jew.

Having read the reply more than once, I must say that I see no reason to change the opinion I expressed in my article. It is highly probable that, as the writer says, "a Jewish Gandhi in Germany, should one arise, could function for about five minutes and would be promptly taken to the guillotine". But that will not disprove my case or shake my belief in the efficacy of *ahimsa*. I can conceive the necessity of the immolation of hundreds, if not thousands, to appease the hunger of dictators who have no belief in *ahimsa*. Indeed the maxim is that *ahimsa* is the most efficacious in front of the great himsa. Its quality is really tested only in such cases. Sufferers need not see the result during their lifetime. They must have faith that if their cult survives, the result is a certainty. The method of violence gives no greater guarantee than that of non-violence. It gives infinitely less. For the faith of the votary of *ahimsa* is lacking.

The writer contends that I approached the Jewish problem "without that fundamental earnestness and passionate search for truth which are so characteristic of his usual treatment of problems". All I can say is that to my knowledge there was lack neither of earnestness nor of passion for truth when I wrote the article.

The second charge of the writer is more serious. He thinks that my zeal for Hindu-Muslim unity made me partial to the Arab presentation of the case, especially as that side was naturally emphasised in India. I have often said that I would not sell truth for the sake of India's deliverance. Much less would I do so for winning Muslim friendship. The writer thinks that I am wrong on the Jewish question as I was wrong on the *Khilafat* question. Even at this distance of time I have no regret whatsoever for having taken up the *Khilafat* cause. I know that my persistence does not prove the correctness of my attitude. Only it is necessary for everyone concerned to know where I stand today about my action in 1919-20.

I am painfully conscious of the fact that this writing of mine will give no satisfaction either to the Editor of *Jewish Frontier* or to my many Jewish friends. Nevertheless, I wish with all my heart that somehow or other the persecution of the Jews in Germany will end and that the question in Palestine will be settled to the satisfaction of all the parties concerned.

*Harijan*, 27-5-1939 (75: 415-16)

### Withdrawn

In *Harijan* of December 24 there is a long report of my talk with missionary friends from Tambaram on non-violence and the world crisis. When during the talk I took the illustration of the Jews, I am reported to have said:

"It is true that the Jews have not been actively violent in their own persons. But they called down upon the Germans the curses of mankind, and they wanted America and England to fight Germany on their behalf."

On reading the last sentence a dear friend wrote to me a fiery letter and challenged me to produce my authority for my remark. He said that I had been hasty in making the statement. I did not realise the importance of the rebuke. I did, however, want to produce support for my statement. I put Pyarelal and later Mahadev (*his secretaries - ed.*) on the search. It is not always an easy task to find support for impressions one carries when speaking or writing.

... The searchers were not able to lay hands on any conclusive writing. The manager of *Harijan* put himself in correspondence with the Editor of the *Jewish Tribune*, Bombay, who sent the following characteristic reply:

"This is not the first time that I have come across the imputation made against Jews that they urge countries like England and America to go to war against Germany on account of its persecution of Jews. Jews have never urged the democracies to wage war against Germany on account of its persecution of the Jews. This is a mischievous lie that must be nailed to the counter. If there is a war, Jews will suffer more than the rest of the population. This is a fact gleaned from the pages of history. And the Jew is a great lover and advocate of peace. I hope you will refute any such allegation that is made against them."

In the face of the foregoing weighty contradictions now enforced by the Editor of the *Jewish Tribune* and of the fact that I cannot lay my hands on anything on the strength of which I made the challenged observation, I must withdraw it without any reservation. I only hope that my observation has not harmed any single Jew. I know that I incurred the wrath of many German friends for what

I said in all good faith
*Harijan*, 27-5-1939 (75: 416-18)

## Jews and Palestine

Hitherto I have refrained practically from saying anything in public regarding the Jew-Arab controversy. I have done so for good reasons. That does not mean any want of interest in the question, but it does mean that I do not consider myself sufficiently equipped with knowledge for the purpose. ... I do believe that the Jews have been cruelly wronged by the world. "Ghetto" is, so far as I am aware, the name given to Jewish locations in many parts of Europe. But for their heartless persecution, probably no question of return to Palestine would ever have arisen. The world should have been their home, if only for the sake of their distinguished contribution to it.

But, in my opinion, they have erred grievously in seeking to impose themselves on Palestine with the aid of America and Britain and now with the aid of naked terrorism. Their citizenship of the world should have and would have made them honoured guests of any country. Their thrift, their varied talent, their great industry should have made them welcome anywhere. It is a blot on the Christian world that they have been singled out, owing to a wrong reading of the New Testament, for prejudice against them. "If an individual Jew does a wrong, the whole Jewish world is to blame for it." If an individual Jew like Einstein makes a great discovery or another composes unsurpassable music, the merit goes to the authors and not to the community to which they belong.

No wonder that my sympathy goes out to the Jews in their unenviably sad plight. But one would have thought adversity would teach them lessons of peace. Why should they depend upon American money or British arms for forcing themselves on an unwelcome land? Why should they resort to terrorism to make good their forcible landing in Palestine? If they were to adopt the matchless weapon of non-violence whose use their best Prophets have taught and which Jesus the Jew who gladly wore the crown of thorns bequeathed to a groaning world, their case would be the world's and I have no doubt that among the many things that the Jews have given to the world, this would be the best and the brightest. It is twice blessed. It will make them happy and rich in the true sense of the word and it will be a soothing balm to the aching world.

*Harijan,* 21-7-1946 (91: 272-73)

---

**Interview to Reuters**
**May 5, 1947**

... What is the solution to the Palestine problem?

It has become a problem which is almost insoluble. If I were a Jew, I would tell them: "Don't be so silly as to resort to terrorism, because you simply damage your own case which otherwise would be a proper case." If it is just political hankering then I think there is no value in it. Why should they hanker after Palestine? They are a great race and have great gifts. I have lived with the Jews many years in South Africa. If it is a religious longing then surely terrorism has no place. They should meet the Arabs, make friends with them, and not depend on British aid or American aid or any aid, save what descends from Jehovah.

*Harijan,* 18-5-1947, and *The Hindu,* 6-5-1947 (95: 27-8)

# Love Giveth: Gandhi's Jesus Christ

*Though Gandhi read the New Testament very early in life and had recourse to the language and idioms of the Bible at all times, he experienced the importance of Christ deeply and poignantly during the war years. Faced with destruction all around him, Jesus and his sacrifice figured largely in his conversations with pacifist friends during this period of his life, as these brief extracts indicate.*

## What Jesus Means to Me

Although I have devoted a large part of my life to the study of religion and to discussion with religious leaders of all faiths, I know very well that I cannot but seem presumptuous in writing about Jesus Christ and trying to explain what He means to me. I do so only because my Christian friends have told me on more than a few occasions that for the very reason that I am not a Christian and that (I shall quote their words exactly) "I do not accept Christ in the bottom of my heart as the only Son of God", it is impossible for me to understand the profound significance of His teachings, or to know and interpret the greatest source of spiritual strength that man has ever known.

Although this may or may not be true in my case, I have reasons to believe that it is an erroneous point of view. I believe that such an estimate is incompatible with the message that Jesus Christ gave to the world. For he was, certainly, the highest example of one who wished to give everything asking nothing in return, and not caring what creed might happen to be professed by the recipient. I am sure that if He were living here now among men, He would bless the lives of many who perhaps have never even heard His name, if only their lives embodied the virtues of which He was a living example on earth; the virtues of loving one's neighbour as oneself and of doing good and charitable works among one's fellow-men.

What, then, does Jesus mean to me? To me He was one of the greatest teachers humanity has ever had. To His believers He was

God's only begotten Son. Could the fact that I do or do not accept this belief make Jesus have any more or less influence in my life? Is all the grandeur of His teaching and of His doctrine to be forbidden to me? I cannot believe so.

To me it implies a spiritual birth. My interpretation, in other words, is that in Jesus' own life is the key of His nearness to God; that He expressed, as no other could, the spirit and will of God. It is in this sense that I see Him and recognize Him as the Son of God.

But I do believe that something of this spirit, that Jesus exemplified in the highest measure in its most profound human sense, does exist. I must believe this; if I do not believe it I should be a sceptic; and to be a sceptic is to live a life that is empty and lacks moral content. Or, what is the same thing, to condemn the entire human race to a negative end.

It is true that there certainly is reason for scepticism when one observes the bloody butchery that European aggressors have unloosed, and when one thinks about the misery and suffering prevalent in every corner of the world, as well as the pestilence and famine that always follow, terribly and inevitably, upon war. In the face of this, how can one speak seriously of the divine spirit incarnate in man?

Because these acts of terror and murder offend the conscience of man; because man knows that they represent evil; because in the inner depths of his heart and of his mind, he deplores them. And because, moreover, when he does not go astray, misled by false teachings or corrupted by false leaders, man has within his breast an impulse for good and a compassion that is the spark of divinity, and which some day, I believe, will burst forth into the full flower that is the hope of all mankind.

An example of this flowering may be found in the figure and in the life of Jesus. I refuse to believe that there now exists or has ever existed a person that has not made use of His example to lessen his sins, even though he may have done so without realizing it. The lives of all have, in some greater or lesser degree, been changed by His presence, His actions, and the words spoken by His divine voice.

... And because the life of Jesus has the significance and the transcendency to which I have alluded, I believe that He belongs not solely to Christianity, but to the entire world; to all races and people, it matters little under what flag, name or doctrine they may work, profess a faith, or worship a god inherited from their ancestors.

*Modern Review*, October 1941 (81: 260-62)

---

*Gandhi did not share the pessimism experienced by pacifists in England and Europe. For the latter, their faith in the possibilities of peace was shaken by the political evil uncovered by World War II.*

## On Its Trail

... I am a pacifist still in one sense; that is to say, I realize that Christians should be able to meet material force with spiritual power. It is horrifying to reflect that after nineteen hundred years, we are still unable to do it except in individual cases and on a small scale. But to me it seems merely "wishful thinking" to act as though we had a power which in fact we have not and for which we have neither trained nor disciplined ourselves in the past. ... I am compelled to echo the words of a very dear relative of mine who, loathing war as much as any pacifist that ever breathed, said to me at the beginning of the last war (in which he lost his life): "If you can stop war with spiritual power, do it. If you can't, let me do what I can; and if you are right in thinking that war is so damnable that anyone who takes part in it is damned, then I would rather be damned than let these things go on without doing all I can to stop them, even at the cost of my own life."

The foregoing is the concluding portion of a touchingly sorrowful article contributed to *The Survey Graphic* of December 1941 by the celebrated Dr. Maude Royden of the Guildhouse, London. She is one of the foremost pacifists of the West. Like many she has felt compelled to revise her position and is now most reluctantly but fully ranged on the side of the defenders of the British Isles.

The article demands a considered reply. I have been in constant touch with the Western pacifists. In my opinion Dr. Royden has surrendered her position in the portion I have quoted. If individuals have lived up to the Christian teaching (i.e., on non-violence) and that on a small scale, one would think practice should make such a life possible for many people and on a large scale. It is undoubtedly wrong and foolish "to act as though one had the power which in fact one has not". "But," says the worthy writer, "such power does not come to those who have not disciplined themselves, at the last moment, in the hour of need."

I suggest that with the knowledge of the defect no time should be lost in seeking to remove it. That by itself is doing not only something but the right thing. To deny one's faith by contrary practice is surely the worst thing one can do. ... There is no cause whatsoever for despondency, much less for denial of one's faith at the crucial moment. Why should not British pacifists stand aside and remodel their life in its entirety? They might be unable to bring about peace outright, but they would lay a solid foundation for it and give the surest test of their faith. When, in the face of an upheaval such as we are witnessing, there are only a few individuals of immovable faith, they have to live up to their faith even though they may produce no visible effect on the course of events. They should believe that their action will produce tangible results in due course.

I would also suggest that individuals like Dr. Maude Royden are not mere camp-followers. They are leaders. Therefore, they have to live their lives in strict accord with the Sermon on the Mount, and they will find immediately that there is much to give up and much to remodel. The greatest thing that they have to deny themselves is the fruit of imperialism. The present complicated life of the Londoner and his high living is possible only because of the hoards brought from Asia, Africa and other parts of the world.

The advice that Dr. Royden's relative gave her and which she quotes approvingly is altogether wrong. If the war is damnable, how can he stop the things that go on by taking part in it, even though it may be on the defensive side and at the cost of his own life? For the defence has to resort to all the damnable things that the enemy does, and that with greater vigour if it has to succeed. Such a giving of life is not only not saving it but a mere waste.

I have attended the Doctor's services in her Church where a living belief in the efficacy of prayer is much in vogue. When the impenetrable gloom surrounded her, why did she not find strength and consolation and real action in heart-prayer? It is never too late to mend. She and her fellow-pacifists, many of whom I have the privilege of knowing, should take heart and, like Peter, repent of the momentary loss of faith and return to the old faith in non-violence with renewed vigour. Their return will mean no material loss to the war effort but will mean a great deal to the anti-war effort which is bound to succeed sooner rather than later, if man is to live as man and not become a two-footed brute.

*Harijan*, 15-3-1942 (82: 104-6)

# Concluding the War Years

*The war years reveal a reflective and poignant Gandhi: principled in his opposition to war, as a way of addressing and settling political differences; acute in his understanding of the destructive economic and social effects of militarism; and, finally, Gandhi the moral actor whose non-violence could never rest with verbal protestations, but had to constantly embody itself in practice.*

*Gandhi's involvement in World War II was radically innocent, both the manner in which he chose to address the war and its participants, as well as the deceptively simple arguments he offered in favour of non-violence. It is possible to read in his letters to every Briton, every Japanese, and to Adolf Hitler, an annoying sentimentality and naivete. Some critics read them thus, but it is far more productive to consider these letters for the views they offer on the links between the extreme pathology of war and the everyday oppressions, commandeered by imperialism and racism.*

*Gandhi's faith in the infinite perfectibility of the human soul and his dictum that evil ought not to be judged on its own claims, but on the basis of the capacity for good that it might yet harbour, are daring and amazing ideas. More so, since they were voiced in a context that effectively argued against such good faith—the context of the Nazi killing camps. Was Gandhi naïve in his understanding of Nazism, or was he holding out a fundamental moral message that transcended the historical context of the Holocaust? After all, he himself invoked the New Testament to support his reliance on the eventual loosening of the most hardened heart.*

*This is a complex question. Historians of World War II, troubled theologians and Jewish intellectuals have been appalled by his granting the Nazis the mercy of remorse. On the other hand, post-war German pacifists and theologians have found his faith in the redemptive powers of the individual conscience inspiring. They have come to value his observation that evil acts do not exhaust the moral conscience of the evil-doer and that good might yet find a place in it.*

*In the matter of the Jews, Gandhi's counselling of satyagraha does appear baffling, even self-righteous. His Jewish admirers were stung by his suggestion that they suffer their condition with courage: he had answered their good faith with moral counselling rather than active comfort. They did not feel his reproaches against them to be just—whether this had to do with his sense of what they were capable of, or what they could expect to deserve. Even those who accepted the general moral rightness of his arguments felt that he appeared unmindful of the peculiarities of their present situation, of the acute suffering imposed on them in the present. Gandhi, to his credit, did modify his opinion of the Jewish predicament, and did express his anguish at the enormity of the evil that searched them out. But he refused to renege on his faith in active suffering, especially its long-term effects and implications. In fact it could even be said that the meaning of the phrase he often used in his disquisitions on satyagraha, that one must learn how to die, was amplified and deepened during the war years and informed his understanding of the tragedy of Europe's Jews.*

*It is clear that Gandhi's disinterest in judging moral and immoral acts lay at the heart of his belief that satyagraha could be offered against Hitler. For otherwise, it is difficult to understand the meaning of what he proposed to the Jews. In matters such as untouchability, too, he had desisted from making a moral and juridical indictment of the oppressor and would rather trust to a change of consciousness. This reluctance to judge was of a part with his faith that one's adversary ought to be loved, irrespective of his or her moral sense or the lack of it.*

*Gandhi's opposition to Zionism appears entirely in order with his more general views on justice and violence. He was resolutely opposed to any struggle, however just, that enjoyed the support of imperial authority— a moral position that he relied on with respect to the Hindu-Muslim tangle in pre-independent India. His voicing of it in the manner he did, quite unequivocally and with a sharp sense of what was due to the Arabs, offended and hurt his Jewish friends but he refused to retract his views. Palestine could not be won through British bayonets and American money. The bloody history of the region bears witness to his unerring moral reasoning in this respect.*

## Chapter 8

## The Mercy of Death: Gandhi's Last Call
## 1946-1948

*The end of World War II saw a somewhat hopeful Congress and Gandhi confronting Empire. Britain had no choice but to settle with India. The war had taken its toll of her political strength and she was under pressure to 'Quit India'. Her allies in the war, especially the United States of America, expected her to do so, and the Congress' opposition to the continuation of British rule had to be considered seriously.*

*However, the Congress had to heed other concerns as well. The Hindu-Muslim tangle appeared insoluble, with the Muslim League's demands for a separate state carved out of British India generating a great amount of anger, tension and violence on the streets. For Gandhi, the Congress demand for independence was inextricably linked to the question of Hindu-Muslim unity—as it had always been—but he had to confront a new historical situation. The Muslim League's demand for a separate state had elicited a favourable response from a section of the Muslim community in India, and Gandhi realized that he had to re-think his own position on Hindu-Muslim unity. He did not give up his intent, though, and decided to act on his belief that India was indivisible and that partition would harm its people. On his release from prison in 1944, he and Mohammed Ali Jinnah, the President of the Muslim League, engaged in a series of discussions. Jinnah refused to compromise on his demand for a separate state and though Gandhi brought his persuasive rhetoric and all his negotiating tact into the meetings, they did not go well.*

*The line of distinction between Gandhi and Jinnah ran through their understanding of nationalism and the party of nationalism, the Indian National Congress. Jinnah was convinced that it was a partisan Hindu body and that it sought to build a 'Hindu' nation, whereas Gandhi held firm to his view that the Congress was nationalist and catholic in its views and that its nationalism was inclusive. The British argument supported Jinnah's claims: it noted that the nationalist claims of Congress would be conceded but only if the question of minority rights was reasonably and amicably settled.*

*There were other factors which influenced—and in some cases, impeded—the progress of events. The Congress, as Gandhi sorrowfully noted, did not appear to be interested in working for that 'heart-unity' between Hindus and Muslims that he desired. Since the mid and late 1930s, especially during the period of Congress rule (1937-9), Hindu right-wing opinion had acquired a public presence and legitimacy. The authority the Hindu Right commanded in nationalist circles and its openly partisan attitudes provoked Muslims to adopt militant postures as well. Besides, an emergent Hindu capitalist class did not wish to countenance a politically unstable India in the future, and in subtle ways threw its weight behind a potential partition of the country. The British, for their part, did not want to lose out on their long-term economic interests in India and, in keeping with the historical logic of colonial rule, desired a legacy that would enable them retain their influence in the region. So they did nothing to help the cause of an already floundering Indian unity.*

*Meanwhile, as World War II ended, a new Labour government came to power in Britain. It immediately announced its intention to quit India sooner or later and requested Viceroy Wavell (1945-47) to initiate the desired political reforms to enable Indians to participate in government and the British to transfer power to them. However, the final political offer from the British—the Cabinet Mission Plan (1946)—complicated the communal issue even more. The Plan attempted to build safeguards for minority populations in a federal India through instituting autonomous political and administrative units within a loose federal unity. These units were to be defined on the basis of their majority populations, whether Hindu or Muslim. In effect communal divisions were to be written into administrative and political fiat. Jinnah and the Muslim League felt cheated of their demand for a separate State, but eventually decided to support the offer. The Congress was not sure if it wished to endorse the Plan. Gandhi was uncertain as to the Plan's implications for a division of hearts, and frustrated with its attempts to resolve a matter of heart-disunity through political administrative fiat. The British, for their part, insisted on a settlement and finally chose the Congress to lead the new interim government, though the Congress was had been decisive about the Plan than the Muslim League.*

*A thoroughly frustrated Jinnah, angered by what he understood as the Congress' doublespeak and British cunning, decided to take his call for Pakistan to the streets—this lead to violent rioting in Bengal, Bihar and then the Punjab. Meanwhile, the British, eager to quit, were insisting on a solution. A rush of events and decisions thus led both the Congress and the League towards seeking and attaining independence, but the cost paid was partition. Gandhi, who had read the signs well—even while he negotiated for a different India— was left by the wayside in the mad march of history.*

*The years 1946-48 reveal a Gandhi who literally walked the length and breadth of riot-struck India to preach a message of forgiveness, reconciliation and non-violence. Tired, desperately lonely and filled with the sorrow of failure, he was ready to die. The day of freedom did not appear meaningful to him—the price that had been paid for it seemed too dear. Freedom also lacked substance, when all around him he could only see displaced people and vengeful crowds. Conscious, though, that his non-violent creed still had a role to play, he began to tend bruised and hurt Hindu and Punjabi Sikh refugees from what was now Pakistan and bewildered and frightened Muslims in India, now the target of vicious attacks by Hindus.*

*Even as he wandered the refugee camps in Delhi, a Hindu assassin, Nathuram Godse, belonging to a violent right-wing group, chose to misread his message of peace and reconciliation as being directed against Hindus. Fearful and full of hatred for Gandhi's ecumenical nationalism, and convinced that India ought to remain 'Hindu', he shot him dead on January 30, 1948.*

# A State of Hatred: The Road to Pakistan

*The last years of British rule in India were vastly difficult ones. With the Congress and the Muslim League unable to agree on anything— from the composition of the interim Ministry that the British wished to constitute, to the political future that awaited either party— independence appeared a sober proposition. However it did look as if communal divisions had come to stay. The results from the provincial elections held during this time showed that everywhere except in the north-west of the Indian subcontinent, Muslims had voted for candidates of the League. Congress Muslims were all defeated. Jinnah's Pakistan did not seem a distant reality.*

*Gandhi spoke of the need to canalize hatred into good deeds, but he appeared a lonely voice. There were other problems that needed to be addressed as well. The end of the war saw anger against the British burst out. Soldiers of the Royal Navy mutinied and Englishmen were attacked in the city of Bombay where the mutineers were supported enthusiastically by trade unions and socialists from the Congress. The latter saw mass struggle, which they felt was imminent, as a way of uniting Hindus and Muslims, but Gandhi did not believe that unity could be forged 'at the barricades' and counselled the socialists to await a gradual transfer of power.*

*Just at this time (1946), a British delegation arrived in India, comprising members nominated by the British cabinet. The Cabinet Mission Plan (of May 16, 1946), as it unfolded after discussions with political leaders, parties and individuals, refused to concede Jinnah's idea of Pakistan. He desired a contiguous territory, comprising areas where Muslims were in a majority—in the north-west (the Punjab), the north-east (Bengal and Assam), the Sind and the North-west frontier, on the Afghan border. Instead, the Plan offered him a compromise: provinces would be grouped on a communal basis—into three sections, in this case—and could evolve their own constitutions. But a loose Federal government would unite the sections.*

*The Congress and the Muslim League interpreted the terms of the Plan in the light of their individual demands and ideologies. In the battle of wills and words that ensued, the Viceroy held it prudent to entertain the Congress' claims to form a Ministry, though it was the Muslim League which had expressed its support of the Plan first. Jinnah had initially rejected the Plan. But, when he was assured by the British that it did contain the basis of a separate state—sectional constituents of the Federal structure could renew the Federal constitution and decide on their future at some point in time—he had accepted it. So he was naturally outraged when the British decided to placate the Congress, which had been equivocal about the Plan, and called it into government. Declaring his intention to stay out of the government and the proposed Constituent Assembly, he called on the Muslim League to undertake direct action—on the streets—to make Pakistan a reality.*

*Gandhi did not favour the plan; he thought it endorsed partition and after reviewing it finally rejected it. He was apprehensive of what would happen, given the manner in which the Congress had arrogated power to itself. In Jinnah's anger he could discern the shape of things to come.*

---

*On August 16, 1946, the Muslim League declared that Muslims had to prepare themselves for 'Direct Action' if they were to acquire Pakistan. This was widely interpreted as a call to violence. Savage riots broke out in Calcutta. During four days of rioting, according to official estimates, some five thousand were killed and fifteen thousand wounded. In other provinces where Muslims constituted a majority of the population, such as Sind, violence held the day.*

## What Can Violence Do?

If newspaper reports are to be believed, responsible ministers in Sindh and other equally responsible Leaguers almost all over, are preaching violence in naked language. Nakedness is itself a virtue as distinguished from hypocrisy. But when it is a hymn of obscenity, it is a vice to be shunned, whether it resides in a Leaguer or any other person. Any Muslim who is not in the League is a traitor, says one. The Hindu is a *kafir* deserving the fate of such, says another. Calcutta has given an ocular demonstration of what direct action is and how it is to be done.

Who is the gainer? Certainly not the Muslim masses nor the sober followers of Islam which itself means sobriety and peace. The very salute *salaam alaikum* means "peace be unto you".

Violence may have its place in life but not that which we have witnessed in Calcutta, assuming of course that newspaper accounts are to be trusted. Pakistan of whatever hue does not lie through senseless violence. ... I believe that the authors of the State Paper issued by the Cabinet Mission desire peaceful transfer of power to representative Indian hands. But if *we* need the use of the British gun and bayonet, the British will not go or, if they do, some other foreign power will take their place. We will make a serious mistake, if, every time the British bayonet is used, we trot out the agent provocateur. No doubt he has been at work. Let us not ride that horse to death. ... Would that the violence of Calcutta were sterilized and did not become a signal for its spread all over. It depends upon the leaders of the Muslim League of course, but the rest will not be free from responsibility. They can retaliate or refrain. Refraining is easy and simple, if there is the will. Retaliation is complicated ...

*Harijan*, 25-8-1946 (92: 44-45)

---

*Gandhi decided to go to Bengal in November 1946. The region had witnessed some of the worst rioting in recent times. He wished to heal hatred and foster unity between Hindus and Muslims. His presence was resented by a section of Muslims, who angrily pointed to rioting in Bihar, where a large number of Muslims had been killed by Hindus, and advised him to go to Bihar instead. Gandhi responded in anguish.*

### To Bihar
### Sodepur, November 6, 1946

Bihar of my dreams seems to have falsified them. I am not relying upon reports that might be prejudiced or exaggerated. The continued presence of the Central Chief Minister (*of Bihar, that is; Bihar had a Congress government and Bengal was under Muslim League rule - ed.*) and his colleagues furnishes an eloquent tale of the tragedy of Bihar. ... I must confess, too, that although I have been in Calcutta for over a week I do not yet know the magnitude of the

Bengal tragedy. Though Bihar calls me, I must not interrupt my programme for Noakhali (*a Bengali village that witnessed terrible incidents of terror - ed.*). And is counter-communalism any answer to the communalism of which Congressmen have accused the Muslim League? Is it Nationalism to seek barbarously to crush the fourteen per cent of the Muslims in Bihar?

I do not need to be told that I must not condemn the whole of Bihar for the sake of the sins of a few thousand Biharis. ...I am afraid, if the misconduct in Bihar continues, all the Hindus of India will be condemned by the world. That is its way, and it is not a bad way either. The misdeeds of Bihari Hindus may justify Qaid-e-Azam Jinnah's taunt that the Congress is a Hindu organization in spite of its boast that it has in its ranks a few Sikhs, Muslims, Christians, Parsis and others. Bihari Hindus are in honour bound to regard the minority Muslims as their brethren requiring protection, equal with the vast majority of Hindus ...

... I do not want in this letter to talk of *ahimsa* to you. I do want, however, to tell you that what you are reported to have done will never count as an act of bravery. For thousands to do to death a few hundreds is no bravery. It is worse than cowardice. It is unworthy of nationalism, of any religion. If you had given a blow against a blow, no one would have dared to point a finger against you. What you have done is to degrade yourselves and drag down India. ...You should not rest till every Muslim refugee has come back to his home which you should undertake to rebuild and ask your Ministers to help you to do so. ...

*Harijan*, 10-11-1946 (92: 451-52)

---

*In Muslim League-ruled Bengal, Gandhi encountered a demoralized Hindu population. He had to literally talk his way into people's hearts, counsel courage and dignity.*

**Talk to Relief Workers, Chandpur**
**November 7, 1946**

GANDHIJI: What goes against my grain is that a single individual can be converted or a single woman can be kidnapped or raped. So long as we feel we can be subjected to these indignities, we shall continue to be so subjected. If we say we cannot do without police or military protection, we really confess defeat even before the battle has begun. No police or military in the world can protect people who are cowards. Today you say thousands of people are terrorizing a mere handful, so what can the latter do? But even a few individuals are enough to terrorize the whole mass, if the latter feel helpless. Your trouble is not numerical inferiority but the feeling of helplessness that has seized you and the habit of depending on others. The remedy lies with you. That is why I am opposed to the idea of your evacuating East Bengal *en masse*. It is no cure for impotence or helplessness.

A WORKER: East Bengal is opposed to such a move.

G. They should not leave. 20,000 able-bodied men prepared to die like brave men non-violently might today be regarded as a fairy tale, but it would be no fairy tale for every able-bodied man in a population of 20,000 to die like stalwart soldiers in open fight. ... I will proclaim from the housetops that it is the only condition under which you can live in East Bengal. You have asked for Hindu officers, Hindu police and Hindu military in the place of Muslim. It is a false cry. You forget that Hindu officers, Hindu police and Hindu military have in the past done all these things— looting, arson, abduction, rape. I come from Kathiawar—the land of petty principalities. I cannot describe to you to what depths of depravity human nature can go. No woman's honour is safe in some principalities and the chief is no hooligan but a duly anointed one.

W. These are cases of individual depravity. Here we have got this on a mass scale.

G. But the individual there is not alone. He is backed by the machinery of his little State.

W. He is condemned even by his compeers. Here such acts are not condemned by the Muslims.

G. I have heard nothing but condemnation of these acts from Shaheed Suhrawardy (*the Chief Minister of Bengal - ed.*) downwards since I have come here. Words of condemnation may tickle your ears, but they are no consolation to the unfortunate women whose houses have been laid desolate or who have been abducted, forcibly converted and forcibly married. What a shame for Hindus, what a disgrace for Islam! No, I am not going to leave you in peace. Presently you will say to yourself, "When will this man leave us and go?" But this man will not go. He did not come on your invitation and he will go only on his own, but with your blessings, when his mission in East Bengal is fulfilled.

W: It is a part of their plan for Pakistan.

G. It is midsummer madness and they (*the Muslim League - ed.*) have realized it. They will soon sicken of it. They have already begun to.

W. Why do not they come here then and set this right?

G. That stage will come. Sickness only marks the crisis. Convalescence must precede cure. You see I am a nature-curist. ... There is not a man, however cruel and hard-hearted, but would give his admiration to a brave man. A *goonda* is not the vile man he is imagined to be. He is not without his noble traits.

W. A *goonda* does not understand reason.

G. But he understands bravery. If he finds that you are braver than he, he will respect you. You will note that for the purposes of our present discussion I have not asked you to discard the use of arms. I can't provide you with arms. It is not for me to provide arms to the Chittagong Armoury Raid men (*Bengali militants who raided a government armoury during the 1930s; they were part of the crowd that Gandhi addressed - ed.*). The most tragic thing about the Armoury Raid people is that they could not even multiply themselves. Their bravery was lop-sided. It did not infect others.

W. ... I am myself an Armoury Raid man.

G. You are no Armoury Raid man or, you should not have been here to tell these things. That so many of them should have remained living witnesses of the things that have happened is in my eyes a tragedy of the first order. If they had shown the same fearlessness and courage to face death in the present crisis as they did when they made that raid, they would have gone down in history as heroes. As it is, they have only inscribed a small footnote in the page of history. You will see I am not, as I have already said, asking you just now to unlearn the use of arms or to follow my type of heroism. I have not made it good even in my own case. I have come here to test it in East Bengal. I want you to take up the conventional type of heroism. You should be able to infect others— both men and women—with courage and fearlessness to face death when the alternative is dishonour and humiliation. Then the Hindus can stay in East Bengal, not otherwise. After all, the Mussalmans are blood of our blood and bone of our bone.

W. Here the proportion of Mussalmans and Hindus is 6 to 1. How can you expect us to stand against such heavy odds?

G. When India was brought under British subjection, there were 70,000 European soldiers against 33 crores of Indians.

W: So we are to fight with arms anyhow?

G. Not anyhow. Even violence has its code of ethics. For instance, to butcher helpless old men, women and children is not bravery but rank cowardice. Chivalry requires that they should be protected even at the cost of one's life. The history of early Islam is replete with such instances of chivalry and Islam is all the stronger for them.

W. Would you permit the Hindus to take the offensive?

G. The people of Bihar did and brought disgrace upon themselves and India. They have set the clock of India's independence back. I have a right to speak about Bihar. In a sense I feel closer to Bihar than to Bengal as fortune enabled me to give a striking demonstration of the non-violence technique in Champaran. I have heard it said that the retaliation in Bihar has "cooled" the Muslims down. They mean it has cowed them down for the time being. They forget that two can play at a game. Bihar has forged a link in the chain of our slavery. If the Bihar performance is repeated or if the Bihar mentality does not mend, you may note down my words in your diary: *Before long India will pass under the yoke of the Big*

*Three with one of them probably as the mandatory power. The Independence of India is today at stake in Bengal and Bihar (emphasis as in the original - ed.).* The British Government entrusted the Congress with power not because they are in love with the Congress but because they had faith that the Congress would use it wisely and well, not abuse it. Today Pandit Jawaharlal Nehru finds the ground slipping from under his feet. But he won't let that happen. That is why he is in Bihar. He has said he is going to stay there as long as it may be necessary. Biharis have behaved as cowards. Use your arms well, if you must. Do not ill-use them. Bihar has not used its arms well. If the Biharis wanted to retaliate, they could have gone to Noakhali and died to a man. But for a thousand Hindus to fall upon a handful of Mussalmans—men, women and children —living in their midst is no retaliation but just brutality. It is the privilege of arms to protect the weak and helpless. The best succour that Bihar could have given to the Hindus of East Bengal would have been to guarantee with their own lives the absolute safety of the Muslim population living in their midst. Their example would have told. And I have faith that they will still do so with due repentance when the present madness has passed away. Anyway that is the price I have put upon my life if they want me to live. Here ends the first lesson.

*Harijan*, 1-12-1946 (93: 1-4)

---

## Speech at Prayer Meeting, Dattapara
## November 10, 1946

Whether you believe me or not, I want to assure you that I am a servant of both the Hindus and the Mussalmans. I have not come here to fight Pakistan. If India is destined to be partitioned, I cannot prevent it. But I wish to tell you that Pakistan cannot be established by force. In the *bhajan* that was just sung the poet has likened God to the philosophers' stone. The proverbial philosophers' stone is said to turn iron into gold. ... That philosophers' stone is within us all. All that I wish to tell my Muslim brethren is that, whether they live as one people or two, they should live as friends with the Hindus. If they do not wish to do so, they should say so plainly. I would in that case confess myself defeated. The refugees (*Hindus who had fled their homes and were now in refugee camps - ed.*) cannot stay on as refugees for ever. The Government cannot go on feeding them. ... It is not possible for them to exist like this for any length of time. If, therefore, the Muslims do not want them back in their villages, they must go elsewhere.

But even if every Hindu of East Bengal went away, I will still continue to live amidst the Muslims of East Bengal and eat what they give me and what I consider lawful for me to partake of. I will not bring my food from outside. I do not need fish or flesh. All that I need is a little fruit, vegetables and some goat's milk ...

... For a thousand Hindus to surround a hundred Mussalmans or for a thousand Mussalmans to surround a hundred Hindus and oppress them is not bravery but cowardice. Fair fight means even numbers and previous notice. That does not mean that I approve of their fighting. It has been said that the Hindus and Mussalmans cannot stay together as friends or cooperate with each other. No one can make me believe that, but if that is your belief, you should say so. I would in that case not ask the Hindus to return to their homes. They would leave East Bengal, and it would be a shame for both the Mussalmans and the Hindus. If, on the other hand, you want the Hindus to stay in your midst, you should tell them that they need not look to the military for protection but to their Muslim brethren instead. Their daughters and sisters and mothers are your own daughters, sisters and mothers and you should protect them with your lives ...

*Harijan*, 1-12-1946 (93: 17-18 )

---

*The scenes he was witness to in Naokhali, where rioting had been intense and barbarous, the fact of Hindu-Muslim disunity and mistrust, the sense of failure that he experienced with regard to several aspects of his life's work: all these made Gandhi feel despondent.*

**A Talk**
**[On or before November 20, 1946]**

When I was in detention in the Aga Khan Palace (*where he was interned following the 'Quit India' call - ed.*), I once sat down to write a thesis on India as a protagonist of non-violence. But as I proceeded with my writing, I could not go on. I had to stop.

There are two aspects of Hinduism. There is, on the one hand, the historical Hinduism with its untouchability, superstitious worship of sticks and stones, animal sacrifice and so on. On the other, we have the Hinduism of the *Gita*, the *Upanishads* and Patanjali's *Yoga Sutra* which is the acme of *ahimsa* and oneness of all creation, pure worship of one immanent, formless imperishable God. *Ahimsa* which to me is the chief glory of Hinduism has been sought to be explained away by our people as being meant for sannyasis only. I do not share that view. I have held that it is *the* way of life and India has to show it to the world. Where do I stand? Do I represent this *ahimsa* in my person? If I do, then deceit and hatred that poison the atmosphere should dissolve. It is only by going into isolation from my companions, those on whose help I have relied all along, and standing on my own feet that I shall find my bearings and also test my faith in God.

*Harijan,* 8-12-1946 (93: 43)

---

## Discussion with Amiya Chakravarty
## December 4, 1946

At meal time Prof. Amiya Chakravarty of the Calcutta University, who had come to him on a visit, asked him the question as to what should be the technique for approaching the wrongdoers so that their resistance should be dissolved. "The chief difficulty with the callous perpetrators of crimes is," Dr. Chakravarty remarked, "that they are not only unrepentant but defiant and even jubilant over their misdeeds."

Gandhiji replied :

Yes, they have their own reason to be jubilant and the only way to meet their attitude is not to succumb to it but to live in their midst and retain one's sense of truth. Goodness must be joined with knowledge. Mere goodness is not of much use as I have found in life. One must cultivate the fine, discriminating quality which goes with spiritual courage and character. One must know, in a crucial situation, when to speak and when to be silent, when to act and when to refrain. Action and non-action in these circumstances become identical instead of being contradictory. I am groping for light. I am surrounded by darkness; but I must act or refrain as guided by truth. I find that I have not the patience and the technique needed in these tragic circumstances; suffering and evil often overwhelms me and I stew in my own juice. Therefore, I have told my friends that they should bear with me and work or refrain as guided by wisdom which is now utterly demanded of us. This darkness will break and, if I see light even those who created the tragedy of the recent communalism in Bengal, will.

The new basis has to be built here in the villages where the Hindus and the Muslims have lived and suffered together in the land of their forefathers and must live together in the future. For the time being I have become a Bengali and a Noakhali man. I have come to live and share their task, to cement the two together or to perish in the attempt. I am in the midst of a raging fire and will stay here till it is put out. For this reason, I do not want to leave these parts. Life must be made livable for the sorely afflicted men and women. The work of organization must go on and the physical as well as moral rescue achieved ...

*Harijan*, 12-1-1947; and *Hindustan Standard*, 8-12-1946 and 9-12-1946 (93: 102-3)

---

*Gandhi's strategy of building trust in the Bengal villages that he visited in the course of his healing journey was to begin his prayer meetings with songs and chants from both Hindu and Islamic scripture. When some Muslims objected to the chanting of the god Rama's name, he gently reprimanded them.*

### Speech at Prayer Meeting, Masimpur
### January 7, 1947

... I am sorry because some of my friends had not been able to bear any name of God except Khuda but I am glad because they have had the courage of expressing their dissent openly and plainly. This small incident probably gives an inkling of the mentality which had prevailed during the fateful October disturbances in the district. I am extremely careful not to wound the susceptibilities of anyone unnecessarily. It is essential that my Muslim brethren should realize as also the Hindus that it does not matter by what name God is addressed. It is the same Creator whom people worship through many tongues. I appeal to the Muslim brethren to assure me of that freedom which is true to the noblest traditions of Islam. Even from the Muslim League platforms it has been repeatedly said that in Pakistan there will be full tolerance of the practice of their faiths by the minorities and that they will enjoy freedom of worship equally with the majority ...

*Hindustan Standard*, 9-1-1947; *The Hindu*, 9-1-1947; and *Amrita Bazar Patrika*, 20-1-1947 (93: 247-48 )

---

*To build trust amongst those who were not sure about his mission, Gandhi decided to do away with the support of armed police in his tour through riot-affected Bengal.*

**Letter to H.S. Suhrawardy**
**Kazirkhil, Ramganj P. S., Noakhali**
**January 9, 1947**

... In this village (Dashpara) Muslims told some Hindu friends that all my attempts at bringing about real friendship between the two communities must fail so long as I go about fully protected by armed police or military, by whatever name these guards may be called. The fright of the military keeps them from coming to me and asking all sorts of questions for the resolution of their doubts.

I do see some force in their argument. There will be none if either community was really brave. Unfortunately both lack this very necessary human quality. I would, therefore, like you to reconsider the position and if you feel convinced, to withdraw this escort. I do not need it. I even feel embarrassed and it certainly interferes with my *sadhana*. If you think that a firm and unequivocal written absolution from me will solve your difficulty I would be quite prepared to consider any draft that you may send me for signature. Failing that I suggest your making a declaration that on a satisfactory assurance being given to you by the Muslims in the area through which I may pass regarding my safety, you will withdraw the escort. If this happens it will be a dignified procedure. I will certainly appreciate it and it will produce a good effect all round ...

From a copy: *Pyarelal Papers*. Nehru Memorial Museum and Library Courtesy: Beladevi Nayyar and Dr. Sushila Nayyar (93: 253)

---

*Noakhali witnessed several instances of sexual assault of Hindu women by Muslim men. Since the assault of women was often viewed by the perpetrator and the victim as a sign of dishonouring, the practice seemed hard to undo. Gandhi's response to this crime was characteristic.*

## A Woman's Dilemma

Q. What is a woman to do when attacked by miscreants—run away or resist with violence? Have boats in readiness to fly or prepare to defend with weapons?

A. My answer to this question is very simple. For me there can be no preparation for violence. All preparation must be for non-violence if courage of the highest type is to be developed. Violence can only be tolerated as being preferable always to cowardice. Therefore I would have no boats ready for flight in emergency. For a non-violent person there is no emergency but quiet dignified preparation for death. Hence whether it is a man or a woman he or she will defy death even when he or she is unassisted; for the real assistance is from God. I can preach no other thing and I am here to practise what I preach. Whether such an opportunity will come to me or be given to me I do not know. If there are women who when assailed by miscreants cannot resist without arms they do not need to be advised to carry arms. They will do so.

There is something wrong in this constant enquiry as to whether to bear arms or not. People have to learn to be naturally independent. If they will remember the central teaching, namely, that the real effective resistance lies in non-violence, they will model their conduct accordingly. And that is what the world has been doing although unthinkingly. Since it has not the highest courage, namely courage born of non-violence, it arms itself even unto the atom bomb. Those who do not see in it the futility of violence will naturally arm themselves to the best of their ability. In India, since my return from South Africa, there has been conscious and constant training in non-violence with the result we have seen.

Q. Can a woman be advised to take her own life rather than surrender?

A. This question requires a definite answer. A woman should most certainly take her own life rather than surrender. In other words, surrender has no room in my plan of life. But I was asked in what way to take one's own life. I promptly said it was not for me to prescribe the means and behind the approval of suicide under such circumstances was and is the belief that one whose mind is prepared for even suicide will have requisite courage for such mental resistance and such internal purity that her assailant will be disarmed. I could not carry the argument any further because it does not admit of further development. It requires positive proof which, I own, is lacking ...

*Harijan*, 9-2-1947 (93:331)

---

*Reconciliation and rehabilitation meant that Muslims and Hindu engage with each other in everyday contexts, and bring to their experiments a practical sensitivity. Gandhi was all too aware of this and addressed this issue in diverse ways.*

### Speech at Prayer Meeting, Panchgaon
### January 28, 1947

On my way here I was taken to three homes, one Hindu and two Muslim. It gave me very great pleasure as all I crave for is love. I was not informed in advance of the places I would be taken to, but I saw love in the eyes of those who invited me, and so I went. At all the three places I was offered something or other to eat, but it was not the time when I usually ate, so I said I would gladly accept some fruit if they sent any to my next halt. My granddaughter accompanies me. The women welcomed her with love and an old lady embraced her on knowing who she was. A Muslim sister who had made fish curry and rotis at the time, pressed her to partake of the fare. What was the poor girl to do? She refused the offer on the ground that she did not take anything at that early hour. The Muslim women thereupon suspected that this Hindu girl was not willing to eat, because at heart she felt she would be polluted. So, to allay their suspicion, she broke a piece from their roti and ate it. The sisters were satisfied. Neither I nor those who associate with me make any distinctions of caste or creed and we have no inhibitions against dining with anybody.

But I appeal to my Muslim friends to look kindly upon those Hindus who think they would lose their religion if they ate at the hands of a Muslim. I understand that that belief is wrong. But the test of brotherly love does not lie only in eating together. This erroneous belief is sure to wear off with time. Much has been achieved already in this direction. But till that attitude changes please learn to appreciate love wherever you find it. Only in this way will you come near one another. The Pressmen who follow me had arranged a mass dinner of all castes and creeds. Muslim brothers did not join in it. But the host of the Pressmen begged them earnestly not to insist on his participation in the common dinner. "You will leave me in a day", he said "but calamity will beset me after you go. The people here will bring pressure to bear upon me saying that I had lost caste by eating with you and so I must become a Muslim."

I felt that the man's fear was well founded. So I had to request the Pressmen not to hold the common dinner in the poor man's hut. I don't know when Hindus and Muslims will shed their weakness and come close to one another. But I am prepared to give up my very life, if need be, to see this object realized, and I appeal to you all to pray with me: "O! God ! bring that golden day soon."

*Eklo Jane Re*, (from Gujarati) pp. 100-1 (93: 338-39)

---

*In spite of his best efforts, Gandhi found that the general distrust and hatred between Hindus and Muslims in Noakhali showed little signs of disappearing or even retreating. He wondered if he was at fault, if there was not a measure of residual impurity in him that compromised his message of heart-unity and non-violence and rendered it ineffective. To test himself, he undertook an experiment in sexual control, while camping in the Bengal hinterland. He requested his grand-niece Manu Gandhi to sleep next to him. He would lie stark naked—his was to flush out, whatever fugitive and illicit desire he harboured within him. The experiment was severely criticized. He sought absolution from an old friend.*

## Discussion with A.V. Thakkar
## February 24, 1947

BAPA: Why this experiment here?

GANDHIJI: You are mistaken, Bapa; it is not an experiment but an integral part of my *yajna*. One may forgo an experiment, one cannot forgo one's duty. Now if I regard a thing as a part of my *yajna*—a sacred duty—I may not give it up even if public opinion is wholly against me. I am engaged in achieving self-purification. … Ever since my coming to Noakhali, I have been asking myself the question, "What is it that is choking the action of my *ahimsa*? Why does not the spell work? May it not be because I have temporized in the matter of *brahmacharya*?"

B. Your *ahimsa* has not failed. Do not miss the wood for the trees. … Just think what would have been the fate of Noakhali if you had not come. The world does not think of *brahmacharya* as you do.

G. If I accept your contention, then it would amount to this that I should give up what I hold to be right for me, for fear of displeasing the world. I shudder to think where I should have been if I had proceeded like that in my life. I should have found myself at the bottom of the pit. You can have no idea, Bapa, but I can well picture it to myself. I have called my present venture a *yajna*—a sacrifice, a penance. It means utmost self-purification. How can there be that self-purification when in my mind I entertain a thing which I dare not put openly into practice? Does one need anyone's approval or permission to do what one holds with all one's being to be one's duty? Under the circumstances, there are only two courses open to friends. Either they should have faith in me, in the purity of my motives and my *bona fides*, even though they are unable to follow or agree with my reasoning, or they should part company with me. There is no middle course. I dare not shrink from putting into action the logical implications of my conviction when I am launched on a sacrifice which consists of the full practice of truth. Nor must I hide or keep my convictions to myself. That would be disloyalty to friends. Let X, Y and Z, therefore, go the way they choose, but how can I run away from the test? My mind is made up. On the lonely way to God on which I have set out, I need no earthly companions.

Let those who will, therefore, denounce me, if I am the impostor they imagine me to be, though they may not say so in so many words. It might disillusion millions who persist in regarding me as a Mahatma. I must confess, the prospect of being so debunked greatly pleases me. Thousands of Hindu and Muslim women come to me. They are to me like my own mother, sisters and daughters. But if an occasion should arise requiring me to share the bed with any of them I must not hesitate, if I am the *brahmachari* that I claim to be. If I shrink from the test, I write myself down as a coward and a fraud.

*Mahatma Gandhi: The Last Phase,* Vol. I, Bk. II, pp. 224-6 (94: 36-37)

---

*Not entirely sure if he had managed to heal divisive hearts, Gandhi left Bengal and travelled to Bihar. He had resisted visiting that site of violence, since he had heard that the Congress government that was in power there was handling matters rather well. When reports to the contrary reached him, he immediately set out for Bihar.*

### Speech at Prayer Meeting, Patna
### March 5, 1947

... This Bihar of ours has today committed a heinous crime. The atrocities perpetrated on a handful of Muslims have no parallel, so say the Muslims, in the annals of history. I too have read some history. I know that the world has witnessed greater brutality by man on man. But it is no use repeating them here. We must not compete in doing evil and that too against whom? Those who cry for avenging Noakhali in Bihar do not know the meaning of vengeance. Is it manliness to return barbarism for barbarism? We ought to overcome violence by love. ... It had been reported to me that some Congressmen had a hand in these crimes. It would be wrong even today to say that there was not a single Congressman involved in the mad upheaval. In India the Congress has to accept the responsibility for the misdeeds of all communities and all individuals. I had claimed in London on your behalf that the Congress represented the whole of India by right of service. Hence any sin committed by India comes to the door of the Congress. You who are listening to me may not have done any evil, yet you have to accept the responsibility.

I have become hard-hearted now. I have not come here to shed tears or to make you cry. I would rather wish to steel your hearts. I could make you cry if I chose. But I do not wish to do so. We should not disown responsibility by saying that our hands are clean. India consists of many communities. ... The way to achieve independence consists in all Indians saying with one voice that unless they gave to the whole world all that was good in them, their survival would be meaningless. Are we going to compete in [making] atom bombs? Are we going to match barbarism with even more barbarous acts?

India has placed before the world a new weapon. ... We have been insisting that we will attain independence through non-violence. I do not claim that all Indians have accepted non-violence as a matter of creed. But even when we accept anything as a matter of policy, it becomes our duty to act upon it. ... Those who are under the illusion that Bihar has saved other people by committing these barbarities are talking nonsense. This is not the way to attain freedom. If Muslims believe that they would annihilate the Hindus or if Hindus believe that they would annihilate the Muslims, I should like to ask them what they would gain thereby? Muslims will not serve Islam if they annihilate the Hindus; rather they would thereby destroy Islam. And if the Hindus believe that they would be able to annihilate Islam it means that they would be annihilating Hindu *dharma*. ... All religions are equal and they are founded on the same faith. ... Scriptures have said that one who condemns other religions, condemns one's own religion... We should not gloat over the massacre of Muslims by Bihar Hindus. ... The Hindus of Bihar have committed a grave sin. They will raise the head of Bihar much higher if they do honest reparations, greater in magnitude than their crimes ...

*Gandhijike Dukhe Dilki Pukar*: I, pp. 1-6, and *Harijan*, 23-3-1947 (94: 74-75)

---

*Gandhi held several public meetings during his stay in Bihar, as he had done in Bengal, where he spoke of matters that had been brought to him, or of letters he had received with regard to the rioting and violence.*

### Speech at Prayer Meeting, Patna
### March 8, 1947

... I have received a telegram from a Hindu brother. It says that I must not condemn the Hindus in Bihar. It warns me that due to my influence over them I may mislead them and prevent them from taking revenge. Look at the cheek of this gentleman who is trying to teach me my duty! He calls himself a Hindu but does not act like one. ... We have committed a dirty crime and I have come here to cleanse the dirt and brighten the image of Hinduism. Am I going to flinch from my duty if someone beats me up or abuses me for doing it? It is my duty to speak out the truth and if I withhold it, I shall be disloyal to Hindus, to Muslims and to India. I shall therefore advise you not to listen to those who incite and misguide you.

I wish to tell you one thing more. ... The Hindus in Bihar ... should do their duty by contributing to a fund for the relief of Muslims by way of repentance. No one should think that he need not lift his little finger since there is already a Congress ministry with a Congress majority here, which will do everything that needs to be done. ... I did not beg for money in Noakhali because I received unsought about three lakh rupees. Today I thought I should hold out the begging bowl here and awaken the conscience of the people. ... I can only remind you of your duty. I cannot perform your duty. Hence you must contribute generously to the Bihar fund. A Muslim child must feel entirely safe in a Hindu locality and the Muslims should be convinced of this change of heart. A friend came to me and asserted that there was a time in Bihar when Hindus and Muslims lived together and called each other uncles. Today it is no longer like that. We must atone for this ...

*Gandhijike Dukhe Dilki Pukar*: I, pp. 136, and *Harijan*, 30-3-1947 (94: 85-86)

---

## Speech at Prayer Meeting, Patna
## March 12, 1947

... Today I visited a village where Hindus had caused great damage. An old Muslim showed me his own house and those of his relations with broken door-frames where bricks were removed from the door-sill. I was shocked and shaken to see that the Hindus had caused these depredations. I had wept when I saw the ruins caused by Muslims in Noakhali. Today also I might have wept. But my tears cannot render any succour to the sufferers. What I witnessed today does not behove human beings. We are all responsible for this vandalism so close to the city of Patna. Even if you did not participate personally in the loot, you cannot escape the charge of abetting the marauders. A mosque was also damaged in the village Kumarahar. ... Those who desecrated the mosque were not men but devils; because mosques, temples or churches are all houses of the Lord.

I have come here today to convey to you my grief. You may perhaps be smiling and thinking that whatever happened was all very good. But I assert that this is potent injustice. I am grieved when I hear that Muslims have desecrated a temple. Should I retaliate by damaging a mosque? How can such damage save the temple or benefit the Hindu religion? If Muslims are about to desecrate a temple, it becomes my duty to prevent them from their vandalism, irrespective of my not being an idol-worshipper. I should hug the idol and request them not to demolish the temple. I should lay down my life to protect the idol but refuse to hand it over to them. My entreaties will impress them, they will realize that I mean no harm to them and then they will become my friends ...

*Gandhijike Dukhe Dilki Pukar*: I, pp. 23-5, and *Harijan*, 30-3-1947 (94: 102-03)

## Discussion with Relief Committee Members
## March 15, 1947

QUESTION: Will you advise Muslims to return to their villages in the prevailing disturbed conditions ?

ANSWER: If you have the courage and if you have the requisite faith in God, I shall advise you to return to your villages. I do realize that it is a difficult task. If I had under gone such harrowing experience, perhaps I myself would not have been able to go back; it would have made me a raving lunatic. The memory of murdered men and women would have haunted me. But I aspire to reach a stage when I shall have such abiding faith in God that I would go and stay in the midst of people who had become my enemies.

Q. If there is no change of heart in the majority community, what should the suffering minority do ? Should they live in small pockets or leave the province for ever?

A. If you do not return and since it was the fault of the Hindus, the Government is bound to compensate you for the loss of your property. But I do not understand your demand that the Government should allot land somewhere else. Well, if you can arrange mutual exchanges, no one can prevent you. But if the Government arranges this, it will not lead to a purification of hearts. Many people are talking of pockets. I simply do not understand this. If those villages where the Muslims are in majority welcome you, who can prevent you from going there? Similarly, no one can prevent you from leaving the province if you decide to go in spite of my promises of affection. ...

Q. Should or should not those who have committed murder, rape, arson and other heinous crimes receive appropriate punishment? If you think they should, how will you advise the Government of Bihar?

A. Of course, those responsible for devilish deeds must be

punished. The Government of Bihar has not abjured the principle of punishment. There is no such government anywhere in the world today. When such a government comes into being, I shall listen to their argument. But a government which believes in the theory of crime and punishment but does not punish the criminal has no right to call itself a government ...

Q. ... How will it be possible to make good the historical, cultural, social and religious damage done by the madness of the majority?

A. This has been a cruel and terrible tragedy. Such holocausts have shaken the world earlier and will do so even in the future. Only when we are reformed and tolerant enough to realize that all religions lead to the same God called by various people by various names, will the world change for the better. Till then the earth not be a habitable place. Till that change comes about, it is impossible to prevent such barbarity and the irreparable losses resultant from it.

Q. What should be done with those officers who openly helped the rioters and deliberately helped one side against the other?

A. Those officers against whom such charges can be proved can have no place in the government.

Q. What do you propose to do to prevent the repetition of riots at places where the Muslims have suffered? Even now the houses and properties of Muslims are being damaged.

A. I am doing my best to prevent a repetition. I shall continue to stay here till I succeed in my effort. I have already declared that I shall do or die. God will either grant me success or put an end to my life. I believe that a change of heart is essential if I am to succeed. As I have been telling the Hindus in Noakhali, this is not a work where the army or police can be of much help. You must gather courage and fear no one except God. I shall advice the Ministers to frame a law making Hindus responsible for the safety of the Muslim minority. Such laws will not in fact be needed where hearts have been purified.

Q. Can the cruelties and injustices meted out to us detain you for long in Bihar? Your prolonged presence is needed for the help of the refugees.

A. You need not worry on that account. I shall not leave Bihar so long as Hindus and Muslims do not jointly allow me to do so on the basis of their brotherly feelings.

Q. Will you call them Congressmen who organized and led the recent riots? If not, what action will be taken against them to preserve the prestige of the Congress?

A. How can those who participated in riots be called Congressmen? Before condemning them, I must listen to their versions of the story. I am a devotee of truth and shall lay down my life in serving truth.

*Gandhijike Dukhe Dilki Pukar*: I, pp. 35-8 (from Urdu) (94: 113-115)

---

*Gandhi called Congress workers to a meeting, where he interrogated their alleged role in the rioting.*

### Discussion with Congress Workers, Bir
### March 19, 1947

... Is it or isn't it a fact that quite a large number of Congressmen took part in the disturbances? I ask this question because people are making this allegation. But the Congressmen assembled here can themselves tell the truth. How many of the 132 members of your Committee (*district Committee of the Congress party - ed.*) were involved? It would be a very great thing if all of you assert that none of you was involved. But this assertion cannot be made. ... I wish to ask you, how could you live to see an old woman of 110 years being butchered before your eyes? How could you tolerate it? I do not wish to talk about anything else. I have vowed to do or die. I will not rest nor let others rest. I would wander all over on foot and ask the skeletons lying about how all that had happened. There is such a fire raging in me that I would know no peace till I have found a solution for all this. You know what happened when I reached Sodepur (*in Bengal, where Gandhi was until he hurried to Bihar - ed.*). ... I had not gone there for rest. I proceeded to Srirampur. It was a predominantly Muslim area with only a sprinkling of Hindu houses which had been burnt down. The Muslims welcomed me. Even then I hurried from there and wandered from village to village. I am afraid I will have to go through the same ordeal in Bihar. If I find that my comrades are deceiving me, I will be furious and I shall walk barefoot on and on through hail or storm.

... When Muslims in Noakhali taunted me to go to Bihar, I used to feel hurt. Some Muslims look upon me as an enemy of Islam. Some people expressed doubts whether I could achieve what I wanted to in Noakhali. But I had no doubts. ... The work in Bihar this time is far more difficult and significant. This time it seems I will have to strive to the utmost to prove that Hinduism and Islam can exist side by side. This is being put to the test today. Many people believe that they cannot and one will have to remain subordinate to the other. I do not think so. ... There are people today who declare that I am out of date and that I should give up all politics. I do not agree with this. This region is teeming with Hindus. We will not rely upon the police for our work although they are our police. We must do this work ourselves. ... The Government here have also deployed the police. I ask them, what is the police for? Muslims are not going to kill me here; the Hindus may probably think of doing so. That is why I wish that the task of establishing peace should be undertaken by you all and not only by the Government although it is our Government. You should either achieve success in your mission or die in the attempt.

*Gandhijike Dukhe Dilki Pukar*: II, pp. 13-6 (from Urdu) (94: 147-150)

---

*Gandhi felt that one could not talk enough about forgiveness and repentance. His Bihar prayer meetings are singular in this respect.*

### Speech at Prayer Meeting, Chorhuan
### March 21, 1947

... You should go to the Muslim brethren and tell them to forget the past, that it will never be repeated and persuade them to return and live peacefully as before. Tell them that their misery is your misery, that you are their brothers, that both Hindus and Muslims are sons of the same soil, both eat and drink from the same source and breathe the same air, hence there should be no ill will between them. Tell them that you will not get any peace of mind until they return to their homes. It is possible that the Muslims may turn round and ask how they can go back and live in the houses where their kith and kin have been done to death. They will be justified in saying so. But if the guilty persons go to the Muslims with truly penitent hearts, I am sure, they will be persuaded. Human hearts melt before love. When the murderers themselves go to them in sackcloth and ashes and promise them never to repeat such deeds, even a stony heart will melt.

You should not depend on the Government to do this work. The Government will of course lend a hand. But it is mainly your task. The Government can give you tools and materials; but the cleaning has to be done by you.

Amidst this mad upheaval there were some Hindus, like oases in a desert, who risked the wrath of the violent mobs and saved the lives of many Muslims and gave them shelter. They deserve congratulations though they do not need any. ... Since we have become strangers to human sentiments these days, we are impelled to congratulate any evidence of human love. Those who gave shelter to Muslims did not do so from any selfish motives. If I have not gone to meet them, let them not think that I have no regard or respect for them. I would love to meet them and know how they saved the lives of Muslims. I have been unable to go to them in spite of my admiration because I have come here like a physician who goes only to those who are suffering. I have come to lighten the sufferings of Muslims in Bihar. I have been told that the Hindus have also suffered in the riots at some places. If there are any such Hindus, they too will be given relief. But I pay more attention to Muslims because there are quite a few of them here who are willing to help the Hindus ...

*Gandhijike Dukhe Dilki Pukar*: II, pp. 29-32 (from Urdu) (94: 165-66)

422 | Soul Force

## Division and Death: Gandhi's Martyrdom

*Gandhi left Bihar in April 1947 for Delhi, to meet the new Viceroy, Lord Mountbatten. He was troubled by news of violent acts in the Punjab, which had prompted the Congress to press for a partition of the Punjab into west (Muslim) and east (Hindu and Sikh) Punjab. While in Delhi, he attempted yet again to address the question of India's unity. He suggested that Jinnah be invited to form the national government. The Viceroy was taken aback, and wondered if this was not a ploy on the part of the astute Gandhi, who perhaps knew full well that the League would not be able to get any of its ministry's decisions through in a Constituent Assembly where they would necessarily have been in a minority. But Gandhi was serious and discussed the matter with the Congress, whose leadership, including Nehru and Patel, turned it down.*

*However, Gandhi and Jinnah met and signed a joint appeal for peace (The Muslim League was now part of the interim ministry. After the declaration of Direct Action day and the killings in Bengal, Lord Wavell had decided to call them into the Ministry to bring a measure of order and responsibility into a context, where both were sorely needed.) Gandhi even wondered if this signing was not a good omen, and if perhaps, Jinnah would eventually agree to a national government. But this was not to be. The Congress, under pressure from its own cadres who were eager to experience the power of rule, and from its financial supporters, who desired to end matters soon and did not want a competing Muslim capitalist class to engage with, decided to accept a partition of the Punjab and Bengal. This was still not the Pakistan of Jinnah's dreams. It did not include east Punjab and west Bengal, which, being predominantly Hindu, would remain with India. Gandhi was disconsolate when the decision was ratified by the Viceroy himself. He knew that Bengal resented partition, and he was even sympathetic to a plan for a united Bengal, autonomous of the Union of India, and supported by Muslims and Hindus. But though the plan enjoyed currency amongst a variety of Bengali political leaders, it did not really acquire political form—the logic of division had already been decided on by the League and the Congress.*

*As lines were drawn and measured in Delhi, lives continued to be lost. A massive movement of populations began in the Punjab, leading to unprecedented violence and death. Gandhi moved from Calcutta to Delhi, speaking of mercy and forgiveness and was prepared to go to the Punjab, if he succeeded in bringing peace in Bengal and Delhi. He was determined that the fact of political division be overcome through a free and frank exchange of love and concern between Hindus, Muslims and Sikhs. He refused to accept the reality of partition, and instead looked to the future, when Pakistan and India could actually exist in amity. In these last days of his life, his public life was pared down to an ascetic severity. Though he continued to keep in touch with the Congress and its leadership, he had moved away from the world of rule and authority. He had become all too aware of the cunning of power and the abuses it invited: it was not his world.*

*Gandhi never did make it to the Punjab. He was all set to go to west Punjab—to Pakistan—to speak to Muslims there of their duty to the minority Hindus and Sikhs. But a Hindu assassin's bullet ended his life. The assassin argued in court that he had decided to kill Gandhi to save Hindus and Hinduism.*

---

*Gandhi was very disturbed by the fact that the Congress had voted to partition the Punjab—the first sign of a reality that would soon come to pass.*

## Letter to Jawaharlal Nehru
## March 20, 1947

I would like you ... (*ellipsis as in the original - ed.*) to tell me what you can about the Punjab tragedy. I know nothing about it save what is allowed to appear in the Press which I thoroughly distrust. Nor am I in sympathy with what may be termed by the old expression of "hush hush policy". It is amazing how the country is adopting almost the very measures which it criticized during the British administration. Of course, I know the reason behind it. It makes no appeal to me. I have long intended to write to you asking you about the Working Committee resolution on the possible partition of the Punjab. I would like to know the reason behind it. I have to speak about it. I have done so in the absence of full facts with the greatest caution. ... I was asked by a Muslim Leaguer of note ... (*ellipsis as in the original - ed.*) if it was applicable to the Muslim-majority provinces, why it should not be so to a Congress-majority province like Bihar. I think I did not know the reason behind the Working Committee's resolution, nor had I the opportunity. I could only give my own view which was against any partition based on communal grounds and the two-nation theory. Anything was possible by compulsion. But willing consent required an appeal to reason and heart. Compulsion or show of it had no place in voluntariness.

*Mahatma Gandhi: The Last Phase*, Vol. II, pp. 34-5 (94: 153-54)

---

*From Bihar, Gandhi returned to Delhi to meet with the new Viceroy, Lord Mountbatten. He was confronted by Hindu refugees from the Punjab who demanded to question him on his work in Bihar. By this time partition of the Punjab appeared more or less inevitable.*

## Talk with Refugees
## April 4, 1947

Q. You tell people to discard arms, but in the Punjab the Muslims kill the Hindus at sight. You have no time even to go to the Punjab. Do you want us to be butchered like sheep?

GANDHIJI: If all the Punjabis were to die to the last man without killing, the Punjab would become immortal. It is more valiant to get killed than to kill. Of course my condition is that even if we are facing death we must not take up arms against them. But you take up arms and when you are defeated you come to me. Of what help can I be to you in these circumstances? If you cared to listen to me, I could restore calm in the Punjab even from here. One thousand lost their lives of course, but not like brave men. I would have liked the sixteen who escaped by hiding to have come into the open and courted death. More is the pity. What a difference it would have made if they had bravely offered themselves as a non-violent, willing sacrifice! Oppose with *ahimsa* if you can, but go down fighting by all means if you have not the non-violence of the brave. Do not turn cowards.

There was a time when the most casual remark from me was honoured as a command. Such is not the case today. Man after all is mortal. We are born only to die. Death alone is the true friend of man. [Birth and death] are like the two sides of a coin. How did we react in Bihar? Man's claim to humanity consists in his magnifying his own fault a million times and minimizing others' faults correspondingly. You ought to know that I have been to villages where death reigned supreme. But in spite of it if I feel like it I would certainly go to the Punjab. But now I am doing the same work from here. I believe I have calmed down Bihar to some extent. Naturally it could be only with God's grace, without which nothing happens ...

*Mahatma Gandhi: The Last Phase,* Vol. II, p. 97, and *Biharni Komi Agman,* pp. 137-8 (94: 230-31)

---

*Gandhi's sorrow over partition and the manner in which the Congress agreed to it hurt him deeply and made him wonder what had gone wrong.*

## Talk with Manu Gandhi
## June 1, 1947

The purity of my *yajna* will be put to the test only now. Today I find myself all alone. [Even the Sardar and Jawaharlal] think that my reading of the situation is wrong and peace is sure to return if partition is agreed upon. The Viceroy is a nice and intelligent man. They did not like my telling the Viceroy that even if there was to be partition, it should not be through British intervention or under the British rule. They wonder if I have not deteriorated with age. But if I did not show myself as I am, I would prove a hypocrite. And I must speak as I feel, if I am to prove a true and loyal friend to the Congress. Never mind if I am not a four-anna member of the Congress. But they all come an consult me, seek my advice. Similarly I am also a friend of the British. I must therefore tell the British what is good for them. Else, of what use is my being their friend? If I were to prove my true and loyal friendship to them it becomes my bounden duty to lay bare the facts before them and show them the right way, regardless of whether my advice is appreciated or resented. I see clearly that we are setting about this business the wrong way. We may not feel the full effect immediately, but I can see clearly that the future of independence gained at this price is going to be dark. I pray that God may not keep me alive to witness it.

And I have left you in this vast field to fend for yourself. I have done it with full deliberation because you share my burden in this sacrifice although you are a little girl with no experience of life. In order that God may give me the strength and wisdom to remain firm in the midst of universal opposition and to utter the full truth, I need all the strength of purity that you will have in your sincere work, whether in thought or act, while waking or asleep or even when you are not conscious of yourself. ... But somehow in spite of my being all alone, in my thoughts, I am experiencing an ineffable inner joy and freshness of mind. I feel as if God himself was lighting my path before me. And it is perhaps the reason why I am able to fight on single-handed. ... I shall perhaps not be alive to witness it, but should the evil I apprehend overtake India and her independence be imperilled, let posterity know what agony this old man went through thinking of it. Let not the coming generation curse Gandhi for being a party to India's vivisection. But everybody is today impatient for independence. Therefore there is no alternative. This is like eating wooden *laddoo*s, if they eat it they die of colic; if they don't they starve.

*Bihar Pachhi Dilhi,* pp. 50-2 (from Gujarati) (95: 182-83)

---

*Though the imminent reality of the country's partition saddened Gandhi, his mind turned to practical matters and he wondered aloud how Pakistan and India would deal with their respective minorities.*

### Speech at Prayer Meeting, New Delhi
### June 10, 1947

... I now assume that the division of India is a fact and the Congress has been forced to accept it. But if the partition cannot make us happy, why should it make us unhappy? Only we should not let our hearts be sundered. We must save our hearts from being fragmented. Otherwise Jinnah Saheb's claim that we are two nations will stand vindicated. I have never believed in it. When we are descended from the same ancestors, can our nationality change simply from our changing our religion? When Sind, the Punjab and maybe the Frontier Province too go to Pakistan will they no more belong to us? I for one do not regard even Britain as an alien country, why should I then regard Pakistan as another nation? It may be said that I belong to India and in India to the Bombay Presidency, there again to Gujarat, in Gujarat, particularly to Kathiawar, where again to a small town of Porbandar. But because I belong to Porbandar I also belong to the whole of India, that is, I am also a Punjabi and if I go to the Punjab I shall live there regarding it as my home and if I am killed I shall accept death.

I am happy that Jinnah Saheb has said that Pakistan will not belong to an emperor, but that it will belong to the people and the minorities too will get a square deal there. I would only like to add that he should put into practice what he says. He should also impress this upon his followers and tell them to forget all talk of war. We too will not think of suppressing the minorities in our part of the land. Even the handful of Parsis in India shall be our co-sharers. It would be bad if the Hindus and Muslims joined hands and threatened to annihilate the Parsis saying they were drink-addicts. The Parsis are my friends and I tell them that if they do not give up drinking they will kill themselves. But we shall not kill them. In the same manner Hindus and Sikhs should be protected in the Punjab. The Muslims should treat them kindly and in a brotherly way and reassure them. If the Muslims start tyrannizing over them, the Hindus and Sikhs should tell them, without fear of death, that they will not accept Islam under duress nor partake of [beef]. The Hindus should not think that they have become a new community which cannot accommodate Muslims. We are in a majority in this part of India. We must enlighten the majority and work with courage. Courage does not reside in the sword. We will become truthful, we will become servants of God and, if need be, we will lay down our lives. When we do this India and Pakistan will not be two separate entities and the artificial partition would become meaningless. If we fight among ourselves the charge of our being two nations will be proved. Let us all therefore pray to God that although India and Pakistan have become separate nations our hearts may not be divided.

*Prarthana Pravachan*: I, pp. 142-6 (from Hindi) (95: 251-3)

---

**Speech at Prayer Meeting, New Delhi**
**June 29, 1947**

BROTHERS AND SISTERS,

... Whether it is the Hindus living in a place or Muslims or both, they will come to acquire rights if they do their duty. Then they do not have to demand rights. ... If Hindus consider Muslims their brothers and treat them well, Muslims too will return friendship for friendship. Take a village for example. If there are in it five hundred Hindus and five Muslims, then the five hundred Hindus come to have certain obligations towards the five Muslims which *ipso facto* gives Hindus certain rights. In their arrogance they should not think that they can crush the Muslims and kill them for it cannot be anyone's right to kill. There is no bravery in killing. It is cowardice and a disgrace. The duty of the Hindus is to share with the Muslims in their joys and sorrows even if they wear beards and face towards the West during *namaaz*. They should see whether they are getting enough food and water and whether their other needs are being satisfied. When the five hundred Hindus do their duty, then they earn the right to expect that the five Muslims also would do theirs. ... Today we do not do our duty. The work goes on because God has so made the world that its progress does not stop.

But supposing the five Mussalmans are bent on mischief, supposing you give them food and water and treat them well and they still abuse you, what then will be the duty of the five hundred Hindus? It certainly is not their duty to cut them down. It would be bestial, not human, to do so. If a brother of mine has gone mad, shall I then start beating him up? I shall not do so. I shall confine him in a room and stop others from treating him roughly. This is the human way.

Similarly if the Muslims in question do not want to behave in a friendly manner and keep on saying that they are a separate nation, that though they are only five, they can summon five crores of Muslims from outside, the Hindus should not let themselves be frightened by such a threat. They should tell the Muslims outside that they want to be friends with the five Muslims, but that they don't reciprocate. That if they want to help them it is their affair, but the Hindus would not be frightened or subdued by force. The world will understand that the five hundred Hindus are good people and want to do their duty. The same thing applies to a village where there are five hundred Muslims and only five Hindus. There are many such villages in Pakistan. Some people from the Jhelam area had been to see me. They were concerned about their future in their home country. I told them that if the Muslims there were good people, could exercise self-control in doing their duty, then they would have nothing to fear. But if the few Hindus there were wicked, then even if Hindus from all over India went to help them nothing would be gained ...

*Prarthana Pravachan*: I, pp. 205–8 (from Hindi) (95: 359-61)

---

*Partition threatened lived reality. Hindu nationalists wondered if they should not abandon Hindustani, the common tongue of the people which contained Persian and Urdu words in the main, since these two languages were 'Islamic' in origin.*

## Speech at Prayer Meeting, New Delhi
## June 12, 1947

... Today someone asked me why we should still continue with Hindustani. Such a question should not be raised. If we adopt the attitude that since Urdu will be the language of Pakistan we should have Hindi as our language then the charge of separatism against us also will be proved. Hindustani means an easy language to speak, read and write. It used to be one language at one time but lately we have Urdu loaded with Persian expressions which the people cannot understand and Hindi crammed with Sanskrit words which also people cannot understand. If we used that language we should have to eject from our midst people like Sapru. Although a Hindu, his mother tongue is Urdu. If I start talking to him in

Sanskritized Hindi he will not be able to make head or tail of it. We should therefore continue the work of Hindustani—of the Hindustani Sabha—and prove our love for those whose language is Urdu. I see God's will in what has happened. He wants to test us both to see what Pakistan will do and how generous India can be. We must pass the test. I am hoping that no Hindu will be so mad as to show inadequate respect for things the Muslim consider sacred or fail to accord the same status to the Aligarh University as he does to Malaviyaji's Hindu University. If we destroy their sacred places we shall ourselves be destroyed. Similarly we should protect the fire temples of Parsis and the synagogues of Jews as we protect Hindu temples ...

*Prarthana Pravachan*: I, pp. 150-4 (from Hindi) (95: 266-67)

---

*Though very unhappy with the Congress for agreeing and hastening the partition of Bengal and the Punjab, Gandhi did not have the heart to blame his friends and colleagues who now headed the party. But he did want to impress upon the ordinary Congressman and woman that it was very important that they asked themselves how communal, or not, they were and how committed they were to a democratic polity.*

### Speech at All-India Congress Committee Meeting, New Delhi June 14, 1947

... The Working Committee has on your behalf accepted partition. Now we have to consider what our duty is. If you want to throw out the resolution you can do so. But you cannot make any changes in it. If the Congress Working Committee has done this, it has done so deliberately and for certain weighty reasons. And this decision has been taken jointly by the Congress, the Muslim League and the British Government. The Working Committee does not approve of the scheme in its entirety. But even so it has accepted it. ... If you want to reject it, you must remember that what the country needs most today is peace. If you are sure that your rejecting the scheme will not lead to further breach of the peace and further disorders you can do so. Whatever you decide to do, you must do after a great deal of deliberation.

So many things are happening today which bring to mind the English saying about swallowing a camel and straining at a gnat. The decision that has been arrived at has been reached with your complicity and yet you complain of the Working Committee, the Working Committee which has men of such great calibre on it. Those people had always said that the Congress would not accept Pakistan and I was opposed to Pakistan even more. However we may leave aside my position. The decision has not been mine to take and the Working Committee has accepted it because there was no other way. They now see it clearly that the country is already divided into two camps.

But our constitution permits it and your duty demands it that if you feel that the Working Committee is in the wrong you should remove it, you should revolt and assume all power. You have a perfect right to do so, if you feel that you have the strength. But I do not find that strength in us today. If you had it I would also be with you and if I felt strong enough myself I would, alone, take up the flag of revolt. But today I do not see the conditions for doing so.

We have great problems to tackle and mere criticism cannot help in the solution of great problems. It is easy to criticize but doing some work is not so easy. ... I criticize them, of course, but afterwards what? Shall I assume the burdens that they are carrying? Shall I become a Nehru or a Sardar or a Rajendra Prasad (*Congress leaders, at the forefront of the initiatives for independence and partition - ed.*) ? Even if you should put me in their place I do not know what I should be able to do.

But I have not come here to plead for them. Who will listen to my pleading? But the President said that I should at least show my face here. Hence I have come to show my face and to speak a few words. It is most important that you should understand the times. The demand of the times is that we should bridle our tongues and do only what will be for India's good. ... In the three-quarters of the country that has fallen to our share Hinduism is going to be tested. If you show the generosity of true Hinduism, you will pass in the eyes of the world. If not you will have proved Mr. Jinnah's thesis that Muslims and Hindus are two separate nations, that Hindus will for ever be Hindus and Muslims for ever Muslims, that the two will never unite, and that the Gods of the two are different. If, therefore, the Hindus present at this meeting claim that India is their country and in it Hindus will have a superior status, then it will mean that the Congress has not made a mistake and that the Working Committee has only done what you secretly wanted.

But if you want to save *dharma* you must be true Hindus. There are only a hundred thousand Parsis in India. Our ancestors gave them shelter and set an example in world history. Must we now kill them? And what shall we do with the Jews? We must so treat them that they will enjoy perfect freedom here. And what about the untouchables? It is said that Islam has risen to abolish untouchability. If you say that untouchables are nothing, the Adivasis are nothing, then you are not going to survive yourselves. But if you do away with the distinction of *savarna* and *avarna*, if you treat the Shudras, the untouchables and the Adivasis as equals then something good will have come out of a bad thing. There should be no distinction of high and low in a democratic polity. But if we oppress them and oppress those following other faiths then it will mean that we do not want India to survive, that we are out to destroy it. It does not matter if the land is divided. But if we divide the hearts then what the Congress Working Committee has done has been well done.

*Bihar Pachhi Dilhi*, pp. 142-6 (from Hindi) (95: 279-82)

---

## Speech at Prayer Meeting, New Delhi
## July 14, 1947

BROTHERS AND SISTERS,

It is said that my speeches these days are such as to generate a feeling of pessimism. Indeed I am advised by some not to speak at all. It reminds me of a story about a painter. He placed a painting on display with a notice that critics might mark the spot where they found the painting faulty. The result was that the painting was soon reduced to a blur of colours. The painter had wanted to show that it was not possible to please everyone and he was satisfied that he had created a good painting. I am in a similar situation. I never speak merely for the sake of speaking. I speak because I feel that I have a message to deliver.

It is true that today there are differences between me and my closest colleagues. I do not approve of certain things that they have done or are doing. But it is not possible for me while I am in Delhi not to express my views on the present situation. What is at the root of these differences? If you go into it you will find that there is only one thing at the root of it. Non-violence is a creed with me while it has never been so with the Congress. The Congress accepted non-violence only as a policy—a policy has the status of a creed only so long as it is pursued. The Congress has a perfect right to change its policy the moment it feels that it is no longer necessary to pursue it. But it is different with a creed. It remains for ever and it cannot be changed ...

*Prarthana Pravachan*: I, pp. 246-8 (from Hindi) (96: 49)

---

*Partition also implied a partition of the British Indian army. Gandhi was not interested in the nature of the division or its significance. But he had his own plans for the Army.*

## Message to Army Officers
## New Delhi, July 27, 1947

I have only one message for you. You have got your guns and sten-guns and you are proficient in killing men and all living things. Instead of that you should learn the art of using the sickle, ploughing the land and producing the food necessary for men and other living beings. Forget violence and gain proficiency in non-violence. Maybe from this you will think that I have gone mad. But look at the way Capt. Shahnawaz and Col. Jiwansingh (*ex-soldiers of the Indian National Army, the force raised from amongst Indians in the Empire's south-eastern colonies by Subash Chandra Bose and who were trained by the Germans and the Japanese - ed.*) live and work today. They have ceased to be army officers and have become public servants and farmers. Thus they have become more powerful. They are themselves happy and have made people happy. One of them is a Muslim and is doing wonderful work in Bihar. The other, in spite of being a Punjabi and orthodox Sikh, has identified himself with the Muslims of Noakhali.

I mention just these two names because I happen to remember them. But many such persons have come to me. They have changed their lives and have become happy. Such a time is now coming. You note down in your diary that the world will curse the scientist who has made the atom bomb. People have wearied of bloodshed. They would like to follow the path of non-violence and peace. India alone can give a lesson in that. America has great riches. Even other countries have more money than we have. Because they have money, they are investing in devices of mass destruction. That is why our scriptures and the *Gita* teach us not to hoard wealth. The right way of becoming happy is the observance of truth, non-violence, non-hoarding, celibacy, non-stealing and physical labour. This is as true as a geometrical theorem. Our army will lead the world if it adopts non-violence instead of violence.

*Bihar Pachhi Dilhi*, pp. 429-30 (from Gujarati) (96: 156-67)

---

*The eve of independence found Gandhi in Calcutta, where violence was all set to follow in the wake of independence and partition. Gandhi's presence was resented by young Hindu militants who questioned his motives.*

### Discussions with Representatives of Demonstratrors, Hydari Mansion, Calcutta
### August 13, 1947

Presently the representatives of the demonstrators were ushered in to meet Gandhiji. One of them began: Last year when Direct Action was launched on the Hindus on August 16, you did not come to our rescue. Now that there has been just a little trouble in the Muslim quarters, you have come running to their succour. We don't want you here.

GANDHIJI: Much water has flown under the bridge since August 1946. What the Muslims did then was utterly wrong. But what is the use of avenging the year 1946 on 1947? I was on my way to Noakhali where your own kith and kin desired my presence. But I now see that I shall have to serve Noakhali only from here. You must understand that I have come here to serve not only Muslims but Hindus, Muslims and all alike. Those who are indulging in brutalities are bringing disgrace upon themselves and the religion they represent. I am going to put myself under your protection. You are welcome to turn against me and play the opposite role if you so choose. I have nearly reached the end of my life's journey. I have not much farther to go. But let me tell you that if you again go mad, I will not be a living witness to it. I have given the same ultimatum to the Muslims of Noakhali also; I have earned the right. Before there is another outbreak of Muslim madness in Noakhali, they will find me dead. Why cannot you see that by taking this step I have put the burden of the peace of Noakhali on the shoulders of Shaheed Suhrawardy and his friends ... this is no small gain. ...

An eighteen-year-old youngster interposed: History shows that Hindus and Muslims can never be friends. Anyway, ever since I was born I have seen them only fighting each other.

GANDHIJI: Well, I have seen more of history than anyone of you, and I tell you that I have known Hindu boys who called Muslims "uncle". Hindus and Muslims used to participate in each other's festivals and other auspicious occasions. You want to force me to leave this place but you should know that I have never submitted to force. It is contrary to my nature. You can obstruct my work, even kill me. I won't invoke the help of the police. You can prevent me from leaving this house, but what is the use of your dubbing me an enemy of the Hindus ? I will not accept the label. To make me quit, you have to convince me that I have made a mistake in coming here ...

*Mahatma Gandhi: The Last Phase,* Vol. II, pp. 365-7 (96: 220-21)

---

*Gandhi resolved to stay on in Calcutta despite threats to his life. He and Suhrawardy, Chief Minister of Bengal whose name had been associated with the Calcutta killings of 1946, appeared in public and apologised for the killings of the year before, and this helped to ease the tension in the city.*

### Miracle or Accident?

Shaheed Saheb Suhrawardy and I are living together in a Muslim manzil in Beliaghata where Muslims have been reported to be sufferers. We occupied the house on Wednesday the 13th instant and on the 14th it seemed as if there never had been bad blood between the Hindus and the Muslims. In their thousands they began to embrace one another and they began to pass freely through places which were considered to be points of danger by one party or the other. Indeed, Hindus were taken to their *masjids* by their Muslim brethren and the latter were taken by their Hindu brethren to the *mandirs.* Both with one voice shouted "Jai Hind" or "Hindu-Muslims! Be one". As I have said above, we are living in a Muslim's house and Muslim volunteers are attending to our comforts with the greatest attention. Muslim volunteers do the cooking ...

Is this to be called a miracle or an accident? By whatever name it may be described, it is quite clear that all the credit that is being given to me from all sides is quite undeserved; nor can it be said to be deserved by Shaheed Saheb. This sudden upheaval is not the work of one or two men. We are toys in the hands of God. He makes us dance to His tune. The utmost therefore, that man can do is to refrain from interfering with the dance and that he should render full obedience to his Maker's will. Thus considered, it can be said that in this miracle He has used us two as His instruments and as for myself I only ask whether the dream of my youth is to be realized in the evening of my life.

For those who have full faith in God, this is neither a miracle nor an accident. A chain of events can be clearly seen to show that the two were being prepared, unconsciously to themselves, for fraternization.

In this process our advent on the scene enabled the onlooker to give us credit for the consummation of the happy event. Be that as it may, the delirious happenings remind me of the early days of the *Khilafat* movement. The fraternization then burst on the public as a new experience. Moreover, we had then the *Khilafat* and *swaraj* as our twin goals. Today we have nothing of the kind. We have drunk the poison of mutual hatred and so this nectar of fraternization tastes all the sweeter and the sweetness should never wear out. In the present exuberance one hears also the cry of "Long Live Hindustan and Pakistan," from the joint throats of the Hindus and the Muslims. I think it is quite proper. ... Indeed, if the two have become friends, not to wish long life to both the States would probably be an act of disloyalty.

*Harijan,* 24-8-1947 (96: 236-27)

---

*The 'miracle' of peace that Gandhi thought he witnessed in riot-ready Calcutta turned out to be a false omen. Rioting broke out again and Gandhi decided to go on a fast until he was assured that such things would not happen again. A citizens' group tried to dissuade Gandhi from his fast.*

## Discussion with Citizens' Deputation, Calcutta
## September 4, 1947

The deputation told Gandhiji that they had been to all the affected parts of the city and there was quiet everywhere. They would hold themselves responsible for anything untoward that might happen thereafter. They had every reason to hope that there would be no recrudescence of trouble which they maintained was "really not communal" but "the work of the *goondas*". They requested him to terminate his fast. After some reflection Gandhiji spoke. He deprecated the suggestion that the outbreak of violence was not communal in character but really the work of the *goondas*.

It is we who make the goondas and we alone can unmake them. *Goondas* never act on their own. By themselves they cannot function. It was the cowardice or passive sympathy of the average citizen or "the man with a stake" that gave the so-called *goondas* the power to do mischief. My fast should make you more vigilant, more truthful, more careful, more precise in the language you use. You have all come here out of affection for me to ask me to give up my fast. The ringleaders also have been to see me and have apologized for what they have done.

But before I can accede to your request, I want to ask you two questions: (1) Can you in all sincerity assure me that there never will be repetition of trouble in Calcutta? Can you say that there is a genuine change of heart among the citizens so that they will no longer tolerate, much less foster, communal frenzy? If you cannot give that guarantee, you should rather let me continue this fast. It won't hurt me. When a man fasts like this, it is not the gallons of water he drinks that sustains him but God; and (2) if trouble breaks out—since you are not omnipotent or even omniscient—would you give me your word of honour that you would not live to report failure but lay down your life in the attempt to protect those whose safety you are pledging? You should remember, too, that if you break your pledge after giving it to me, you will have to face an unconditional fast unto death on my part. I do not wish to live in a fool's paradise. If you deceive me, if you say one thing and mean another in your heart, my death will be upon your heads. I want a clear and straight answer. Your assurance must be in writing.

SUHRAWARDY: You had said that you would break the fast when Calcutta returned to sanity. That condition has already been fulfilled. In asking us to give a guarantee for the future, are you not imposing a fresh condition ?

... What I have spoken now is only a home truth to make you know what is what. If there is complete accord between your conviction and feeling, there should be no difficulty in signing that declaration. It is the acid test of your sincerity and courage of conviction. If you sign it merely to keep me alive, you will really be compassing my certain death ...

*Mahatma Gandhi: The Last Phase*, Vol. II, pp. 421-2; also *Harijan*, 14-9-1947 (96: 337-38)

---

*After exacting a promise from the citizens of Calcutta that peace would be maintained at all costs, Gandhi left for Delhi in September 1947. There, he immediately began a tour of free India's capital city, home to some of the worst rioting. He inspected the refugee camps in the city—both Hindu and Muslim camps.*

### Speech at Prayer Meeting, New Delhi
### September 10, 1947

... The reports of traumatic events in the West Punjab are heart-rending. The leaders of the Indian Union and Pakistan cannot fling their hands in despair and say that it is all the doing of the goondas. It is the duty of the Dominions to accept full responsibility for the actions of its people—their duty is "not to reason why" but "to do and die". Now they are not forced to do anything against their will under the crushing burden of Imperialism. Today they can do anything they choose. But if they wish to face the world with honesty, freedom should not mean that there need be no rule of law in both the Dominions. Would the Union Ministers declare their bankruptcy and shamelessly say that the people of Delhi and the refugees who are staying there do not, of their own free will wish to abide by the law of the land? As for me, I would expect the Ministers to stake their own lives in fighting this madness rather than submitting to it. Even at the house where I am staying, fruits or vegetables are not available ...

... I visited the camp of the Meos (*a Muslim community from Rajasthan - ed.*) near the Humayun's Tomb. I was told that they had been turned out from the States of Alwar and Bharatpur. They said they had nothing to eat except what the Muslim friends had sent to them. I know that the Meos are an easily excitable community and can create a lot of trouble. But the remedy does not lie in driving them out to Pakistan against their wishes. The real remedy lies in treating them as human beings and their weaknesses should be treated as any other illness.

Then I went to the Jamia Millia. I had lent a big hand in building up that institution. Dr. Zakir Husain is a dear friend of mine. He narrated his experiences with great anguish. But he had no bitterness in his heart. Recently he had to visit Jullunder. Had a Sikh Captain and a Hindu railway official not come to his help in time, the Sikhs in their mad fury would have killed him for being a Muslim. Dr. Zakir Husain thanked those people as he narrated his experiences to me. Just imagine, the national institution where many Hindus have been educated, is now afraid that angry refugees and the people who instigate them may attack it. I met the refugees who have been somehow accommodated in the compound of the Jamia Millia. When I heard their tragic tales I hung my head in shame.

Then I went to the refugees camps at Diwan Hall, Wavell Canteen and Kingsway (*Hindu refugee camps - ed.*). I met the Sikh and Hindu refugees there. They had not yet forgotten my past services to the Punjab (*from the early days of the freedom movement, presumably - ed.*). But I noticed some angry faces in all those camps. Those people can be forgiven. They talked to me in sharp tones for being harsh to the Hindus. They said that I had not undergone the hardships that they did, and not lost my kith and kin. They said I had not been compelled to beg at every door. They asked me how I could comfort them by saying that I had been staying at Delhi to do my utmost to establish peace in the capital of the country. True I cannot bring back the dead. But death is a gift of God to all living things—human beings, animals. The difference is only of time and manner. Hence right conduct is the royal path to be followed, which makes life beautiful and worth living ...

*Prarthana Pravachan*: I, pp. 294-8 (from Hindi) (96: 356-58)

---

*Hindu and Sikh refugees from the Punjab refused to be comforted by Gandhi's appeals to not harbour ill-will towards Muslims, and much of his time was spent trying to engage them in a meaningful dialogue.*

## Speech at Prayer Meeting, New Delhi
### September 12, 1947

... If any Hindu or Sikh from the Punjab comes and tells me that his anguish is greater than mine because he has lost his brother or daughter or father, I would say that his brother is my brother, his mother is my mother, and I have the same anguish in my heart as he has. I am also a human being and feel enraged but I swallow my anger. That gives me strength. What revenge can I take with that strength? How should I take revenge so that they feel repentant for their crimes and admit that they have committed grave crimes? You all know what the Muslims have done in West Punjab. What can we do if Muslims are destroying religion? What are we going to do about it? Should I say that the Hindus and Sikhs of Delhi and those who have come from outside should become barbarians because Muslims are becoming barbarians? I had gone to the Jama Masjid today. I met the residents of that area. I also met their womenfolk. Some of the women wept before me and some brought their children to indicate their sad plight. Should I narrate to them the plight of the Hindus and Sikhs in West Punjab and in the Frontier Province? Will it mitigate the sorrow of the Hindus and Sikhs of the Punjab in any way?

... Let us know our own *dharma*. In the light of our *dharma* I would tell the people that our greatest duty is to see that the Hindus do not act in frenzy, nor the Sikhs indulge in acts of madness. I wish to tell you that all those Muslims who have left their places should be sent back. I do not have the courage to send them back right now. But we must keep it in mind that they have got to be sent back. Till the Muslims are able to return to the places from which they have fled, we cannot have peace of mind.

... I would tell the Muslims and I am telling everybody in Delhi that they should declare with God as witness, that there is no reason for them to be killed for the crimes committed in Pakistan. We are your friends and we all belong and shall ever belong to India. Delhi is no small place. It is the capital of the country. Here we have the grand Jama Masjid and also the fort. You have not built these nor have I built them. They have been built by the Mughals who ruled over us. They had become part of India. By telling the Muslims today to leave the country do you mean to say that you are going to take possession of the Jama Masjid? And if that is your intention, do you know the implication? Just think about it. Are we going to stay in the Jama Masjid? I cannot agree to any such proposal. The Muslims must have the right to visit that place. It belongs to them. We are also proud of it. It is full of great artistic beauty. Shall we raze it to the ground? That can never be.

I appeal to the Muslims that they should open-heartedly declare that they belong to India and are loyal to the Union. If they are true to God and wish to live in the Indian Union, they just cannot be enemies of the Hindus. And I want the Muslims here to tell the Muslims in Pakistan who have become the enemies of the Hindus, not to go mad: "If you are going to indulge in such madness, we cannot cooperate with you. We will remain faithful to the Union, and salute the tricolour. We have to follow the order of the Government." These Muslims themselves should tell all the other Muslims to surrender all their arms. ... The Hindus too should surrender all their arms. There should be no mutual fear. We should tell them that whatever happens outside, we in Delhi would live like brothers. The same thing happened in Calcutta and the

Hindus and the Muslims have started living like brothers. The Hindus in Bihar have adopted the same attitude. You must soon create such a situation in Delhi that I can immediately go to the Punjab and tell the people there that the Muslims of Delhi are living in peace. I would ask for its reward there ...

*Prarthana Pravachan*: I, pp. 298-305 (From Hindi) (96: 362-65)

---

*Gandhi was particularly moved by the plight of Muslims from the city of Delhi, who had fled their homes, or had been forced to flee their homes, in fear of marauding Hindu and Sikh gangs. Gandhi invoked the cosmopolitan history and culture of Delhi as he went about counselling forgiveness.*

### Speech at Prayer Meeting, New Delhi
### September 13, 1947

... I went to the Purana Quila today. I saw thousands of Muslims there. Other trucks loaded with Muslims were proceeding towards the Quila. All of them were Muslim refugees. Why did they have to live in the fort? Of whom were they frightened? Were they afraid of you, of me? I know that I do not frighten anyone, but my brothers, who consider themselves Hindus and Sikhs, are frightening them. But if they have frightened them it means that I have frightened them, you have frightened them. Thus I cannot bear to see them escaping to Pakistan out of panic. It is not as if there is heaven in Pakistan and hell here. Why do we find ourselves in such hell? I know that neither Pakistan nor India is hell. If we wish we can turn either into heaven or by our own deeds into hell. And if both the countries become hell, an independent man has no place there. After that we are only doomed to slavery.

This thought is gnawing at my heart. My heart trembles and I wonder how I will make any Hindu, Sikh or Muslim understand all this. Quite a few Muslims in the fort were enraged, but others stopped them. There was love in their hearts. They persuaded their enraged brethren saying: "This old man has come to serve us, to wipe our tears. We are hungry and he has come to see if he can find bread for us somewhere. We are without any water, he has come to see if he can get us water from somewhere." I do not know whether they get food and water there. Some of them told me there was no food, no water for them. I had gone there to find out. Some of them talked to me with great affection. I felt happy. No one would ever want to leave behind his house and property.

The Hindu refugees are in the same situation. They have left behind their homes and properties. Some of them died; this is not a happy situation. It is a matter of shame for everybody. I was trying to convince them also. Through you I want to speak to everyone who cares to listen to me. It is said that in the *Mahabharata* period the Pandavas used to stay in this Purana Quila. Whether you call it Indraprastha or Delhi, the Hindus and the Muslims have grown here together. It was the capital of the Mughals. Now it is the capital of India. There is no survivor of the Mughal dynasty. The Mughals came from outside. They identified themselves with the manners and customs of Delhi. From among them some happened to be Ansari Sahebs, Hakim Sahebs and some became Hindus too. The Hindus also joined their services. In such a Delhi of yours the Hindus and the Muslims used to live together peacefully. They did fight occasionally. But they would fight for a short while and then be united again.

... People tell me that the Muslims are supposed to be Fifth Columnists, that is, they are traitors, disloyal to the present Government. There are 4 crore Muslims in India. If 4 crore people are traitors, who would be the loser? They themselves will be the losers. They would be burying Islam that way. But they cannot do harm to the Hindus and the Sikhs. But you should not harass those 4 crore Muslims. It is not proper to tell them that they should be either ready to die or go to Pakistan. Why should they go? And under whose protection? I tell you that they are under your protection, and under my protection. At least I am not prepared to see that sight. I would rather pray to God that He should take me away before that. He has kept me alive long enough. A life of 78-79 years is not a short one. I am fully satisfied. I have served to the best of my capacity. If God wishes to keep me alive, let Him take from me the work that will satisfy my heart. Let both the communities tell me that I am their friend, that is why they listen to me and would continue to do so ...

*Prarthana Pravachan*: I, pp. 305-10 (from Hindi) (96: 368-370)

---

*Ever concerned about the details of living, and the nature of the everyday, Gandhi worried about the insanitary conditions in the camps and the absence of enough warm clothing to help people tide over the oncoming winter days.*

## Speech at Prayer Meeting, New Delhi
## September 14, 1947

... Our camps should not be kept so dirty. I was very much pained. There is so much police and military arrangement and why do they tolerate such stink and stench? They would say cleaning the place is not their job, and that they have only orders to shoot, if necessary and to maintain peace and order in the camps. They say that if the refugees quarrel among themselves, they brush them away with their guns.

They have orders only to do this much and they cannot go beyond what they have been ordered to do. That is all right. But they are now our soldiers and our police. In my view they must have a pickaxe and also a spade. They must clear the dirt wherever they find it. Their primary function should be to keep the places clean. To keep the camps in good condition both the Hindu and Muslim friends themselves have to clean them ...

... Just as it is the duty of the Government to reach food to the camps, it is also its duty to make arrangements for sanitation, drinking water and water for washing purposes. Because there is no proper sewage arrangement, cholera spreads. Camp sanitation should never be imperfect. I must admit that I have learnt this thing from the British. ... Here people are living in chaos. They are all lying helterskelter. Whom can I blame? The commander of the Muslim camp is a Muslim. He can tell his people and make them understand what they should do. He has to be persuasive. They must be told that they would all die if they continued to live in filth, that their children can't remain unclean. So it is much better that they keep the camp clean. We can do a lot there if we train those people in sanitation. If you see the camp of the Hindus, you will find filth there too. ... After all, neither the Muslims nor the Hindus are animals. But today we have turned into beasts ...

*Prarthana Pravachan*: I, pp. 305-10 (From Hindi) (96: 371-72)

---

*Even as Gandhi wandered about the refugee camps, talking healing words and attending to matters of sanitation and comfort, he was alert to the call of violence that might rouse tired and exhausted minds into frenzy. This set him wondering about the turn of historical events.*

## Speech at Prayer Meeting, New Delhi
## September 15, 1947

During the night as I heard what should have been the soothing sound of gentle life-giving rain, my mind went out to the thousands of refugees lying about in the open camps at Delhi. I was sleeping snugly in a verandah protecting me on all sides. But for the cruel hand of man against his brother, these thousands of men, women and children would not be shelterless and in many cases foodless. In some places they could not but be in knee-deep water. They have no other choice. Was it all inevitable? The answer from within was an emphatic "No."

Was this the first fruit of freedom, just a month-old baby? These thoughts have haunted me throughout these last twenty hours. My silence has been a blessing. It has made me enquire within. Have the citizens of Delhi gone mad? Have they no humanity left in them? Have love of the country and its freedom no appeal for them? I must be pardoned for putting the blame first on the Hindus and Sikhs. Could they not be men enough to stem the tide of hatred? I would urge the Muslims of Delhi to shed all fear, trust God and disclose all the arms in their possession which the Hindus and the Sikhs fear they have. Not that the former too do not have any. The question is one of degree. Some may have more, some less.

Either the minority rely upon God and His creature man to do the right thing or rely upon their fire-arms to defend themselves against those whom they must not trust. My advice is precise and firm. Its soundness is manifest. Trust your Government to defend every citizen against wrongdoers, however well-armed they may be. Further trust it to demand and get damages for every member of the minority wrongfully dispossessed. All that neither Government can do is to resurrect the dead. The people of Delhi will make it difficult to demand justice from the Pakistan Government. Those who seek justice must do justice, must have clean hands. Let the Hindus and the Sikhs take the right step and invite the Muslims who have been driven out of their homes to return. If they can take this courageous step, worthy from every point of view, they immediately reduce the refugee problem to its simplest terms.

They will command recognition from Pakistan, nay from the whole world. They will save Delhi and India from disgrace and ruin. For me, transfer of millions of the Hindus and the Sikhs and the Muslims is unthinkable. It is wrong. The wrong of Pakistan will be undone by the right of a resolute non-transfer of population. I hope I shall have the courage to stand by it, even though mine may be the solitary voice in its favour.

*Harijan*, 28-9-1947 (96: 375-76)

---

*Gandhi's apprehensions about violence were well-founded. Militant Hindus claimed that since Pakistan did not want Hindus, India should not worry about keeping its Muslim population inside its borders. Gandhi vehemently protested this argument.*

### Speech at Prayer Meeting, New Delhi
### September 19, 1947

... The note which I have received says that since the non-Muslims are not going to live in Pakistan, why should the Muslims live in India? But I say that if there is one man doing something wrong let us not imitate and do similar things ourselves. Pakistan or Islam cannot mean that non-Muslims cannot live there. The Muslim empire has spread far and wide; but nowhere was it laid down that non-Muslims cannot live there. Non-Muslims used to live there and lived in peace. They also possessed money. Is Islam now coming to India as a new phenomenon? Islam has lived on for the last 1,300 years. There have been great renunciations and sacrifices for its sake. If any other type of Islam emerges, it would not be genuine and acceptable to all Muslims as good. Think over this. It means that true India is not that in which none but the Hindus can live. True Christianity is not that which does not accept in its fold anyone who is not a Christian. That is not religion but irreligion. The world has not followed that path, is not following it at present nor will follow it in future. Why should we then, try to write a new history?

Let us not ruin India and allow Pakistan to be ruined. There are 4 crore Muslims in India. Where can all of them go? And should they take the Jama Masjid, the Aligarh University and all those Muslim tombs to Pakistan? And should all the gurdwaras in West Punjab be brought to East Punjab? If the Hindus cannot live in Pakistan, their temples will then have to be brought here. This means that everybody wants to ruin himself and destroy religion. I have no desire to be a witness to it. Let God take me away before that. And I would say that all those young men should die doing their duty. Let not India be ruined while they are alive. I do not want to see the country ruined. If anything, I only want to see that we all die in the attempt to remove the evils in the country.

*Prarthana Pravachan*: I, pp. 305-10 (From Hindi) (96: 392-93)

---

*In spite of Gandhi's best efforts, Muslims continued to migrate to Pakistan. Gandhi's response was gently accepting of the fact, but he did not, therefore, stop remonstrating with the Hindus and Sikhs about their attitudes towards Muslims.*

### Speech at Prayer Meeting, New Delhi
### September 23, 1947

... The Muslims who have gone away in panic have left behind their houses and their lands. Should I tell them that they should occupy the houses of those Muslims? I cannot say anything of the kind. Those houses still belong to their Muslim owners as they did in the past. They have run away in fear. If they have gone away of their own accord and if they feel that they will be happy in Pakistan, let them be happy there. Do not harm them. Let them go in peace. They should take their property and jewellery with them. The houses they leave will be in the possession of the Government and it can do whatever it chooses about them. It would not be proper if our refugees go and occupy them on their own. One thing I know for certain is that you should be strong and do as I tell you so that you can let me go from here.

I want to go to the Punjab. I want to go to Lahore. I do not want to go with any police or military escort. I want to go alone, depending only on God. I want to go with faith and trust in the Muslims there. Let them kill me if they want. I would die smiling, and silently pray that God should be kind to them. And how can God be kind to them? By making them good. With God, the only way of making them good is by purifying their hearts. God will listen to me if I do not have a feeling of animosity even for one who regards me as his enemy. Then that man would ask himself what he would have gained by killing me. He would wonder what harm I had done him. If they kill me they have a right to do so. That is why I want to go to Lahore. I want to go to Rawalpindi (*both cities had become part of Pakistan - ed.*). Let the Government stop me if they will. But how can the Government stop me? They will have to kill me if they want to stop me. If they kill me, my death will leave a lesson for you. It will make me very happy. What will be that lesson? It will be that you may have to die but you will not wish evil to anybody ...

*Prarthana Pravachan*: I, pp. 337-40 (from Hindi) (96: 411-12)

---

*Knowing as he did how hatred and prejudice could enshrine themselves in argument and rhetoric, Gandhi spoke out against the separation of a common culture into 'Hindu' and 'Muslim'.*

## Of New Universities

... Assume that the unthinkable has happened and that not a single Muslim can remain in the Union safely and honourably and that neither Hindu nor Sikh can do likewise in Pakistan. Our education will then wear a poisonous form. If, on the other hand, Hindus, Muslims and all the others who may belong to different faiths can live in either Dominion with perfect safety and honour, then in the nature of things our education will take a shape altogether pleasing.

Either people of different faiths having lived together in friendship have produced a beautiful blend of cultures, which we shall strive to perpetuate and increasingly strengthen, or we shall cast about for the day when there was only one religion represented in Hindustan and retrace our steps to that exclusive culture. It is just possible that we might not be able to find any such historical date and if we do and we retrace our steps, we shall throw our culture back to that ugly period and deservedly earn the execration of the universe.

By way of example, if we make the vain attempt of obliterating the Muslim period, we shall have to forget that there was a mighty Jama Masjid in Delhi second to none in the world, or that there was a Muslim University in Aligarh, or that there was the Taj in Agra, one of the seven wonders of the world, or that there were the great forts of Delhi and Agra built during the Mughal period. We shall then have to rewrite our history with that end in view. Surely today we have not the atmosphere which will enable us to come to a right conclusion about the conflicting choices. Our two-months-old freedom is struggling to get itself shaped. We do not know what shape it will ultimately take.

Until we know this definitely, it should be enough if we make such changes as are possible in the existing universities and breathe into our existing educational institutions the quickening spirit of freedom. The experience we will thus gain will be helpful when the time is ripe for founding new universities ...

*Harijan*, 2-11-1947 (97:154-5)

---

*Gandhi's work in Delhi rendered him a mediator. He often carried demands to the government, asking for reparations and better living conditions for those displaced by partition. This list of demands was presented to Vallabhbhai Patel, free India's first Home Minister.*

**Letter to Vallabhbhai Patel**

**Birla House, New Delhi**
**November 1, 1947**

CHI. VALLABHBHAI,

When you came to see me yesterday, I simply forgot that it was your birthday. I could not, therefore give you my blessings personally. Such is my plight today. I write this for special reasons:

1. Refugees are crowding near the Birla Mandir. It is not possible for all of them to live there and they huddle together somehow. They must be removed to a camp and that too quickly.

2. I enclose a letter regarding mosques. It is only one of many such. A statement should be issued that all of them will be protected from abuse and whatever damage they might have suffered will be repaired by the Government.

3. It should be announced that those who were forcibly converted to Hinduism or Sikhism will be regarded by the Government as not having changed their religion and will receive adequate protection.

4. No Muslim will be forced to leave the Union.

5. Those who have been compelled to vacate their houses or whose houses have been illegally occupied by others, should be assured that such occupation will be regarded as null and void and that the houses will be reserved for the original owners. I think it is necessary to issue such a statement.

Blessings from
BAPU

*Bapuna Patro 2: Sardar Vallabhbhaine*, pp. 376-7 (from Gujarati) (97: 205)

---

*One of the things that sickened Gandhi's heart and mind during these years was the violence done to women, especially their forced abduction, assault, marriage and conversion. He had encountered such things in Noakhali and now, as then, refused to consider women as being dishonoured by what had happened to them. He appealed to families— over the radio—to take their women back and not abandon them.*

**Speech at Prayer Meeting, New Delhi**

**December 7, 1947**

... We have become barbarous in our behaviour. It is true of East Punjab as well as of West Punjab. It is meaningless to ask which of them is more barbaric. ... Atrocities have taken place on a mass scale and it is irrelevant who took the first step. The need is for women who have been abducted and harassed to be taken back to their homes. It is my belief that the police cannot do this. The army cannot do this. Yes, a team of women workers could be sent to East Punjab and another team to West Punjab but I do not think that would be effective. I can say as a man of experience that this is not the way to do this work. This is a task for the Governments to tackle. I am not saying that the Governments were behind the abductions. It was not the Government of East Punjab which organized abductions. In East Punjab Hindus and Sikhs were responsible for them and in West Punjab Muslims were responsible. What further investigation is required? Whatever the number—I put it at 12,000 at least—East Punjab and West Punjab should return them.

It is being said that the families of the abducted women no longer want to receive them back. It would be a barbarian husband or a barbarian parent who would say that he would not take back his wife or daughter. I do not think the women concerned had done anything wrong. They had been subjected to violence. To put a blot on them and to say that they are no longer fit to be accepted in society is unjust. At least this does not happen among Muslims. At least Islam is liberal in this respect, so this is a matter that the Governments should take up. The Governments should trace all these women. They should be traced and restored to their families. The police and women social workers cannot effectively deal with this. The problem is difficult, which means to say that public opinion is not favourable. You cannot say that all the 12,000 women were abducted by ruffians. I do not think that is the case. It is good men that have become ruffians. People are not born as goondas; they become so under certain circumstances. Both the Governments had been weak in this respect.

Neither Government has shown enough strength to recover the abducted women. Had both the Governments exercised authority, what happened in East Punjab and West Punjab would not have happened ...

Courtesy: All India Radio. Also *Prarthana Pravachan*: II. pp. 178-82 (from Hindi) (98: 9-10)

---

**Speech at Prayer Meeting**
**New Delhi, December 26, 1947**

... Muslims have abducted Hindu and Sikh girls. We want to recover them. In Lahore some Hindu, Muslim and Sikh women met and decided to have these abducted girls recovered and restored to their homes. They decided that Muslim girls carried away by Hindus and Sikhs should also be returned. I have received a long list of girls abducted from Patiala. Some of them come from very well-to-do Muslim families. When they are recovered it will not be difficult for them to be returned to their parents.

As regards Hindu girls it is still doubtful whether they will be accepted by their families. This is very bad. If a girl has lost her parents or husband it is not her fault. And yet Hindu society does not look upon such a girl with respect any more. The mistake is ours, not the girl's. Even if the girl has been forced into marriage by a Muslim, even if she has been violated, I would still take her back with respect. I do not want that a single Hindu or Sikh should take up the attitude that if a girl has been abducted by a Muslim she is no longer acceptable to society. We should not hate her. We should sympathize with her and take pity on her. If a girl is a Sikh, in my eyes she remains a Sikh, if a Hindu, she remains a Hindu. If my daughter has been violated by a rascal and made pregnant, must I cast her and her child away? Nor can I take the position that the child so born is Muslim by faith. Its faith can only be the faith of the mother who bore it. After the child grows up he or she will be free to take up any religion.

Today we are in such an unfortunate situation that some girls say that they do not want to come back, for they know that if they return they will only face disgrace and humiliation. The parents will tell them to go away, so will the husbands. I have suggested that a sort of home should be established for such girls which should take up the responsibility for their food and shelter and education, so that they can stand on their own feet. These girls are innocent. The culprits are those—be they Hindus or Muslims or Sikhs—who have abducted them. Let the Hindus and Sikhs who have abducted Muslim girls return them. Let the Muslims who have abducted Hindu and Sikh girls return them. And let them confess publicly that they are guilty ...

Courtesy: All India Radio. Also *Prarthana Pravachan*: II, pp. 241-3 (from Hindi) (98: 117-18)

---

*Though Gandhi did not see himself as playing an effective role in the Congress anymore, he was called to address the All-India Congress Committee on the responsibilities of independence. This was his last appearance before the Committee.*

## Speech at All-India Congress Committee Meeting
## November 15, 1947

I have come in your midst today. I came to Delhi not to stay for long, but since my arrival many things have happened which should not have happened. And so I have had to prolong my stay here instead of proceeding to the Punjab. This explains my presence in your midst today. I had made a vow to do or die. When the occasion comes I shall indeed either do or die. I have seen enough to realize that though not all of us have gone mad, a sufficiently large number have lost their heads. What is responsible for this wave of insanity? Whatever the cause, it is obvious to me that if we do not cure ourselves of this insanity, we shall lose the freedom we have won. You must understand and recognize the gravity of the plight we are in. Under the shadow of this impending misfortune the A. I. C. C. has met today. You have to face very serious problems and apply your minds to them.

... When we were fighting for our freedom, we bore a heavy responsibility, but today when we have achieved freedom, our responsibility has grown a hundred-fold. What is happening today? Though it is not true of the whole of India, yet there are many places today where a Muslim cannot live in security. There are miscreants who will kill him or throw him out of a running train for no reason other than that he is a Muslim. There are several such instances. I will not be satisfied with your saying that there was no help for it or that you had no part in it. We cannot absolve ourselves of our responsibility for what has happened. I have to fight against this insanity and find out a cure for it. I know and I confess that I have not yet found it. ... Today we are reduced to such a state that not even an old man or a child feels safe, if he happens to be a Muslim. Under such circumstances we have met today.

...We have to recognize that India does not belong to Hindus alone, nor does Pakistan to Muslims. I have always held that if Pakistan belongs to Muslims alone, then it is a sin which will destroy Islam. Islam has never taught this. It will never work if Hindus as Hindus claim to be a separate nation in India and Muslims in Pakistan. The Sikhs too have now and again talked of a Sikhistan. If we indulge in these claims, both India and Pakistan will be destroyed, the Congress will be destroyed and we shall all be destroyed. I maintain that India belongs both to Hindus and Muslims.

You may blame the Muslim League for what has happened and say that the two-nation theory is at the root of all this evil and that it was the Muslim League that sowed the seed of this poison; nevertheless I say that we would be betraying the Hindu religion if we did evil because others had done it. ... You say that you will not allow Muslims to stay in India, but I hold it to be an impossibility to drive away three-and-a-half crores of them to Pakistan. What crime have they committed? The Muslim League indeed is culpable, but not every Muslim. If you think that they are all traitors and fifth-columnists, then shoot them down by all means, but to assume that they are all criminals because they are Muslims is wrong. If you bully them, beat them, threaten them, what can they do but run away to Pakistan? After all, life is dear to them. But it is unworthy of you to treat them so. Thereby you will degrade the Congress, degrade your religion and degrade the nation.

If you realize this, then it is your duty to recall all those Muslims who have been obliged to flee to Pakistan. Of course those of them who believe in Pakistan and wish to seek their happiness there are welcome to migrate. For them there is no bar. They will not need military protection to escort them. They go of their own will and at their own expense. But those who are leaving today have to be provided with special transport and special protection. Such unnatural exodus under artificial conditions must cause us shame. You should declare that those Muslims who have been obliged to leave their homes and wish to return are welcome in your midst. You should assure them that they and their religion will be safe in India. This is your duty, this is your religion. You must be humane and civilized, irrespective of what Pakistan does. If you do what is right Pakistan will sooner or later be obliged to follow suit.

As things are we cannot hold our heads high in the world today and have to confess that we have been obliged to copy Pakistan in its misdeeds and have thereby justified its ways. How can we go on like this? What is happening is a provocation to war on both sides and must inevitably lead to it. …This is the basic issue before you. Until you have faced it, you cannot solve any of the problems that are before you. When your house is on fire you must first put out the flames before you can do anything else. That is why I have taken so much of your time …

… One more point. I understand that a hundred-and-fifty thousand Muslims are about to be sent to Pakistan. You will say, they belong to the criminal tribes who are better sent to Pakistan. Why should they have to go? If there are criminal tribes in India, whose fault is it? We are to blame for not having reformed them. They were here during the British regime. Was there any talk of deporting them then? It is wrong of us to send them away because they are "criminal". Our duty should be to reform them. How shameful it is for us that we should force them to trudge three hundred miles on foot! I am against all such forced exodus.

I claim to be an orthodox sanatanist. I know that my religion does not advocate untouchability. The mission of the Hindu Mahasabha is to reform Hindu society, to raise the moral level of the people. How then can the Sabha advocate the compulsory evacuation of all Muslims from India, as I am told it does? I know what some people are saying. "The Congress has surrendered its soul to the Muslims. Gandhi? Let him rave as he will. He is a washout. Jawaharlal is no better. As regards Sardar Patel there is something in him. A portion of him is sound Hindu, but he too is after all a Congressman." Such talk will not help us. Where is an alternative leadership? Who is there in the Hindu Mahasabha who can replace Congress leadership? Violent rowdyism will not save either Hinduism or Sikhism. Such is not the teaching of *Guru Granthsaheb.* Christianity does not teach these ways. Nor has Islam been saved by the sword. I hear many things about the Rashtriya Swayamsevak Sangh (*A militant Hindu group, known for its militant anti-Islamic, anti-Christian views - ed.*) and I have heard it said that the Sangh is at the root of all this mischief. Let us not forget that public opinion is a far more potent force than a thousand swords.

Hinduism cannot be saved by orgies of murder. You are now a free people. You have to preserve this freedom. You can do so if you are humane and brave and ever-vigilant, or else a day will come when you will rue the folly which made this lovely prize slip from your hands. I hope such a day will never come. You will forgive me for taking so much of your time ...

A. *I. C. C. File No. G. 43/II*, 1947-48. Courtesy: Nehru Memorial Museum and Library (97: 317-23)

---

*Gandhi was in a state of disquiet over the distance that had grown between him and the Congress. He was saddened by reports of Congressmen being corrupt and self-indulgent, and by the fact that in spite of all his counselling of tolerance, Hindus did not appear to mind Muslims leaving India. Veiled charges of Hindu chauvinism that were being brought up against his trusted companion of many decades, the Home Minister, Vallabhbhai Patel also troubled his conscience. To do penance for the ills that attended on the historical moment, he decided to fast but refused to divulge his reasons for doing so.*

### Speech at Prayer Meeting, New Delhi
### January 12, 1948

... Though the voice within has been beckoning for a long time, I have been shutting my ears to it lest it might be the voice of Satan, otherwise called my weakness. I never like to feel resourceless; a satyagrahi never should. Fasting is his last resort in the place of the sword—his or others. I have no answer to return to the Muslim friends who see me from day to day as to what they should do. My impotence has been gnawing at me of late. It will go immediately the fast is undertaken. I have been brooding over it for the last three days. The final conclusion has flashed upon me and it makes me happy. No man, if he is pure, has anything more precious to give than his life. I hope and pray that I have that purity in me to justify the step. I ask you all to bless the effort and to pray for me and with me. The fast begins from the first meal tomorrow (Tuesday). The period is indefinite and I may drink water with or without salts and sour limes. It will end when and if I am satisfied that there is a reunion of hearts of all communities brought about without any outside pressure, but from an awakened sense of duty. The reward will be the regaining of India's dwindling prestige and her fast-fading sovereignty over the heart of Asia ... . I flatter myself with the belief that the loss of her soul by India will mean the loss of the hope of the aching, storm-tossed and hungry world. Let no friend or foe, if there be one, be angry with me.

There are friends who do not believe in the method of the fast for reclamation of the human mind. They will bear with me and extend to me the same liberty of action that they claim for themselves. With God as my supreme and sole counsellor, I felt that I must take the decision without any other adviser. If I have made a mistake and discover it, I shall have no hesitation in proclaiming it from the house-top and retracing my faulty step. There is little chance of my making such a discovery. If there is a clear indication, as I claim there is, of the Inner Voice, it will not be gainsaid. I plead for all absence of argument and inevitable endorsement of the step. If the whole of India responds or at least Delhi does, the fast might be soon ended.

But whether it ends soon or late or never, let there be no softness in dealing with what may be termed as a crisis. Critics have regarded some of my previous fasts as coercive and held that on merits the verdict would have gone against my stand but for the pressure exercised by the fasts. What value can an adverse verdict have when the purpose is demonstrably sound? A pure fast, like duty, is its own reward. I do not embark upon it for the sake of the result it may bring. I do so because I must. Hence I urge everybody dispassionately to examine the purpose and let me die, if I must, in peace which I hope is ensured. Death for me would be a glorious deliverance rather than that I should be a helpless witness of the destruction of India, Hinduism, Sikhism and Islam.

... Just contemplate the rot that has set in in beloved India and you will rejoice to think that there is an humble son of hers who is strong enough and possibly pure enough to take the happy step. If he is neither, he is a burden on earth. The sooner he disappears and clears the Indian atmosphere of the burden, the better for him and all concerned ...

*The Hindustan Times,* 13-1-1948, and *Harijan,* 18-1-1948 (98:219-220)

---

### Speech at Prayer Meeting, New Delhi
### January 13, 1948

... Now that I have started my fast many people cannot understand what I am doing, who are the offenders—Hindus or Sikhs or Muslims. How long will the fast last? I say I do not blame anyone. Who am I to accuse others? I have said that we have all sinned. That does not mean that any one particular man has sinned. Hindus in trying to drive out the Muslims are not following Hinduism. And today it is both Hindus and Sikhs who are trying to do so. But I do not accuse all the Hindus and Sikhs because not all of them are doing it. People should understand this. If they do not, my purpose will not be realized and the fast too will not be terminated. If I do not survive the fast, no one is to be blamed. If I am proved unworthy, God will take me away.

People ask me if my fast is intended for the cause of the Muslims. I admit that that is so. Why? Because Muslims here today have lost everything in the world. Formerly they could depend on the Government. There was also the Muslim League. Today the Muslim League is no longer there. The League got the country partitioned and even after the partition there are large numbers of Muslims here. I have always held that those who have been left behind in India should be given all help. It is only humanity. Mine is a fast of self-purification. Everyone should purify himself. If not, the situation cannot be saved. If everyone is to purify himself, Muslims will also purify themselves. Everyone should cleanse his heart. No one should find fault with the Muslims whatever they may do. If I confess before someone that I have done wrong, then it is a kind of atonement. I do not say this in order to appease the Muslims or anyone else. I want to appease myself which means that I want to appease God. I do not want to be a sinner against God. Muslims also must become pure and live peacefully in India.

What happened was that for election purposes Hindus and Sikhs recognized the Muslim League. I shall not go into that history. Then followed the partition. But before partition became a fact the hearts had already become divided. Muslims were also at fault here, though we cannot say that they alone were at fault. Hindus, Sikhs and Muslims, all are to blame. Now all of them have to become friends again. Let them look to God, not to Satan. Among the Muslims too there are many who worship Satan. Among the Hindus and the Sikhs many worship not Nanak and other Gurus, but Satan. In the name of religion we have become irreligious. Since I have undertaken the fast in the cause of the Muslims, a great responsibility has come to devolve on them. They must understand that if they are to live with the Hindus as brothers they must be loyal to the Indian Union, not to Pakistan. I shall not ask them whether they are loyal or not. I shall judge them by their conduct ...

Courtesy: All India Radio. Also *Prarthana Pravachan*: II, pp. 293-300 (from Hindi) (98: 224-25)

---

*Gandhi broke his fast on being assured that his concerns would be heeded. But his trials were not ended. On January 20, 1948, there was an attempt on his life. One of the assassins was captured. Gandhi pleaded that he be forgiven.*

## Speech at Prayer Meeting, New Delhi
## January 21, 1948

... Let me first deal with the bomb incident of yesterday. People have been sending me wires congratulating me and praising me.

In fact I deserve no congratulations. I displayed no bravery. I thought it was part of army practice somewhere. I only came to know later that it was a bomb and that it might have killed me if God had not willed it that I should live. But if a bomb explodes in front of me and if I am not scared and succumb, then you will be able to say that I died with a smile on my face. Today I do not yet deserve to be so praised. You should not have any kind of hate against the person who was responsible for this. He had taken it for granted that I am an enemy of Hinduism ...

... Let us pray that God may grant him (*the assassin - ed.*) good sense. It seems he had lodged himself in a mosque. In this he had offended against India, against God and against Hinduism. If everyone thus takes to occupying mosques and, when stopped, assails police officers it will never do. This is not the sort of thing that God will prompt anyone to do. When he says he was doing the bidding of God he is only making God an accomplice in a wicked deed. But it cannot be so. Therefore those who are behind him or whose tool he is, should know that this sort of thing will not save Hinduism. If Hinduism has to be saved it will be saved through such work as I am doing ...

... Some Sikhs came to me and asked me if I suspected that a Sikh was implicated in the deed. I know he was not a Sikh. But what even if he was? What does it matter if he was a Hindu or a Muslim? May God bless him with good sense. I have told the Inspector-General of Police not to harass the man. They should try to win him over. I cannot ask that he should be released because that is not my function. If he can realize that he has committed a crime against Hinduism, against India, against the Muslims and against the whole world, we should not be severe with him. We should pity him. ... If you whole-heartedly disapprove of his action his heart will change of itself, because in this world sin cannot stand by itself. It always wants support. Only God and his devotees are self-sustained. This is the premise from which our Non-cooperation is derived. I pray to God to give us enough strength that we may maintain our self-possession and continue the prayer and not budge from our places, even if a bomb should be thrown in our midst, and even if a police party should come and try to make us leave. Only then shall I deserve to be congratulated. I want to go on uttering Ramanama even if there should be shooting taking place all around me ...

Courtesy: All India Radio. Also *Prarthana Pravachan*: II, pp. 328-30 (from Hindi) (98: 281-83)

---

*Gandhi was often reprimanded for his counselling of forgiveness and harmony. In this speech at a prayer meeting held a day before his death he answered his detractors.*

## Speech at Prayer Meeting, New Delhi
## January 29, 1948

... One of them—I did not ask whether he was a refugee—said I had done enough harm already and that I should stop and disappear from the scene. He did not care whether I was a mahatma. I asked him where he wanted me to go. He said that I might go to the Himalayas. I had to rebuke him. He is not as old as I am and is stronger. But I could not afford to become nervous. I asked why I should go to the Himalayas merely because he wished it, when there were many who wanted me to stay. There are many who praise me and there are others who abuse me. What am I to do? I can only do as God bids. You may say that you do not believe in God. But then you must allow me to go my way. God is the help of the afflicted. But an afflicted person is not God. When I claim that every woman is my own sister or daughter, then her suffering becomes my suffering. Why do you presume that I do not understand the sufferings of the refugees? Why do you presume that because I am a friend of Muslims I am an enemy of Hindus and Sikhs? I cannot run away because anyone wants me to run away. I have not taken to service at any one's bidding. I have become what I have become at the bidding of God. God will do what He wills. He may take me away. I shall not find peace by going to the Himalayas. I want to find peace in the midst of turmoil or I want to die in the turmoil. My Himalayas are here ...

Courtesy: All India Radio. Also *Prarthana Pravachan*: II, pp. 352-6 (from Hindi) (98: 331)

---

# Ending the Story

*The last years of Gandhi's life reveal a tormented individual whose life became pared down to what he essentially believed in—that love gives and does not ask questions. Steadfastly opposed to partition and convinced that the nationalism espoused by the Congress did represent the aspirations and needs of diverse peoples, Gandhi struggled during these years to find a solution to the problem of Pakistan and India.*

*He was keenly aware that Jinnah felt his cause passionately, just as he knew that the Congress and Congressmen had not thought through the communal tangle, as he himself had not, at least since the late 1920s. But he was not willing therefore to compromise on his rather ecumenical nationalism, which drew its spiritual strength from a variety of sources, many of which were religious. In his search for a political system, a form of rule that would prove adequate to his broad conception of a nation, he wrestled with the Congress and made it bear the burden of his distinctive vision.*

*But it is clear from the events of this period that, after the war, Congressmen were keen on settling the business of governance with the British so that the transfer of power would be smooth. They were not prepared to heed Gandhi's calls to heart-unity, especially since the mid-1940s witnessed rioting, murders and lynching, the like of which no one had been witness to in the immediate past. Gandhi chose to misread the Congress' will to power as an assertion of the national-popular will of his conception. This is why, time and again, he attempted to gain for Congress the reins of rule, negotiating first with Wavell, and then with Mountbatten. In the end, it was only logical that the Congress, as it rushed past the post to victory, would leave him behind, wondering at its short memory and expedient methods. Besides, he had felt a steady alienation from the Congress since the late 1930s, though he refused to concede that this was so—at least until the mid-1940s, when it was evident that there existed a gulf between Gandhi and the Congress leadership.*

*Gandhi's relationship to Jinnah was complex. Jinnah felt his exclusion from the nationalist project acutely, and his call for a separate Muslim nation was as much strategic as it was ideological. This is clear from the manner in which the League responded to the May 16 Cabinet Mission Plan of 1946—moving from suspicion to acceptance to rejection. Jinnah was critical of the Congress' Hindu core, which Gandhi too addressed and criticized, but Jinnah was equally impatient with Gandhi's complex discourse of faith, god and nation. Gandhi, for his part, did not think it politic or feel it important to engage with the idea of Pakistan. By declaring it sinful, he placed it beyond the pale of his considerate mind. As in the case of separate electorates for the untouchables, he preferred to define the problem in terms of consciousness, feeling and practical acts of everyday love, rather than in terms of a modern language of rights, especially the right to national self-determination. On the other hand, he worked against the notion of Pakistan fairly consciously, putting forth the nationalist claims of the Congress with a fervour which even the Congress found embarrassing. If, instead of doing that, he had actually thought concretely in terms of a coalition that would answer to the heart-unity he was desperate to erect, then perhaps the course of events would have been different. For historians have since shown that Jinnah would have been satisfied with something less than Pakistan, if the Congress had assured him of its willingness to concede power in actual terms, and after a serious weighing of his fears over Hindu domination.*

*Gandhi was aware of the increasingly strident and shrill call to a Hindu nationalism, voiced by Hindu right-wing groups. He refuted their demands and disagreed with their plans and prospects for a free India. Yet, in the earlier years, in the late 1930s for example, when stalwart members of the Hindu Right were influential in the formulation of the Congress' policy, he did not seek to actively interrogate their claims. As always, he pointed to errors and underscored the nature of a wrong, but did not reject those who were responsible for either.*

*But whatever may have been Gandhi's role in the events and decisions that led to partition, his life, after it had happened, kept pace with and, in some senses, directed the march of history. British rule over India ended on August 14, 1947, when, on the stroke of midnight, a free Indian government was formed. But Gandhi was not enthused by a freedom which brought partition in its wake. Neither did he feel a sense of achieved success: on the day of independence, he was in Bengal, doing his utmost to prevent an outbreak of anticipated rioting. In fact his predominant emotion during this time was a sense of desolate failure. The violence that he had witnessed in the months leading to freedom had convinced him that real freedom was still very far away and that the political victory the Congress had won belied the terrible price that had been paid for it. As always, he did not think the end justified the means adopted to attain it, and wondered if the Congress should not start all over again and try and build a new society: he counselled that the party be dissolved.*

*Paradoxically, Gandhi's moment of failure was also his moment of historical reckoning. His magnificent indifference to questions of power and patriotic pride, and to the dubious politics of working human tragedies to political advantage, enabled him to chart an ethic of peace, which is unmatched to this day for the manner in which it engaged with suffering, pain, reconciliation, rehabilitation and most important of all, guilt. Gandhi was concerned as much with the oppressor's soul, as he was with the victim's scarred and hurt mortality, and he held out hope for those who 'sinned', as he did for those who suffered. He did not imagine that the law or the penalty imposed by systems that supervised justice could, in themselves, bring about true penitence or prevent the wrong from repeating itself. He knew that he had to work with the hearts and souls of those who had caused pain, that hatred had to be addressed, not on its own terms but more generously and gently than it warranted.*

*From his days in Noakhali, through the weeks spent in anguished anger in Bihar and finally in his tireless wandering around Delhi's refugee camps, Gandhi distilled a message that was unique: these sites of violence taught him that, at some point in time, the laws of history must heed the laws of the heart and the claims of mutuality, forgiveness and penitence, as much as they did those of justice and right.*

*These last years of his life also constitute a veritable practical lesson in living together—his notions of a cooperative ashram life, of minimal living, of a common labour that implicates high and low, of truth and compassion, were put to use to help Hindus and Muslims come to terms with each other's proclivity for causing hurt and pain. For these were the values he counselled in the refugee camps, where, to an extent at least, he managed to contain hatred and violence.*

*On the eve of his death Gandhi demonstrated to the world how the 'measure of law' could be tempered with the 'measure of mercy', how truth and justice could be modulated with compassion on the one hand and reconciliation on the other.*